CONTENTS

PLATES AND DIAGRAMS

ACKNOWLEDGMENTS

A number of individuals contributed valuable suggestions and critiques which are reflected in the text of this book, but of course the responsibility for any errors of fact or interpretation, if such be found, is entirely my own. I also wish to reserve for myself any problems that may arise on account of the reaction to this book, and for this reason I refrain from making the applicable personal acknowledgments here.

Institutional acknowledgments are made to the U.S. National Archives, the U.S. Army Audio-Visual Agency and the Foreign Affairs Document and Reference Center of the U.S. Department of State, Washington, D.C., to the Panstwowe Museum, Oswiecim, and to the Library of the University of Chicago and the Center for Research Libraries, Chicago.

Special acknowledgment is made to the staffs of the Imperial War Museum, London, the national office of the Netherlands Red Cross, The Hague, and the Library of Northwestern University (especially the inter-library loan department), Evanston, all of whom contributed more than routine services without, of course, being aware of the exact nature of the research involved.

A. R. BUTZ

FOREWORD

In common with virtually all Americans who have had their opinions formed since the end of World War II I had, until not very long ago, assumed that Germany had given the world a particularly murderous outburst during World War II. This view has ruled Western opinion since 1945 and earlier, and I was no exception in accepting the essentials of it.

An important qualification in the preceding is the term "essentials", for the collection of crimes of which the Germans were supposedly guilty in World War II grows rapidly smaller as one examines the evidence and arguments assembled in readily available "revisionist" books. An elementary critical examination reveals that most of the crimes that are real even in the minds of "intellectuals" (e.g. lampshades manufactured by some Germans from the skins of human beings killed in concentration camps for the purpose) obviously had no basis in fact. Likewise with legends about mistreatment of American and British prisoners of war. Moreover, the general problem is elaborated considerably when one weighs, as the revisionists do, the appalling wartime and postwar brutalities of the Western allies.

Such an investigation does not overturn the "holocaust" legend, however, and the "six million" Jews murdered, mainly in "gas chambers", can seem immovable fact. The revisionist books which overturn some of the most popular misconceptions seem to accept the gas chambers as factual. All educated opinion that the investigator consults accepts the "extermination" story. Professors of history who have specialized in Germany, if asked, seem to consider the charge as established as the Great Pyramid. Liberal and conservative publicists, though they have very different attitudes toward World War II and America's entry into it, and though they squabble with each other on almost everything else, close ranks on the reality of the "holocaust".

Noting the obvious ways in which this legend is exploited in contemporary politics, notably in connection with the completely illogical support that the U.S. extends to Israel, I had long had lingering doubts about it, and there was also the fact that there existed a small number of respected observers whose views had not been formed entirely after World War II and who, in the very limited channels open to them and with various degrees of explicitness, denied even the approximate truth of the legend. A good example is the distinguished American scholar John Beaty, who was called to active duty in the Military Intelligence Service of the War Department General Staff just before the entry of the U.S. into the war and attained the rank of Colonel by the end of the war. Among other things, Beaty was one of the two editors of the daily secret "G-2 Report", which was issued each noon to give persons in high places, including the White House, the world picture as it existed four hours earlier. In his book *Iron Curtain Over America,* published in 1951, he ridiculed the six million legend with a few remarks that were unfortunately brief and inconclusive but, coming from a man who was one of the best informed in the world during the war, carried some amount of authority.

Elementary investigation into the question, of the sort the non-historian customarily does, led me nowhere. The meager amount of literature in the English language which denied the truth of the legend was not only unconvincing; it was so unreliable and unscrupulous in the employment of sources, when sources were employed, that it had a negative effect, so that the case for the truth of the essentials of the legend (disregarding quantitative problems, e.g., whether it was six million of four million or only three million) seemed strengthened. At the time I became aware that there existed additional literature in French and German but, being quite unaccustomed to reading texts in those languages except on rare occasions when I consulted a paper in a French or German mathematics journal, I did not undertake to acquire copies of the foreign language literature. Moreover, I assumed that if such literature was worth more than what was being published in English, somebody would have published English translations.

Still possessing my lingering doubts I sat down, early in 1972, and started to read some of the "holocaust" literature itself rather more systematically than I had previously, in order to see just what claims were made in this connection and on what evidence. Fortunately, one of my first choices was Raul Hilberg's *The Destruction of the European Jews.* The experience was a shock and a rude awakening, for Hilberg's book did what the opposition literature could never have done. I not only became convinced that the legend of the several million gassed Jews must be a hoax, but I derived what turned out to be a fairly reliable "feel" for the remarkable cabalistic mentality that had given the lie its specific form (those who want to experience the "rude awakening" somewhat as I did may stop here and consult pp. 567-571 of Hilberg).

Although my long-lingering skepticism in regard to the legend was no longer on the defensive, my information could not, early in 1972, be considered conclusive and my knowledge of the subject was not comprehensive so I set out, at first in my "spare time", to investigate the subject with the thoroughness that was required.

The reader will have surmised that my "spare time" eventually expanded considerably. Several, for me startling, discoveries made the subject irresistible in a purely intellectual sense. I acquired the foreign language literature. Ultimately I spent the entire summer of 1972 working on an exposé of the hoax, since by then I had penetrated and demolished the whole sorry mess so that, while the book you are holding differs considerably in quantity of factual content and general quality from the picture I had formed by the summer of 1972, that picture, whose essentials are transmitted here, was in such overwhelming contradiction to the lies that Western society had equipped me with that my attention could not be drawn from the subject by any appeal to prudence or any such practical calculation. Since, even early in the summer of 1972, it was evident that my research had carried the subject beyond the existing literature, I felt an inescapable obligation and an intellectual imperative to put forward for society's evaluation what I knew about this most pernicious hoax. It quickly became clear that only a book would do; the subject could not, given the years of propaganda, be treated in a research paper or pamphlet and, a *fortiori,* it could not be treated in the form of a lecture.

The body of a text was written in the summer of 1972 and then the manuscript was gradually improved in the course of the next two years. A trip to Europe in the summer of 1973 was very rewarding, as was a trip to

Washington later in the year. The book was essentially finished in late 1974.

There will be those who will say that I am not qualified to undertake such a work and there will even be those who will say that I have no right to publish such things. So be it. If a scholar , regardless of his specialty, perceives that scholarship is acquiescing, from whatever motivation, in a monstrous lie, then it is his duty to expose the lie, whatever his qualifications. It does not matter that he collides with all "established" scholarship in the field, although that is not the case here, for a critical examination of the "holocaust" has been avoided by academic historians in all respects and not merely in the respect it is treated in this book. That is, while virtually all historians pay some sort of lip service to the lie, when it comes up in books and papers on other subjects, none has produced an academic study arguing, and presenting the evidence for, either the thesis that the exterminations did take place or that they did not take place. If they did take place then it should be possible to produce a book showing how it started and why, by whom it was organized and the lines of authority in the killing operations, what the technical means were and that those technical means did not have some sort of more mundane interpretation (e.g. crematoria), who were the technicians involved, the numbers of victims from the various lands and the timetables of their executions, presenting the evidence on which these claims are based together with reasons why one should be willing to accept the authenticity of all documents produced at illegal trials. No historians have undertaken anything resembling such a project; only non-historians have undertaken portions.

With these preliminary remarks, therefore, I invite your study of the hoax of your century.

Evanston, Illinois
August 1975

I
TRIALS, JEWS AND NAZIS

The "war crimes trials" which the victors in World War II conducted, mainly of Germans but also of many Japanese, were precedent shattering in their scope and in the explicitness of the victorious powers' claims to some sort of legal jurisdiction in respect of laws or understandings which did not exist at the time they were allegedly broken by the Axis powers. Thus in disregard of European honor conventions which had been respected for centuries, German civilian and military prisoners, many of the highest rank, met violent deaths while in Allied captivity as a supposed consequence of these extraordinary proceedings.

Nothing resembling the trials of 1945–1949 which were conducted by the wartime enemies of Germany has ever occurred before. The case of Joan of Arc comes to mind, but that involved a solitary prisoner, not an entire state, and the English who were, in the last analysis, responsible for the trial did everything to make the issue appear to be one of heresy and witchcraft, already formally proscribed, to be decided by an impartial and universal church according to pre-existing rules of evidence and procedure.

In the United States, the real progenitor of the trials, opinion on the appropriateness of having conducted such trials has always been divided, but the balance has varied. In the immediate post-war period, opinion generally favored the trials with, however, some significant voices in opposition. In the middle of the heated election campaign of 1946, just before the major Nazis Goering, Ribbentrop *et. al.* were to be hanged, Sen. Robert A. Taft delivered a speech attacking both the legal basis for the trials and the sentences which had been imposed; his speech seems to have hurt his Republican Party in those elections.

A decade later views had evidently changed somewhat, since at that time the then obvious presidential candidate John F. Kennedy published a book, *Profiles in Courage* (a survey of various people whom Sen. Kennedy thought courageous) in which he commended Taft for taking this stand, adding that Taft's views "are shared . . . by a substantial number of American citizens today."[1]

With the Eichmann abduction in 1960 and subsequent "trial" and with the associated later publicity, opinion seemed to move again, however slowly, toward approval of the trials. Many reasons may be offered for this extraordinary reversal but it seems to me that what had happened was that in a peacetime, generally non-hysterical atmosphere the world's attention had been focused on one tale of a peculiarly macabre sort: the killing, mainly in "gas chambers", of several (usual figure, six) million Jews, of all ages and conditions, by the Nazis during the war, as part of a program of ridding Europe of Jewry. Gerald Reitlinger's *The Final Solution*, 2nd edition (1968) is generally accepted as the most detailed and useful presentation of this claim, and Raul Hilberg's *The Destruction of the European Jews* (1961) tells essentially the same story. Other writings are Nora Levin's *The Holocaust*

9

(1968), several books by Léon Poliakov, and the very recent *The War Against the Jews, 1933–1945*, by Lucy S. Dawidowicz (1975).

Returning to the problem of the appropriateness of the war crimes trials, everybody would agree on the (at least) shaky legal foundations of the trials, but apparently many people would go along with the claim that the trials were appropriate anyway because normal wartime excesses were not involved; the extraordinary nature of the crime, the extermination of the European Jews, called for extraordinary proceedings. Such cruelty must not only be punished but documented as well, the argument goes.

I do not propose in this book to settle the question of what degree of cruelty justifies what degree of legal irregularity. Rather, a rarely heard point which is at least relevant to the debate is insisted upon here; it is a fact that without the evidence generated at these trials, there would be no significant evidence that the program of killing Jews ever existed at all. One has only to examine the sources employed by Hilberg and by Reitlinger to see this. If the trials had not been held, a person claiming the existence of the extermination program could not, if challenged, produce any evidence for this save a few books (not including Hilberg or Reitlinger) whose claims are just as unsupported as his original claim. Thus the problem that had been involved in deciding whether or not to hold trials on the Jewish extermination aspect was not a simple question of whether or not to try mass murder; unlike the usual murder case there was legitimate and very solid doubt that the deed had been committed at all.

This may surprise the reader who regards the tale of Jewish extermination as a near certainty; such is simply not the case. There are many considerations supporting this view and some are so simple that they may surprise the reader even further. The simplest valid reason for being skeptical about the extermination claim is also the simplest conceivable reason; at the end of the war they were still there.

This must be qualified only slightly. Consider a West European observer, who had been familiar with the status of European Jewry prior to the war, making a survey of West European Jewry in, say, late 1946 (East European Jewry was out of bounds). He would have found Italian, French, Belgian and Danish Jewry essentially unscratched (these points will be discussed more fully in later chapters). On the other hand he would have found that large numbers of Jews, possibly majorities, were missing from Luxembourg, the Netherlands and Czechoslovakia (then accessible from the West). German-Austrian Jewry was confused since, although most had emigrated before the war, it was difficult to be precise about what numbers had emigrated to where. In any case large numbers, possibly majorities, of those who had remained were no longer resident in their former homes.

However, the absences were offset by the obvious facts that displaced persons' camps in Germany were full of Jews (a figure of more than 250,000 has been given[2]) and that many European Jews had emigrated to the U.S. or Palestine or elsewhere since the beginning of the war. The facts available to the West European observer in late 1946 argued very strongly against the extermination claims which had received such wide publicity during the war and at the recent trial at Nuernberg.

The passage of a quarter of a century has, despite superficial developments, gradually strengthened this view of the extermination tale, although for many years there was only one serious writer in the field, the late French geographer Paul Rassinier. In 1948 he published a book, *Passage de la Ligne*, on his experiences as a left wing political prisoner at Buchenwald, 1943–1945, "generally received with sympathy, provoking only muffled and inconclusive gnashings of teeth on a certain side." Then in 1950 he published *Le Mensonge d'Ulysse*, a critical study of the concentration camp literature in which he challenged the certainty of the gas chambers: "it is yet too early to pronounce a definitive judgment on the gas chambers." This provoked a violent press campaign which led ultimately to legal actions in which author, preface author and publisher were first acquitted, then found guilty with judgments involving fines, damages and suspended prison sentences, and finally acquitted again. In 1955 the two books were combined as *Le Mensonge d'Ulysse,* 2nd edition, in which material increasingly critical of the gas chamber claim had been added. The most common (but not very common) edition today is the fifth (referenced here), published in 1961, in which year Rassinier also published a short "complementary" volume, *Ulysse Trahi par les Siens,* consisting of three essays showing that he had moved rather strongly in the direction of a negative judgment on the gas chambers; the last essay is the text of a speech given in several German and Austrian cities in the early spring of 1960 (just before the Eichmann affair). In 1962 followed *Le Véritable Procès Eichmann,* a study of the entire range of alleged German crimes in their historical and political contexts; by this time he had reached a definitive conclusion on the tale of extermination of the Jews: "a historic lie: the most tragic and the most macabre imposture of all time."[3] Rassinier employed two basic approaches to reach this conclusion, the material and the demographic. By the material approach we mean the analysis of the evidence that mass executions of Jews by gassings or other specific means were in fact conducted by the Germans during World War II. The material approach is nearly synonymous with analysis of the war crimes trial evidence, or of the trials evidence as interpreted by Hilberg and by Reitlinger, and as supplemented by them with similar evidence. Rassinier only tentatively explored the demographic approach in *Le Véritable Procès Eichmann,* but in his final general work on the Jewish extermination problem, *Le Drame des Juifs Européens,* 1964, he presented a lengthy analysis of the question from a demographic point of view. In 1965 he published *l'Opération "Vicaire",* a critique of Rolf Hochhuth's play, *The Deputy.* One must comment that it is necessary to check up on Rassinier in his interpretation of sources; some do not check out and, in addition, he employs some clearly unreliable sources at a few points. There are also some glaring but relatively irrelevant errors of fact, such as characterizing Hanson Baldwin as the *N.Y. Times* "expert in matters of Jewish population" (it is doubtful that the *Times* ever had a staff member who could be characterized thus), and in asserting that the majority of American Jews are anti-Zionist and support the outlook of the anti-Zionist American Council for Judaism (which was never a politically significant organization). However Rassinier was a courageous pioneer in an ignored area and, despite the various shortcomings of his work, no fair minded person could read it without becoming at least skeptical about the "exterminations". Rassinier passed away in July 1967. His books had appeared in German, Spanish and Italian translations, but no English translation was published for some years.

Rassinier's books were followed by three books which Josef Ginsburg published under the pseudonym J. G. Burg: *Schuld und Schicksal* (Debt and Destiny), 1962, *Suendenboecke* (Scapegoats), 1967, and *NS-Verbrechen* (National Socialist Crimes), 1968. Ginsburg's books are not particularly well researched since his views are based mainly on what he has read in the newspapers plus his personal experiences as a Jew who, together with his family, was deported during the war to occupied eastern territory by the Nazis and the Rumanians. After the war Ginsburg took his family to Israel but he eventually became very anti-Zionist and moved back to Europe, eventually setting up a bookbindery in Munich. While he believes that many Jews perished as a result of the combined effects of Nazi policies and wartime conditions, he denies that the German Government ever contemplated the extermination of the Jews of Europe and he is particularly scornful of the six million figure. He is unsure of the existence of gas chambers, but he believes that many Jews perished on account of epidemics, pogroms, air raids and executions of partisans, and offers an estimate of about three million as the maximum possible number of victims, although he believes the correct figure is much lower. As a reward for his efforts to get at the truth Ginsburg, a small man and not young, was beaten up by Jewish thugs while visiting his wife's grave in the Israelite cemetery in Munich.

In 1969 a short book was published in the United States, *The Myth of the Six Million,* attributed to an anonymous author. The book has had a confused history and a legal litigation forced the withdrawal of the book shortly after its appearance. However, in 1973 it was again being offered for sale. I will only comment here that, in my opinion, the book is terrible and a clear retrogression in relation to the prior work of Rassinier.

The next development was the publication in Germany of a book by Emil Aretz, *Hexen-Einmal-Eins einer Luege* (The Witches' Multiplication Table is a Lie), of which only the third edition, Munich, 1973, seems to have attained significant circulation. Aretz carries the case against the exterminations only slightly beyond Rassinier. He depends heavily on Rassinier in this respect, although he provides some new material. A major function of his book is the presentation of a remarkably bold and forthright general defense of the German nation.

The unreasonable continuation of war crimes trials in West Germany, and the absence of any statute of limitations with respect to alleged war crimes by Germans, have had a seldom remarked implication; people who "were there" have been afraid to come forward and report what, to their knowledge, actually happened. They would rather not call attention to the fact that they "were there". However it was inevitable that a few courageous individuals would come forward nevertheless. The first significant such person was Thies Christophersen, who was at Auschwitz in 1944, and who in 1973 published his booklet *Die Auschwitz Luege* (The Auschwitz Lie), wherein he reported his recollections and his firm view that no exterminations took place there. Christophersen was soon followed by Dr. Wilhelm Staeglich, a Hamburg judge, who was also at Auschwitz in 1944, and who published his recollections in the German monthly *Nation Europa.* Subsequent events confirmed the fears of many. Staeglich soon retired, but he was punished in July 1975 with a twenty percent reduction of his pension for five years. A few months later the publisher of Christophersen's booklet, the lawyer Manfred Roeder, was punished with a fine and suspended prison sentence. Such episodes make it perfectly clear why it has taken so long for the truth to come out.[4]

In 1973 and 1974 there were short works published by Austin J. App in the U.S.A. and by Wolf Dieter Rothe and Heinz Roth in Germany. However the most consequential such publication in this period was Richard Harwood's *Did Six Million Really Die?,* a British booklet that, while not perfect, is quite effective in stimulating serious thought on its subject. It was favourably reviewed by Colin Wilson in the November 1974 issue of the influential British monthly, *Books and Bookmen,* setting off a months-long controversy in the pages of that journal.

In early 1975 Harry Elmer Barnes' translation of one of Rassinier's books, *Drama of the European Jews,* was issued by a small publisher in the

United States.

In this introductory chapter we quickly review the principal problems that arise when demographic questions are asked. We then indicate how demographic problems are resolved in this book, but indicate that the specific task of resolution must be deferred until late in the book.

The problems inherent in a demographic study are formidable. First, all sources of post-war primary data are private Jewish or Communist sources (exclusively the latter in the all important cases of Russia and Poland). Second, it appears that one can get whatever results desired by consulting the appropriately selected pre-war and post-war sources. Consider world Jewish population. The 1939 study of Arthur Ruppin, Professor of Jewish Sociology at the Hebrew University of Jerusalem, gave 16,717,000 Jews in the world in 1938.[5] Since Ruppin (who passed away in 1943) was considered the foremost expert on such matters, on account of many writings on the subject over a period of many years, the estimates of other pre-war sources tend to agree with him. Thus the American Jewish Committee estimate for 1933, which appears in the 1940 *World Almanac,* was 15,315,359. The *World Almanac* figure for 1945 is 15,192,089 (p. 367); no source is given but the figure is apparently based on some sort of religious census. The 1946 *World Almanac* revised this to 15,753,638, a figure which was retained in the editions of 1947 (p. 748), 1948 (p. 572) and 1949 (p. 289). The 1948 *World Almanac* (p. 249) also gives the American Jewish Committee estimate for 1938 (sic), 15,688,259, while the 1949 *World Almanac* (p. 204) reports new figures from the American Jewish Committee which were developed in 1947–1948: 16,643,120 in 1939 and 11,266,600 in 1947. However Hanson Baldwin, *N.Y. Times* military expert, in an article written in 1948 dealing with the then forthcoming Arab-Jewish war on the basis of information available at the UN and other places, gave a figure of 15 to 18 million world Jewish population, as well as figures for such things as Jews in Palestine, Jews in the Middle East, Arabs in Palestine, total Arabs, total Moslems, etc..[6]

Such a sketch illustrates some of the simpler uncertainties that exist in a demographic study. To carry the matter further, the 11–12 million post-war world Jewish population figure which it is necessary to claim in order to maintain the extermination thesis is very vulnerable on two points. The first is the set of statistics offered for the U.S. and the second is the set offered for Eastern Europe. Both, especially the latter, are subject to insuperable uncertainties. Let us first consider the United States. Census figures for the total U.S. population are:[7]

Year	Population
1920	105,710,620
1930	122,775,046
1940	131,669,275
1950	150,697,361
1960	179,300,000

while U.S. Jewish population figures, as given by the Jewish Statistical Bureau (subsidiary of either the American Jewish Conference or the Synagogue of America), H. S. Linfield, Director are:[8]

Year	Jewish Population
1917	3,388,951
1927	4,228,029
1937	4,770,647
1949	5,000,000
1961	5,530,000

It is important to note that all of the U.S. Jewish population figures are given by the same source (Linfield).

The indicated growth of U.S. Jewish population, 1917−1937, is 40.8% while the growth of total U.S. population, 1920−1940 is 24.6%. This contrast is generally reasonable since in the period under consideration Jewish immigration was fairly heavy. However Jewish immigration into the U.S. raises some problems of its own. The American Jewish Yearbook gave a net Jewish immigration for the years 1938−1943 and 1946−1949 (inclusive) of 232,191.[9] Figures for 1944 and 1945 do not seem to be available. It was in those two years, incidentally, that an indeterminate number of Jews were admitted to the U.S. "outside of the regular immigration procedure." It was claimed that there were only 1,000 such Jews quartered at a camp near Oswego, N.Y., and that they were not eligible for admission to the U.S.. This was supposed to be a U.S. contribution to relieving the problems of refugees, but the whole episode seems most strange and suspicious.[10]

Rather than attempt to settle the problem of the extent of Jewish immigration, suppose one allows the Jewish population a growth rate in 1937−1957 at least equal to that of the U.S. Jewish population of 1917−1937, as seems at least reasonable in view of various facts, e.g., the reasons which sent 1.5 million Jews to Palestine during the World War II and aftermath period appear to motivate immigration to the U.S. just as well, and no national or racial immigration quotas were applicable to Jews as such. In such a case there should be at least 6,678,000 Jews in the U.S. in 1957, not the 5,300,000 that are indicated. There are about 1,400,000 Jews missing from the interpolated figures for 1957, and we consider this a conservative figure for the reason given. The period 1937−1957 was one of Jewish movement on an unprecedented scale.

On the other hand we can adopt an equally conservative approach and assume that the 4,770,647 Jews of 1937 grew in 1937−1957 at the same rate as the U.S. population in 1940−1960. Under this assumption these should have become 6,500,000 Jews in the U.S. in 1957. If one adds the reasonable figure of 300,000 more due to immigration we have 6,800,000 in 1957. Thus by either method of extrapolation the figures offered for post-war U.S. Jewish population are at least approximately 1.5 million short for 1957.

The specific major fault of the U.S. Jewish population figures is the inexplicably small claimed growth from 1937 to 1949 despite record Jewish movement and a very open U.S. immigration policy.

Eastern Europe, however, presents the core of the demographic problem. In order to avoid very serious confusion, one must first recognize that there have been extensive border changes in Eastern Europe in the course of the twentieth century. A map of Europe on the eve of World War I (1914−1918) is given as Fig. 1. A map for January 1938 showing, essentially, Europe organized according to the Treaty of Versailles, before Hitler began territorial acquisitions, is given in Fig. 2, and Fig. 4 shows the post-war map of Europe. The principal border change at the end of World War II was the moving westward of the Soviet border, annexing the three Baltic countries (Lithuania, Latvia and Estonia) and parts of Rumania, Czechoslovakia, Poland and East Prussia. Poland was compensated with the remainder of East Prussia and what used to be considered eastern Germany; the effect was to move Poland bodily westward.

Pre-war (1938) Jewish population estimates for Eastern Europe were offered by H. S. Linfield and the American Jewish Committee in the 1948 (sic) *World Almanac* (p. 249). Post-war (1948) figures were published in the 1949 *World Almanac* (p. 204):

	1938	*1948*
Bulgaria	48,398	46,500
Hungary	444,567	180,000
Poland	3,113,900	105,000
Rumania	900,000	430,000
U.S.S.R.	3,273,047	2,032,500
Totals	7,779,912	2,794,000

The claimed Jewish loss for Eastern Europe is thus 4,985,912. The figures for the U.S.S.R. include, in both cases, the three Baltic countries and the Jews of Soviet Asia. The pre-war figures are in all cases in close agreement with the figures that Ruppin published shortly before the war. To the extent that the extermination legend is based on population statistics, it is based precisely on these statistics or their equivalents.

The trouble is that such figures are absolutely meaningless. There is no way a Western observer can check the plausibility, let alone the accuracy, of such figures. He must either be willing to accept Jewish or Communist (mainly the latter) claims on Jewish population for Eastern Europe or he must reject any numbers offered as lacking satisfactory authority.

It is possible to reinforce our objection on this all important point, and simultaneously deal with a reservation that the reader may have; it would appear excessively brazen to claim the virtual disappearance of Polish Jewry if such had not been essentially or approximately the case, or if something like that had not happened. This seems a valid reservation but one must recall that much of the territory that was considered Polish in 1939 was Soviet by 1945. It was possible for Polish Jewry to virtually disappear if, during the 1939—1941 Russian occupation of Eastern Poland, the Soviets had dispersed large numbers of Polish Jews into the Soviet Union, and if, during 1941—1944, the Germans had concentrated Polish Jews eastwards, with the Soviet Union ultimately absorbing many of these Jews into the Soviet Union, with those who did not wish to remain in the Soviet Union emigrating, mainly to Palestine and the U.S., but also to some extent to the new Poland and other lands. This, in fact, is what happened to the Jews who had resided in Poland before the war.

Whatever may be said about Soviet Jewish policy after, say, 1950, it is clear that the earlier policies had not been anti-Jewish and had encouraged the absorbing of Jews into the Soviet Union. It is known that many Polish Jews were absorbed during and immediately after the war, but of course numbers are difficult to arrive at. Reitlinger considers this problem and settles on a figure of 700,000, without giving reasons why the correct figure might not be much higher. He then notes that the evidence that he employs of extermination of Jews in Russia (documents alleged to be German) indicates about the same number of Soviet Jews exterminated, from which he correctly infers that, in the period 1939—1946, the Soviet Jewish population may have actually increased.[11] This important concession, coming from the author of *The Final Solution,* shows that our unwillingness to accept the Communist figures need not be regarded as motivated merely by the necessities of our thesis. The figures are unarguably untrustworthy. It is claimed by the Soviets that their Jewish population declined by 38%, despite the acquisition of territory containing many Jews. Since the U.S.S.R. is one of the lands where "Jew" is a legally recognized nationality the Soviets do, indeed, possess accurate figures on the number of Jews they have but have chosen (in Reitlinger's opinion if you choose not to accept this author's) to claim an utterly mythical Jewish population loss of 38%.

Likewise with the value to be attached to the remainder of the figures offered.

The most relevant research by a demographer appears to be that of Leszek A. Kosinski of the University of Alberta (*Geographical Review*, vol. 59, 1969, 388–402 and *Canadian Slavonic Papers*, vol. 11, 1969, 357–373), who has studied the changes in the entire ethnic structure of East Central Europe (i.e. excluding Germany and Russia) over the period 1930–1960. He explains the extreme difficulties with basic statistics:

> The criteria used in compilation differ from country to country and are not always precise. In principal, two types are used: objective criteria, such as language, cultural affiliation, and religious denomination, and subjective criteria, based on the declaration of the persons themselves. Each type has virtues and deficiencies. Objective criteria define nationality only indirectly and are difficult to apply in marginal cases (for example, bilingual persons). The same criticism applies even more to subjective criteria. External pressure and opportunism can influence the results, especially where national consciousness is not fully developed or where an honest answer can bring undesirable consequences. Official data are not always reliable, then, even when they are not forged, as has also occurred. However, criticism of the official data cannot be applied in the same degree to all the countries, and reliability is very much a function of national policy.

Jews are of course one of the groups Kosinski is interested in and he presents various figures, generally comparable to those given above, for numbers of pre-war Jews. However his post-war data is so useless from this point of view that he does not even attempt to offer specific post-war numbers for Jews, although he offers post-war figures for other groups, e.g. gypsies, giving numbers less significant, statistically, than the numbers of Jews who, according to the extermination mythologists, survived in Eastern Europe. It is true that he accepts the extermination legend in a general way and presents a bar graph showing a catastrophic decrease in the Jewish populations of Poland, Hungary, Rumania and Czechoslovakia. He also remarks that the combined war caused population losses for Jugoslavs, Jews, Poles and east Germans was about 12.5–14 million, not breaking the total down, and referring the reader to the statistical summary *Population Changes in Europe Since 1939* by Gregory (Grzegorz) Frumkin, whose figures for Jews come from the American Jewish Congress, the Zionist Organization of America, and the *Centre de Documentation juive contemporaine* (Center for Contemporary Jewish Documentation) in Paris. However the point is that Kosinski arrives at no figures for Jews, as he obviously should not, given the problems he has noted. The ethnic population figures from Communist Hungary are based on language, and the figures from Communist Poland, Communist Czechoslovakia and Communist Rumania are based on "nationality", whatever that means in the various cases. Naturally he apologizes for his use of "official statistics, imperfect as these may be."

We will return to demographic problems, especially those which involve the Polish Jews, in Chapter VII.

We must also remember that the problem of counting Jews in Western countries contains enormous difficulties on account of the lack of any legal, racial or religious basis for defining a "Jew". As an example, the statistics available to Reitlinger indicate to him that early in World War II there were 300,000 Jews in France, including refugee German Jews.[12] The Nazis, on the other hand, thought that there were 865,000, and I see no motivation for deliberate inflation of this figure; other figures used by the Nazis were not wildly inflated compared to the figures of other sources.[13] I should add that I really have no idea how many Jews there are in the U.S.. I can consult the *World Almanac*, which will tell me that there are about 6,000,000, but I cannot see how that figure was arrived at, and have little confidence in it. As far as I know, the correct figure could as easily be 9,000,000. There must be at least 4,000,000 in the New York City area alone.

To summarize what has been said with respect to Jewish population statistics: the problem of compiling such statistics is formidable even without political interference or pressure. Moreover, in the demographic argument for a five or six million drop in world Jewish population, the sources and authorities for the figures used are Communist and Jewish and thus, by the nature of the problem we are examining, must be considered essentially useless. In addition, the post-war figures for the United States are demonstrably too low by a significant amount.

One should not form the impression that it is essential to my argument that any demographic conclusions seemed to be reached above be accepted by the reader. It has only been shown what sorts of problems arise if one attempts a too direct demographic approach; it is not possible to settle anything in such a manner. In the final analysis the difficulty is that the figures available amount to nothing more than statements, from Jewish and Communist sources, that millions of Jews were killed. Such claims are to be expected, but they must certainly not deter us from looking deeper. We will take up the demographic problem late in the book, however, since the nature of the situation is such that reasonably useful demographic conclusions are possible once it is understood what, in general, happened to the Jews.

Rassinier's demographic study, in fact, does not really even attempt to settle the problem, strictly speaking. His basic approach is to analyze the inferences that have been drawn from two different sets of data, that of the *Centre de Documentation juive contemporaine* and that of Hilberg, both of whom infer from their data five to six million Jewish victims of the Nazis. Rassinier's conclusion is that the former can only claim 1,485,292 victims from its data, and the latter 896,892.[14] Rassinier accepts the reality of about a million Jewish *victims of Nazi policies,* while rejecting the claims of *extermination.* For example, it is known that some East European peoples took advantage of general political-military conditions to persecute Jews. Also, many Jews who were deported from their homes no doubt perished as a result of generally chaotic conditions which accompanied the latter part of the war.

Believing that the task is not possible, I will offer here no definite estimate of Jewish losses. However, I have no strong reason to quarrel with Rassinier's estimate.

As stated, the "material" approach will be extended here and, in addition, a "historical-political" approach will be "introduced". This is just a fancy way of saying that we will grasp that there are two political powers involved in the problem, not just one. That is to say, we have a tale of extermination and we should inquire into the circumstances of its generation. Clearly, there are two states involved in the problem. Germany had an anti-Jewish policy involving, in many cases, deportations of Jews from their homes and countries of citizenship. That is certain. The wartime policy of Washington was to claim extermination and the post-war policy was to hold trials at which there was generated the only evidence that we have today that these wartime claims had any foundation. That is also certain. The policies of both states are necessarily of interest and, if there is any respect in which this book may be breaking fundamentally new ground on the problem, it is in its insistence in seeing Washington as an active agent in the generation of the story. Thus we are interested not only in what Hitler, Himmler, Goering, Goebbels and Heydrich were doing during the war in regard to these matters, but also what Roosevelt, Hull, Morgenthau and the *N.Y. Times* and associated media were doing during the war, and what the various tribunals controlled or dominated by Washington did after the war. This is not only a fair but, more importantly, an illuminating historical approach.

The conclusion is that Washington constructed a frame-up on the Jewish extermination charge. Once this is recognized, the true nature of German Jewish policy will be seen.

Before we review the details of the story it should be pointed out that there are excellent *a priori* grounds for expecting a frame-up. There is of course the very general argument that political enmity of a magnitude to bring on armed conflict between two states necessarily excludes the impartiality on the part of one of them which is a necessity for a fair trial, and for which there exists no substitute. The judges had pursued political careers in the contexts of the internal politics of the Allied powers hostile to Germany and after the trials would, assuming they had not done anything highly improbable at the war crimes trials, return to these careers. They had, in addition, for several years heard only the anti-German viewpoint. In sitting on the military tribunals, they were *ad hoc* political appointees. Such considerations exclude approximate impartiality.

There are, however, much more specific reasons for expecting a frame-up. In order to see this it is only necessary to consider the easily obtainable facts concerning the various tribunals involved.

First there was the "big trial" conducted by the "International Military Tribunal" (IMT) at Nuernberg immediately after the war. This was the trial of the top Nazis Goering, Hess, Ribbentrop *et. al.* which ran from November 1945 to October 1946. The judges and prosecutors were American, British, French and Russian. As with all "military" tribunals, there was no jury. There were three acquittals, seven prison sentences and eleven death sentences. The latter were carried out almost immediately after the trial except that Goering escaped the noose by swallowing a potassium cyanide capsule just before the hangings. It was never determined where Goering had obtained the poison, or how he had managed to hide it for any length of time. A unique sequel to this episode was that the first Nuernberg prison psychiatrist, Dr. Douglas M. Kelley, a leader in the treatment of psychiatric disorders with drugs, shortly later published a book on his experiences at Nuernberg, giving Goering and Goering's last act a laudatory treatment:

> He stoically endured his long imprisonment that he might force down the Allied Tribunal and browbeat the prosecuting lawyers on their own terms . . . His suicide . . . was a skillful, even brilliant, finishing touch, completing the edifice for Germans to admire in time to come. . . . History may well show that Goering won out at the end, even though condemned by the high court of the Allied powers.

A decade later Dr. Kelley followed Goering by taking one of several potassium cyanide capsules which he possessed, said to be "souvenirs" taken off Goering's body.[15]

The IMT trial was the only one that received very great attention. It was important in the sense that the Allied powers committed themselves to a specific version of the extermination claim, but there was little evidence presented of any substantial nature, relative to Jewish extermination; it was almost entirely testimony and affidavits, not at all difficult for the victorious powers to produce under the circumstances. The only relative merit of the IMT trial, for our purposes, is that the complete transcript and a reasonably complete selection of the documents put into evidence are readily available (see References) in numerous libraries as a 42 volume set with a very complete subject and name index.

From 1946 to 1949 a series of twelve superficially less important trials were held by the Americans before what is here called the Nuernberg Military Tribunal (NMT). They are referred to variously according to the "case number", the major defendant, or a more descriptive title:

Case No.	U.S. vs.	Description	NMT vols.
1	Brandt	Medical Case	1, 2
2	Milch	Milch Case	2
3	Alstoetter	Justice Case	3
4	Pohl	Concentration Camps Case	5, 6
5	Flick	Business Men Case	6
6	Krauch	I.G. Farben Case	7, 8
7	List	Hostages Case	9
8	Greifelt	RuSHA Case	4, 5
9	Ohlendorf	Einsatzgruppen Case	4
10	Krupp	Krupp Case	9
11	Weizsaecker	Wilhelmstrasse, or Ministries, Case	12–14
12	von Leeb	High Command Case	10, 11

Several death sentences resulted from these trials but the great majority received prison sentences, in many cases rather lengthy ones. However, almost all were free by the early Fifties.

The only cases among these that will concern us here in any way are Case 1, a trial of medical personnel involved in euthanasia and medical experiments, Case 4, a trial of concentration camp administration, Cases 6 and 10, self explanatory, Case 8, dealing with German resettlement policies, Case 9 (the *Einsatzgruppen* were used for rear security in Russia) and Case 11, a trial of officials of various ministries. The U.S. Government published a fifteen volume set of books, referred to here as the "NMT set", in which may be found "summaries" of the cases, along with very limited "selections" of the documents put into evidence. The volume numbers corresponding to the various cases are listed in the above table.

On this point the student encounters a significant difficulty because, as can be seen by consulting Hilberg and Reitlinger, almost all the evidence for the extermination claim was developed at the NMT, not the IMT. That is to say the important documents, those which, for better or for worse, constitute major source material for writing any history of Nazi Germany, are those of the NG, NI and NO series, and these documents were put into evidence at the NMT trials. Documentary evidence is, especially in view of the irregular legal and political circumstances which prevailed, immeasurably more weighty than testimony, as has been suggested. The relevant documentary evidence generated at the NMT consists of certain kinds of material allegedly supporting the extermination charges: documents dealing with concentration camp administration, with crematoria construction, with deportations, with certain Farben and Krupp operations which employed prisoner labor, with general Jewish policies of the German Government, etc.. There is of course no direct documentary evidence for an extermination program. As Dr. Kubovy of the Center for Jewish Documentation in Tel-Aviv admitted in 1960, "there exists no document signed by Hitler, Himmler or Heydrich speaking of exterminating the Jews and . . . the word 'extermination' does not appear in the letter from Goering to Heydrich concerning the final solution of the Jewish question."[16]

The difficulty for the normally circumstanced person is that only small fractions of the NMT testimonies and documents are widely accessible, in English translations (in the fifteen volume NMT set). Additionally, these translations cannot always be trusted, as will be seen. Also, the extracts which are published have been selected by unknown criteria. Finally, the fifteen volume NMT set is likely to be found only in cities of moderately large size.

The situation is better if one lives in a very large city, since reasonably complete collections of documents together with the mimeographed trial transcripts (almost always in German) exist in certain library centers. However the normally circumstanced person may encounter trouble in arranging to examine specific pieces which he may call for, and in some cases general browsing even by university faculty is not welcome. In addition, no subject or name indexes exist for the NMT trials (indexes of testimonies of witnesses, with many errors, appear in the NMT volumes).

The IMT and NMT trials are almost the only ones of significance here. Of general significance are a series held by the British; of these, only the Belsen case and the Zyklon B case interest us to any extent. The Poles, Russians, French, Dutch and Italians have all held trials of no significance except to the victims. The Bonn Government has held some trials of slight interest, for example the "Auschwitz trial" of 1963–1965, reported on by Langbein, by Laternser and by Naumann.

The manners in which the IMT and the NMT were constituted can be set forth with sufficient completeness for our purposes. Since the autumn of 1943, there had been in existence a United Nations War Crimes Commission, headquartered in London. However this Commission never really did anything except realize, at one point, that if anything was to be done, it would be done by the individual Allied governments.

The first serious moves started in the United States. In August 1944 the Joint Chiefs of Staff considered a proposed program for dealing with war crimes. The proposal had been approved by the Judge Advocate General of the U.S. Army. On 1 October 1944 the Joint Chiefs approved this proposal and, at about the same time and in accordance with directives of the Secretary of War, a "War Crimes Branch" was established in the Department of the Judge Advocate General. The War Crimes Branch, headed by Brig. Gen. John M. Weir, with Colonel Melvin Purvis as his assistant, was responsible for handling all war crimes matters for the State, War and Navy Departments.

The proposal which had been approved by the Joint Chiefs did not survive for very long, for its character had been rather traditional, in that it contemplated, basically, the trial of persons who had broken the accepted laws of war in the field. Thus, offenses committed before the war or acts by enemy authorities against their own nationals were not considered to be under Allied jurisdiction. Thus, for example, all measures against German Jews were considered outside the jurisdiction of the planned war crimes trials. The concept of war crimes was, at this point, strongly under the influence of the principle, never questioned, that a belligerent may try enemy soldiers for the same sorts of offenses for which he may try his own soldiers.

The Secretary of War, Stimson, had a conference with President Roosevelt on 21 November 1944, at which Roosevelt made it clear that he had in mind a much broader idea of war crimes, and that the proposals approved by the Joint Chiefs were completely unsatisfactory. Accordingly, in January 1945, Roosevelt designated Judge Samuel Rosenman as his personal representative in discussions on war crimes problems. A meeting of 18 January between Stimson, Rosenman, Attorney General Francis Biddle and others resulted in general agreement on very much expanded conceptions of war crimes to be tried.[17]

Biddle was later to sit as a judge at the IMT although, for Roosevelt's use at the Yalta conference, he had written in January 1945 that "the chief

German leaders are well known and the proof of their guilt will not offer great difficulties." The Russian IMT "justice" Nikitchenko was slightly more direct in declaring before the trial that "we are dealing here with the chief war criminals who have already been convicted."[18]

In early May 1945 President Truman approved the revised proposals and appointed Robert H. Jackson, an Associate Justice of the Supreme Court, to act as Chief of Counsel for the U.S. in the forthcoming trial, and also to represent the U.S. in negotiations with foreign governments relative to constituting the trial. On 6 June 1945 Jackson made an interim report to the President and later in June Jackson and his staff set up headquarters in London, where much of the preliminary work for the IMT was done.

A key member of Jackson's London staff was Colonel Murray C. Bernays, who was one of the first people who had been involved in war crimes problems. Graduated from Harvard in 1915, he established a law practice in New York. He was given a commission in the Army in 1942 and, in October 1943, he was made chief of the Special Projects Branch, Personnel Division, Army General Staff. His major project in this position was the preparation of plans for trials of German "war criminals". After each stage of negotiations with the White House and others he made the appropriate revisions in the plans being considered although, if one is to credit his account, he was the author of the plan that was eventually settled on. In any case, shortly after the appointment of Jackson, Bernays was awarded the Legion of Merit, the citation reading in part:

> Early recognizing the need for a sound basis in dealing with the problem of war criminals and war crimes, he formulated the basic concept of such a policy and initiated timely and appropriate action which assured its adoption as the foundation of national policy.

Bernays returned to the U.S. in November 1945 and immediately resigned from the Army. Since, as we have seen, there was considerable dialogue at higher levels relating to plans for war crimes trials, it is doubtful that one can take Bernays' claims at full value, but he no doubt had a great deal to do with the drafting of the plans for the trials. Moreover, he had certainly been an appropriate choice for something as novel as the formulation of the "legal" structure for the war crimes trials, since his views of justice were equally novel. After his return to the U.S. he had a chat with some editors (who characterized him as "the man behind the gavel"), and in answer to their queries as to "how the small fry are going to be hooked," he replied:[19]

> There are a good many Nazi criminals who will get off if the roundups aren't conducted efficiently. But if we establish that the SS, for example, was a criminal organization, and that membership in it is evidence *per se* of criminality, the Allies are going to get hold of a great many more criminals in one swoop. You know, a lot of people here at home don't realize that we are now the government of Germany in our zone and that no judicial system can exist other than one we approve. We *are* the law. If we wanted to, for instance, we could try Germans for crimes twenty, thirty, forty years old. We'll be too busy with the current crop of war criminals, though, to have much time to look into ancient wrongdoings.

In London, Jackson negotiated with the Allies on the trials, and his interim report of 6 June became the basis for the "London Agreement" of 8 August, signed by the U.S., Britain, Russia and France. An "indictment" was filed against twenty four individuals and six organizations (the SS, the General Staff, etc.) on 18 October and the trial opened at Nuernberg on 20 November 1945. Three of the listed defendants did not stand trial. Martin Bormann was never found, Robert Ley committed suicide before the trial, and Gustav Krupp was too ill and too old to stand trial. An attempt was made by the prosecution to substitute Krupp's son as defendant, but this was too much even for that court, so the trial of Alfred Krupp had to wait until the NMT.

In passing we should note that Justice Jackson, in addition to being the American chief prosecutor at the trial, was also in a formal sense the leading personality in the London negotiations relative to the formulation of the legal system under which he was to operate at the trial. A rare opportunity for a prosecutor, and probably an utterly unprecedented one in respect to proceedings that civilized people have seriously considered to be trials. Equally unique features of the final charter of the IMT were that its jurisdiction was not restricted to acts taken in connection with the war but extended over the entire life of the Nazi Party, that the defense of superior orders was inapplicable and that defendants could be compelled by the prosecution to testify.

The War Crimes Branch that had been set up in 1944 did not cease to operate, since in connection with the IMT trial Jackson had "enlisted the cooperation and participation of the War Crimes Branch of the Judge Advocate General's Department." Moreover, in the early months of the IMT trial (and perhaps also later), the ordinary prosecution staff, exclusive of Jackson, was "on the payroll of the Judge Advocate General."[20]

A significant role for the Judge Advocate General's Department (JAG Dept.) was most natural under the circumstances since the JAG Dept. was the legal agency of the Army, and the basic American administrative machinery in Germany immediately after the war was that of the U.S. Army. The traditional role of the JAG Dept. had been the administration of military justice: court martials and related matters. However during World War II the operations of the JAG Dept. had spread to all phases of military activity where legal matters arose; it even got involved in litigations relative to war production contracts. The Judge Advocate General, Maj. Gen. Myron C. Cramer, had given a speech in May 1945 in which he declared that the pursuit and arraignment of Nazis was to tax to the utmost the capacity of the War Crimes Branch and become a major activity of the JAG Dept., whose resources he pledged to Jackson. This was not, one can be sure, a vacuous promise, since the organization that Cramer headed had much more substance than that headed by Jackson. While it is not specified exactly what the War Crimes Branch did in connection with the IMT, it is most likely that it effectively supervised the American (hence major) role in the screening and selection of prosecution and defense lawyers and staff, in the selection of other staff such as translators, and in interrogations. Of course, Jackson formally held much of this authority, but it is reasonably sure that such responsibilities were, in fact, exercised by the War Crimes Branch.[21]

The involvement of the War Crimes Branch in trials was, however, much deeper. While the IMT and NMT trials were being conducted, several lesser trials were taking place. Among these were the trials held at the Dachau camp (outside Munich, and thus not far from Nuernberg) of the staffs of some concentration camps (Buchenwald, Flossenburg, Dachau) which had been captured by the Americans, and of the Germans accused of killing 83 American prisoners at Malmédy during the Battle of the Bulge. These trials were supervised by the War Crimes Branch.[22] They were perhaps the most shameful episodes in U.S. history.

The entire repertoire of third degree methods was enacted at Dachau: beatings and brutal kicking, to the point of ruining testicles in 137 cases, knocking out teeth, starvation, solitary confinement, torture with burning splinters, and impersonation of priests in order to encourage prisoners to "confess". Low rank prisoners were assured that convictions were being sought only against higher ranking officers, and that they had absolutely nothing to lose by cooperating and making the desired statements. Such "evidence" was then used against them when they joined their superiors in the dock. The latter, on the other hand, had been told that by "confessing" they had taken all responsibility onto themselves, thereby shielding their men from trial. A favorite strategem, when a prisoner refused to cooperate, was to arrange a mock trial. The prisoner was led into a room in which civilian investigators, dressed in U.S. Army uniforms, were seated around a black table with a crucifix in the center, with two candles providing the only light. This "court" then proceeded to hold a sham trial, at the conclusion of which a sham death sentence was passed. The "condemned" prisoner was later promised that, if he cooperated with the prosecutors in giving evidence, he would be reprieved. Sometimes interrogators threatened to turn prisoners over to the Russians. In many cases the prisoner's family was threatened with loss of ration cards or other hardships if cooperation was not obtained.

The official, as distinct from the mock, trials were also an apparently deliberate mockery of any conception of due process. The mockery started with the "indictment", which made only general reference to very broad categories of crimes allegedly committed in the years from 1942 to 1945 (in the cases of concentration camp personnel), and then proceeded to present a long list of defendants accused of being criminal in the extremely general sense stated. Specific crimes by specific people on specific dates were not part of the indictments (e.g. document 3590-PS).

In some cases, the "defense counsel" was an American with no legal training, who could not speak German. Competent interpreters were not provided at the trial. The "prosecution" also lacked legal training, as did the "court", which consisted of ten U.S. Army officers. There was one person with legal training present, all of whose rulings on the admissibility of evidence were final. There were 1,416 convictions out of 1,672 tried, with 420 death sentences.

While the prosecution could hunt all over Europe for witnesses and, if necessary, torture or otherwise coerce Germans in order to get "evidence", the accused, cut off from the outside world and without funds, were rarely able to summon anybody to their defense. In addition, the "Association of Persons Persecuted by the Nazis," by a propaganda campaign, forbade former concentration camp inmates to testify for the defense.

The American lawyer George A. McDonough, who had had the rather peculiar experience of having served as both a prosecutor and defense counsel in the war crimes program, and later on as a member of a reviewing board and an arbiter on clemency petitions, wrote to the *N.Y. Times* in 1948 complaining about the lack of legal basis for the trials, and remarking that "in nine problems out of ten the authorities and the textbooks had no answer" to the legal questions that regularly and consistently came up for anybody seriously concerned with matters of legality. For McDonough, the major problem was whether or not a defense of superior orders should be accepted in war crimes trials. In respect to the Dachau trials he wrote:

> At the Dachau trials, the claim of the accused that he would have been shot himself if he had not obeyed his superior's order to commit an act which he, in ignorance, may have believed to be a legal order, or knew to be illegal, seemed to be handled by the courts as an issue of fact. The availability of this defense seemed to depend upon the age and the rank of the accused, and the state of battle existing at the time of the offense. Again it would seem high-handed procedure to hold an enlisted man to the knowledge of the illegality of a particular act when the international authorities themselves are in disagreement as to its illegality or have never defined the act at all.
> . . . Hearsay evidence was admitted indiscriminately and sworn statements of witnesses were admissible regardless of whether anybody knew the person who made the

statement or the individual who took the statement. If a prosecutor considered a statement of a witness to be more damaging than the witness' oral testimony in court he would advise the witness to go back to his home, submit the statement as evidence, and any objection by defense counsel would be promptly overruled.

One notable incident occurred when investigator Joseph Kirschbaum brought a certain Einstein into court to testify that the accused Menzel had murdered Einstein's brother. When the accused was able to point out that the brother was alive and well and, in fact, sitting in court, Kirschbaum was deeply embarassed and scolded poor Einstein: "How can we bring this pig to the gallows, if you are so stupid as to bring your brother into court?"

The U.S. Army authorities in charge admitted some of these things. When the chief of the Dachau War Crimes Administration Branch, Colonel A. H. Rosenfeld, quit his post in 1948 he was asked by newspapermen if there was any truth to the stories about the mock trials, at which sham death sentences had been passed. He replied: "Yes, of course. We couldn't have made those birds talk otherwise...... It was a trick, and it worked like a charm."[23]

The Malmédy defendants had had a competent defense attorney, Lt. Colonel Willis M. Everett, Jr.. It was Everett's repeated appeals to, among others, the U.S. Supreme Court, plus a chorus of protests from German clergymen and others, plus such details regarding what was going on that managed to get into the press by various routes, that persuaded the American military governor, General Lucius D. Clay, to request an investigation of the trials at Dachau. On 29 July 1948 the Secretary of the Army appointed a commission consisting of two American judges, Gordon Simpson of Texas and Edward Van Roden of Pennsylvania, both JAG Department reserve colonels. They were assisted by JAG Department Lt. Colonel Charles Lawrence, Jr.. The commission submitted its report to the Secretary of the Army in October 1948, and selected portions were made public in January 1949. Subsequent public remarks by Van Roden and also, to some extent, by Simpson, plus an independent investigation by a review board appointed by Clay, decisively exposed the whole affair, to the point where the defenders of the trials could only haggle about the numbers of German prisoners subjected to brutalities. The review board confirmed all that Van Roden claimed, taking exception only in respect to the frequencies of the brutalities.[24] Oddly, in his book, *Decision in Germany*, Clay denies the brutalities, but he is contradicted by his own review board.

The cases, especially the Malmédy case, attracted a good deal of attention through 1949, and a subcommittee headed by Senator Baldwin conducted an investigation. One witness, formerly a court reporter at the Dachau trials, testified that he was so repelled by what had gone on there that he quit the job. He said that the "most brutal" had been Lieutenant Perl, Frank Steiner and Harry W. Thon. He explained that both Perl and his wife had been in Nazi concentration camps, and that the Nazis had killed Steiner's mother. Judge Gordon Simpson (unlike Van Roden, trying to put the best interpretation, even if very strained, on the sorry facts that had come out) conceded that this was probably "a poor team", and explained that the shortage of German speaking American lawyers and interpreters had forced the Army to "draw on some of the German refugees." Steiner, Kirschbaum and Thon (later chief of the evaluation section of the civil administration division of the U.S. military government) appeared later and denied all, but they were shaken by the testimony of investigator Bruno Jacob, who admitted a few things. Speaking for the press, investigators Dwight Fanton and Morris Elowitz also denied all. Colonel Rosenfeld denied almost all. He charged that Lt. Colonel Harold D. McGown, commander of the American soldiers massacred at Malmédy, had fraternized with SS Colonel Joachim Peiper, the German commander, and this explained why McGown had appeared at Dachau as a defense witness for Peiper and had testified that Peiper had held talks with him and had been responsible for saving a number of Americans. As evidence for the fraternization, Rosenfeld claimed that McGown and Peiper had been "entirely too friendly during those nights they spent talking together" and that, when Peiper and his men were later able to escape a U.S. Army trap, "McGown was with them." Of course, McGown was Peiper's prisoner.[25]

It will, of course, be argued that these nightmarish Dachau "trials" have little to do with our subject because the standards maintained in the trials at Nuernberg were not comparable and because the bearers of the extermination legend do not cite any of the "evidence" produced at these trials. There is partial truth to these contentions; brutality and coercion were not nearly as extensive at the prominent Nuernberg trials as they were at the Dachau trials, and mass exterminations were not emphasized in the Dachau trials (although gas chambers made occasional appearances in testimony). However the Dachau trials cannot be waved aside so easily because the administering agency, the War Crimes Branch, was also deeply involved in the Nuernberg trials, as we have noted, and as we are to reconfirm shortly in a particularly striking respect. In addition coercion was, in fact, employed in order to get evidence at the Nuernberg trials, but that subject is discussed in a later chapter.

None of the four powers were happy with the IMT arrangement and after the "big trial" they split up and held the kinds of trials they were interested in. The British trials reflected a general interest but on points of relatively minor significance here. The only major French trial was of Saar industrial magnate Hermann Roechling, whom the French had also tried, *in absentia,* after World War I. Planning for the American NMT trials had actually started in 1945, and in March 1946 a division of Jackson's office, headed by Telford Taylor, had been created for this purpose.

It is worth noting that in all of these trials of Nazis, from the IMT through the Eichmann "trial" of 1961 (in which defense witnesses were not permitted) to the "Auschwitz trial" of 1963–1965 (which the Bonn Government would not allow Rassinier to attend as observer), the defense lawyers had no staff of trained research assistants to go through the documents and, in addition, almost all of the documents which were available to them were controlled by the prosecuting powers.[26] Whatever the legalistic evaluation of such a situation, it can produce a very distorted historical picture if not approached skeptically.

Under the legalistic schema of the occupation, there was an important constraint on the NMT and other single nation tribunals:

The determination of the International Military Tribunal in the judgments . . . that invasions, aggressive acts, aggressive wars, crimes, atrocities or inhumane acts were planned or occurred, shall be binding on the tribunals established hereunder and shall not be questioned except insofar as the participation therein or knowledge thereof by any particular person may be concerned. Statements of the International Military Tribunal in the judgment . . . constitute proof of the facts stated, in the absence of substantial new evidence to the contrary.

Two administratively distinct organizations functioned at the NMT. One was the collection of "Military Tribunals", the judges, functioning administratively through a Secretariat, headed by a Secretary General. The judges were recruited in the U.S. "by the Department of the Army." There were three or more judges at any one trial.

25

The second organization was the Office, Chief of Counsel for War Crimes (Telford Taylor) which had come into existence on 24 October 1946, immediately after Ribbentrop *et. al.* had been killed. It filed its first indictment the next day. Although there was a trivial difference in their titles, Taylor, who had been an associate trial counsel at the IMT, was really the successor to Jackson in the trials being staged in the Nuernberg courthouse.[27]

We will have much to say of the NMT trials in this volume. However the reader can grasp much of the spirit of these proceedings even from remarks made by some of the American judges who had been recruited by the U.S. Army to serve at Nuernberg. Understandably, these people were normally very reluctant to speak out publicly against what they observed. Thus, the remark of one of the judges in the Farben trial, that there were "too many Jews on the prosecution", was a privately expressed hint to the prosecution, certainly not intended for publication. However the presiding judge in Case 7 (trial of German generals for alleged wholesale murder of hostages), Charles F. Wennerstrum, spoke out publicly and forcefully, immediately after sentences had been pronounced:[28]

If I had known seven months ago what I know today, I would never have come here.

Obviously, the victor in any war is not the best judge of the war crime guilt. Try as you will it is impossible to convey to the defense, their counsel, and their people that the court is trying to represent all mankind rather than the country which appointed its members.

What I have said of the nationalist character of the tribunals applies to the prosecution. The high ideals announced as the motives for creating these tribunals has not been evident.

The prosecution has failed to maintain objectivity aloof from vindictiveness, aloof from personal ambitions for convictions. It has failed to strive to lay down precedents which might help the world to avoid future wars.

The entire atmosphere here is unwholesome. Linguists were needed. The Americans are notably poor linguists. Lawyers, clerks, interpreters and researchers were employed who became Americans only in recent years, whose backgrounds were imbedded in Europe's hatreds and prejudices.

The trials were to have convinced the Germans of the guilt of their leaders. They convinced the Germans merely that their leaders lost the war to tough conquerors.

Most of the evidence in the trials was documentary, selected from the large tonnage of captured records. The selection was made by the prosecution. The defense had access only to those documents which the prosecution considered material to the case.

Our tribunal introduced a rule of procedure that when the prosecution introduced an excerpt from a document, the entire document should be made available to the defense for presentation as evidence. The prosecution protested vigorously. Gen. Taylor tried out of court to call a meeting of the presiding judges to rescind this order. It was not the attitude of any conscientious officer of the court seeking full justice.

Also abhorrent to the American sense of justice is the prosecution's reliance upon self-incriminating statements made by the defendants while prisoners for more than 2½ years, and repeated interrogation without presence of counsel. Two and one-half years of confinement is a form of duress in itself.

The lack of appeal leaves me with a feeling that justice has been denied.

. . . You should go to Nuernberg. You would see there a palace of justice where 90 per cent of the people are interested in the prosecution.

. . . The German people should receive more information about the trials and the German defendants should receive the right to appeal to the United Nations.

Ironically, the validity of Wennerstrum's attack on the low or non-existent standards of integrity maintained by the Nuernberg prosecution was confirmed even by the nature of Telford Taylor's reaction to Wennerstrum's statements, which were made in supposed privacy in Nuernberg, for publication in the *Chicago Tribune*. The *Tribune* reporter, Hal Foust, sent the message to Berlin for transmission to the U.S., on a wireless channel which was supposedly secure from prying. However the prosecution, apparently by employment of a ruse, managed to obtain a copy of the message. Ernest C.

Deane, Taylor's press officer, immediately phoned Foust in order to attempt "to talk him out of sending the story." However the story had already been sent, and Foust replied that "Taylor could not properly have knowledge of the article until its publication." Taylor thereupon prepared a reply to Wennerstrum's remarks, and the reply was actually made public before the *Tribune* published the Foust story containing Wennerstrum's attack. Taylor accused the judge, among other things, of making remarks "subversive to the interests and policies of the United States." Wennerstrum, on arrival in the U.S. shortly after the publication of Taylor's "reply" and of the *Tribune* story, stood firm on his remarks and again criticized Taylor.

This incident was one of the notable "government spying" incidents of the year 1948. The Army issued an order against such spying, and there was much speculation that Taylor might be court martialed. When reporters asked Taylor for his opinion on the legality of his action, the following exchange occurred:

"I don't know whether it was legal or not," he replied.

"Weren't you general counsel of the federal communications commission for two years before being commissioned in the army?"

"Yes, but what does that have to do with it?"

Taylor steadfastly refused to express an opinion of the legality of his action but

off the record indicated he was as pleased with himself as a field officer . . . which he never was . . . who had just scored against the enemy by a trick outside the rules of warfare as prescribed by the 1907 Geneva convention.

The quote is from Hal Foust's story about the Taylor press conference. Foust claimed that this was the second instance of Army interference with his messages to his newspaper, and that in the first instance he had been picked up by Army agents for interrogation after his story had been sent.

In our examination of the Nuernberg trials we are naturally interested in who supervised the NMT proceedings. *Pro forma,* Taylor supervised almost everything except the appointments of the judges, since the Chief of Counsel's formal responsibilities were not confined to the mere prosecution of cases. His Office was also charged with determining who should and who should not be tried (there was no separate proceeding for formulating indictments, such as a grand jury), what the former were to be charged with and how the latter were to be disposed of. The Office also took over the functions of the Nuernberg staff and hence one may assume that the Office took over, at least formally, the (expanded) Nuernberg staff itself. Thus the Office was responsible for interrogations, field work, examination of documents, court reporting, and translating and interpreting.[29]

We have given reasons why one should expect that this Nuernberg staff had been under the effective supervision of the War Crimes Branch and it will shortly be seen that, whatever Taylor's formal powers, his actual functions do not suggest that he ever took over the Nuernberg staff in any effective sense. The War Crimes Branch, although quartered in far-off Washington, continues to be involved in our consideration of the Nuernberg trials.

On 12 June 1948 the American press carried a story which reported that an officer of the U.S. Army, Colonel David "Mickey" Marcus, a West Point graduate operating under the alias "Mickey Stone", had been killed in action while serving as supreme commander in the Jerusalem sector in the Jewish-Arab war for the control of Palestine (actually, Marcus had been erroneously shot by one of his own sentries). The *N.Y. Times* summarized his career. He had been Commissioner of Corrections in N.Y. before the war and, as an Army officer, had helped draft the German and Italian surrender terms. He was a legal aid at the Potsdam conference (summer of 1945), after which point, if one judges from the adulatory *N.Y. Times* article only, his career ended, since we are told of no other activity of Marcus' until he turns up with the Haganah in Palestine in January 1948, visits the U.S. in April, receiving a medal at a ceremony in the British Embassy in Washington (probably a cover for negotiations on the details of the final British capitulation), and then returns to Palestine after three weeks to take over in Jerusalem. The only hint we get of any activity in the period August 1945 to January 1948 is a story on 24 June, p. 15, reporting that the London *Daily Telegraph* of the same date said that

> He was at the time of his death a full colonel in the Judge Advocate General's office of the organized reserve of officers ... Although not subject to military discipline he had agreed to remain subject to recall.

Marcus had, in fact, been Weir's successor as head of the War Crimes Branch. Immediately after the war, he had been "number three man in making American policy" in occupied Germany, but was taken out of this position early in 1946 in order to take the war crimes job. His appointment was effective as of 18 February 1946, but he spent a few months in Japan after leaving Germany and then moved into the Washington office of the War Crimes Branch in June. He remained the chief of the War Crimes Branch until April 1947, when he retired from the Army and went into private law practice.[30]

Our previous observations obviously suggest that it was in reality the War Crimes Branch that exercised the crucial functions in respect to the NMT. This is the case, as is made clear by a careful reading of Taylor's official final report on the NMT trials, although the fact is not emphasized there.[31] The fact is confirmed by the remarkable book by Josiah E. DuBois, who headed the I.G. Farben NMT prosecution, and Berkman's book about Marcus provides some sketchy information on this aspect of Marcus' career.[32]

Marcus was made head of the War Crimes Branch primarily in order "to take over the mammoth task of selecting hundreds of judges, prosecutors and lawyers" for the NMT and Far East (Tokyo) trials. In December 1946 DuBois had been summoned to Marcus' office in Washington to discuss the possibility of DuBois' taking over the prosecution of leading officials of the great German chemicals firm, I.G. Farben. DuBois had been undecided so he conferred at length with Marcus on the problems involved; one of the problems being whether or not there was sufficient evidence to charge Farben with an "aggressive war" plot and, if so charged, the possible political repercussions that might ensue. They discussed the general advantages of bringing the Farben men to trial. One point Marcus made was that a trial might show how Farben managed to develop certain weapons in total secrecy. Then too, if they went free, they might start working for the Russians. Marcus displayed great knowledge of Farben. He pointed out that there was a "warehouse full" of Farben records in nearby Alexandria, Virginia, a fact which DuBois forgot until later events forced him to recall and act on it during the pre-trial investigation.

They got around to the required length of the pre-trial investigation. Said Marcus, "As far as I'm concerned, you could go over there for as long or as short a time as you liked." DuBois suggests that he would need about four months, and Marcus replies, "I have no objection to that. Within a few days after you get home, you should get a wire from Telford Taylor agreeing to it."

Taylor, of course, was in Europe in his capacity of Chief of Counsel. DuBois records Taylor's activities relative to the Farben trial. He responded favorably to a staff member's suggestion that DuBois (under whom the staff member had worked in the Treasury Department during the war) be appointed to prosecute Farben. He passes the recommendation on to Washington. After DuBois had taken the job, he had plans to see Taylor to get his OK for adding another man, specified by DuBois, to the prosecution staff. The OK was granted. Taylor went to Paris to plead before the French cabinet for the extradition of a key Farben man. Taylor gave the opening speech at the Farben trial and then disappeared from the proceedings. Taylor was not involved in the pre-trial investigation or in the formulation of the specific charges made by the prosecution.

All of this suggests rather strongly that Taylor's role was in public relations and that he was not deeply involved in the details of the running of the trials which were his formal responsibility. Somebody or some others must have exercised effective responsibility. Such situations are not unusual in large scale operations.

The facts show that the real organizers of the NMT trials were not as much in the public eye as Taylor was; in effect and possibly in intention Taylor was a front man. Marcus, as head of the War Crimes Branch, no doubt exercised effective control of much of the Nuernberg staff, and he selected the judges and lawyers for the trials (with only a handful of exceptions). The book by DuBois shows that Taylor was not involved with the trials on the working level so the inescapable conclusion is that the substantial powers of Taylor's office were actually exercised either by the War Crimes Branch or by persons subordinate to Taylor. In examining the prominent persons in the latter group one encounters Robert M. W. Kempner, who is discussed in Chapter V.

Marcus seems to have had a real importance quite incommensurate with his relatively common rank of Colonel, since we are told that during the war he had made a "favorable impression on F.D.R. . . . he was one of the anonymous handful who charted American policy behind the scenes." A man whose career was remarkably intertwined with that of Marcus was General J. H. Hilldring, who headed the Army Civil Affairs Division that Marcus was assigned to in 1943. The CAD had been created in 1943 within the Army General Staff in anticipation of a need for a group to concern itself with policies to be followed in occupied territories. It had been thought that Fiorello LaGuardia was to head the CAD, but the job went to Hilldring. Marcus became a member, and later the chief, of the Planning Branch of the CAD. It was as a consequence of Marcus' activities in the CAD that he made his mark; his assignment to the military government of Germany was a direct result of his CAD responsibilities. It was Hilldring who, several months later, pulled him out of his military government position and assigned him to head the War Crimes Branch (which was transferred from the JAG Dept. to the CAD on 4 March 1946). Then Hilldring immediately moved over to the State Department as an Assistant Secretary of State in charge of occupied areas problems; in this capacity he headed a secretariat which coordinated Army, Navy and State Department policies in Germany. In September 1947 he left the State Department and became an Adviser to the U.S. delegation at the United Nations, where the diplomatic battle between the Zionists and the Arabs was being waged. Hilldring "was a tower of strength from the outset . . . as information link with the Jewish representatives, he frequently conversed with Zionist strategists." Then, at about the time that Marcus was made supreme commander in Jerusalem, Hilldring was appointed back to the State Department as Assistant Secretary of State for Palestine. Zionist sources have subsequently boasted that both the U.N. and second State Department appointments were direct results of Zionist lobbying.[33] Quite a pair, Marcus and Hilldring.

The filling of the War Crimes Branch position with a fanatical Zionist, the "first soldier since Biblical times to hold the rank of General in the Army of Israel," is not only significant in terms of what the Zionist might do in the position, but also significant in revealing, in a simple way, the nature of the overall political forces operating at the trials. This is the important point. It is simply not possible to imagine an appointment that would make these trials more suspect.

Under these political conditions it is simply silly to expect anything but a frame-up at the "trials". The associated "extermination" hoax will be exposed with complete clarity in these pages.

This book is written for people who are already informed on the European side of World War II and the immediately preceding years. We have no intention of reviewing the nature of the Nazi state, the roles of Goering, Himmler, Goebbels, etc., or the anti-Jewish measures that were taken prior to the war, except that these matters will be touched upon here and there as a matter of course. The major events and approximate dates associated with the war are assumed known by the reader.

When Europe was dominated by the Germans it was not organized according to the plan of the Treaty of Versailles; Fig. 3 presents a map of Europe as it was organized in the autumn of 1942, at the apex of Hitler's power. Germany had annexed Austria, Alsace-Lorraine, part of Czechoslovakia, and a great deal of Poland (essentially the part that had been taken from Germany after World War I). The part of Poland that remained was called the "General Government" and had the status of a subject province governed by the Germans, as did the three Baltic states of Lithuania, Latvia and Estonia. In the same subject status were White Russia, the Ukraine, Bohemia-Moravia (formerly western Czechoslovakia), and Banat (long a part of Hungary dominated by ethnic Germans). The eastern part of Czechoslovakia had become the independent state of Slovakia, and Yugoslavia had been reorganized as Croatia and Serbia, corresponding to the two dominant of the five nationalities that had constituted Yugoslavia. Italy also had an interest in this area of Europe, controlled Albania, and shared influence in adjoining countries with her German ally. Finland, Hungary, Rumania and Bulgaria were also allied with Germany, and the Waffen SS (regular military units within the SS) recruited troops all over Europe, particularly in the Baltic states, in the Ukraine, in Scandinavia, and in the Netherlands and Belgium.

Norway, Denmark, the Netherlands, Belgium and much (later all) of France were occupied by the Germans. Sweden, Switzerland, Spain and Portugal remained neutral throughout the war.

It is convenient to review, at this point, some matters pertaining to the SS, a strange bureaucracy which had responsibility for certain improbable combinations of functions. Only three of these functions, security, concentration camp administration and resettlement policies, are of interest in our study.

The best known agency of the SS was the RSHA, Reich Security Main Office, which embraced the Gestapo (Secret State Police, headed by SS Lt. General Mueller), the SD (Security Service, headed by SS Lt. General Schellenberg), the Kripo (Criminal Police, headed by SS Lt. Generals Nebe and, later, Panzinger) and related functions. The first head of the RSHA had been SS General Reinhard Heydrich, an ambitious and ruthless young man whose methods generated many enemies for him.

Ever since the Roehm purge of 1934, the substantial ambitions of the SS in respect to military matters had resulted in growing conflict between the

30

SS and the regular military establishment, the Wehrmacht, and Heydrich was not in the least bit delicate in the methods he employed to prosecute the conflict. In 1938 he had forced the resignation of the Minister of War, General Blomberg, by showing that Blomberg's new wife had been a prostitute. Blomberg's obvious successor was General von Fritsch, so Heydrich constructed a frame-up of von Fritsch, based on perjured allegations of homosexuality. Although von Fritsch was eventually exonerated, his career had been ruined, and the bitterness toward Heydrich swelled.

The SS had a second basis for rivalry with the military establishment. The German intelligence services were the *Abwehr*, German military intelligence, responsible to the military high command and headed, since 1935, by Admiral Wilhelm Canaris, and the SD, the political intelligence arm, responsible to Heydrich and Himmler. Since the two types of intelligence activity cannot be strictly separated, Canaris and Himmler inevitably became rivals. Heydrich appears to have attempted to be cooperative with Canaris, at least at first; this may have been due to Heydrich's own background as a naval intelligence officer who, during the Twenties, had served and trained under Canaris and had even been a frequent visitor to his home.

More significantly, the Admiral was a traitor; he is one of the awesome mysteries of World War II. During, and even before (he was in contact with Churchill in 1938), the war Canaris betrayed Germany at every opportunity. A British official has expressed the role of Canaris most succinctly: "we had Admiral Canaris." The man's motivations remain as mysterious as his personality and his antecedents. Ian Colvin, one of the authorities on World War II intelligence operations, wrote a whole book about Canaris and, yet, never deciphered him:

> The readers will have to judge for themselves whether Admiral Wilhelm Canaris was a German patriot or a British spy, a European statesman or a cosmopolitan intriguer, a double agent, an opportunist, or a seer. It will not be easy for them to make up their minds.

It may be of some relevance that the man whom Colvin, in his 1951 book, characterized as one of Canaris' "close personal friends," Otto John, the *Abwehr* man in the all important neutral capital of Lisbon during World War II, later became Chief of State Security for the Bonn Government, and was subsequently exposed (in 1956) as a Soviet agent.[34]

The Canaris case is sometimes confused by grouping Canaris with the men behind the abortive coup d'état of 20 July 1944. This is utterly erroneous since Canaris used all his powers to betray Germany, whereas the men of 20 July merely betrayed Hitler, and would never have betrayed Germany. No Englishman, after the war, could have truthfully said, "we had Erwin Rommel." The most one can say about Canaris' involvement is that he was no doubt aware of the conspiracy in its early stages, and naturally gave its members the impression that he was with them. Canaris was a grand master at giving such impressions.

To return to Heydrich, great ambition had gotten the young SS General appointed Deputy Protector of Bohemia-Moravia in late 1941; he was thus starting to look bigger than his superior, Reichsfuehrer-SS Heinrich Himmler. It might also be interesting to speculate that, at about this time, Heydrich may have started to grasp Canaris' game; as chief of the RSHA and as a former associate of Canaris, no man was better situated and motivated to penetrate Canaris' secret than Heydrich was. When one considers the long burning antagonism of the Army, it appears that Heydrich, by early 1942, had accumulated a very long list of powerful enemies in Germany. It was thus remarkable that at this point in Heydrich's career the English, it is said, fortuitously removed him in May 1942 by dropping two assassins from the sky. In accord with the all-too-common scenario for political assassinations (e.g. the Abraham Lincoln and John F. Kennedy assassinations), the alleged assassins were said to have been killed before they got an opportunity to talk.

In an appointment that caused general astonishment, Heydrich was succeeded in early 1943 by the relatively obscure and much less ambitious Dr. Ernst Kaltenbrunner. Evidently desirous of avoiding repetition of the situation that had developed with Heydrich, Himmler retained a rather more direct control of the Gestapo and the SD than he had held previously. However both agencies continued to be formally responsible to the head of the RSHA, now Kaltenbrunner. Himmler also charged Kaltenbrunner with a special task: to build up the intelligence service of the SD. This was a particularly timely decision on the part of Himmler since Canaris fell from power (without being fully exposed) in February 1944 and, by a special Hitler decree, all military and political intelligence functions were taken over by the RSHA, thus uniting all intelligence activity under SD chief Schellenberg. Canaris was arrested after the 20 July coup and he was executed shortly before the end of the war.

Concentration camp administration was under the WVHA, Economic-Administrative Main Office, headed by SS General Oswald Pohl. As its name suggests, the WVHA was concerned with the economic role of the SS which had arisen, for the most part, on account of the availability of the labor of concentration camp inmates. The commandants of the concentration camps reported to the Inspectorate of Concentration Camps, headed by SS Brigadier General Gluecks, who reported to Pohl. Pohl reported to Himmler and was formally equal in rank to Kaltenbrunner and Heydrich.

It is convenient to state at this point, in very general terms, what was going on with respect to the Jews of Europe during the life of the Nazi regime. Before the war, the German Government had used all means to encourage the emigration of Jews from Germany, and most German Jews had left Germany before the outbreak of the war. The persistent problems in connection with this emigration program were, first, the dislocations of the economy which were entailed in moving the Jews out and, second, the difficulty in arranging for other countries to take the Jews. By the summer of 1941 Germany was at war with Russia and huge numbers of Jews, i.e., the greater part of all the Jews of Europe, were in the German sphere of influence. However the war had also opened up, temporarily, vast new territories for the Germans and, consequently, a program of Jewish resettlement got under way in the autumn of 1941. Through the course of the war, as long as Germany controlled any significant amount of eastern territory, European Jews were being resettled in the East. There were also a certain number of young, adult Jews conscripted for labor.

On account of certain political problems and the priority of war requirements, the resettlement program was only partially carried out and, of course, nowhere near six million Jews were involved. Excluding Polish and Rumanian Jews, perhaps 750,000 Jews were resettled, primarily in the Ukraine, White Russia and Latvia. Not all Polish Jews fell under German domination. Apart from those who managed to flee before or after the German occupation, several hundred thousand or perhaps a million Jews had been deported from Poland by the Russians in 1940 and had been dispersed in the Soviet Union. For the most part, the Polish Jews who came into German hands were crowded into ghettoes in eastern Poland (1939 boundaries).

What happened to all of these people can be established only in a very general way, because all of the territory that the Jews had been resettled onto became Soviet territory after the war, and because the victorious powers engaged in considerable suppression of the data. However there is sufficient evidence to permit us to see approximately what happened. Although it is very likely that a fair number perished in the disorderly and chaotic conditions that accompanied the German retreats, it is established that a large number of Jews, predominantly of pre-war Polish nationality, were absorbed into the Soviet Union, and the remainder of the Jews who had been uprooted ultimately resettled in Palestine, the U.S., Europe and elsewhere.

These general remarks are supplied here to serve as a background to assist the reader in interpreting the analysis of the "extermination" claims, which is the task of the next few chapters. However, the major evidence for these remarks concerning what actually happened to the Jews will not be presented until Chapter VII.

The RSHA was responsible for carrying out most aspects of this Jewish policy. Within the Gestapo there was an office, "B4", which designated the "religions and cults division — Jewish religion subdivision," headed by one Karl Adolf Eichmann, whose highest attained rank had been Lieutenant Colonel or Colonel.[35] Eichmann did the routine chores associated with the Jewish emigration and resettlement policies of the German Government; most of his time was spent arranging with the various Jewish Councils to draw up transport lists of Jews, and arranging for transportation for the deportees. There is no evidence that Eichmann ever participated in formulating policy and, since he was not involved in concentration camp administration, he could not have been directly involved in whatever it was that happened in those camps.

It is, therefore, quite ridiculous that it was possible to get so many people excited about the case of a person such as Eichmann, who had performed completely routine functions in Nazi Germany. Those functions were carried out in accordance with specific orders transmitted by his superiors. His Jerusalem testimony was given "after consulting Reitlinger and Poliakov, (producing) seventeen multicolored charts, which contributed little to a better understanding of the bureaucratic machinery of the Third Reich."[36] I see no point in viewing the Eichmann affair as anything but a publicity stunt on the part of a state accustomed to disregarding the constraints that other states feel bound to respect. A short discussion of the Eichmann case, and of Eichmann's Jerusalem testimony, is provided in a later chapter.

Other departments of the SS which were involved in resettlement activities were the RKFDV (Reich Commission for the Strengthening of Germandom, headed by SS General Ulrich Greifelt), the RuSHA (Race and Settlement Main Office, headed by SS Generals Otto Hofmann and, later, Richard Hildebrandt) and the VoMi (Liaison Office for Ethnic Germans, headed by SS General Werner Lorenz). The most important responsibility of these departments was the resettlement of ethnic Germans on conquered territories, and Greifelt was the main personality in this program. However they inevitably got involved in the program of Jewish resettlement to some degree.

II
CAMPS

When Germany collapsed in the spring of 1945 it was after a long Allied propaganda campaign which had repeatedly claimed that people, mainly Jews, were being systematically killed in German "camps". When the British captured the camp at Bergen-Belsen in northern Germany they found a large number of unburied bodies lying around the camp. Photographs such as Fig. 10 and pictures of guards with unfortunate facial expressions, such as Fig. 12, were accordingly reproduced all over the world.

It is, I believe, Belsen which has always constituted the effective, mass propaganda "proof" of exterminations, and even today you will find such scenes occasionally waved around as "proof".

In fact these scenes, repeated in varying degrees at other German camps, e.g. Dachau and Buchenwald, were much less related to "extermination" than the scenes at Dresden after the British-American raids of February 1945, when many, many times as many bodies were found lying around[1]. The deaths at Belsen were the result of a total loss of control, not a deliberate policy. Equivalent scenes could easily have existed in any country invaded on all sides by enemy armies, crippled by powerful "strategic" bombings which had caused all sorts of shortages and chaotic conditions.

The major cause of the deaths at Belsen was a typhus epidemic. Everybody agrees that typhus was a constant menace in all German camp and eastern military operations; for this reason there was a real fear of typhus spreading throughout Germany and vigorous countermeasures were applied[2]. The typhus problem will play a most significant role in our story because it was not merely at the end of the war that it manifested itself; the scenes at the end of the war were due to the total collapse of all measures against a disease that had plagued the German concentration camps since early in the war. The typhus was of the sort carried by the body louse and consequently defensive measures consisted in killing the lice, whose spread was due mainly to the constant rail traffic with the East. Thus all "survivor literature", sincere or inventive, and regardless of the type of camp involved, report the same basic procedure involved in entering a German camp: disrobe, shave hair, shower, dress in new clothes or in old clothes after disinfection[3].

At Belsen, the trouble had started in October 1944 with a breakdown of these measures. In the account of a political prisoner there:[4]

> Towards the end of February 1945 my own situation changed completely. By that time typhus had become a serious danger for the whole camp. It was the species of typhus which is transmitted by lice. At one time all the transports which arrived at Belsen had had to pass through a "human laundry" and this disinfection seems to have been effective enough to keep the camp free from lice until the autumn of 1944.
>
> At the end of October a big transport had for the first time been admitted to the camp without being disinfected, because there had been some damage to the machinery of the shower-baths. Unfortunately the people of this transport were louse carriers, and from that day the lice gradually spread over the whole camp . . . Typhus broke out in Camp I about the end of January. At first there were only a few

34

cases, but a month later a dozen had appeared, and it became impossible to check the disease . . .

Another serious complication was that, in the final months, Belsen was considered a *Krankenlager,* a sick camp, so that many people entering were sick to begin with.[5] The British could not check things at once and over a quarter of those alive when they took over the camp were to perish in the first four weeks.[6]

Despite the very effective propaganda role of the Belsen scenes, nobody acquainted with the most easily obtainable facts claims exterminations at Belsen and the British military court which tried the commandant, SS Captain Kramer, never accused him of supervising an extermination camp at Belsen.[7] Today in fact, exterminations at any of the concentration camps in Germany are not claimed by anybody trying to be serious; Belsen, Buchenwald, Dachau, etc. were not extermination camps. The extermination camps are all supposed to have been in occupied Poland, namely the camps referred to as Auschwitz, Belzec, Kulmhof (Chelmno), Lublin (Majdanek), Sobibor and Treblinka.[8] Also, exterminations of Jews were supposed to have been conducted in Russia by the *Einsatzgruppen,* employing either mass shooting or "gasmobiles". The camps in Poland are also claimed to have employed "gas chambers" but, except for the case of Chelmno, stationary rather than mobile ones.

Thus the exterminations are supposed to have taken place only at locations which had been abandoned before being captured by the Russians, not at camps which were still functioning, however disastrously, when captured by Western troops.

Although six extermination camps are claimed one of them, Auschwitz, is the key to the whole story. It is for Auschwitz that quantities of even documentary evidence are offered; there is little of any sort offered for the others. It was Auschwitz, as will be seen, that got the very special attention of Washington long before the end of the war. Thus much of this work is necessarily concerned with the claim that at Auschwitz Jews were being exterminated during World War II.

The subject of this book is the question of whether or not the Germans attempted to exterminate the European Jews. We are not concerned with considering in any detail the general question of alleged Nazi brutalities of all sorts or with presenting a complete picture of the functioning of German camps. However it has been found that many people have such distorted views of these camps that, since at Auschwitz there were camps, it is difficult to separate Auschwitz at the outset and consider it in isolation from other camps. Thus a few general words about the camps are in order. Figure 23 presents a map (January 1938 boundaries) which shows the locations of a few of the most frequently referred to camps together with the locations of a few large cities.

There were many types of German camps and only a fraction of them were called "concentration camps". There were thirteen German concentration camps, each of them actually being a collection of neighboring camps. Only two of the six alleged "extermination camps", Auschwitz and Lublin, were "concentration camps". A table of many types of German camps, which includes many ordinary prisons, is given by Aronéanu, pp. 203-251, who lists about 1,400 "camps", together with their locations and "characters". While this table gives some idea of the scope and diversity of the German prison and camp systems, it has obvious major errors, such as giving the "character" of Birkenau as "medical experiments".

The major significance of Oranienburg, near Berlin, was that it quartered the Inspectorate of Concentration Camps, and was thus in direct communication with all concentration camps.

The typical inmate of a German concentration camp was a person being detained for punitive or security reasons. There were five major categories and they were distinguished by colored insignia which were associated with their uniforms:[9]

Green — Criminals
Red — Political prisoners (mainly communists)
Pink — Homosexuals
Black — Asocials (vagrants, drunkards, etc.)
Purple — Considered disloyal on account of religious views (mainly Jehovah's Witnesses)

At Auschwitz and some other camps a triangle of the appropriate color was attached to the uniform. If the prisoner was Jewish a yellow triangle was superimposed on the first triangle, forming a star of David. This is referred to as the Auschwitz "star system".

Economic conditions being what they were, the German Government made every effort to use concentration camp inmates for labor. Prisoners of war (POW) were also used to the extent that such use did not conflict with the relevant conventions, as the Germans interpreted their obligations under them. Thus Russian POW were used freely, since Russia did not respect the conventions. Employment of western POW was restricted to cases where certain legalistic "transformations" into civilian workers were possible, as with many French POW,[10] or to cases where the work was not considered to be ruled out by the conventions, as with some British POW employed under conditions to be discussed.

The number of inmates in the entire German concentration camp system was about 224,000 in August 1943 and 524,000 a year later.[11] These figures include only camps referred to by the Germans as concentration camps, and do not include any transit camps or camps referred to in other terms, such as the Theresienstadt ghetto, or any other establishments intended for quartering families.

It is generally accurate to say that there was no such thing as a "concentration camp" for Jews as such, but this remark must be clarified; there are three distinct categories of Jews which must be considered in this connection.

First, a fraction of those interned for punitive and security reasons were Jews and under the national socialist system it was natural, in the camps, to segregate them from the "Aryan" inmates. Thus sections of the camps could, in this sense, be considered "for Jews".

Second, specific legislation existed for the labor conscription of Jews and many selected specifically for labor found their ways into concentration camps on this basis.

The third category was Jewish families, but the closest they got to "concentration camps" was in certain *Durchgangslager*, transit camps, which in some cases were independent camps such as Westerbork in the Netherlands[12] and others (to be mentioned) and in some cases were separate compounds which existed at some concentration camps, e.g. Belsen, possibly Dachau,[13] and others (to be mentioned). The transit camp, as its name suggests, was intended only for temporary quartering pending transport to some other destination.

In addition to the transit camps there were "camps" for some Jewish families, such as Theresienstadt in Bohemia-Moravia and others far to the East, but the most pejorative term applicable in these cases would be "ghetto", not "concentration camp". In addition, as we shall see, toward the end of the war, as the Russians were approaching on the eastern front, the Germans put many formerly free Jews into ghettos for security reasons.

The full story regarding the position of Jews relative to German controlled camps of all types is rather complicated. Rather than attempt to say here exactly what that position was, the subject will be touched at many points in the book and the reader will be able to form a reasonably complete picture.

There is no point in attempting to discuss the entire German camp system here. For our purposes it will suffice to discuss the three that are referred to most frequently (excluding Auschwitz): Belsen, Buchenwald and Dachau (inmate populations in August 1943 3,000, 17,600 and 17,300 respectively[14]). Then we will pass on to preliminary discussion of the alleged "extermination camp" Auschwitz in Poland.

Belsen had only a very brief history. It had originally been a Wehrmacht camp for wounded POW. In mid-1943 the SS took over half the camp for the purpose, among others, of turning it into an "exchange camp", a transit camp· for foreign nationals and Jews whom the Germans contemplated exchanging for Germans held abroad. Some new grounds and buildings were also added to the camp. Jews from Salonika, Greece who possessed Spanish passports were the first Jewish arrivals (it was hoped to send them to Spain) but eventually the Dutch Jews predominated (about.5,000). A fraction of the Dutch Jews were there on a semi-permanent basis since they numbered many of the skilled craftsmen of the essential Amsterdam diamond cutting industry and thus their diamond cutting operations had merely been moved to Belsen. The quarters for Jews at Belsen formed what was called the "Star Camp", which was strictly separated from the rest of the camp and was essentially untouched by the typhus epidemic of the last months[15].

The Dutch Jews were particularly heavily hit by deportations; reasons for this will be given later. It was at Belsen in March 1945 that Anne Frank is said to have perished[16]. Since there were many Dutch Jews at Belsen this could easily be true but it is difficult, to say the least, to guess the cause of death in such a case. There were no exterminations and the Jewish families were isolated from the typhus epidemic. The question of the authenticity of the diary is not considered important enough to examine here; I will only remark that I have looked it over and don't believe it. For example, already on page 2 one is reading an essay on why a 13 year old girl would start a diary, and then page 3 gives a short history of the Frank family and then quickly reviews the specific anti-Jewish measures that followed the German occupation in 1940. The rest of the book is in the same historical spirit.

The remainder of the Belsen concentration camp contained the usual assortment of inmates, and the fate of the camp has been seen. Bergen-Belsen never had a significant economic-industrial aspect, except for the diamond cutting.

The major significance of Buchenwald was industrial; its satellite camps at Beuchow, Dora, Ellrich, Elsing, Gandersheim and Halberstadt existed primarily for the sake of an underground aircraft factory which employed the usual concentration camp and foreign labor in addition to regular German labor.[17] There were however two other aspects, the medical experiments conducted at the main camp Buchenwald and the activities of commandant Koch; these offer quite perfect illustrations of how the meanings of facts have been distorted in speaking of these camps. We are fortunate in having a book by Christopher Burney, a former inmate; this book not only indulges in some of this distortion but also offers us some facts or hints which enable

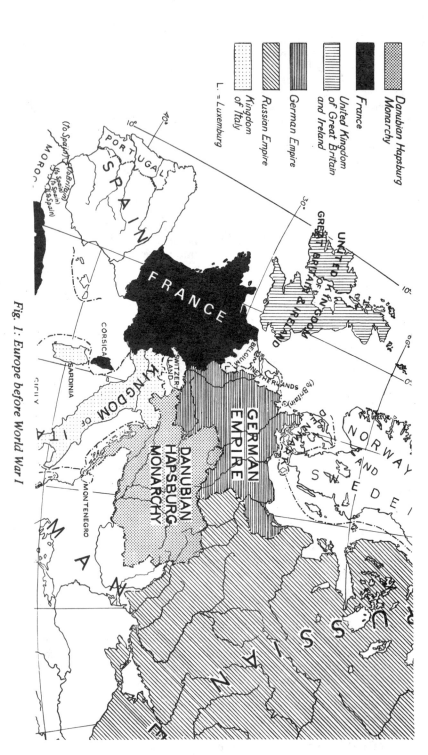

Fig. 1: Europe before World War I

Legend:
- Danubian Hapsburg Monarchy
- France
- United Kingdom of Great Britain and Ireland
- German Empire
- Russian Empire
- Kingdom of Italy

L. = Luxemburg

38

62. THE GREAT POWERS OF THE WESTERN WORLD IN EUROPE, A.D. 1925

France

Territories under French control

United Kingdom of Great Britain & Northern Ireland

Territories under British control

Germany

Union of Soviet Socialist Republics

Italy

L. = Luxemburg

E.P. = East Prussia (to Germany)

(to It.) = to Italy

Fig. 2: Europe between the two World Wars

39

Fig. 3: Nazi dominated Europe

Legend:
- Subject provinces outside frontiers of the Reich
- German-administered occupied territories
- Self-administered territories
  - A: occupied
  - B: non-occupied
- Italy and Italian-administered territories
- Satellites other than Italy
- German Reich

40

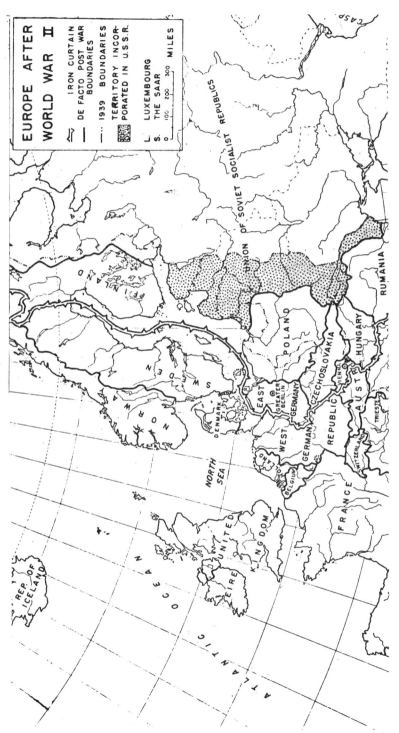

Fig. 4: Europe after World War II

EUROPE AFTER WORLD WAR II

≈ IRON CURTAIN
— DE FACTO POST WAR BOUNDARIES
···· 1939 BOUNDARIES
▓ TERRITORY INCORPORATED IN U.S.S.R.

L. LUXEMBOURG
S. THE SAAR
0 100 200 300 MILES

us to see through the distortion. Burney's book should illustrate to any reader the necessity, when reading "personal experience" literature of this sort, of sharply and rigorously distinguishing between the scenes the author actually claims to have witnessed or the claims he has read or heard, on the one hand, and the inferences he has drawn or pretended to draw on the other. The differences are often most stark. Describing commandant Koch:[18]

No cruelty was foreign to him, no single cell of his brain had not at some time or other contributed to the planning of new refinements of anguish and death for the rats in his trap.

Burney goes on to explain that, since Koch was a homosexual, Frau Koch used to make out with the prisoners, "who were then sent to the crematorium", except that highly valued tattooed skin was saved for lampshades. At this point in Burney's book things obviously look real bad for him, especially if he has tattoos and Frau Koch finds him but, happily, all of that had happened before he arrived there in early 1944. Koch had been arrested in 1943 for embezzlement and was succeeded by Pister who was "one of the mildest concentration camp commanders in history" so that:

in the last year of its existence a casual observer who came to the camp and looked generally at it without probing its corners, would have seen little or no beating, a large number of men doing no work, a much larger number working with a lethargy taught them by the Russians . . . , living blocks which were clean, kitchens with huge, horrifyingly modern soup-cookers and a hospital which would just pass muster at first glance.

The Koch arrest had, in fact been part of the breaking of a ring of corruption which had spread through the German concentration camp system and had involved the murder of some prisoners who knew too much. It was exposed through the efforts of SS Judge Konrad Morgen. Koch was executed by the SS.[19]

The tattooed skin was undoubtedly due to the medical experiment role of Buchenwald. As remarked by Burney, when a Buchenwald inmate died the camp doctors looked his body over and if they found something interesting they saved it.[20] It is fairly certain that the collection of medical specimens thus gathered was the source of the tattooed skin and the human head that turned up at the IMT as "exhibits" relating to people "murdered" at Buchenwald. What is probably the greater part of the collection is pictured in Figure 32. The head is normally pictured, without any explanation, in the company of some soap (Fig. 24), allegedly made from human bodies, which was submitted as evidence by the Russians who, when they learned there was to be a trial, evidently read up on what the Germans had been charged with in World War I.[21] By the time the IMT was done "developing" the fact about the tattooed skin found at Buchenwald, we had an official deposition:[22]

In 1939 all prisoners with tattooing on them were ordered to report to the dispensary. No one knew what the purpose was, but after the tattooed prisoners had been examined, the ones with the best and most artistic specimens were kept in the dispensary and then killed by injections . . . the desired pieces of tattooed skin were detached from the bodies and treated. The finished products were turned over to Koch's wife, who had them fashioned into lampshades and other ornamental household articles. I myself saw such tattooed skins with various designs and legends on them, such as "Haensel and Gretel", which one prisoner had on his knee, and designs of ships from prisoners' chests.

Frau Koch was convicted of such crimes at her trial before a U.S. military court but in 1948 the American military governor, General Lucius Clay, reviewed her case and determined that, despite testimony produced at her trial, Frau Koch could not be related to the lampshades and other articles which were "discovered" (i.e. planted) in the Buchenwald commandant's residence when the camp was captured in 1945. For one thing, she had not lived there since her husband's, and her own, arrest in 1943. Also her "family journal", said to be bound in human skin, and which was one of the major accusations against her, was never located, and obviously never existed. Clay thus commuted her life sentence to four years imprisonment, for ordinary sorts of brutalities.

What happened after the commutation provided one of the many episodes which, together with the 1948-1949 revelations of what had transpired at the Dachau "trials", exposed quite effectively the lawlessness that prevailed in the war crimes trials. Rabbi Wise and other influential people protested the commutation so strongly that there was a Senate investigation into the matter, which concluded that:

military authorities say they have been unable to find evidence of any other crime Ilse Koch committed on which she could be tried without violating the rule of double jeopardy. However . . . since the trial conducted by our special military government court was based on charges that the various accused had mistreated "non-German nationals", the German courts might well try Ilse Koch under their law for crimes committed against German nationals. . . . Should the German people bring Ilse Koch to trial on such charges, the subcommittee is convinced that it would then be the duty of our military authorities to give complete cooperation to the German authorities.

This distinction between crimes against Germans and crimes against non-Germans was merely a bit of sophistry that was trotted out for the occasion. Not only had the U.S. war crimes courts always assumed jurisdiction in cases of alleged crimes against German Jews, but the distinction was irrelevant anyway, for Clay's commutation of her sentence was based on a conclusion that she was not guilty of the major charges against her, which had to do with lampshades and the like, irrespective of the nationality of the alleged victims. Clay did not change his position throughout the long public controversy concerning efforts to try Frau Koch a second time on essentially the same charges, a controversy which, according to the *N.Y. Times,* "rocked the United States and Europe". Clay was firm on his decision in the Ilse Koch case, and explained that:

examination of the record, based upon reports which I received from the lawyers, indicated that the most serious charges were based on hearsay and not on factual evidence. For that reason the sentence was commuted.

I hold no sympathy for Ilse Koch. She was a woman of depraved character and ill repute. She had done many things reprehensible and punishable, undoubtedly, under German law. We were not trying her for those things. We were trying her as a war criminal on specific charges.

Despite this emphatic stand of the American military governor, pressures from the U.S. induced the German authorities to move against Frau Koch after she was released from American detention in October 1949. She was again tried on the familiar "lampshade" charges. Although the defense was able to show that the testimonies of two of the prosecution witnesses contradicted declarations that they had made in connection with earlier proceedings, thus forcing the German court to strike their testimonies from the record, Ilse Koch was found guilty and sentenced to life imprisonment. She hanged herself in her cell in 1967.[23]

Burney reports some Belsen-like scenes at Buchenwald, but mainly among incoming prisoners evacuated from more eastern locations during the final chaotic weeks. So much for Buchenwald.[24]

Dachau was one of the oldest Nazi concentration camps, with an emphasis on Austrian political prisoners, Roman Catholic priests (detained for reasons which need not be examined here) and old and semi-employable people of all categories. The camp also had its group of ordinary criminals. Work was mainly at outside factories but a herb plantation was being built up at the camp and some prisoners worked at draining swamps.[25]

It is useful here to go into some detail on how, at the end of and immediately after the war, Dachau was misrepresented as an extermination camp with gas chambers. In showing that such events never took place at Dachau we are not, of course, contradicting the present story put forward by the bearers of the extermination legend, who do not claim Dachau in this connection, and build their story around the camps in Poland, with Auschwitz occupying the central position in this respect. The point of exploring these details regarding Dachau is that the credibility of the U.S. occupation is thereby demolished. The U.S. propaganda had claimed exterminations in the German camps and Dachau was the major camp taken over by the Americans (Buchenwald was later surrendered to the Russians). Thus an effort was made to distort and misrepresent what had happened at the Dachau concentration camp. A recognition of the amazing crudeness and clumsiness of that effort, and the ludicrous nature of the "evidence" put forward, will prime the reader quite suitably for our analysis of the central part of the hoax, the Auschwitz lie.

The conditions in the camps had forced the German Government, in March 1945, to take the final step in reversal of its earlier policy of absolute exclusion of the International Committee of the Red Cross (ICRC) from the concentration camps (existing conventions covered POW's, not concentration camp inmates). On 29 March 1945 SS General Kaltenbrunner authorized the ICRC to place one delegate in each camp for the purpose of distributing relief supplies, on the condition that the delegate remained there until the end of the war.[26] The ICRC organized road transport for relief supplies (use of the railways was out of the question) but its effectiveness was to a degree influenced by the attitudes of individual concentration camp commanders; for example the reception at Mauthausen on 23-30 April was at first negative. SS Colonel Ziereis claimed that he had not heard of the Kaltenbrunner order.[27]

At Dachau the ICRC had gotten a relatively warm reception on 27 April (after some coolness on 26 April) and a delegate was allowed to establish himself in the camp. By Sunday 29 April it was found that most of the German officers, guards and employees had fled and the effective command of the camp had fallen to a certain SS Lieutenant Wickert who had similar intentions of leading a flight of the remaining guards. Since this raised many dangers, notably violence by prisoners against German civilians of the area and the spread of epidemics, the delegate talked Wickert out of this. They came to an agreement regarding surrender of the camp which the ICRC delegate was to do his best to have respected. First, guards would remain in the towers to prevent the escape of prisoners. Second, the soldiers not standing guard would assemble, unarmed, in one of the courtyards. Third, the garrison would be allowed to withdraw to its own "battle lines", after the transfer of the camp to the Americans.

The ICRC delegate then affixed a white towel to a broomstick and, taking a German officer with him, left the camp to hunt up some Americans. After a while they encountered an American motorized unit and the delegate presented himself to the American general (not named in the delegate's report on these events) who, on learning the identities of his new guests, immediately asked that the delegate and the German officer accompany them for the purpose of taking press photos at the camp, particularly of a certain train which was full of dead bodies. Although the Red Cross delegate had been at the camp for two days, he had apparently been too busy to learn of this train while at the camp, and learned of it from the general.

With its mission thus defined, the column set off for the camp. On the way, the delegate was able to ask a Major Every to communicate to the general the agreement for the transfer of the camp, but apparently this attempt to communicate with the general was not successful.

On arrival at the camp they found that some Americans had already arrived, the German guards in the towers had been replaced and all the Germans had surrendered. The inmates were in great disorder and some were armed; shots were fired at SS guards and this resulted in some killed on both sides. The delegate was finally able to gain the attention of the general to present the plan for the transfer of the camp. The general assented to the plan, but the German prisoners were not allowed to leave anyway, and many of them suffered at the hands of inmates seeking vengeance. As many of the inmates were disarmed as possible, but this did not end the disorders. Some inmates embraced the American soldiers while others tore down barbed wire fences and escaped. Some shots were fired by the Americans over the heads of inmates and an uneasy calm was finally reached by 10 PM. There were, however, occasional shots fired during the following night. The following day, 30 April, it was possible to pass out adequate food and on the next day, Tuesday 1 May, some members of the ICRC legation arrived and, according to the delegate, they visited not only piles of corpses but "equally the execution chamber, the gas chamber, the crematory ovens, etc.".[28]

The preceding is a summary of the report of the Red Cross delegate. It contains no assertions similar to later assertions made independently by former inmates Fr. Lenz and Nerin E. Gun, both of whom claim that the Americans, on arrival, started killing all SS guards in sight (unquestionably at least an exaggeration). Gun claims that this policy even extended to the dogs in the kennels, while Lenz claims that the general ordered a two hour bombardment of the defenseless town of Dachau (he was eventually dissuaded from this) in retaliation for the bodies which had been found lying around.[29] If there is any truth to these claims, the ICRC delegate made a fairly significant omission in his report.

It is very important to recognize what the Red Cross delegate refers to as the "gas chamber" in his report. The tone of the delegate's report is tongue-in-cheek and contemptuous at several points, for it was written in defensive awareness of all the drivel that was being given mass circulation in the press. Thus he remarks, in connection with the bodies found on the train at Dachau, that "many of these men had been killed while the others were probably dead of hunger". Also, while the delegate is happy to pass along the names of *le lieutenant* Wickert and *le major* Every and others, he refuses to mention the name of the U.S. commander (apparently either Linden or Patek), who is referred to only as *"le general"*.

There were two types of rooms which were claimed as gas chambers by the U.S. propaganda after the camp was captured, and Gun reproduces the relevant photographs. Here we present Figs. 16 and 22. The former shows an ordinary shower which the U.S. propagandists had the audacity to claim was a gas chamber disguised as a shower. Figure 19 shows the entrance to this *"Brausebad"* ("shower bath").

The second type of room which was claimed as a gas chamber was, indeed, a gas chamber, the door of which is shown as Fig. 22. This door certainly appears to be genuine and not manufactured for the propaganda. To see what is involved, examine Fig. 13. On the left one can perceive the very same door and, near the door, a heap of dirty prisoner clothing. That "gas chamber" was obviously a chamber for disinfecting clothing; such equipment was necessary and existed at all of the German concentration camps. The interior of the disinfection room is shown in Fig. 6.

The building shown in Fig. 13 housed disinfection chambers, the shower bath of Fig. 16, and the crematorium of Fig. 17. This building has been maintained and is regularly visited by tourists. It is removed from the main part of the camp, located in a relatively isolated spot. It was perfectly logical to locate both the disinfection chamber and the crematorium in such a way that inmates did not come into frequent contact with such things (the former for reasons of health and the latter for reasons of morale). The shower was necessary, obviously, to decontaminate the people who worked in this building before they returned to the main part of the camp. I do not know whether this shower bath also serviced incoming prisoners, or if a separate shower existed for that purpose. As suggested by Fig. 16, and confirmed by the literature, it was almost always the shower bath, rather than the disinfection chamber, which served the propaganda as a "gas chamber".[30] The latter was probably considered too small to represent as a gas chamber which had claimed countless victims.

Naturally, the "war crimes trials" produced witnesses who claimed gassings at Dachau (e.g. IMT witness Franz Blaha, who also claimed tattooed skin scenes as at Buchenwald[31]). Naturally, the people whose bodies had been found at the camp when it was captured, especially those on the train, were always represented as having been murdered.

The number of bodies on the train at Dachau was approximately 500. Finding dead people on trains in Germany toward the war's end was not unusual even on ordinary passenger trains; in January 1945 800 Germans, frozen to death, had been found on a train which had arrived in Berlin.[32] The German rail system was in utter chaos and conditions in April 1945 are difficult to imagine, but some attempt should be made to see some of these corpse-laden trains in context. Some thought might also be given to the possible conditions of people as they started their journeys on these trains. It is entirely possible that the typical individual concentration camp commander, presented with what he considered insane orders to "transfer" N inmates to X camp, reasoned that putting the half-dead on the train had the double merit of minimizing numbers of deaths and also getting some of the dying off his hands. However, such problems are not of essential or central interest here.

The truth about Dachau was not long in coming out, but did not receive wide publicity. The causes for the dead bodies which were found at the camp when it was captured were described in a 1948 publication of the American Association for the Advancement of Science. As the U.S. Army advanced into Germany, it encountered the sorts of conditions which its medical services had anticipated and for which they had prepared counter-measures:[33]

Germany in the spring months of April and May was an astounding sight, a mixture of humanity travelling this way and that, homeless, often hungry and carrying typhus with them. . . . The more territory that was uncovered, the greater was the number of reported cases; for Western Germany in the area of the American advance was rather uniformly seeded with typhus. To be sure, there were heavily involved communities and others lightly affected. There were great accumulations of cases in the concentration and prison camps, and in nearby small communities.

An estimated 35,000-40,000 prisoners were found in (Dachau), living under conditions bad even for a German camp of this kind and worse than any other that came into American hands. Extreme filthiness, louse infestation, and overcrowding prevailed throughout the camp buildings. Several car-loads of human bodies were found packed in box cars in the railroad yards adjacent to the camp, the vestiges of a shipment of prisoners from camps further north who were transferred to Dachau in the late days of the war to escape the advancing United States troops.

The number of patients with typhus fever at the time the camp was first occupied will never be known. Days passed before a census of patients could be accomplished.

Several hundreds were found in the prison hospital, but their number was small compared with the patients who continued to live with their comrades in the camp barracks, bedridden and unattended, lying in bunks 4 tiers high with 2 and sometimes 3 men to a narrow shelf-like bed; the sick and the well; crowded beyond all description; reeking with filth and neglect – and everywhere the smell of death.

It is not surprising that Dachau had experienced catastrophies very similar to those at Belsen. Since the beginning of 1945, there had been an estimated 15,000 prisoner deaths from typhus, mostly in the final two months.[34]

The Americans brought the camp under control and it served, as we have seen, as an American camp and center of "war crimes trials". An American lawyer, Stephen S. Pinter, who was stationed there and evidently disapproved of what had been carried out there in the name of the United States, wrote in 1959:[35]

I was in Dachau for 17 months after the war, as a U.S. War Department Attorney, and can state that there was no gas chamber at Dachau. What was shown to visitors and sightseers there and erroneously described as a gas chamber, was a crematory. Nor was there a gas chamber in any of the other concentration camps in Germany. We were told that there was a gas chamber at Auschwitz, but since that was in the Russian zone of occupation, we were not permitted to investigate, since the Russians would not permit it. . . . uses the old propaganda myth that millions of Jews were killed by the national socialists. From what I was able to determine during six postwar years in Germany and Austria, there were a number of Jews killed, but the figure of a million was certainly never reached, I interviewed thousands of Jews, former inmates of concentration camps in Germany and Austria, and consider myself as well qualified as any man on this subject.

In 1960, the *Institut fuer Zeitgeschichte* of Munich, "the paragon of hostility and resistance to nazism", declared that[36]

The gas chamber in Dachau was never completed and put into operation. . . . The mass extermination of Jews by gassing started in 1941/1942, and took place . . . with the aid of installations technically designed for this purpose, above all in occupied Polish territory (but nowhere in the Old Reich) . . .

This is essentially the Dachau myth as it stands today. In the summer of 1973 the information given the visiting tourist at Dachau correctly identified the disinfection room as such, without any attempt to represent it as a gas chamber for exterminating people. In regard to the shower bath the leaflet explained that

This gas chamber, camouflaged as a shower room, was not used. The prisoners selected for "gassing" were transported from Dachau to the Hartheim Castle, near Linz (Austria) or to other camps.

So much for Dachau, a close examination of which was necessary in order to evaluate the general credibility of the U.S. propaganda.

The camps at Auschwitz were, of course, part of the same concentration camp system as the camps we have just discussed. However the operations referred to with the term "Auschwitz" were really, in many ways, in a class by themselves. This is so much the case that, in order to see the role of Auschwitz clearly, it is necessary to go back considerably in time. It is also necessary, unfortunately, to indulge in a certain amount of discussion that may seem excessively technical at first.

The principal cause of the German defeat in World War I in 1918 had been shortages brought about, chiefly, by the British blockade. Shortages of such things as oil and rubber had been crippling the Army, and near starvation conditions in Germany had made the internal political situation unpredictable and unstable. Germany capitulated, a victim of, among other things, the twentieth century's first "energy crisis".

The extreme vulnerability of Germany in respect of raw materials had, of course, been realized by the German chemical industry during the war, and after the war the popularity of the concept of "autarky", non-reliance on imports or foreign aid, was partially based on this consideration. The only raw materials that concern us here are oil and rubber, of which there was essentially none in Germany. In Europe, only Rumania had significant oil resources, and there was no natural rubber anywhere in Europe. There were, however, huge sources of coal in Germany and elsewhere in Europe.

The great German chemicals company, I.G. Farben, was in 1918 a collection of six smaller companies which later combined in 1925 to form Farben. The principal predecessor company, *Badische Anilin und Soda Fabrik* of Ludwigshafen-am-Rhein had, starting early in World War I, been working on processes for producing synthetic oil and synthetic rubber from coal. These investigations continued after the formation of Farben and also after the rise of Hitler in 1933. The Nazi government soon adopted a policy of subsidizing these autarky oriented developments.[37] Thus on account of government encouragement, the real need for the synthetics, and the general German scientific-technological pre-eminence of the time, especially in chemistry and chemical engineering, Germany was substantially ahead of the rest of the world in these areas.

Synthetic oil was by far the easier of the two problems. Coal is mainly carbon; the general principle is that coal treated with hydrogen gas at high pressure and temperature ("hydrogenation") resulted in oil. The usual range of chemical products could be made from this oil: dyes, explosives, drugs, etc. Another stage of hydrogenation yielded gasoline. The idea was basically simple, although the process was inherently expensive, and most research consisted in a search for the most effective catalysts. During World War II there were many synthetic oil plants in and around Germany; they produced about 75% of the oil available to the Germans; the rest came mainly from Rumania.[38]

Synthetic rubber was a different matter; the technical problems in developing a sufficiently economic synthetic rubber suitable for tires were most severe and were not really resolved until approximately the beginning of the war.

The basic steps in making a rubber are first making long chains of molecules of some sort, polymerization, and then causing these chains to "cross-stitch", to join each other at various points, vulcanization. One needed a molecule congenial to polymerization and vulcanization and it was found that butadiene was particularly suitable. In the late Twenties it had been found that sodium was an excellent catalyst for polymerization of the butadiene, and consequently the synthetic rubber which was being made from butadiene with sodium (Na) as catalyst was called "Buna" rubber. The sodium had been dropped by 1935, but the term "Buna" was retained. By replacing 25 per cent of the butadiene with styrene "Buna-S" rubber, the type particularly suited for tires, was obtained.[39]

The earliest serious German Buna-S plant, and the largest, was the Schkopau plant, started in 1937 and completed in 1939. It had a capacity of 6,000 tons per month. A second plant was started at Huels in 1938 and was in operation in August 1940; its capacity was 4,000 tons per month. A third plant was started in January 1941 at Ludwigshafen, Farben research headquarters, and it was producing Buna in March 1943; its capacity was 2,500 tons per month. The fourth, at Auschwitz, was begun in 1941 and was designed for a capacity of 3,000 tons per month.

During all this plant construction, research on new processes continued and the differences in the processes used in the four plants reflected this. All started from coal but at Schkopau the butadiene was produced via a classical

48

calcium carbide-acetylene-butadiene sequence; at Huels the carbide stage was replaced by one involving hydrocarbon gases. Ludwigshafen reverted to the classical sequence but the superior Reppe process was introduced for the acetylene-butadiene stage. The Buna plant at Auschwitz also used a version of the classical sequence.[40]

The reason for the appearance of Auschwitz in this context is very simple; Auschwitz was a huge industrial operation.

When Germany annexed a large part of Poland after the partitioning of Poland in 1939 by Germany and Russia, it came into the possession of the great coal fields of Polish Upper Silesia. It was naturally decided to exploit this and the possibilities for a hydrogenation and Buna plant were examined. It was found that the little town of "Oswiecim" (population 13,000), translated into German as "Auschwitz" (Auschwitz had been a duchy of the Hapsburg Empire before World War I), was ideally located since the three rivers that joined there could provide the necessary power, while a fourth river for carrying off the waste was nearby. In addition, Auschwitz was on the southern border of the Silesian coal fields, the Kattowitz (Katowice) mining region of Poland.[41]

In early 1941 it was decided to build a hydrogenation and a Buna plant at Auschwitz employing both free and prisoner labor. By pure chance there was already near the town a partisan–POW camp holding 7,000 prisoners (it had formerly been a Polish artillery barracks); this camp became the nucleus for expansion via its own enlargement and also the construction of additional camps. It was quickly transformed into and remained to the last a camp for political prisoner-workers; it is usually referred to as Auschwitz I. The terms "main camp", *"Hauptlager"* and *"Stammlager"* are also sometimes used.[42]

Sometime in 1941 work had begun on a second camp, Auschwitz II, generally referred to as Birkenau. It was one to one and a half miles northwest of Auschwitz I and was initially referred to as a POW camp. Part of it was completed by April 1942; Russian POW labor was used for constructing the camp. Its functions will be examined at length.

Some 4,000 Jews were moved out of the town to another town to make room for free labor attached to the industries. On 16 November 1941 it was decided to build a third camp, generally referred to as Monowitz, three miles east of the town and close to the Farben plant, for quartering labor working on and in the plant. Russian POW's were again used for constructing the camp.[43] The relative locations of the three camps are shown in Figure 5.[44]

There were also a large number of smaller camps in the outlying region, most of them within a radius of 25 miles. These "outer camps", of which "Raisko" and "Harmense" were two relatively close-in examples, were administered by the Auschwitz camp administration and their number has been variously given as 13 to 39, depending upon what is considered a single camp. The smaller or outer camps were mainly for those who worked at the five blast furnaces or five coal mines. Monowitz and the collection of all outer camps taken together are sometimes referred to as Auschwitz III. The collection of all camps, Auschwitz I, Birkenau (Auschwitz II) and Auschwitz III, together with the industries which employed the inmates, is usually what is referred to under the blanket term "Auschwitz".[45]

The prisoner population of Auschwitz III was nothing unusual except that there was a significant number of British POW's.[46] The NMT judgment was that the use of British POW was not contrary to the Geneva Convention since the Buna factory had an ultimate peaceful purpose.[47] The Red Cross apparently concurred since, although it was specifically aware of this situation, it did not mention the employment of British POW in its later report on the problems it had encountered during the war in respect to the use of POW for war related work.[48]

Typical camp strengths were 20,000 for Auschwitz I, 35,000 for Birkenau (30 to 60 per cent women) and 15,000 for Auschwitz III. By a wide margin, Auschwitz was the largest complex of concentration camps in the German system; in August 1943 the second largest was Sachsenhausen with a population of 26,500.[49] There were also many free laborers working and living in the area. For example, less than thirty per cent of the workers at the Farben plant were in the "prisoner" category; more than half were free foreign workers who had enlisted voluntarily for labor and the remaining approximate twenty per cent were ordinary German employees.[50]

Auschwitz I was the administrative center for all SS functions at Auschwitz. These SS functions included the guarding, feeding, clothing, housing, recreation and disciplining of the prisoners, and also their medical services. The working hours at Auschwitz were those standard for the German concentration camps: eleven hours per day, six days a week, with extra work on Sunday mornings in "emergencies".[51] As a large establishment Auschwitz was able to supply relatively diverse recreational activities: concerts, cabaret performers, movies and athletic contests. There was even a brothel for the male prisoners.[52] Medical services will receive further comment later on.

The providing of such extensive services naturally meant that companies using the labor of the prisoners "rented" them for the SS; a typical rate seems to have been RM 4.00 – RM 6.00 ($1.00 – $1.50) per day and up.[53] Thus the prisoners were at the basis of Himmler's bureaucratic and economic empire and accordingly this resource, together with the supporting functions of feeding, clothing, etc. were jealously guarded. Nevertheless Farben had been big enough to get a special arrangement for those at Monowitz; it was granted full authority for the care of the prisoners there and consequently the payments to the SS were reduced. This led to the expected scraps between the SS and Farben. The SS complained of beatings and other mistreatments such as unsanitary conditions at the Monowitz hospital. Also, one-fifth of the people who had been registered at this hospital were discharged by being sent to Birkenau, at which time the Farben appropriations for their care immediately ceased and they became the responsibility of the SS which, already wounded by not being accorded its customary rights in regard to employable prisoners, was incensed at receiving in return only the unemployables from Monowitz. The SS therefore demanded that the Monowitz hospital, which had only 300 beds, be enlarged, but the reply to this, of course, was that "if they aren't strong enough to work, they don't belong on the factory grounds".[54]

Birkenau, like Auschwitz I, had a responsibility of supplying labor for Farben and for sub-contractors to Farben. It also supplied labor for other enterprises such as the Krupp fuse plant and the Siemens electrical factory. In addition inmates worked at clearing demolished structures, draining the marshy land, road construction, operating an establishment for the cultivation of special plants (Raisko), building and operating a model farm (Harmense), clothing manufacture, etc.[55] Birkenau had other functions, as will be seen. It will be particularly necessary to examine the claim that at Birkenau a program of mass killings of Jews via gas chamber was in operation, the Jews having been transported to Auschwitz primarily for this purpose.[56]

The rough figures given above for camp populations are only illustrative; actually the Birkenau figure varied a great deal and, in addition, the Birkenau camp was never completed. The projected capacity of Birkenau

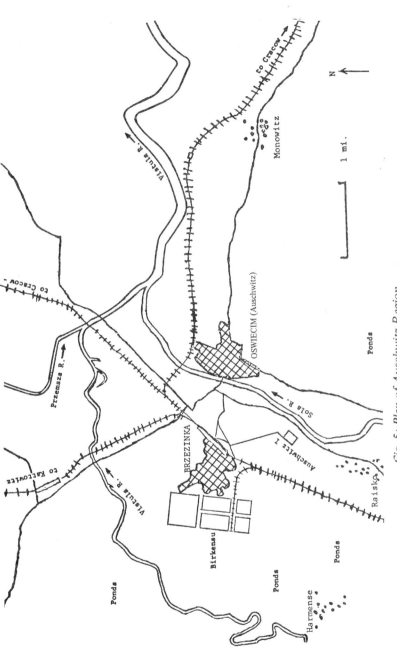

Fig. 5: Plan of Auschwitz Region

51

seems to have been 200,000 prisoners while Auschwitz I expanded to a capacity of about 30,000 and then stabilized.[57] Thus, on the basis of seniority and also on account of quartering the Auschwitz SS administrative offices, Auschwitz I was indeed the "main camp", but Birkenau, designed for the specific requirements of the Auschwitz operations, was clearly intended as the "principal camp" in terms of inmate accommodating functions.

While the Auschwitz-Kattowitz region was ideal from a technical point of view, it was also wretched from a human point of view. The ground was extremely flat with no means of draining away water in many places; it was dotted with stagnant ponds which poisoned the air and caused the area to be constantly muddy. Malaria and typhus were natural, not wartime created, dangers in this region; the war conditions greatly aggravated matters. It is said that "motor cars were disinfected after each journey carrying prisoners or their clothing".[58]

After 1942, the hydrogenation plant at Auschwitz produced oil and gasoline and other chemicals, but by the time the camp was evacuated in January 1945 it had not produced any Buna; it was only at the point of producing acetaldehyde from acetylene.[59] This relative slowness in plant construction was no doubt due to the initially virgin character of the area, the use of prisoner labor and the bad health of many prisoners; the latter had further implications which will be seen later in proper context.

I do not know whether the Auschwitz Buna plant was to have been essentially the same as the Ludwigshafen plant, an improved version of the latter, or a new generation in Buna plant construction. In any case, if it had been finished, there would have been no more advanced Buna rubber plant in the world at the time.

III
WASHINGTON AND NEW YORK

The military situation of the Allied powers in 1942 was superficially a desperate one. After the winter of 1941-1942 the German armies continued their advance across Russia. The destruction of most of the American Pacific fleet at Pearl Harbor on 7 December 1941 had made the Pacific a virtual Japanese lake. America was suddenly faced with a problem which was, for her, a strange one: lack of a crucial raw material without which no war effort appeared possible. Japan controlled what had been the source of ninety per cent of America's rubber, Malaya and the East Indies, and the source of the other ten per cent, Central and South America, was hopelessly inadequate.[1]

The manner in which America extricated herself from this grave situation will go down as one of the great ironies of history. America, one would expect, could not resolve this problem since nobody in America had thought in terms of "autarky".

Standard Oil of New Jersey had the essentials of the I.G. Farben Buna rubber process. This was on account of a series of agreements between the two companies, commencing in 1927, covering technical cooperation and mutual licensing arrangements. Standard was quite interested in Buna rubber since it could also be made (more easily) from oil. The cooperation continued, with the consent of the German Government, right up to the outbreak of war and even, to some extent, after the outbreak of war. The American side benefited hugely from these arrangements, but the German side got almost nothing out of them.[2]

The outbreak of war in September 1939 between Germany on the one hand and England and France on the other threw these arrangements between Farben and Standard into a certain amount of legal confusion which need not be explored here. Farben wished to clarify the confusion and so a meeting was arranged at the Hague, 22 September, at which certain legal arrangements were made. Standard official Frank A. Howard was puzzled by all of this:[3]

I could not escape the conviction, however, that the Germans themselves were the only people who could profit from a military standpoint by leaving the relations between Standard and the I.G. in the situation into which the war had thrown them.

The arrangements which had been made at the Hague soon proved to be inadequate so it was decided in the spring of 1940 that another meeting was necessary. Howard saw another motivation for an additional meeting:

... we intended also to ask them to supply some of their detailed designs of manufacturing equipment and technique for Buna. We hoped that I.G. might obtain permission of its government to sell to us the plans for the Buna polymerization plants they had erected in Germany under the government program.

These hopes were dashed at the conference between Standard and Farben which finally took place in Basle, Switzerland in mid-April 1940, during the German occupation of Norway which signalled the end of the *Sitzkrieg*. The new political conditions arising from the German realization that the situation was a serious one brought about at the conference the effective termination of the relations between Farben and Standard. Naturally Standard got nowhere with its proposals to buy plant designs. However, as Howard explains:

> One other point was very much on our minds. We wanted to make sure, if possible, that the Germans had not, since the outbreak of the war in Europe, made any radical change in their Buna manufacturing processes or formulas. Direct questions were out of order, since the I.G. men could not discuss any phase of Germany's industrial war effort. But during the settlements of patent transfers and discussions of license definitions needed to implement the Hague agreement, we obtained sufficient data to feel sure that all of the fundamentals of the Buna operation had remained unchanged. This conclusion was later fully confirmed.

This was the "last direct contact Standard had with the Germans on Buna rubber".[4]

All American knowledge of the Buna processes, which made the American war effort possible, came from these relationships with I.G. Farben, and this is accepted fact in the rubber industry.[5] Nevertheless, Standard later came under some rather stupid criticism and even later legal action on account of them.[6]

The sudden inavailability in 1942 of a source of rubber set off a major political crisis in the United States. There had been a Buna program in existence since mid-1940, when the Rubber Reserve Corporation had been created within the Reconstruction Finance Corporation. This agency, headed by Jesse H. Jones, supervised the stockpiling of reserve crude rubber and also sponsored the construction of Buna plants, which started in 1941. However, nobody in authority had foreseen the complete loss of the Far East rubber, so the synthetic rubber program had been modest in scope. Consequently, in 1942 there was almost no practical experience with large scale use of the Farben processes.

The emergency had been realized immediately after the attack on Pearl Harbor since, three days later, the U.S. Government had banned the sale of new automobile tires for civilian purposes. General rationing of rubber followed quickly. Early in 1942 it became realized that, if there was to be any American war effort, a gigantic synthetic rubber industry would have to be created in record time. The apparently dismal prospects for such an achievement were the cause of some amount of panic and, naturally, scapegoats were sought. Jesse Jones was a favorite target, and his claim that 300,000 tons of synthetic rubber would be produced in 1943, and 600,000 tons in 1944, was jeered at (U.S. rubber consumption in 1940 was 648,500 tons). Standard Oil also came in for outrageously unfair abuse by people who interpreted the Farben-Standard agreements as a conspiracy to retard synthetic rubber development in the U.S. Harry S. Truman, chairman of a Senate committee which investigated war production problems, first became prominent in connection with the rubber crisis of 1942.

The crisis also set off internal political conflicts. The big oil interests had a long lead in the production of Buna-S, but the farm bloc was dominant in Congress. Now, Buna can be made not only from coal and oil, but also from alcohol, an agricultural product. Forseeing the birth of a major new industry, the farm interests started arguing in favor of making Buna from alcohol (the most expensive method). They cited the fact that the Russians, also long active in the synthetic rubber field, started from alcohol. They also produced a Polish refugee who was supposed to have made some revolutionary invention in connection with making Buna from alcohol.

There was another political bloc tied up with South American interests, which proposed subsidies for plantations. There was also a small farm bloc which pressed for more extensive planting of the guayule plant in the southwest. The effect of these internal political battles was to generate massive confusion and retard the progress of the existing U.S. Buna program.

The rubber crisis filled the press in 1942 and was, in fact, the major crisis which the U.S. faced in connection with the war. There was constant lamenting that Germany was well ahead of the U.S., and that the U.S. lacked the vital experience with the processes that the Germans possessed. Methods being used in Germany were cited in connection with discussing the prospects of the U.S. program.[7]

The farm bloc's battle against what it called the "oily interests" achieved a temporary major success in July 1942 when the Congress passed the weird "Rubber Supply Act of 1942". The Act would have established a new agency for rubber production, entirely under the control of Congress and outside the domain of the War Production Board, the Army, the Navy or any executive agency of the Government. Of course, the Act also specified that the rubber was to be made from grain alcohol. President Roosevelt vetoed this bill on 6 August and announced the appointment of a committee to study the rubber problem and make some recommendations in regard to the organization of an American synthetic rubber program: "probably the most widely acclaimed action on the domestic front in the history of the war program". The members of the committee were Dr. James D. Conant, President of Harvard, Dr. Karl T. Compton, President of M.I.T., and the financier and political leader Bernard M. Baruch, who served as Chairman. The committee is normally referred to as the Baruch Committee.[8]

These three men were chosen partially because they were not considered connected with any specific interests in the conflict, and also because of their expertise. The appointment of Baruch as Chairman of such a technically oriented group may seem peculiar at first, but this is not the case. Besides being a man of diverse talents and important financial, industrial and political connections, he had chaired the War Industries Board during World War I. Moreover, for a period of more than thirty years he had been interested in industrial ventures involving rubber and had independently inventoried, with war requirements in mind, American rubber stocks in the spring of 1941. As a consequence he had gotten into fights with various people, mainly Jesse H. Jones. In addition, unlike the usual chairman of a "name" Washington *ad hoc* committee, Baruch threw all his energy into the work of the Committee. His assistant Sam Lubell also was put to work on the Committee's assignment. Even after the issuing of the final report Baruch maintained interest since Howard reports that Baruch later expressed a wish to speak to the Standard people, and that a meeting was accordingly held, at which the major technical-economic problems were discussed.[9]

The work of the Baruch Committee was completed with remarkable speed and the final report was issued on 10 September 1942; the best explanation for this speed would appear to be Baruch's independent prior involvement in the problem.

We must attempt to see this problem as the Committee must have seen it in 1942. Primarily, it was a political problem requiring the reconciliation of the various interests contending for the synthetic rubber business. Thus the final report of the Committee recommended the creation of a capacity to produce 100,000,000 gallons of additional grain alcohol per year. A second problem involved the lack of practical American experience with the Buna processes. Technical specifications were at hand, but there existed many questions on many details and quite a few alternative versions of the processes. Thus, in order to accelerate the American synthetic rubber program, the Baruch Committee saw a need to learn as much as possible of the experiences of others. It made a specific recommendation that an immediate effort be made to learn the experiences of the Russians in the production of synthetic rubber and make use of them in the American program (Jesse Jones had been charged with overlooking this possibility). The effort was made but yielded no results of any value.[10] Under such conditions it is necessary to assume that somebody in America looked into new developments in Germany in as close detail as possible at the time, and the new German development in rubber in 1942 was Auschwitz, the site of the most advanced developments in Buna rubber at that time.

The point to be made in our discussion of the American rubber crisis of 1942 is that American intelligence must have known what was going on at Auschwitz in that year. Clearly, it would be delightful if we could learn exactly what U.S. military intelligence knew about events in and around Germany during the war. However, intelligence agencies are notoriously reluctant to release such information, even many years after the events in question. With respect to World War II intelligence operations, a few sensational episodes are known but, on the whole, the content of Allied intelligence information has not been divulged. The intelligence relative to Auschwitz will be a long, long time in being made public, if it is ever made public.

In attempting to estimate, therefore, what information was possessed by Allied intelligence agencies, one must proceed very much on the basis of common sense. The difficulty is that my common sense may differ very much from another's, and that agreement on such matters may be most difficult to arrive at. Now, my common sense tells me that, quite apart from the rubber crisis, Allied intelligence would have known, in mid-1942, what was happening at the largest German concentration camp. If additionally, as every version of the extermination legend asserts, there had been anything as outré as a program of systematic extermination of Jews at Auschwitz in the summer of 1942, then my common sense tells me that it is a certainty that U.S. military intelligence would have known about it.

If another's common sense does not lead him to the same conclusion it is very doubtful that the disagreement could be settled by discussion. However with Auschwitz we have the fact that it was of interest not only as a large concentration camp (and also, if the extermination claims were correct, an extermination camp), but also as the site of the most advanced developments in synthetic rubber. In 1942, no location in the German Reich was of greater interest, and no industrial operations of greater strategic importance. Therefore, if one wishes to claim that U.S. (or the closely related British) intelligence did not know what was happening at Auschwitz in the summer of 1942, then I am afraid that one must logically claim the complete ignorance and incompetence of these intelligence agencies.

Auschwitz was of the greatest interest to the U.S. in mid-1942 on account of its enormous technological significance. Above we saw Howard's great interest, in 1940, in any information about possible new developments that could be obtained directly or inferred indirectly. A similar interest on the part of the Americans in 1942 must be assumed. It is a certainty that intelligence had developed the basic facts about the industry at Auschwitz: a plant for hydrogenation and other chemical processes aimed at producing gasoline and rubber. It has been seen that each one of the German Buna rubber plants employed processes differing in important details from the others and that the Auschwitz processes were to be the beneficiary of accumulated experiences with several different versions. We are thus justified in assuming, on account of the peculiar urgency of the rubber problem and the peculiar position of Auschwitz relative to this urgency, that the intelligence had gone into unusual detail in regard to Auschwitz, probably going over every inch via aerial photographic intelligence, and that the assembled information was available to various people in the U.S. The information probably included many details not greatly relevant to the rubber problem, such as the employment of prisoner and POW labor at Auschwitz.

Although concealment of information has been the rule in the area of military intelligence, we can nevertheless assume that the means of gathering intelligence data on Auschwitz included more or less conventional methods: exploitation of contacts with commercial representatives of Farben who were stationed in neutral countries (Portugal, Spain, Turkey, Sweden, Switzerland), aerial photographic intelligence (aircraft used for such purposes may always have longer ranges than bombers on account of their lack of armaments), general knowledge of German industrial and economic matters, spies and informers in German industry and in the German Government (e.g. Admiral Canaris), and informers in the employ of advantageously situated neutral organizations (such as the Swiss and Swedish diplomatic corps and also firms doing business in Germany). Although all of these means no doubt played a role, photographic intelligence was probably particularly important; the technology of photographic intelligence had attained a respectable level in 1942 so that a "you are there" effect was possible in blown-up aerial photos of even heavily defended positions. There were other channels of information, whose nature and existence are of some particular importance here, and which will be discussed in due course.

Not being sufficiently acquainted with the technical problems that were associated with Buna at the time, we have no idea what information the Americans might have been after and how it could be inferred from the intelligence data, any more than we have an understanding of what questions were on the minds of the Standard people at the Basle meeting and how partial answers could be inferred from the legal ritual that took place at that meeting. We can, however, offer one possibility by way of example without any claim that such was the specific case.

We have seen that the first German Buna plant at Schkopau employed a carbide-acetylene-butadiene process and that at the Huels plant the process was hydrocarbons-acetylene-butadiene. The new plant at Ludwigshafen, nearing completion when the Baruch Committee was meeting, had reverted to making the acetylene from carbide and had modernized the acetylene to butadiene stage. Since either a carbide or a hydrocarbons process was potentially applicable to the processes to be employed in the U.S. (which could have started from oil or grain alcohol) it was no doubt of great interest whether Auschwitz was to employ a carbide process (as was the case), suggesting abandonment of the hydrocarbons version on the basis of the Huels experience, or was to employ a hydrocarbons or other process, suggesting failure to make a commitment to carbide processes. Moreover the carbide *vs.* hydrocarbons question could probably be answered on the basis of aerial intelligence, if necessary.

What was the ultimate value, in terms of the problems the Americans faced, of the detailed information about contemporary German Buna developments which, we feel certain, they examined closely approximately in middle-late 1942? Perhaps none, as was the case with most categories of information; it is just that you don't miss a bet in the sort of situation in which the Americans found themselves regarding rubber in 1942.

Consideration of technical matters has been necessary here because it was in a technical context that Auschwitz first became prominent in

Washington. However it is not the technical matters that have been our objective here but simply the fact of prominence, or heavy exposure, in U.S. inner circles in the summer of 1942; this is the only point relevant to our subject. We have no direct evidence of this but we have reviewed reasons why such exposure must be assumed. It remains to show that events at Auschwitz at this time were such as to actually suggest an "extermination factory" charge to those in the inner political circles, who were alert to the appearance of semi-factual bases for atrocity stories. The events at Auschwitz in late 1942– early 1943 will be covered in a second context in the next chapter, and hence are not annotated here.

The eeriest aspect that Auschwitz must have presented while the Baruch Committee was meeting was that of the site of a ghost factory; starting around 1 August the Buna plant had been closed. There was no activity to be seen except possibly on occasional watchman. This must have excited great curiousity and no doubt special steps were taken to find out what was going on.

Our ugly old friend typhus was at Auschwitz; an epidemic had shut the Buna plant down for two months, so that work did not resume until late September. By this time there were a number of dead which must have been a few thousand, although there is a large degree of uncertainty here. The German policy was to cremate the bodies of camp inmates who died, but the epidemic caught the Auschwitz authorities with inadequate crematory facilities. There was a small crematory at Auschwitz I but more extensive facilities at Birkenau, plans for which existed in January 1942, were yet under construction in 1942 and the first complete new unit, consisting of fifteen conventional crematory ovens, was not to be available until January 1943. It appears that many of the victims of the epidemic were immediately cremated in pits, but it is possible that many were buried, at least temporarily. That the Germans were constructing crematoria at Birkenau was probably evident to continued Allied surveillance (which we assume existed) in the autumn of 1942. The buildings which the Birkenau ovens were installed in had certain halls, rooms or cellars which the accusations say were the "gas chambers".

Several books offer versions of Fig. 7, which is claimed to be a photograph of gassed victims about to be burned in pits, taken by an Auschwitz inmate in 1944.[11] We have no way of knowing when, where or by whom it was taken. However such scenes were common at Auschwitz in 1942, when the camp presumably attained some prominence in Allied intelligence. Indeed the poor quality of the picture caused some initial speculation on my part that it is an aerial intelligence photograph; the low angle does not rule out the possibility since such angles were frequently attained even with highly defended positions.[12] Also, the versions I examined in the various books do not have the border material which tends to support the claim that it was taken on the ground. Our Fig. 7 is reproduced from a print obtained in 1973 from the museum operated by the Polish Government at Auschwitz, and there remain a number of mysteries concerning it. The version reproduced here is the only one, so far as I know, that is not obviously falsified to some extent. However such an observation does not settle the matter because of the strange fact that the falsified (or, at least, retouched) versions display more apparently genuine background detail (e.g. the fence and trees).

In any case Birkenau was, in a very real sense, a "death camp"; dead, dying and sick people were sent there and, after the crematoria were built, the dead were disposed of in them. If one is to claim an "extermination camp" when there is none, what better choice is there but a "death camp"?

While the preceding adequately suggests how the Auschwitz lie originated, it is not relevant to the circumstances under which the more general extermination legend originated. The claims of exterminations of Jews have their origin not in Allied intelligence information but in the operations of the World Jewish Congress, whose leaders were at first either unconcerned with, or uniformed about, the facts pertaining to Auschwitz.

In this connection one must reject two possible fallacious expectations. The first is that Allied propaganda would strive to maximize Auschwitz propaganda after it was realized that the propaganda possibilities were excellent. The second is that the claims made in the Allied propaganda relative to Auschwitz would be almost completely devoid of real fact.

If, as is claimed here, there was no German extermination program but certain propagandists in the U.S. wished the acceptance of the thesis that there was, it would have been a most serious blunder for the propagandists to give maximum emphasis to Auschwitz or any other place as an alleged extermination camp for this would amount to making a charge that the Germans could answer. If high U.S. officials, such as Roosevelt or his cabinet members, had made specific remarks about exterminations, naming sites where exterminations were taking place, under circumstances where their remarks received the wide publicity normally given to public statements by officials of their rank, then both the Germans and the Allies would have been put on the spot on the question and the truth would not have been long in coming out. On the contrary, as we shall see in a later chapter, the first period in which there was a persistence of references to Auschwitz as an extermination camp, appearing even under obscure circumstances, was immediately after D-Day (6 June 1944), when nobody was paying any attention to such stories. Later in the summer of 1944, the emphasis shifted to the Lublin camp, which the Russians had just captured. The first reference to emerge from a U.S. Government source which was high enough so that it could not be ignored, and which charged exterminations at Auschwitz, came in late November 1944, after the exterminations are supposed to have been terminated.[13] Otherwise, people such as Roosevelt and Churchill and their ministers spoke only in very general moralistic terms about exterminations. It is only if one believed there actually were exterminations taking place at Auschwitz, and one wanted to stop them, that one would have made a specific charge concerning Auschwitz to which the Germans would have felt obliged to respond. No such challenge ever materialized. Despite the fact that in all versions of the extermination legend the Auschwitz exterminations had certainly started by the late summer of 1942, and despite the fact that U.S. military intelligence must have known whatever it was that was going on at Auschwitz at that time, no specific extermination charges came from any high source until much later.

The second fallacious expectation is that American propaganda relative to Auschwitz would be almost free of fact. We have indicated already that this should not be expected. Washington had excellent and accurate information about Auschwitz, as it had about all important phases of German industrial activity, and it has been remarked above that the real facts about Birkenau seemed to invite distortion of interpretation.

The first "inside" events relative to the extermination propaganda were in the context of a conflict involving the U.S. State and Treasury Departments and the World Jewish Congress (and American Jewish Congress), headed by Rabbi Stephen S. Wise. The prominent characters in the story are Treasury Secretary Morgenthau, later the nominal author of the notorious

"Morgenthau Plan" for the despoliation of Germany, Secretary of State Cordell Hull and Undersecretary of State Sumner Welles, who were mildly reluctant to be carried along by the propaganda, and Assistant Secretary of State J. Breckenridge Long, who was very resistant to the propaganda. Also involved are the World Jewish Congress representatives in Switzerland, Gerhard Riegner and Professor Paul Guggenheim, who transmitted stories of supposedly European origin to Wise or to other persons in the U.S., notably to the State Department through the U.S. Ambassador to Switzerland, Leland Harrison, or through the U.S. Consul in Geneva, Paul C. **Squire**. The principal work that has set forth the events surrounding the birth of the extermination legend is Arthur D. Morse's *While Six Million Died,* a book which is supplemented to some extent by Henry L. Feingold's *The Politics of Rescue.* Additional material has been contributed by post-war accounts given by Morgenthau, by historians J.M. Blum and Anthony Kubek (in interpreting Morgenthau's papers, the latter for the U.S. Senate publication *Morgenthau Diary*), historian F.L. Israel (in summarizing the papers of J. Breckenridge Long), and J. DuBois, who was at first Chief Counsel of the Treasury's Foreign Funds Control, involved in these matters chiefly in connection with efforts to extend assistance to refugees.[14]

The first extermination claim appears to have been made by the London section of the World Jewish Congress in June 1942. It was claimed that one million Jews had been killed in some undesignated and unlocated "vast slaughterhouse for Jews" which had been established in Eastern Europe. The only attempt to provide evidence for this claim was a remark that the Polish government in exile in London had received confirming information. The allegation was carried in the *New York Times* in a story that will be reviewed below.

The evidence for this London claim was obviously too flimsy to serve as effective propaganda, so an effort was made to improve matters slightly. On 8 August 1942 Riegner and Guggenheim approached the U.S. Consulate in Geneva, which had been cooperating with the World Jewish Congress to the extent of allowing it to use diplomatic channels for messages, with a story that some anonymous German industrialist had informed them that he had learned of a decision to kill all non-Soviet Jews under German control. Discussions, which the industrialist had overheard, were being held in the Fuehrer's Headquarters regarding the methods to be employed. One method under discussion was gassing with Prussic acid (hydrogen cyanide gas) after the Jews had been concentrated at camps in Eastern Europe. This story was forwarded to Washington by the Consulate, via U.S. diplomatic channels, and to London via British diplomatic channels. The "industrialist" has remained anonymous to this day.

When the U.S. State Department received the message, it was evaluated and it was decided that

it does not appear advisable in view of the . . . fantastic nature of the allegations and the impossibility of our being of any assistance if such action were taken, to transmit the information to Dr. Wise as suggested.

The message was accordingly suppressed, but Wise learned of its contents anyway. It is said that he learned from London, but it is also possible that he had composed the message in the first place, and learned of its transmission and suppression through his various connections.

Wise immediately contacted Welles, who had approved the decision to suppress, in order to protest the State Department's handling of the matter. Welles replied that the "information" was somewhat too unsubstantiated to be taken seriously, and that some confirmation should be obtained before any public announcement was made. Welles then instructed the U.S. representative in the Vatican to attempt to check the allegations with Vatican sources. At the time, almost nobody in Washington pretended to take these claims seriously, and even President Roosevelt assured Justice Felix Frankfurter that the Jews who had been deported to the East were merely being used to help build fortifications.

In September two anonymous persons showed up in Geneva, claiming to have escaped from German controlled areas. They reported the extermination of Polish Jews and the utilization of the Jewish corpses for the manufacture of fertilizer. This was forwarded to Washington through diplomatic channels, and again an attempt was made to get confirmation by the Vatican (which had thus far ignored the first request for confirmation). At about the same time, Wise had received a message from a World Jewish Congress official in Europe reporting on the "manufacture of soap and artificial fertilizer" from Jewish corpses.

In late September Riegner came forward with two new documents. The first had, he said, been prepared by an (anonymous, naturally) officer attached to the German High Command, and had reached Reigner through several intermediaries. The anonymous officer claimed that there were at least two factories in existence which were manufacturing soap, glue and lubricants from Jewish corpses, and that it had been determined that each Jewish corpse was worth 50 Reichsmarks. The second document consisted of two coded letters which had, it was said, been written by a Swiss Jew resident in Warsaw. The anonymous Jew reported wholesale exterminations of Warsaw Jews deported to the East. All of these messages were forwarded to Washington and then filed.

In passing we should note the resemblance of such claims to World War I propaganda, and the appalling lack of originality and creativity on the part of the World Jewish Congress. It scarcely requires remarking that the soap and glue factories were a very transient propaganda phenomenon, and that the only similar charges made at Nuernberg were made by the Russians. These charges were largely ignored even then and nobody, to my knowledge, has since come forward with the locations of these factories, the identities of the persons who managed them, or similar information. Reitlinger does not claim the existence of such factories, and Hilberg (p. 624) does not believe they existed. using H to support

On 10 October the Vatican finally informed the U.S. representatives that it had been unable to confirm the many reports it had heard of severe measures against the Jews.

On 22 October Riegner met with Ambassador Harrison and presented him with more of the same sort of "evidence", this time reporting "information" provided by yet another anonymous German Informant (whose name, however, is said to have been presented to Harrison in a sealed envelope, and to have been kept secret from everybody but the OSS) and also an anonymous official of the International Red Cross. Harrison forwarded this material to Washington, but also wrote two personal letters to Welles in late October, claiming that he knew the name of the German industrialist, and also claiming that the anonymous Red Cross official was Karl Jacob Burckhardt, the distinguished Voltaire-Goethe scholar who was prominent in the International Red Cross during the war. He enclosed an affidavit that Guggenheim had deposed before Squire on 29 October, in which Guggenheim claimed that he had obtained from an anonymous German informant information confirming Riegner's claims. The anonymous German informant had gotten his information from an anonymous official of the German Foreign Ministry, and from an anonymous official of the German Ministry of War. Moreover, an anonymous Swiss informant, resident in Belgrade, had also given information to Guggenheim supporting the claims.

In order to confirm the claims, Squire arranged an interview with Burckhardt, which took place in Geneva on 7 November. On 9 November Squire communicated to Harrison his memorandum on the interview, in which he had recorded that Burckhardt's information was that Hitler had signed an order that before the end of 1942 Germany must be free of all Jews. Squire's account of the interview explains:[15]

I then asked him whether the word *extermination,* or its equivalent, was employed, to which he replied that the words *must be Juden-frei* (free of Jews) were utilized. He then made it clear that since there is no place to send these Jews and since the territory must be cleared of this race, it is obvious what the net result would be.

This, the report of an ambiguous remark, made by an imperfectly informed Swiss citizen, reported by an intermediary who was friendly to the World Jewish Congress and eager to discover a sinister interpretation to such facts as were available, is as solid as this "evidence" ever got. To my knowledge, Burckhardt never spoke out publicly, during or after the war, in connection with these matters. He answered some written questions which were put to him by Kaltenbrunner's defense during the IMT trial, but these questions, relating to Kaltenbrunner's efforts to permit the Red Cross to enter the German camps toward the end of the war, were not relevant to our subject. Nobody asked Burckhardt about exterminations.[16]

Late in November, the State Department received "information" from an anonymous Vatican source, consisting of a three page description, in French, of events allegedly transpiring in Poland. The document is unsigned and the only sort of endorsement is a handwritten notation, "from Mr. F at Vatican City", which appears in an unknown hand on the first page. The document reports, *inter alia*[17]

Farms for the breeding of human beings are being organized to which women and girls are brought for the purpose of being made mothers of children who are then taken from them to be raised in Nazi establishments. ... Mass execution of Jews continues. ... They are killed by poison gas in chambers especially prepared for that purpose (often in railway cars) and by machine gun fire, following which the dead and the dying are both covered with earth. ... Reports are being circulated to the effect that the Germans are making use of their corpses in plants manufacturing chemical products (soap making factories).

During the late summer and autumn of 1942, Wise had continuously campaigned for the Allied governments to take a public position directly condemning the alleged exterminations of Jews in Europe. On 8 December Wise led a delegation to the White House and presented to President Roosevelt a twenty page document entitled *Blue Print for Extermination,* which was based on the sort of "information" we have reviewed. Related Jewish pressures finally brought capitulation to Wise on the mythical exterminations, and on 17 December 1942 the Allies, led by Washington, issued a statement condemning the exterminations. A related statement, released two days later, claimed exterminations at Belzec and at Chelmno, but Auschwitz was not mentioned (the relevant news stories are reviewed below).

Despite this public declaration, the group headed by J. Breckenridge Long continued to resist the propaganda. On 19 January 1943 Reigner gave Harrison the "information" that "in one place in Poland 6,000 Jews are killed daily". On 21 January Harrison communicated this material to the State Department and also to certain unspecified "private Jewish agencies", apparently meaning Wise. The message was merely filed and the Department made no public mention of it. For a time, the private Jewish agencies were also silent about the message. On 10 February Long's group took a further step in suppression of such propaganda. It instructed Harrison, in a message signed by Welles (who is said to have not read the message), and with particular reference to Harrison's cable of 21 January,

in the future, reports submitted to you for transmission to private persons in the United States should not be accepted unless extraordinary circumstances make such action advisable. It is felt that by sending such private messages which circumvent neutral countries' censorship we risk the possibility that neutral countries might find it necessary to take steps to curtail or abolish our official secret means of communication.

Finally, on 14 February, the *N.Y. Times* published the story. For explanation of the delay of four weeks in publishing the story, despite its being received by "private Jewish agencies" on 21 January, and despite the evident policy of publishing the unsupported claims of such agencies, we can only conjecture that certain unknown persons were hoping that the State Department, given the precedent of the declaration of 17 December, would release the "information" so as to confer a greater credibility than would have been granted to the story as it eventually appeared: a claim indistinguishable in terms of authority from the average sort of atrocity claim.

The Treasury (which, because of Morgenthau's long crusade against Germany, had repeatedly interfered in the conduct of foreign affairs since at least 1936[18]) was soon to come into conflict with State over this suppression. A second and more substantial basis for conflict between the two Departments was also established in February 1943. It was learned that the Rumanian Government was prepared to transfer 70,000 Jews to Palestine on Rumanian ships bearing Vatican insignia (it is unlikely that the Rumanians really cared where the Jews sent to, so I assume that the Palestine destination must have been somehow specified by Zionists involved in the formulation of the proposals). An important condition was specified by "officials who were in charge in Rumania of Jewish interests". A cost of 250 pounds (about $1200) per capita was specified. There were other difficulties. The British policy at the time was not to antagonize the Arabs, especially in view of the potentially catastrophic consequences of an Arab uprising in wartime, and thus the British at first refused to consider the admission of so many Jews to Palestine. The British took the position that if such Jews were to be taken out of Europe, the U.S. should provide camps in North Africa for them. In addition, both the British Foreign Office and the U.S. State Department took the position that there would inevitably be spies in such a large group of people, that the logistical problems involved in transporting and accomodating such numbers were formidable, and that the money demanded might fall into the hands of the enemy (who valued Allied currency for various purposes). The Treasury was eager to get into the business of aiding Jewish refugees and thus it sought to overcome such objections. By July 1943 there was said to be bribe money demanded for the Rumanian Jews, $170,000, and the Treasury and the World Jewish Congress proposed that Rumanian Jewish businessmen could produce the bribe money if they could be reimbursed after the war with money to be held in escrow in Switzerland. However the British objections to admitting Jews to Palestine stood, and efforts to circumvent them by proposing other destinations for the Jews ran into the opposition of various candidate countries and also into U.S. immigration laws.

The State Department, especially J. Breckenridge Long and associates, considered all the talk about "exterminations" to be just wartime propaganda invention, in the same spirit as the stories invented during World War I. They were, after all, continually considering proposals to move these exterminated people out of Europe; as late as January 1944 the Department was taking steps to encourage Jews to leave Poland for Hungary. Long wrote that one danger in supporting the proposals of Wise was that it "may lend color to the charges of Hitler that we are fighting this war on account of and at the instigation and direction of our Jewish citizens". State considered the whole project pointless and, indeed, in conflict with the requirements of an optimum war effort. Long wrote that

> Wise always assumes such a·sanctimonious air and pleads for the "intellectuals and brave spirits, refugees from the tortures of the dictators" or words to that effect. Of course only an infinitesimal fraction of the immigrants are of that category – and some are certainly German agents . . . I did not allude to the *Navemar* – en route from Lisbon to Havana and New York – a freight boat, passenger accomodations for 15 and 1200 poor Jews above and below decks with no sanitary arrangements, no service, no kitchen facilities, at from $700 to $1500 apiece, 4 dead before reaching Bermuda, 6 hospitalized there, 1 of which died, victims of the greed of their fellows – not of Germany or the United States policy. The vessel is a ,menace to the health of any port where it stops and a shame to the human greed which makes it possible. But I did not allude to it in reply to Rabbi Wise. Each one of these men hates me. I am to them the embodiment of a nemesis. They each and all believe every person, everywhere, has a *right* to come to the United States. I believe *nobody,* anywhere has a *right* to enter the United States unless the United States desires.

The State Department either procrastinated on the matter or actively sabotaged the proposed project. At the end of the summer of 1943 it was learned that 6,000 Jewish children could be taken out of France, and this possibility got involved in the problem.

The people from the Treasury and the World Jewish Congress kept pressing for the proposed projects and continually asserted, with apparent complete seriousness, that the only alternative was the death of the people in question at the hands of Hitler. It was evenly openly charged that the failure to approve the projects was "acquiescence of this Government in the murder of the Jews". Pressure was also put on the British by various people. Long had become a whipping boy both publicly and within Government circles, and he wrote bitterly that "the Jewish agitation depends on attacking some individual. Otherwise they would have no publicity. So for the time being I am the bull's eye".

As a result of this campaign, a breakthrough was achieved by Wise and Morgenthau in December 1943, when arrangements were finally made for the ,evacuation of Rumanian Jews and money was put into a Swiss account controlled by Riegner and the U.S. Treasury. Moreover, in December Rumania put out peace feelers and was assured it would be treated well if it treated its Jews well; Rumania immediately decided to repatriate Jews it had resettled by the Sea of Azov in Russia.

This Morgenthau victory had been achieved at a 20 December meeting of Hull, Long, Morgenthau and John Pehle, chief of the Treasurv's Foreign Funds Control. Morgenthau had evidently decided on a showdown with State over the entire matter for at that meeting he casually showed a copy of the complete text of the 10 February message from Welles to Harrison (the suppression instruction). The Stage Department complied, but deleted the reference to Harrison's message of 21 January, thereby causing the message of 10 February to appear utterly routine. In thus editing the message, State was obviously unaware that the complete contents of this correspondence had already been leaked to DuBois in the Treasury by Donald Hiss of the State Department (brother of Alger Hiss and later identified in Bentley-Chambers testimony as a Communist, although he denied it), who had acquired copies of the messages only with great difficulty and, in complying with DuBois' request, nevertheless cautioned the latter that the messages

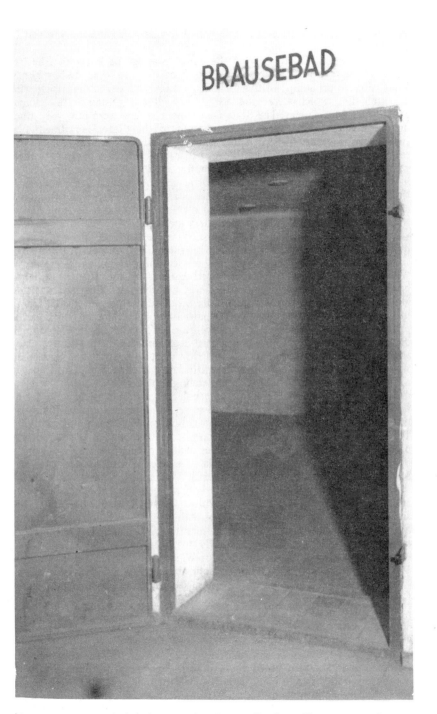

Fig. 6: Interior of disinfection chamber at Dachau. Photograph taken by author August 1973.

were "none of Treasury's business" and that Hiss could lose his job for the leak.[19]

When Morgenthau received the edited message he knew that he had another weapon to use against Long and associates and, thus, he brought on a collision by charging editing of the message and demanding to see the unedited files, which were produced shortly later, exposing State's clumsy attempt at concealment. The State Department people were now very much on the defensive, and further examination of the State Department files (which the Treasury was now in a position to insist on) revealed that, in response to a request by Wise, Welles had cabled Harrison in April to meet with Riegner and transmit new information that Riegner was supposed to have obtained. The confused Harrison did as requested (Riegner's information had to do with proposals to assist Jewish refugees in France and Rumania) and also remarked to Welles that such material should not be subjected to the restriction imposed by the 10 February message.

Morgenthau was victorious in the State-Treasury collision; Roosevelt, drawn into the issue, sided with him by establishing in January 1944 the so-called War Refugee Board consisting of Morgenthau, Hull and Secretary of War Stimson. However the executive director was "Morgenthau's fair haired boy", John Pehle, and Josiah DuBois was the general counsel. It was thus Morgenthau's Board. The WRB naturally acquired the powers that had been held by the three Government Departments that were involved in the proposed projects for taking Jews out of Europe. Thus, the State Department became committed to appointing special attachés with diplomatic status on the recommendation of the Board (the UNRRA, set up the previous November, was to have a similar function but only after the war ended).[20]

In order for the reader to completely grasp the nature of this development, and its import in terms of our subject, we should go beyond noting the obvious fact that the WRB was to serve, to a great extent, as simply an instrument of the World Jewish Congress and other Zionist organizations. The Communist apparatus was also one of the directors involved, for the person to whom Morgenthau had delegated all of the Treasury's powers in the areas relevant to the WRB was Harry Dexter White, later exposed as a Soviet agent. White became a member of Morgenthau's inner circle in the spring of 1938. A week after Pearl Harbor, Morgenthau announced that "on and after this date, Mr. Harry D. White, Assistant to the Secretary, will assume full responsibility for all matters with which the Treasury Department has to deal having a bearing on foreign relations . . ." The extreme generality of the wording of this order, especially the phrase "having a bearing on", were to create grand opportunities for White in the years ahead. In early 1943 Morgenthau amplified White's responsibilities:

> Effective this date, I would like you to take supervision over and assume full responsibility for Treasury's participation in all economic and financial matters . . . in connection with the operations of the Army and Navy and the civilian affairs in the foreign areas in which our Armed Forces are operating or are likely to operate. This will, of course, include general liaison with the State Department, Army and Navy, and other departments or agencies and representatives of foreign governments on these matters.

White, who became an Assistant Secretary of the Treasury in early 1945, took full advantage of these powers, especially in connection with occupation policy in Germany. It is also evident that, since the WRB was to a large degree an arm of the Treasury, its operations fell into White's domain. It is also worth remarking that the general counsel of the WRB, DuBois, was "closely associated" with the Communist agent, William L. Ullmann, and was also a witness of White's will.[21]

Long had mixed and, as it developed, prescient thoughts about the implications of these developments:

it will be only a few more days now before I relinquish jurisdiction in connection with refugees and let somebody else have the fun. And it has been a heavy responsibility— domestic as well as foreign, because there are 5 million Jews in the country, of whom 4 million are concentrated in and around New York City. And we have *no* Arab or Moslem population, but we do have increasingly important commercial interests — principally oil — in the Moslem countries. In addition our ally England has hardly any Jewish citizenship but a very large political interest in the Near East. So our policy is increasingly based in part — a large part — on a domestic situation, while England's is based entirely on a foreign affairs base — and the two are hard to reconcile . . . it is good news for me . . . this ensures me staying out. What they can do that I have not done I cannot imagine.

Long miscalculated on the last point for the WRB eventually did a considerable amount of Jew relocation, and its acts on behalf of refugees are of great importance in this book and are discussed in a later chapter. It also aided concentration camp inmates, through the Red Cross, in the final weeks of the war.[22] As an instrument of Wise and other Zionists, the WRB also did considerable propagandizing[23] and its most consequential propaganda achievement was a booklet, *German Extermination Camps: Auschwitz and Birkenau,* Executive Office of the President, Washington, November 1944. The booklet is hereafter referred to as the WRB report.

The WRB report constituted the formal birth of the "official" thesis of exterminations via gas chamber at Auschwitz. In it all of the essentials and many of the details of the later Auschwitz hoax are found. The Nuernberg charges grew out of the WRB report. There does not seem to have been any particularly strong reaction, one way or the other, to the WRB report at the time that it was issued. However, an American journalist, Oswald F. Schuette, wrote a critical letter to Stimson (one of the signers of the report), but Schuette did not get a satisfactory reply.[24]

Of course the WRB report failed to change the opinions of the State Department people who had scoffed at the extermination propaganda from the very beginning. In private with DuBois, they were blunt in their opinion of the WRB report: "Stuff like this has been coming from Bern ever since 1942 . . . Don't forget, this is a Jew telling about the Jews". . . . "This is just a campaign by that Jew Morgenthau and his Jewish assistants."

The WRB report was said to have been transmitted from Bern to Washington. The report will be discussed in depth after we have surveyed a key part of the wartime propaganda, in its public aspect. First, however, we should point out that some otherwise keen observers misinterpret the role of Auschwitz in the extermination legend. The distinguished American journalist and historian, Harry Elmer Barnes, wrote in 1967 that the extermination[25]

camps were first presented as those in Germany, such as Dachau, Belsen, Buchenwald, Sachsenhausen, and Dora, but it was demonstrated that there had been no systematic extermination in those camps. Attention was then moved on to Auschwitz, Treblinka, Belzec, Chelmno, Jonowska, Tarnow, Ravensbruck, Mauthausen, Brezeznia, and Birkenau, which does not exhaust the list that appears to have been extended as needed.

The basis for Barnes' misunderstanding, of course, is that at the end of the war the mass media, for the sake of sensation mongering did, indeed, seize on the scenes found in the German camps as proof of exterminations, and it is also true, as we indicated in the previous chapter, that these scenes have served as the mass propaganda "proof" of exterminations. However our analysis shows that Auschwitz had been carefully chosen in 1944 as the core for the extermination hoax. This point will be supported by material to be reviewed below and also in a later chapter. By publishing the WRB report in November 1944, Washington committed itself to a specific form of the hoax. That form was maintained in the trials in Nuernberg and, even today, the form of the hoax does not differ in any significant respect from the WRB report.

After his WRB victory, Morgenthau busied himself with other things, particularly with the policies to be followed in occupied Germany. He found that existing plans actually paid regard to the Hague and Geneva Conventions, to which the United States was signatory, and which prohibited such things as the seizure of private personal property of no military significance, the detaining of POW's long after the end of hostilities, and the needless imposition of starvation rations. He therefore campaigned for the harsher policies which later became known as the Morgenthau Plan, and of which many were actually adopted and put into practice. David Marcus, in the CAD, sponsored Morgenthau's objectives there and kept him informed about his opponents. Colonel Bernard Bernstein, long associated with Morgenthau, performed a similar function for him at SHAEF headquarters in London. Baruch also helped out.[26]

The thesis of this book is that the story of Jewish extermination in World War II is a propaganda hoax. Obviously, therefore, we must examine the origins of the hoax in wartime propaganda. We have already discussed many of the "inside" aspects, and the public aspects remain to be examined.

The enormity of the task plus the "controversial" nature of the subject seem to have discouraged a thorough study of the propaganda. There have been studies of special aspects. John T. Flynn, in *While You Slept*, surveyed the propaganda in respect to communist and pro-communist influences, especially in regard to Asia. James J. Martin made a study of the manner in which the American media treated the Soviet Union, the negotiated peace question, and the Allied terror bombings during the war.

It would be quite out of the question to survey all of the atrocity and extermination propaganda pertaining to the European theater in World War II. Here we may economize on the magnitude of the survey to be undertaken by noting that we are interested only in the Jewish extermination question, and only in what important people were doing. We will therefore find that examination of stories concerning alleged Jewish extermination which appeared in the *N.Y. Times*, spring 1942 through 1943, together with a summary of 1944 propaganda which will be presented in a subsequent chapter, is all that is required to get a satisfactory conception of the propaganda. Therefore we start here with spring 1942 stories. Concurrent commentary will be made. In many cases there is involved a story, allegedly originating in Europe, claiming mass killings and the matters of particular interest in such cases are the source of the story, the location of the alleged killings and the method of killing allegedly employed. It should also be kept in mind that the post-war extermination legend claims only three varieties of mass exterminations: gassing at six sites in Poland, "gasmobiles" in Russia, and mass shootings in Russia.

6 April 1942, p.2   REPORTS NAZI SLAUGHTER OF JEWS

KUIBYSHEV, Russia, April 5 (AP) — The Anti-Fascist Jewish Committee reported today that the Germans have killed 86,000 Jews in and around Minsk, 25,000 at Odessa and "tens of thousands" in Lithuania, Latvia and Estonia. In Estonia, the report said, the entire Jewish population numbering 4,500 was wiped out.

13 June 1942, p.7   NAZIS BLAME JEWS FOR BIG BOMBINGS

BERLIN, June 12 (From German Broadcast Recorded by the United Press in New York) — Propaganda Minister Joseph Goebbels said tonight that Germany would carry out a mass "extermination" of Jews in reprisal for the Allied air bombings of German cities which, he acknowledged, have caused heavy damage.

Dr. Goebbels, in an article in the publication The Reich, said the Jews would be exterminated throughout Europe "and perhaps even beyond Europe" in retaliation against the heavy air assaults.

Goebbels' remark was directed against the Jewish controlled press, which he regarded as largely responsible for the propaganda atmosphere which made the terror bombings possible. His remark in *Das Reich* was:

> In this war the Jews are playing their most criminal game, and they will have to pay for that with the extermination *(Ausrottung)* of their race in Europe and perhaps far beyond. They are not to be taken seriously in this conflict, since they represent neither British nor American, but exclusively Jewish, interests.

Now this is indeed an extermination threat, since the primary meaning of the term *"Ausrottung"* is "extermination" (the English "uprooting", to which the word is related etymologically, is only a secondary meaning). Similar totally public utterances were also made occasionally by Hitler. Examples are "the result of this war will be the destruction of Jewry", and "it will not be the Aryan peoples that will be annihilated but it will be Jewry."[27]

In reaction to this one should observe that (a) extreme statements were a pervasive feature of Nazi oratory and rhetoric, and (b) the extermination mythologists find it necessary to claim that the exterminations were carried out in the most extreme secrecy, which makes it somewhat untenable to take such occasional references in the public declarations of Nazi leaders as evidence of exterminations, and (c) it is necessary to fully grasp the specific circumstances of the Goebbels remark, i.e. it was a reaction to Allied terror bombings, and (d) people can say heated things in wartime, and bloodthirsty statements were made by supposedly responsible people on both sides during the war, and (e) it is often the case that a complete understanding of context is necessary when interpreting the specific meaning of a reference to "extermination" or "annihilation" (or, in German, *"Ausrottung"*, *"Vernichtung"*, respectively). Moreover, the German word for "Jewry", *das Judentum,* is ambiguous in meaning. Let each of these five points be examined in order.

(a) It is well known that Nazi oratory and rhetoric tended to have a provocatively inflammatory character whose origins go well back into the days when the Nazis were a minor party in Weimar Germany. It appears that this was a result of a deliberate and studied policy, for in 1931 Hitler explained the reasons for it in a private interview;[28]

> What some madman of an editor writes in my own press is of no interest to me. . . . We can achieve something only by fanaticism. If this fanaticism horrifies the bourgeoisie, so much the better. Solely by this fanaticism, which refuses any compromise, do we gain our contact with the masses.

Put more simply, he often found that he could get attention by making wild statements. Naturally, all of the Nazi leaders, especially Goebbels, were infected with this attitude to some degree. It is true that after the Nazis came to power and assumed responsibility for ruling Germany, their public declarations became much more moderated in tone, but the tendency never entirely departed from them, and of course the war and the problem of attempting to reach public opinion in the Allied countries revived the feature somewhat. Under the circumstances, it is actually remarkable that Hitler and Goebbels only rarely made such declarations.

(b) We shall see in following chapters that the extermination mythologists are forced to take the position that the Nazis went to extremes to preserve the secrecy of their killing program of continental scope, and did in fact preserve this secrecy to a most remarkable extent. What is known of the behavior of European Jews during those days, for example, despite the claims

69

of some individual authors and the indubitable fact that there were all sorts of rumors current, shows that the Jews were not conscious of any extermination program. When they were told to pack up for transport, they did just that, and went without resistance. In Chapter IV we shall note Theresienstadt Jews *volunteering* for transport to Auschwitz as late as August 1944, for the Jews at Theresienstadt knew nothing of any extermination program at Auschwitz or anywhere else. In Chapter VII we shall note that the Nazis were allegedly even unwilling to commit anything to confidential documents for, we are told, "the drafting of circumspect minutes was one of the major arts of Hitler's Reich". Since this is the case put forward by the extermination mythologists, then it is not merely that occurrences of the sort of remarks under consideration do not support their case; the problem becomes that of explaining such occurrences, and it's their problem.

(c) The Goebbels remark should be seen for what it was: a professional propagandist's reaction to the Allied bombings, which obsessed German policy in various ways from May 1940 on. Since the facts in this connection, although well established, are not well known, they are very briefly summarized here but, in order to avoid inexcusably long digression, the summary is indeed brief. The reader interested in a more thorough treatment is referred to Veale and to Colby.

At the outbreak of war in 1939, German air doctrine viewed the bomber as a form of artillery and thus a weapon to be used in support of ordinary ground operations. It was in this connection that the well publicized bombings of Warsaw in 1939 and Rotterdam in May 1940 took place: only after these cities had actually become the scenes of military operations and the laws of siege applied. "Strategic bombing", as we understand the term, played no role in German combat operations (although of course it had been and was under study by German military planners).

This was not the case in Britain, however, for at the time that the Germans were using their bombers as artillery in the Netherlands, the British made the "splendid decision" to bomb German civilian targets, knowing perfectly well that Hitler had no intention or wish to engage in warfare of this sort (Hitler, indeed, did not want war with Britain at all). There was a moderate amount of German bombing of targets in England during the early summer of 1940, but only specifically military targets were attacked, even while such cities as Hamburg and Bremen were undergoing general attack. It was only after three months of this, and with the greatest reluctance, that Hitler felt himself forced to reply in kind, and in this way the well publicized "Blitz" hoax was established. The British people were not permitted to find out that their Government could have stopped the German raids at any time merely by stopping the raids on Germany.

The British raids on Germany, while of no military significance in 1940, had put the German Government on the spot in German popular opinion, since the German people naturally thought that their Government should be able to do something about them, and this was the only reason that the Germans had adopted retaliatory bombing as a last resort. In announcing the policy, Hitler declared in a *Sportpalast* speech of 4 September 1940 that[2]

If the British Air Force drops two or three or four thousand kilograms of bombs, we will drop a hundred and fifty, a hundred and eighty, two hundred thousand, three hundred thousand, four hundred thousand kilograms and more in a single night.

This was a gross exaggeration of his capabilities relative to the British for, although at the time his bombers were numerically superior to the British, they were designed for support of troops and not for the "strategic bombing" that the British bombers were equipped for. Nevertheless violent words are cheap and, after the Luftwaffe, which was never more than a nuisance for the Allied bombing operations, violent words (sometimes coupled with promises of secret new weapons) were about all Hitler and Goebbels were able to come up with, in 1940 or at any subsequent time, to oppose the bombings. It is in this context that the Goebbels remark should be grasped.

(d) There were bloodthirsty remarks made on both sides during the war. In the U.S. there were many examples of wild views earnestly put forward by apparently civilized persons, which were received with apparently thoughtful reactions of approval by equally respected persons. Since there were so many such people, it will suffice to remark only on Clifton Fadiman, the well known author and critic who, at the time, was the book review editor of the *New Yorker* weekly magazine.

Fadiman was the principal luminary of the Writers War Board, a semi-official government agency that did volunteer writing for government agencies in connection with the war. The Board was chaired by Rex Stout. The thesis that Fadiman and Stout carried to the writers' community in 1942 was that writings on the war should seek "to generate an active hate against all Germans and not merely against Nazi leaders". This generated some heated controversy and writers and observers took sides in what became debate hot enough for Fadiman to declare that he knew of "only one way to make a German understand and that's to kill them and even then I think they don't understand".

These were not isolated outbursts for, through his column in the *New Yorker,* Fadiman welcomed the opportunity to set down his views on Germans in a more organized context. In April 1942 he had found the juvenile concept he needed in a book by de Sales, *The Making of Tomorrow.* Taking for granted the reader's concurrence that the Nazis were at least the worst scourge to come along in centuries, he wrote that de Sales'

argument is simply that the present Nazi onslaught is not in the least the evil handiwork of a group of gangsters but rather the final and perfect expression of the most profound instincts of the German people. "Hitler is the incarnation of forces greater than himself. The heresy he preaches is two thousand years old". What is the heresy? It is nothing more or less than a rebellion against Western civilization. Mr. de Sales traces five such German rebellions, beginning with Arminius. At first you are inclined to be skeptical of the author's grand indictment – his anti-Germanism may conceivably stem from his French ancestry – but as you follow his argument it becomes more and more cogent and the true proportions of this war emerge with great clarity.

His reviews of books on the war expressed the historical concept that he had found in de Sales' nonsense. Scoffing at Howard K. Smith's claim that "If we can offer (the Germans) a real alternative to extermination, the nation, though it may not succumb to actual revolution, will fall into our hands", Fadiman wrote that "The world has been appeasing the Germans ever since their human wolf packs broke out of their forest lairs in the time of Arminius. The result is a Europe on the verge of suicide". This was followed by his obvious approval of Hemingway's "extraordinary . . . suggestion that 'the only ultimate settlement' with the Nazis is to sterilize them. He means just that, in a surgical sense". Of course, Fadiman also saw no distinction between Nazis and other Germans and ridiculed Dorothy Thompson's "passionate argument" for such a distinction, as well as her conviction "that our postwar efforts must be directed toward the construction of a European federation of states, with Germany, under democratic leadership, occupying a leading position". Although Fadiman never advocated the killing of all or most Germans, at least not in so many words, this was the clear sense of his declarations. After all, what else can be done with "wolf packs who broke out of their forest lairs", are now trying to enslave the rest of the world, "understand" only if you "kill them" and must not be given "a real alternative to extermination"?[30]

Clifton Fadiman was only a very prominent and semi-official example of a "school of thought" that existed among leaders of opinion in the U.S. during the war. James J. Martin and Benjamin Colby have published longer studies of Allied propaganda based on hatred of all Germans, the latter presenting a particularly thorough study of the Writers War Board.

The climate of wartime opinion in Britain, of course, was about the same and, on account of England's earlier entry into the war, of longer standing. In reacting to Hitler's Berlin *Sportpalast* speech on the initiation of German air raids on British cities (quoted above), the London *Daily Herald* gloated that Hitler had made "a frantic effort to reassure his raid-harassed people" who "are in an extremely nervous condition and stay awake even when there is no alarm". The same issue of the *Herald* goes on to present the recommendations of the Reverend C.W. Whipp, Vicar of St. Augustine's, Leicester:

"The orders ought to be, 'Wipe them out', and to this end I would concentrate all our science towards discovering a new and far more terrific explosive.

"These German devils (that is the only word one can use) come over our cities and turn their machine-guns on women and children.

"Well, all I hope is that the R.A.F. will grow stronger and stronger and go over and smash Germany to smithereens.

"A Minister of the Gospel, perhaps, ought not to indulge in sentiments like these.

"I go further, and I say quite frankly that if I could I would wipe Germany off the map.

"They are an evil race and have been a curse in Europe for centuries.

"There can be no peace until Hitler and all those who believe in him are sent to the hell which is their place of origin and their final home."

The *Herald* remarked that Whipp "has aroused considerable local controversy", so it is evident that in Britain, as in the U.S., there were many people who kept their heads despite the Fadiman types.

The peculiar *ad hoc* philosophy of history enunciated by de Sales and promoted by Clifton Fadiman also made its apparently independent appearance in England. An article by Reginald Hargreaves in the June 1941 issue of the respected journal *National Review* (not to be confused with the *National Review* that was founded in the U.S. in 1955) proposed as a war aim (as distinct from an unavoidable consequence of the war) that "at least three million Nazi soldiers (be) put permanently out of action", it being

an absolutely vital prerequisite to the laying down of arms that a sufficient number of the present-day corrupted, brutalised and delirious young dervishes of Nazidom should be left dead upon the field.

The necessity for this arose from the consideration that

throughout her whole history Germany has shown herself as utterly uncivilised and worthy of nothing but detestation and disgust. From the very beginning the behaviour of the Teutonic peoples has qualified them for the role of pariahs — the outcast mad dogs of Europe . . .

Our real war aim must be, not only military triumph in the field, but the reduction of the German people to such a shrunken and delimited condition that never again will they be in such a position to "start anything" to the detriment of generations yet to come. Our conflict, despite mushy affirmations to the contrary, is with the German *people;* a race so savage, so predatory, so unscrupulous and so utterly uncivilised that their elimination as a major power is the only hope for a world that has no choice but to take the surgeon's knife and cut out this cankerous growth from its body-politic, thoroughly, relentlessly, once and for all.

Such declarations seem even more extraordinary when one considers that they came from a nation noted for *understatement.*

The point of this discussion is not that there had grown up any consensus in the U.S. and Britain that all Germans are by nature monsters and should be killed or at least sterilized. Everybody would agree that no such consensus existed (and even the extermination mythologists would agree, I think, that no consensus favoring extermination of the Jews existed in Germany). Moreover, as we all realize, the genocidal policies advocated or implied by many leaders of opinion in the U.S. and Britain were not, in their literal form, within the bounds of the possible; the American and British people would never have permitted such deeds to be done in their names. The point is that during the heat of wartime the most extraordinary things were said. For the most part (unfortunately, one can only say for the *most* part) such lunacies were not realized in events, but they were expressed nevertheless.

Murderous things were said on both sides and, in my opinion and dim recollection of the times, the rhetoric in the U.S. (especially in regard to the Japanese) seems to me to have been more violent than anything that now seems to have been current in Germany during the war, although such a comparison is difficult and perhaps should not be attempted in regard to degree, on account of the very different roles played by "public opinion" and by the statements of political leaders in the two political systems involved.

On the Axis side, one should also note that Fascist Italy had various anti-Jewish laws which were however very mild in application and certainly never approached murder. Nevertheless the anti-Jewish rhetoric in the Fascist press was at least as violent as anything generated in Germany and, assuming the *N.Y. Times* (22 Oct 1941) reported accurately, it even advocated that all Italian Jews be "annihilated as a danger to the internal front" since "this is the moment to do away with half way measures."

(e) A final point is that one must use some common sense and a feeling for the context in interpreting references to "extermination" and "annihiliation" properly. In the American Civil War, many wanted Lincoln to "annihilate" the South, and it is not inaccurate English to say that Lincoln did just that, but it was understood, then as now, that the killing of all Southerners was not contemplated.

Naturally the same observation may be made in connection with public declarations of Nazi leaders, but there is an additional point to be made in this connection. Very often the Jews were referred to via the German word *das Judentum*, one of whose correct translations is "Jewry", but which can also mean "Judaism" or even "Jewishness" or "the idea of Jewishness". Thus a Hitler reference to *"die Vernichtung des Judentums"*, if lifted out of context and interpreted in a purely literal way, can be interpreted as meaning the killing of all Jews, but it can also be interpreted as meaning the destruction of Jewish influence and power, which is what the politician Hitler actually meant by such a remark, although it is true that he could have chosen his words more carefully. Alfred Rosenberg made specific reference to this ambiguity in his IMT testimony, where he argued that *"die Ausrottung des Judentums"*, a term he had used on occasion, was not a reference to killing in the context in which Rosenberg had used it.

The lengthy digression made necessary by Goebbels' *"Ausrottung"* remark being concluded, we return to the survey of stories in the *N.Y. Times* for 1942-1943.

14 June, 1942, p.1

258 JEWS REPORTED SLAIN IN BERLIN FOR BOMB PLOT AT ANTI-RED EXHIBIT

By George Axelsson
By Telephone to THE NEW YORK TIMES

STOCKHOLM, Sweden, June 13. At the Gross Lichterfelde Barracks in the

Fig. 7: Bodies being cremated in open pits. This photograph is said to have been taken at Auschwitz.   Photo: Panstwowe Museum, Oswiecim

western suburbs of Berlin 258 Jews were put to death by the S.S. on May 28, and their families deported, in retaliation for an alleged Jewish plot to blow up the anti-Bolshevist "Soviet Paradise" exhibition at the Lustgarten . . .

If there were any bombs, they evidently were discovered before they had time to explode . . .

The S.S. wanted the executions to be published . . . Instead . . leaders of the Jewish colony were called in . . .

30 June 1942, p.7   1,000,000 JEWS SLAIN BY NAZIS, REPORT SAYS

LONDON, June 29 (U.P.) . . . spokesmen for the World Jewish Congress charged today.

They said Nazis had established a "vast slaughterhouse for Jews" in Eastern Europe . . .

A report to the Congress said that Jews, deported en masse to Central Poland from Germany, Austria, Czechoslovakia and the Netherlands were being shot by firing squads at the rate of 1,000 daily.

Information received by the Polish Government in London confirmed that the Nazis had executed "several hundred thousand" Jews in Poland.

No such "slaughterhouse" where executions were by "firing squad" is claimed today. As noted above, this was the start of the World Jewish Congress' campaign of extermination propaganda. It is quite possible that this first story was inspired by Goebbels' then recent *"Ausrottung"* remark.

22 July 1942, p.1   NAZI PUNISHMENT SEEN BY ROOSEVELT

. . . President Roosevelt declared last night in a message read to 20,000 persons at Madison Square Garden . . .

President's Message

The White House
Washington   July 17, 1942

Dear Dr. Wise:

. . . Citizens . . . will share in the sorrow of our Jewish fellow-citizens over the savagery of the Nazis against their helpless victims. The Nazis will not succeed in exte-minating their victims any more than they will succeed in enslaving mankind. The American people . . . will hold the perpetrators of these crimes to strict accountability in a day of reckoning which will surely come . . .

Text of Churchill Message

" . . . you will recall that on Oct. 25 last both President Roosevelt and I expressed the horror felt . . . at Nazi butcheries and terrorism and our resolve to place retribution for these crimes among the major purposes of this war . . . "

Such vague statements of the wartime leaders, while devoid of any specific charges, carried more weight among the public than any of the more specific stories that the leaders may have seemed, by their statements, to be endorsing. We shall see that the specific claims of the time, at least for several months, did not very much resemble the claims made at the later trials. Nevertheless the politics of the situation, as perceived by Roosevelt and Churchill, made it opportune for them to "go along", at least to the extent of making vague public statements supporting the propaganda.

3 Sept. 1942, p.5   50,000 JEWS DYING IN NAZI FORTRESS

LONDON, Sept. 2 (U.P.) – Fifty thousand Jews from Germany and Czechoslovakia have been thrown into the fortress at Terezin and several thousand who are ill or charged with "criminal" acts are in underground dungeons where they are "dying like flies" a Czech Government spokesman said tonight.

"All hope for them has been abandoned," the spokesman said . . .

The spokesman said the Germans had launched a campaign to exterminate Jews from the protectorate and that of 40,000 Jews formerly in Prague only 15,000 remain. Pilsen and Bruenn have been cleared of Jews, he said, many of them being sent to Terezin, largest concentration camp in Nazi-controlled Europe.

A European observer said the Germans planned to exterminate the Jews not only in Europe, but throughout the world. He declared the Nazis had executed 2,000,000 Jews in the past three years . . .

The only truth in this story lies in the fact that the death rate of Jews was rather high at Terezin (Theresienstadt) due to the German policy of sending all Reich Jews over sixty five there. Another category at Theresienstadt was the "privileged" Jews — the war veterans — especially those with high decorations. There were other Jews, many of whom were eventually moved out but, if they suffered, it was not at Theresienstadt. The place was visited by the Red Cross in June 1944 and the resulting favorable report angered the World Jewish Congress.[31] There will be more to be said about Theresienstadt in subsequent chapters. While it was not the "largest concentration camp in Nazi-controlled Europe", it nevertheless plays an important role here.

5 Sept. 1942, p.3   U.S. REBUKES VICHY ON DEPORTING JEWS

WASHINGTON, Sept. 4 — The State Department has made the "most vigorous representations possible" to the French Government through the American Embassy in Vichy over the mass deportation of Jews from unoccupied France, it was announced today by the American Jewish Committee.

The protest followed representations by four Jewish organizations, and the action was communicated to them in a letter by Sumner Welles, Under-Secretary of State.

.... Mr. Welles said:

"I have received your communication of Aug. 27, 1942, enclosing a letter ... in regard to the mass deportation of Jewish refugees from unoccupied France.

"I am in complete agreement with the statements made concerning this tragic situation, which provides a new shock to the public opinion of the civilized world. It is deeply regretted that these measures should be taken in a country traditionally noted for adherence to the principles of equality, freedom and tolerance.

"The American Embassy at Vichy ... has made the most vigorous representations possible to the highest authorities at Vichy ... "

. . . The letter of the four organizations to the Secretary of State follows:

On behalf of the organizations we represent . . . the undersigned respectfully request our government to transmit to the government of France a solemn protest against the action taken recently by that government to turn thousands of refugees over to the agents of the Nazi government for deportation to Poland and to other Nazi-occupied regions in Eastern Europe.

Reports reaching us ... (state) that the government of France is permitting the ... deportation by the Nazis of Jewish refugees who have been interned in a number of camps in the south of France. This action began about Aug. 8, when a total of 3,600 men, women and children were rounded up, loaded on trains and sent off without any word regarding their destination.

The reports agree that these 3,600 were the first contingent of a total of 10,000 Jewish refugees which the French government has agreed to deport to eastern territories ...

. . . Mass deportations of Jews from Germany and from territories under German occupation have been going on ever since the conquest of Poland. In accordance with the announced policy of the Nazis to exterminate the Jews of Europe, hundreds of thousands of these innocent men, women and children have been killed in brutal mass murders. The rest are being herded in ghettos in Eastern Europe under indescribably wretched conditions, as a result of which tens of thousands have succumbed to starvation and pestilence.

We should only note at this point that even the four Jewish organizations are not completely secure in claiming exterminations, since they allow themselves an "out" by referring to those being "herded in ghettos". Welles' reply, while "in complete agreement" with the letter, avoids direct endorsement of the extermination claim.

24 Nov. 1942, p.10   HEBREW PAPERS MOURN

JERUSALEM, Nov. 23 (U.P.) — The Hebrew press appeared today with black borders around reports of mass murders of Jews in Poland. The reports, received by the Jewish Agency, asserted that systematic annihilation of the Jewish population was being carried out by a special German "destruction commission" . . . on the former frontier between German and Russian Poland, thousands were thrown into the Bug river and drowned.

13 Dec. 1942, p.21   TARDY WAR REPORT HELD AID TO FAITH

. . . Rabbi Israel Goldstein declared: "Authenticated reports point to 2,000,000 Jews who have already been slain by all manner of satanic barbarism, and plans for the total extermination of all Jews upon whom the Nazis can lay their hands. The slaughter of a third of the Jewish population in Hitler's domain and the threatened slaughter of all is a holocaust without parallel".

11 ALLIES CONDEMN NAZI WAR ON JEWS
Special to THE NEW YORK TIMES

WASHINGTON, Dec. 17 — A joint declaration by members of the United Nations was issued today condemning Germany's "bestial policy of cold-blooded extermination" of Jews . . .

. . . The declaration was issued simultaneously through the State Department here, and in London . . .

Text of Declaration

. . . From all the occupied countries Jews are being transported in conditions of appalling horror and brutality to Eastern Europe. In Poland, which has been made the principal Nazi slaughterhouse, the ghettos established by the German invader are being systematically emptied of all Jews except a few highly skilled workers required for war industries. None of those taken away are ever heard of again. The able-bodied are slowly worked to death in labor camps. The infirm are left to die of exposure and starvation or are deliberately massacred in mass executions. The number of victims of these bloody cruelties is reckoned in many hundreds of thousands of entirely innocent men, women and children.

This was the beginning of the State Department involvement in the extermination legend, and that it came from such a seemingly official source was the basis for special comment in the *Times* editorial of the same day:

18 Dec. 1942, p.26   HITLER'S TERROR

Despite all that has been written about Nazi persecution of the Jews, the facts in the joint statement issued yesterday in Washington, London and Moscow in the name of the United Nations will come as a shock to all civilized people who have preserved a modicum of human decency. For this statement is not an outcry of the victims themselves to which many thought it possible to close their ears on the ground that it might be a special plea, subject to doubt. It is the official statement of their own Governments, based on officially established facts . . .

Clearly, it was believed that atrocity claims apparently coming from the State Department were more credible than claims coming from such groups as the World Jewish Congress, which is no doubt what is meant by the "victims themselves". However we have seen that Wise was also behind the "joint declaration".

The 17 December statement marked the start of U.S. and British Government complicity in the extermination legend. The German Government did not see the event as laden with import, and von Stumm of the Foreign Office's press section flippantly explained to the neutral press that the Allied declaration was for the purpose of helping the Christmas sales of the Jewish department stores of New York and London.[32]

20 Dec. 1942, p.23   ALLIES DESCRIBE OUTRAGES ON JEWS

What is happening to the 5,000,000 Jews of German-held Europe, all of whom face extermination, is described in a statement released yesterday by the United Nations Information Office. . .

. . . Novel methods of mass execution by shooting and lethal gas are cited in the main body of the report, which states that this destruction of the Jews is not "isolated in one country but is continent-wide. Early in December 1942 the State Department in Washington gave some figures showing that the number of Jewish victims deported and perished since 1939 in Axis-controlled Europe now reached the appalling figure of 2,000,000 and that 5,000,000 were in danger of extermination . . .

The document concludes:

"The means employed in deporting from the ghetto all those who survive murders and shooting in the street exceeds all imagination. In particular, children, old people and those too weak for work are murdered. Actual data concerning the fate of the deportees is not at hand, but the news is available — irrefutable news — that places of execution have been organized at Chelmno and Belzec, where those who survive shootings are murdered en masse by means of electrocution and lethal gas."

The alleged electrocutions at Belzec appeared a few times in the propaganda and will be mentioned again in Chapter V. They are one of the versions of exterminations that were quickly forgotten about after the end of the war. Nevertheless we can see, at this point, a clear tendency of the propaganda to resemble the claims which have become the fixed features of the legend, the gas chambers and the approximate 6,000,000 killed during the course of the war. We will have more to say a bit later on the origin of the six million figure.

28 Dec. 1942, p.21   DEMAND JEWS BE SAVED

ALBANY, Dec. 27 (AP) . . .

Dr. Wise, president of the American Jewish Congress and the World Jewish Congress . . . (urged) formulation of an Allied program to halt the Nazi slaughter of civilians.

8 Jan. 1943, p.8   93 CHOOSE SUICIDE BEFORE NAZI SHAME

Ninety three Jewish girls and young Jewish women, the pupils and the teacher of a Beth Jacob School of Warsaw, Poland, chose mass suicide to escape being forced into prostitution by German soldiers, according to a letter from the teacher, made public yesterday by Rabbi Seth Jung of the Jewish Center of New York City.

7 Feb. 1943, VI, p.16   IN THE VALLEY OF DEATH
                                  (magazine article by Sholem Asch)

. . . gas chambers and blood poisoning stations which are established in the out-lying countryside, where steam shovels prepare community graves for the victims.

14 Feb. 1943, p.37   TYRANNY OF NAZIS SHOWN

Warsaw is being subjected to a deliberate Nazi pattern of death, disease, starva-tion, economic slavery and wholesale elimination of population, the Office of War Information states in a twenty-four page pamphlet, "Tale of a City", published today.

Declaring that Warsaw has been the testing ground for Nazi plans of world conquest . . .

. . . "there is no way of telling at this time exactly how many Poles have been murdered by the Nazis in Warsaw". The execution spot is now Palmiry, near Warsaw, where mass shootings occur either at dawn or during the night.

14 Feb. 1943, p.37   EXECUTION "SPEED-UP" SEEN

Mass executions of Jews in Poland on an accelerated tempo was reported by European representatives of the World Jewish Congress in a communication made public by Rabbi Stephen S. Wise, president of the American Jewish Congress.

In one place in Poland 6,000 Jews are killed daily, according to the report, dated Jan. 19. Jews left in Poland are now confined in fifty five ghettos, some in the large towns and some in the smaller towns that have been transformed into ghettos.

This was the propaganda story involved in the conflict between State and Treasury. As noted in connection with the remarks on the *Times* editorial of 18 December, if this story had managed to emerge from the State Depart-ment, greater credibility would, apparently, have been attached to it. Unfor-tunately for the propaganda inventors at the time, they had to settle for Rabbi Wise as ostensible source.

16 Feb. 1943, p.7   NAZIS SHIFT 30,000 JEWS

GENEVA, Switzerland, Feb. 15 (ONA) . . .

All the aged and feeble (from Czestachowa, Poland) were sent to Rawa-Russka, in Galicia, for execution by the Nazis, sources from inside Poland said.

23 Feb. 1943, p.23   ATROCITIES PROTESTED

Thirty five hundred children . . . held a solemn assembly of sorrow and protest against Nazi atrocities in Mecca Temple, 133 West Fifty-fifth Street . . . Six refugee children related their experiences at the hands of the Nazis.

2 Mar. 1943, pp.1,4   SAVE DOOMED JEWS, HUGE RALLY PLEADS

Immediate action by the United Nations to save as many as possible of the five million Jews threatened with extermination . . . was demanded at a mass demonstration . . . in Madison Square Garden last night.

. . . (Rabbi Hertz said) "appalling is the fact that those who proclaim the Four Freedoms have so far done very little to secure even the freedom to live for 6,000,000 of their Jewish fellow men by readiness to rescue those who might still escape Nazi torture and butchery . . . "

. . (Wendell Willkie said) "Two million human beings, merely because they are Jews, have already been murdered by every fiendish means which Hitler could devise. Millions of other Jews . . face immediate destruction . . "

. . . (Chaim Weizmann said) "Two million Jews have already been exterminated . . .

"The democracies have a clear duty before them . . . Let them negotiate with

78

Germany through the neutral countries concerning the possible release of the Jews in the occupied countries . . . Let the gates of Palestine be opened to all who can reach the shores of the Jewish homeland . . . "

7 Mar. 1943, p.30   600 JEWS SENT TO SILESIA

STOCKHOLM, Sweden, March 6 (Reuter) — Nearly 600 Norwegian Jews . . . are now known to have reached Polish Upper Silesia. Most of the men have been sent to work in the mines near Katowice.

10 Mar. 1943, p.12   40,000 HERE VIEW MEMORIAL TO JEWS

Forty thousand persons listened and watched . . . last night to two performances of "We Will Never Die", a dramatic mass memorial to the 2,000,000 Jews killed in Europe . . . The narrator said "There will be no Jews left in Europe for representation when peace comes. The four million left to kill are being killed, according to plan".

1 April 1943, p.2   FRENCH JEWS SENT TO A NAZI OBLIVION
Wireless to THE NEW YORK TIMES

LONDON, March 31 — A system of "death convoys" under which French Jews are being rounded up . . . and then shipped out to various points in Eastern Europe, aftet which they are no longer heard from, was described here today by the British section of the World Jewish Congress, which charged that the "full force" of the Nazi and anti-Jewish terror now was being concentrated in France.

Basing its report on first hand information supplied by a prominent French Jew who has escaped to a neutral country, the Congress declared the last "convoy" left France about Feb. 20. It involved 3,000 Jews of all classes and ages, and all that was known about its eventual destination was that it was somewhere in the East.

In mid-February, the Congress added, the Gestapo raided the Lyon headquarters of the General Union of French Jews, arrested the entire staff, removed them to the Drancy concentration camp and since has shipped them, too, to some "extermination center" on the other side of Europe.

Reitlinger (p. 327) tells us that "less than a tenth of the Jews who were deported (from France) possessed French nationality". By his figures that is perhaps 5,000 of the 240,000 French Jews, suggesting that maybe the 5,000 enlisted for work voluntarily or were actually "politicals" or partisans.[32]

12 April 1943, p.5   NAZIS ERASE GHETTOS IN TWO POLISH CITIES

LONDON, April 11 (AP) — The Polish Telegraph Agency said tonight that the Germans had erased the ghetto at Krakow in a three day massacre that started March 13, and also had eliminated the ghetto in Lodz.

The fate of the Jews in the latter city was unknown, but the agency said it was believed they also were killed.

20 April 1943, p.11   2,000,000 JEWS MURDERED

LONDON, April 19 (Reuter) — Two million Jews have been wiped out since the Nazis began their march through Europe in 1939 and five million more are in immediate danger of execution. These figures were revealed in the sixth report on conditions in occupied territories issued by the Inter-Allied Information Committee.

. . . The report said lethal gas and shooting were among the methods being used to exterminate the Jews.

20 April 1943, p.11   RESCUE OF JEWS URGED

The Jewish Agency for Palestine, in a memorandum addressed to the Bermuda Refugees Conference yesterday, urged that measures of rescue be launched immediately on behalf of 4,000,000 Jews estimated to be still surviving in Nazi-occupied countries.

The Agency, headed by Dr. Chaim Weizmann, is recognized in the Mandate for Palestine as a body to advise and cooperate with the Government of Palestine on matters affecting the establishment of the Jewish National Home.

The memorandum declares that "should the announced policy of the enemy continue unchecked, it is not impossible that by the time the war will have been won, the largest part of the Jewish population of Europe will have been exterminated".

25 April 1943, p.19   SCANT HOPE SEEN FOR AXIS VICTIMS
Special Cable to THE NEW YORK TIMES

HAMILTON, Bermuda, April 24 — The large scale movement of refugees is impossible under wartime conditions, and neither the United States nor Great Britain, alone or jointly, can begin to solve the refugee problem. These two concrete impressions have emerged after almost a week's discussion of the refugee problem by the American and British delegations here.

Since almost all Jews outside the Continent, particularly those in the

U.S., believed the extermination claims, they brought political pressures which resulted in the Bermuda Conference. It was believed,[33] correctly, that the Nazis wished the emigration of the Jews from Europe (under appropriate conditions) and this put the British and American Governments, on account of the propaganda basis for their war, into an awkward position which they were obliged to continually double-talk around.[34] We have described the conflict between State and Treasury in this regard. The British had, at that point, no intention of opening Palestine, and both the British and Americans had no intention of providing the resources, in the middle of the war, for massive operations undertaken for reasons that were valid only to the degree that their propaganda was taken seriously No sane modern statesmen believe their own propaganda. This is the dilemma which J. Breckenridge Long and other State Department officials felt themselves facing.

Another point that should be made here before proceeding with the survey of the propaganda is that, apparently, the six million figure had its origin in the propaganda of 1942-1943. An examination of the problem of the origin of the six million figure could easily lead to the conclusion that it had its origin at the IMT, where the indictment mentioned a figure (supplied by the World Jewish Congress) of 5,721,800 "missing" Jews and Wilhelm Hoettl of the SD signed an affidavit, 2738-PS, asserting that he had gotten a figure of six million from Eichmann. According to Hoettl, Eichmann had visited his Budapest office in a depressed mood because he was convinced that the war was lost, thought that the Allies would punish him as a major war criminal, and then declared, with no other witnesses present, that four million Jews had been killed in extermination camps and that two million had met death in various other ways, mainly through executions carried out by the *Einsatzgruppen* in Russia.

Here we offer a different theory regarding the origin of the six million figure. Its very first appearance seems to be Rabbi Goldstein's statement of 13 December 1942, followed by the story of 20 December to the same effect, except that it specified a potential seven million in danger of being exterminated, rather than the six million implied by Goldstein's statement. However, it could correctly be argued that one must not infer the origin of the six million figure purely on the basis of these stories.

However the appearances of the two million killed – four (or five) million to be killed extermination claim, at the public affairs reported on 2 and 10 March 1943, must be taken much more seriously. More information about the latter affair can be extracted from an advertisement that also appeared on 10 March (p. 10), reporting that the show had been organized by the "Committee for a Jewish Army of Stateless and Palestinian Jews", headed by Senator Johnson of Colorado. The advertisement makes the same extermination claim (two million killed, four million to be killed) and also lists the sponsors of the organization, which included many members of Congress and other notables. The same organization had also run a full page advertisement on 16 February (p. 11), specifying two million killed and four million to go (and also claiming that the only Arabs who objected to massive Jewish immigration into Palestine were Nazi agents). The two stories of 20 April suggest rather widespread usage of the two million killed – four (or five) million to be killed form of the extermination claim in early 1943. We therefore have very general usage of the six (or seven) million figure, long before the end of the war, by the political establishment that wrote the charges at Nuernberg so, I believe, we can take late 1942 – early 1943 propaganda as the origin of the six million figure. The complete independence of that figure of any real facts whatever is reflected in Reitlinger's elaborate apologies for his belief that he can claim only 4.2 to 4.6 million Jews, almost all East European, who perished in Europe during World War II, one third of them dying from "overwork, disease, hunger and neglect".[35] However, Reitlinger's figures are also mostly independent of any real facts, but that matter will be discussed in a later chapter.

It is not at all remarkable that after the war somebody could be found to declare, at Nuernberg, that the propaganda figure was correct. Hoettl, indeed, was a completely appropriate choice, since he was one of those stereotype "operators" that the world of intelligence work is plagued with. Born in 1915, he entered the SD in 1938 and soon acquired a reputation for mixing official business with personal business deals. His teaming up with a Polish countess friend in a Polish land deal led, in 1942, to an SS investigation of his activities. The report of the investigation characterized him as "dishonest, scheming, fawning, . . . a real hoaxer", and concluded that he was not even suitable for membership in the SS, let alone a sensitive agency such as the SD. He was, accordingly, busted down to the ranks, but then the appointment in early 1943 of his fellow Austrian and Vienna acquaintance, Kaltenbrunner, to head the RSHA seems to have reversed his fortunes, and he rose to the rank of Lieutenant Colonel by the end of the war, and played a responsible role in foreign intelligence work. After the war he worked, until 1949, for the U.S. Army Counter-Intelligence Corps in lining up ex-SS personnel to give information. It is said that he managed to make this job rather lucrative. After 1949 he immersed himself in the snake pit of Vienna cold war politics, maintaining links with neo-Nazis, Soviet agents, and nearly everybody else. He had a particularly close relationship with one Soviet agent Kurt Ponger, a naturalized U.S. citizen whom he had met when Ponger was employed as a translator at the IMT (in addition a Kurt Ponger, probably the same person, was a prosecution lawyer in Case 4). Hoettl consequently became suspect in the Verber-Ponger espionage case of 1953, and was arrested by U.S. authorities in March in Vienna but released a few weeks later. In the mid-Fifties, he published two books on his wartime experiences. In 1961, he signed a prosecution affidavit for Eichmann's trial (substantially the same as his IMT affidavits).[36]

Authors on my side have written that, during the war, Hoettl was an Allied agent. This is not correct. The only real fact that is involved in this claim is that Hoettl was in touch with Allen Dulles, of the OSS in Switzerland, towards the end of the war. This was a part of his duties; the RSHA was attempting to arrange a favorable conclusion of the hostilities and Hoettl was one of the persons involved in the secret contacts with the western Allies. No doubt, during the very last weeks of the war many of these intelligence officers started acting with their personal interests in mind and, also without doubt, Hoettl would have been delighted to have been enlisted as an Allied agent at this juncture of the war, and may even have volunteered some favors to Dulles with this development in mind. However, these contacts are no more evidence that Hoettl was an Allied agent than they are that Dulles was an Axis agent (Dulles is even said to have peppered his conversation with anti-semitic remarks when he was trying to win the confidence of some German contacts[37]). If Hoettl had been an Allied agent, it would seem that he would boast about this in one of his two books *(The Secret Front* and *Hitler's Paper Weapon)*, but he makes no such claim. In addition, Ian Colvin, who knows as much about these matters as anybody, wrote the Introduction for *The Secret Front*, and makes no remarks in this connection.

27 April 1943, p.10   NORWEGIAN DEPORTEES DIE

STOCKHOLM, Sweden, April 26 (ONA) — Reports from Oslo said today that most of the Norwegian Jewish women and children deported from the country . . . had died of starvation.

Transports of deportees that left Oslo in November and February were removing them toward an ultimate destination in the Silesian mining region around Katowice . . .

3 May 1943, p.12   BRITAIN SCORED ON JEWS

An audience of 1,500 persons . . . heard Pierre van Paassen . . . assert that Palestine presented the only solution to the refugee problem.

. . . Mr. van Paassen said that Great Britain had made a "hollow mockery" of the refugee conference in Bermuda by excluding discussion of Palestine among the possible solutions.

"Britain feels that the modernization of Palestine by the Jews endangers the pillars of her empire . . . That is the real reason many more Jews face death because Britain wants to keep the doors of Palestine shut to them."

20 May 1943, p.12   EDEN TIES VICTORY TO REFUGEE HOPES
                                          Special Cable to THE NEW YORK TIMES

LONDON, May 19 . . . Eden . . . insisted that it was not fair to accuse the British Government of utterly ignoring the situation.

. . . he disclosed that the war Cabinet had approved the (Bermuda conference) report . . .

LONDON, May 19 (Reuter) — The World Jewish Congress . . . expressed deep disappointment with the results of the Bermuda Conference.

The note . . . pointed out that the way to Palestine is now also free.

22 May 1943, p.4   JEWS LAST STAND FELLED 1,000 NAZIS
                                          Wireless to THE NEW YORK TIMES

LONDON, May 21 — Nearly 1,000 Germans were killed or wounded in the battle in the Warsaw ghetto in the last two weeks when the Nazis undertook the final liquidation of the ghetto.

. . . More news of the anti-Jewish campaign in Poland was picked up today from SWIT, the secret Polish radio station. It said the Nazis had started liquidating the ghetto of Cracow and Stanislawow . . . shooting Jews wherever they were found or killing them in gas chambers.

7 June 1943, p.15   "RALLY OF HOPE" IS HELD

Six-thousand children . . . participated yesterday in a "Rally of Hope" . . .

" . . . Jewish children and their parents are tortured and put to death by a barbarous enemy . . . "

9 June 1943, p.3

LONDON, June 8 (Reuter) — No fewer than 3,500 Jews have recently been deported from Salonika, Greece, to Poland, it was stated here today. Men, women and children were herded indiscriminately into cattle trucks, which were then sealed, it was added.

13 June 1943, p.8   NAZI GAS KILLINGS OF REFUGEES CITED
                                          By Telephone to THE NEW YORK TIMES

STOCKHOLM, Sweden, June 12 — More than 10,000 Jews were killed since last October in the Brest-Litovsk district . . . according to the Swedish language Jewish Chronicle published in Stockholm.

Thousands were gassed to death in hermetically sealed barns and others have been shot in groups of sixty in adjoining woods, the paper says.

. . . When Dr. Robert Ley, chief of the German Labor Front, recently spoke at Koenigsberg, Bialystok and Grodno he said: "The Jews are the chosen race, all right — but for extermination purposes only".

15 June 1943, p.8   NAZIS DEPORT 52,000 BELGIANS

LONDON, June 14 (AP) — The Belgian Government in exile said today that the Germans had removed nearly all 52,000 Belgian Jews to concentration camps in Germany, Poland and occupied Russia.

Reitlinger reports for Belgium the same situation as in France. Among the Jews deported from Belgium, "virtually none" were Belgian Jews. It is worth remarking that essentially the same held for Italy and Denmark.[38]

21 June 1943, p.2   BERMUDA PARLEY SCORED

A resolution condemning the "inaction" of the Bermuda Conference and another calling upon President Roosevelt and Prime Minister Winston Churchill to open the doors of Palestine to refugees were adopted unanimously yesterday by the order of the Sons of Zion . . . at the Hotel Pennyslvania.

21 June 1943, p.3   RUMANIANS BLAMED FOR KILLING OF 5,000

BERNE, Switzerland, June 20 (U.P.) — Swiss newspapers said tonight that 5,000 bodies reported by Axis propagandists to have been buried near Odessa were those of Rumanian Jews killed by the Rumanian secret police.

The Rumanian press announced the discovery of the mass tomb on April 22, claiming the bodies were those of Rumanians killed by the Russians after the latter occupied Bessarabia and Bukovina in 1940.

23 June 1943, p.8   NETHERLAND JEWS OUSTED BY NAZIS

LONDON, June 22 (U.P.) — All Jews in Amsterdam have been deported by the Germans to Poland, thus completing the removal of the entire Jewish population of the Netherlands, the Aneta news agency said today.

This story is not true; nevertheless the majority of Dutch Jews were deported. The reasons for the great differences in policy in the Netherlands (and Luxembourg) on the one hand and in Belgium and France and other countries on the other will be seen in a later chapter. It will be shown that the ultimate, as distinct from immediate, destination of the Jews deported from the Netherlands was most probably not Poland. Of the 140,000 Dutch Jews, about 100,000 were deported.[39]

28 June 1943, p.8

LONDON, June 27 (Reuter) — A German radio broadcast tonight quoted Premier Nicholas von Kallay of Hungary as stating that all remaining property of Jews in Hungary would pass into "Aryan" hands at the end of this year. This property will be distributed among those who have distinguished themselves in the war and families with many children, it is said.

29 June 1943, p.6   NAZIS EXECUTE 150 JEWS

LONDON, June 28 (Netherlands News Agency) — The Germans have launched mass executions of Netherlands Jews deported to Poland, it was reported tonight.

. . . 150 Jews in the village of Turck had been mowed down with machine gun fire . . .

At Socky . . . 340 Netherlands Jews were machine gunned, and 100 women and children were slain near Potok . . .

They were among the thousands of Jews who had been transported from the Netherlands to the notorious Treblinka concentration camp.

It seems odd to transport people out of an extermination camp and then kill them. Whoever composed this story was evidently not only uninformed on what Treblinka was supposed to be, but also on the order of magnitude of the numbers that were supposed to be thrown around.

21 July 1943, p.13   QUICK AID IS ASKED FOR EUROPE'S JEWS

Immediate action to rescue the Jews of Nazi-dominated countries was demanded last night by speakers at the opening session of the Emergency Conference to Save the Jews of Europe, held at the Hotel Commodore.

. . . Representative Rogers pointed out that some 3,000,000 of Europe's 7,000,000 Jews already have perished and insisted that "this is a problem which cannot be solved through the exercise of vocal cords and routine protests".

. . . "Certainly there are enough open spaces and unpopulated areas to accomodate 4,000,000 tortued human beings", he said. "Palestine is the logical place. It is nearer and over land instead of over water . . ."

. . . Count Sforza voiced the hope that Jews and Arabs would be able to cooperate in the future in the building of a great Near East federation, with Palestine as a member.

2 Aug. 1943, p.10   16,000,000 MADE REFUGEES BY AXIS

WASHINGTON, Aug. 1 — A survey of the European refugee problem, published today by the Foreign Policy Association, said that only a collective effort on the part of the great powers or an international organization could deal effectively with the situation that would follow the end of the war.

. . . On the basis of reports from the Governments in exile and other informants, the report said, it was estimated that of the Jews who in 1939 inhabited European countries now held by the Axis, two million already have been deported or had perished from various forms of mistreatment or deliberate extermination.

The Foreign Policy Association does not seem to be very secure in asserting exterminations, since it gives the impression that most of the Jews had been "deported", although by this time the propagandists were speaking of three million dead Jews.

8 Aug. 1943, p.11   2,000,000 MURDERS BY NAZIS CHARGED

LONDON, Aug. 7 – Polish Labor Fights, a publication issued here today, printed an account of a house maintained by the Germans at Treblinka, Poland, for the extermination of Jews. In this place alone, it is said, the Germans have killed 2,000,000 persons.

. . . "When the cells are filled they are closed and sealed. Steam is forced through apertures and suffocation of the victims begins. At first cries can be heard but these gradually subside and after fifteen minutes all is silent. The execution is over.

. . . Often a gravedigger is too weak to carry two bodies, as ordered, so he ties arms or legs together and runs to the burial ground, dragging them behind him.

Of course, the post-war story was that the bodies were burned, not buried, since these millions of buried Jewish bodies simply did not exist.

27 Aug. 1943, p.7   REPORT BARES FATE OF 8,300,000 JEWS

. . . a 300 page survey made public yesterday by the . . . American Jewish Congress and the World Jewish Congress.

More than 3,000,000 Jews have been destroyed by planned starvation, forced labor, deportations, pogroms and methodical murders in German-run extermination centers in eastern Europe since the outbreak of the war in 1939, according to the report, while 1,800,000 Jews have been saved by migration into the interior of the Soviet Union and 180,000 have succeeded in emigrating to other countries.

. . . The survey . . . declares that 1,700,000 Jews have been victims of organized massacres and pogroms, . . . that 750,000 Jews perished as a result of starvation and its consequences, and that 350,000 died in the process of deportation.

. . . A table showing how the process of extermination has been carried out . . . follows:

Country	Number	Country	Number
Germany	110,000	Belgium	30,000
Poland	1,600,000	Holland	45,000
U.S.S.R.	650,000	France	56,000
Lithuania	105,000	Czechoslovakia	64,500
Latvia	65,000	Danzig	250
Austria	19,500	Estonia	3,000
Rumania	227,500	Norway	800
Yugoslavia	35,000		
Greece	18,500	Total	3,030,050

27 Aug. 1943, p.7   DELIBERATE NAZI MURDER POLICY IS
                             BARED BY ALLIED OFFICIAL BODY

LONDON, Aug. 26 (U.P.) – The Inter-Allied Information Committee . . . tonight accused Germany, Italy and their satellites of . . . a deliberate program of wholesale theft, murder, torture and savagery unparalleled in world history.

. . . Poland – Exhaustion, torture, illness and executions have created a life expectancy of only nine months from the time an individual is thrown into a concentration camp. Conditions are particularly severe at the Oswiecim camp, where 58,000 persons are believed to have perished.

At least 1,000,000 Jews have been slaughtered, starved or beaten to death in Poland during the past three years. In Warsaw food rations permit only 23.4 per cent of the calories necessary to keep a human being alive.

This was one of the very few pre-1944 specific references to the Auschwitz concentration camp (although the stories of 7 March and 27 April were oblique references). The interesting thing about this reference to Auschwitz is that it is essentially correct, as shall be confirmed in the next chapter, although one cannot be confident of the accuracy of the 58,000 figure and "torture" and "executions" should not be included as causes of the high death rate. The important point is that this story implicitly rejects the post-war extermination claims, which assert that thousands were killed at Auschwitz almost every day, starting at the latest in the summer of 1942 and continuing to the autumn of 1944.

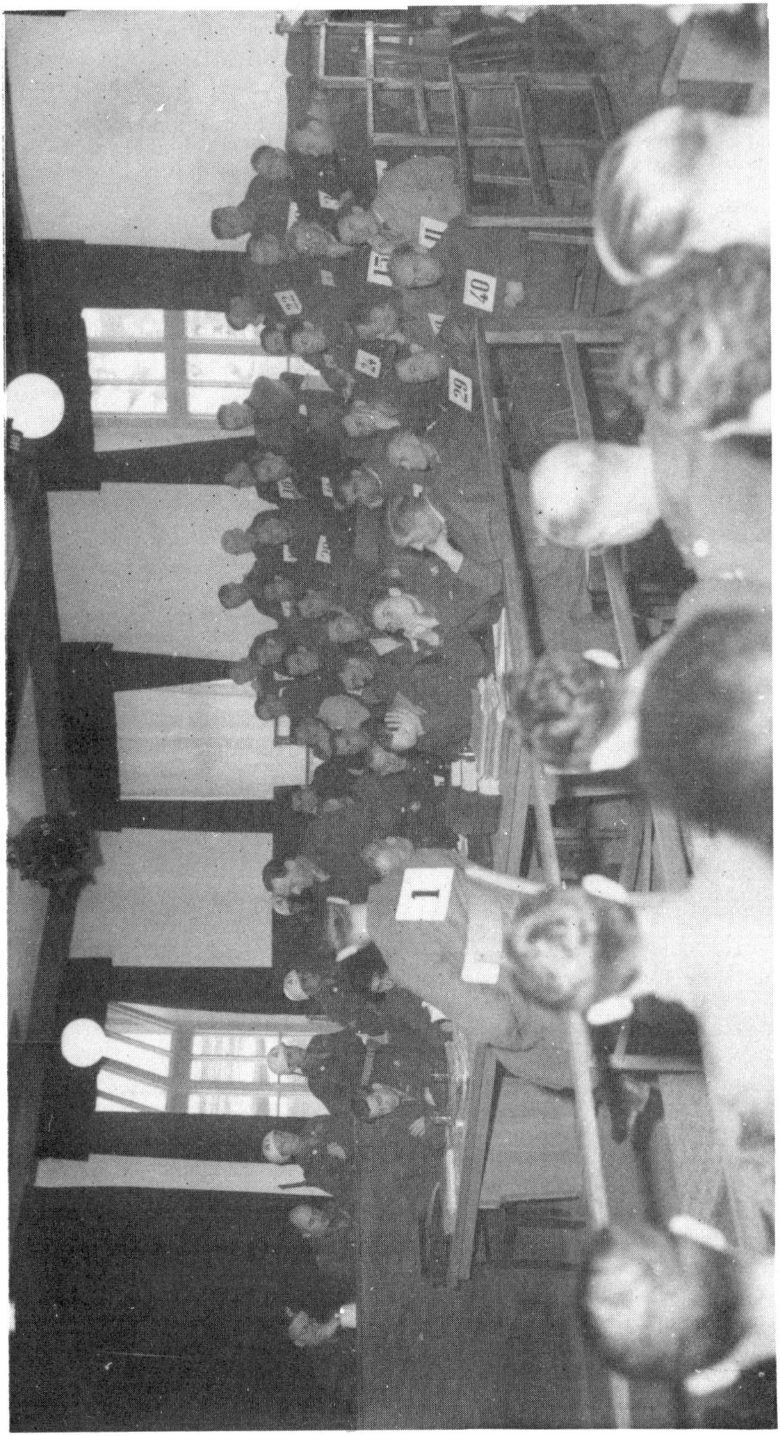

Fig. 8: A trial at Dachau

85

8 Oct. 1943, p.5   ALL-EUROPE PURGE OF JEWS REPORTED

STOCKHOLM, Sweden, Oct. 7 — Well-informed circles here said today that a decree had been issued in Berlin ordering the removal of all Jews from Europe before the end of the war. The source said that the order was issued by Adolf Hitler himself.

. . . The power behind the Nazi persecution of Danish Jews is the so-called "Jew Dictator", Storm Trooper Eighmann (sic) . . . who was born in Palestine of German emigrants and brought up there (and) is known for his sadistic hatred of Jews. He engineered all the extermination action against Jews in Germany and the occupied territories . . .

This seems to be Eichmann's debut in the propaganda and, probably, the source of the myth that he was raised in Palestine (he was born in Solingen, Germany, and raised in Linz, Austria).

23 Nov. 1943, p.4   WIFE OF MIKOLAJCZYK HOSTAGE OF GERMANS

The 43-year-old wife of Premier Stanislaw Mikolajczyk of Poland is being held by the Germans as a hostage in the Oswiecim concentration camp and may be facing imminent execution, the Polish Telegraph Agency reported from London yesterday.

. . . Oswiecim is the most notorious German prison in Poland, where thousands of helpless victims have been tortured to death . . .

The names of the Germans chiefly responsible for the massacre of Polish Jews were given in a Polish statement in London . . .

"There are ten of them, headed by Ludwig Fischer, the Nazi Governor of the Warsaw area . . . A member of the Polish National Council said that most of the Jews in Poland had already been wiped out."

29 Nov. 1943, p.3   50,000 KIEV JEWS REPORTED KILLED
By W.H. Lawrence

KIEV, Russia, Oct. 22 (Delayed) — Kiev authorities asserted today that the Germans had machine-gunned from 50,000 to 80,000 of Kiev's Jewish men, women and children in late September, 1941 and, two years later — when Kiev's recapture by the Red Army seemed imminent — had forced Russian prisoners of war to burn all the bodies, completely destroying all the evidence of the crime.

. . . On the basis of what we saw, it is impossible for this correspondent to judge the truth or falsity of the story told to us . . .

6 Dec. 1943, p.10   CAPTIVE KILLINGS LAID TO GERMANS

LONDON, Dec. 5 (U.P.) — Evidence that Russian prisoners of war were executed and cremated in German concentration camps has been offered to the emigre Czech Government by a Czech Army officer who spent several years in a German prison camp before he escaped to England.

. . . The officer's teeth had been kicked out when he was struck on the mouth, he was deaf in one ear from a blow on the head and on his body was the scar of a swastika that he said had been carved by Germans to whom he went for treatment of an infection.

Jews were chosen at random from those in the camp and shot, he said . . .

This completes the survey of relevant N.Y. Times stories for the period spring 1942 through 1943. Selectivity on my part was, of course, necessary but I believe that an adequate picture has been given of the sort of stories that were in circulation in supposedly intelligent circles.

What cannot be recaptured is the hysterical atmosphere of the time. The unusually critical reader will have noticed the rather high page numbers of many of the stories cited, especially those which report specific instances of mass killings. In practical politics only page one counts, and these things seldom appeared on page one. If Roosevelt said something, it was normally printed on page one, but only because he said it, not because he said anything interesting or significant. The allegations of exterminations of Jews do not appear to have had great importance to the public during the war, if one judges from the lack of any prominence given to such stories. Another way to express it is to say that if one spends some time examining the newspapers of the time, a high degree of hostility to the Nazis is obvious, but the specific basis of the hostility is virtually impossible to distinguish. Thus, there is something of an emotional nature missing from our survey, but this is unavoidable.

Two principal observations should be made in regard to the extermination propaganda. First, the legend has its origin among Zionists and, second,

Auschwitz was not claimed as an extermination camp until very late in the war.

We have seen that the first extermination claims were not based on one scrap of intelligence data. Zionists, principally the World Jewish Congress, merely presented their nonsense to the Allied governments, in particular to the U.S. Government, demanding endorsement of their nonsense. The first reactions in Washington were to scoff at the claims but, on account of various political pressures, and only on account of those pressures and not because corroborating information had been procured from military intelligence, official Washington eventually cooperated with the extermination propaganda to the extent of having high officials make vague public declarations in support of it, and of having propaganda agencies make more specific declarations of an obscure nature. The early propaganda had features which are retained in the legend to this day, such as the six million figure, and also features which were quickly forgotten, such as the soap factories, although both features were authored by the same Zionist circles.

In regard to our terminology, it should be remarked that the word "Zionist" is not being employed here as a code word for "Jewish"; the evidence shows that, while the hoax is certainly a Jewish hoax, in the sense of having been invented by Jews, it is also a Zionist hoax, in the sense of having been invented by Jews who were Zionists, on behalf of Zionist ends. The Zionist character of the propaganda is quite clear; note that, as a rule, the persons who were pressing for measures to remove Jews from Europe (under the circumstances a routine and understandable proposal) coupled such proposals with demands that such Jews be resettled in Palestine, which shows that there was much more in the minds of the Zionist propagandists than mere assistance to refugees and victims of persecution.

We have also noted that Auschwitz was absent from the extermination propaganda in 1942 and 1943 although, if there had been exterminations at such a prominent site, military intelligence and others would certainly have learned of it. To be sure, Auschwitz appeared in the propaganda, but the specific claims, bearing on a high death rate due to more or less normal causes, were in their essentials true, however amplified their content. There were no claims of gas chambers or exterminations. Naturally I make the reservation that this statement is based on the fact that, after a reasonably thorough study, I have not noticed Auschwitz in the 1942-1943 extermination propaganda; Treblinka, Belzec and Chelmno appeared in the newspaper extermination stories, but not Auschwitz.

This view is confirmed by the periodicals and books of the period that I have examined. Three periodical publications are of particular interest. The issue of *Commonweal* for 4 June 1943 carried an article by Jacques Maritain which summarized what he, evidently after some investigation, believed to be the chief features of the extermination program. Auschwitz is not mentioned, although exterminations via "poison gases, electrocution, mass piling into enclosed spaces where asphyxia takes place by degrees, suffocation . . . in sealed freight cars" are mentioned, and particular reference is made to Chelmno.

The *New Republic* for 30 August 1943 was a special issue devoted to the plight of the Jews in Europe, and made no reference to Auschwitz. A two page advertisement, placed by the Jewish Labor Committee (New York), mentions only Treblinka, Belzec and "hermetically sealed cars where Jews are being poisoned".

Survey Graphic for April 1943 carries a two page article by William L. Shirer. The subject is the whole range of alleged German atrocities and thus

Auschwitz (Oswiecim) is mentioned, but only in connection with an alleged high death rate of 250 Poles per day, due to "executions, inhuman treatment, hunger and epidemics". Shirer claims exterminations of Jews at Belzec.

The Shirer story cites a 7 March report from the Polish government in London as the source for the statements about Auschwitz. This is the earliest reference that I know of to Auschwitz in the propaganda. The only candidate for an earlier claim that I know of appears in *The Black Book of Polish Jewry*, J. Apenszlak, ed., 1943. Pages 56 and 59 tell of reports in the *"East London Observer"* in early 1942 that the ashes of Jews who had been sent to Auschwitz were being returned to their relatives (contradicting post-war propaganda). However, as far as I have been able to determine, the *East London Observer* did not exist. The *Black Book* does not claim exterminations at Auschwitz but speaks of exterminations via gasmobile at Chelmno (pp. 115-117, in agreement with later claims), via electrocution in baths at Belzec followed by burial (p. 131, not in agreement), through being left in freight cars for days near Belzec followed by burning (pp. 137-138, not in agreement), via steam baths at Treblinka followed by burial (p. 143, not in agreement; the Diesel engine whose exhaust gases were used for killing in later versions of the story is used for digging the graves in *The Black Book*).

There remains one source which conveys the impression that Auschwitz appeared in the extermination propaganda early in 1943 or even earlier. This is the book *The Devil's Chemists* by Josiah DuBois, whom we have encountered as a wartime Treasury official. At the NMT after the war, DuBois was the chief prosecutor in the Farben trial, and his book is his account of the trial and such other matters that he considered relevant. According to him, a message dealing with Auschwitz crossed his desk in November 1942. The message transmitted the contents of a note, a "crumpled testament of despair", which had allegedly been written by a worker-inmate at Auschwitz and then passed along underground in hand-to-hand relay to Bern:

We worked in the huge "Buna" plant . . . There was a chain of sentry posts overlooking every 10 square meters of workers, and whoever stepped outside was shot without warning as "having attempted to escape". But attempts were made every day, even by some who tried to crawl past the sentries because they could no longer walk.

The note also applied to Farben's Ter Meer "stereotyped images of swastika and riding crop and fixed sneer (which had not characterized Ter Meer at any time during his life)". The claimed origin and history of the note make the whole thing appear rather silly but one should note the strong element of fact in the note; at approximately this time many workers at Auschwitz were indeed not in a condition to work or even walk. Thus this message was not really extermination propaganda, and we cannot be certain that it really existed but, if it did, all it suggests is that the propagandists were well aware, in late 1942, of what was happening at Auschwitz.

DuBois then proceeds to misinform his reader that the two messages of January and April 1943 from Harrison to the State Department, discussed above, dealt with Auschwitz, i.e. it was at Auschwitz that 6,000 were allegedly being killed every day. In reporting thus, DuBois is simply passing along misinformation. His motive seems to be that, as the prosecutor in the Farben case, he was attempting to maximize the significance of Auschwitz in every respect possible, and has thus read in the record something that simply is not there.[40]

It is of passing interest to comment on what the Germans were saying about the Allied propaganda stories. We have seen that von Stumm of the press section of the German Foreign Office ridiculed the extermination claim when it was first made by the Allied governments, but that was a rare reference, on the part of the German Government, to any specific Allied propaganda concoction. The weekly newspaper *Das Reich*, published by the Goebbels Ministry, and the *Voelkischer Beobachter*, the daily newspaper of the Nazi Party, had much comment of a general sort on the *"Greuelpropaganda"*, but there were few references to specific propaganda claims. The usual situation was one of no commentary on the Jewish extermination claim, as well as on other specific propaganda claims, e.g. starvation and torturing of American and British POW's and the various gruesome inventions of Hollywood, such as the draining of the blood of children in occupied countries for the use of the Wehrmacht.

The reason for this relative silence on specific propaganda claims was no doubt that there was no need, from the German point of view, to review its content. They had seen it all before, during World War I. Thus the German press treatment of the *"Greuelpropaganda"* was on a higher level and, rather than concern itself with the specific contents of the stories, it concerned itself with such questions as the nature of the political interests that were served by the propaganda and the extent and means of Jewish influence in the Allied press (e.g. *Das Reich* for 20 December 1942).

The high level Washington commitment to the claim that Auschwitz was an extermination camp came in November 1944, after the claimed termination of the killing program, in the form of the WRB report (the claim had appeared many times in the propaganda earlier in 1944; those stories are reviewed in a later chapter). The issuing of the report was carried by the *N.Y. Times* on 26 November 1944 (p. 1) and some excerpts were given.

The WRB report is described as two reports, one written by "two young Slovakian Jews" and the other by "a Polish major", all of whom had been inmates at Auschwitz from the spring of 1942 until the spring of 1944, when they escaped (the two Jews on 7 April). There is an additional short supplement said to be written by two other young Jews who escaped on 27 May 1944 and made their way to Slovakia (under German domination until 1945) to make their report, which is said to have been received in Switzerland on 6 August 1944. The authors are completely anonymous and this anonymity is duly apologized for — "whose names will not be disclosed for the time being in the interest of their own safety" *no names the same*

Sections 1, 2 and 3 constitute the first part of the report, and section 4 the second part. The first section is the major part of the report. It is said to have been written by a Slovakian Jew who arrived at Auschwitz on 13 April 1942 and was given a registration number (tattooed onto his left breast) in the neighborhood of 29,000. He eventually became registrar in the Birkenau infirmary. The feature of this first section is a detailed record, for the period April 1942 to April 1944, of the transports which arrived at Auschwitz, together with the registration numbers assigned. About 55 groups of transports (sometimes more than one transport are in a group) are reported and the (admittedly approximate) registration numbers assigned to the people in each group are given. The numbers start at 27,400 and run to 189,000 in the consecutive numbering system, in which a number was not used twice. For each group the nationalities represented, as well as other information (Jewish or Aryan, political prisoners or other, occasional names of individuals, numbers "gassed" instead of registered, etc.) is given. The WRB report, if it is approximately correct in these matters (interpreting the people "gassed" as either never having existed or having been sent on to another destination), is one of the two known sources of significant amounts of such information (the other is the referenced set of Netherlands Red Cross reports, which is the subject of Appendix C).

Almost all of this information is given by the author of the first section of the WRB report, but after he escaped the authors of the third, supplemental, section of the report kept an account of this information for the period 7 April – 27 May and have contributed it to the report.

The second section of the report is said to be written by a Slovakian Jew who arrived at the Lublin camp around 4 June 1942, but was sent to Auschwitz around 30 June 1942. According to the first section of the report he then would have received a registration number around 44,000, which was tattooed onto his left forearm (the tattooing system had changed). The two authors of the first two sections of the report are the two young Slovakian Jews who escaped together on 7 April 1944. The third section of the report is the short supplement and the fourth section is the contribution of the "Polish major".

The anonymity of the authors of the report is certainly a vulnerable feature, but the major implausibility is simply the contents of the WRB report. Examination shows that the information given in the report which is most likely true to semi-true is the sort of thing that could have been built up from intelligence data, not from reports of "two young Slovakian Jews and a Polish major" who "escaped". This is exactly as one should expect; Germany's enemies had certain means of gathering information about German camps and about events in Europe and simply used information gathered by such conventional methods, plus a considerable amount of intervention, to compose the WRB report. It is just not believable that they were in such a primitive position with respect to, of all things, the industrial center Auschwitz, that they were obliged to depend for information on miraculous escapes by unusually well informed prisoners. This point will be amplified below. Of course, such an observation does not rule out the possible use of reports of former employees or inmates, escaped or otherwise, as part of the data.

The report presents the following information (or estimates, or guesses, or claims, or inventions):

1. The number of prisoners at Auschwitz I in the month of April 1942, the predominant nationalities present and the main causes of internment. Description of the inmate registration number system and the "star system" of inmate insignia. A list of various factories in the area (pt. I, 1-2).

2. An accurate map of the area, comparable to our Fig. 5 (pt. I, 4).

3. Dimensions related to the Auschwitz I camp size, its fences and its guard towers. Ditto for Birkenau. Description of barracks (pt. I, 5-7).

4. In the case of a natural death of a prisoner, a death certificate was made out and sent to Oranienburg central camp administration. If the inmate was gassed, his name was entered in a special register and marked "S.B." (*Sonderbehandlung*, special treatment) (pt. I, 9).

5. Four buildings, referred to as crematoria I, II, III and IV were in use in Spring 1944 at Birkenau; use of at least one of them had started in February 1943. Each building contained: (A) a furnace room of ovens; (B) a large hall; (C) a gas chamber. The first two buildings each contained 36 ovens and the other two 18 each. Three bodies are put into one oven at a time and the burning took an hour and a half. Thus one could dispose of 6,000 bodies per day. This was considered, at the time, an improvement over burning in trenches (the method previously employed) (pt. I, 14-15).

6. The specific product used for generating the gas for the gas chamber was a powder called "Cyklon", manufactured by a Hamburg concern. When exposed it released cyanide gas and about three minutes were required to kill everybody in the gas chamber. The containers for the Cyklon were marked "for use against vermin" (pt. I, 16).

7. Prominent people from Berlin attended the inauguration of the first

crematorium in March 1943. The "program" consisted in the gassing and burning of 8,000 Cracow Jews. The guests (no names given) were extremely satisfied with the results (pt. I, 16).

8. A detailed breakdown of the numbers and classifications of the inmates at Birkenau in April 1944 (pt. I, 23-24).

9. In the camp, each block has a "block eldest" who "has power of life and death". Until February 1944 nearly 50 per cent of the block eldests were Jews, but this was stopped by order of Berlin. Under the block eldest is the block recorder, who does all the clerical work. If the recorder has noted down a death by mistake, as often occurs, the discrepancy is corrected by killing the bearer of the corresponding number. Corrections are not admitted (pt. I, 25).

10. A passage strikingly similar to the November 1942 "crumpled testament of despair": "We worked in the huge Buna plant to which we were herded every morning about 3 A.M. . . . As our working place was situated outside the large chain of sentry posts, it was divided into small sectors of 10 x 10 meters, each guarded by an SS man. Whoever stepped outside these squares during working hours was immediately shot without warning for having 'attempted to escape'. . . Very few could bear the strain and although escape seemed hopeless, attempts were made every day". (pt. I, 30).

11. A "careful estimate of the numbers of Jews gassed in Birkenau between April 1942 and April 1944", summarized in a tabular form. The numbers showed up in the published record of the IMT trial and are presented here as Fig. 25 (pt. I, 33).

12. Great excitement prevailed as a consequence of the escape of the two young Slovakian Jews (this is supposedly written by the authors of the supplementary section 3), and the friends and superiors of the two escapees were closely questioned. Since the two had held posts as "block recorders", all Jews exercising such functions were removed for punishment and as a precautionary measure. This, of course, contradicts the implication of the "Foreword" of the WRB report that the Germans did not know the identity or even registration numbers of the two escapees, since it withholds such information "in the interest of their own safety" (pt. I, 34).

13. Starting 15 May 1944 Hungarian Jews started arriving at Birkenau at the rate of about 15,000 per day. Ninety per cent were killed immediately and, since this exceeded the capacity of the ovens, the method of burning in trenches which had existed earlier was reverted to. The ten per cent who were not killed were also not registered at Birkenau but sent eventually to camps in Germany: Buchenwald, Mauthausen, Gross-Rosen, Gusen, Flossenburg, Sachsenhausen, etc. (pt. I. 36-37).

14. A new inmate registration number system was also put into effect in the middle of May 1944. At about the same time, a visit by Himmler to nearby Cracow was reported in the Silesian newspapers. These newspaper reports apparently omitted to mention, however, that on this trip Himmler had also visited Birkenau, and that his party made a special visit to crematorium I (pt. I, 37-38).

15. In the late summer of 1943 a commission of four distinguished Dutch Jews had visited Auschwitz for the purpose of inspecting the condition of the Dutch Jews (who were then specially prepared by the Germans with new clothes, better food, etc.). The commission saw only a part of the Dutch Jews sent to Auschwitz but were told that the others were in similar camps. The commission was satisfied with this and signed a declaration that everything had been found in good order at Auschwitz, but after signing the four Jews "expressed a desire to see the camp of Birkenau and particularly

the crematoria about which they had heard some stories . . . The commission was then taken to Birkenau . . . and immediately to crematorium No. 1. Here they were shot from behind. A telegram was supposedly sent to Holland reporting that after leaving Auschwitz the four men had been victims of an unfortunate automobile accident". (pt. I, 38).

16. The area around Auschwitz, within a radius of 100 kilometres, had been evacuated, and the buildings not to be taken over by the camp were to be demolished (pt. II, 6).

17. Description of the Auschwitz I hospital and its procedures. In the autumn of 1942 the hospital mortality rate was so high that Berlin requested an explanation. An investigation uncovered that the "camp doctor" had been administering lethal injections to weak and sick people, certain prisoners condemned to death, and some teenagers considered to be orphans. For "punishment" the camp doctor was simply sent to the same job at the Buna plant (probably meaning Monowitz — the SS continued to provide some services to the camp administered by Farben) (pt. II, 8-10).

18. As a result of bad treatment a Jew, irrespective of his physical condition, could not last more than two weeks (pt. II, 12).

19. In the summer of 1942 Jews were being gassed in the birch forest (*Birkenwald*, where Birkenau was located) in special sealed buildings giving the impression of showers. Since the crematoria were not completed, the bodies were buried in mass graves, causing putrefaction. In the autumn of 1942 the four crematoria were completed and many bodies were exhumed and burned (this is the Polish major's account, contradicting that of the two young Slovakian Jews, who said that part of the new crematoria were put into operation in February 1943 and that prior to that date bodies were burned in trenches) (pt. II, 16-17).

20. Details on how it was decided exactly when to execute somebody already condemned to death (pt. II, 16-17).

The foregoing is effectively illustrative of the contents of the WRB report. It is a mixture of truth, guess-work, and invention, the factual part of which could have been, and obviously was, put together on the basis of inside information available in 1944.

The contradiction in the two accounts of exterminations serves to enhance the credibility of the claim that these are unsolicited reports of escaped inmates, but it is not clear that such increased credibility was the motivation for composing the report thus. The first version, that large crematoria were in operation at Birkenau in early 1943 and that mass cremations took place in trenches before that date, is the one subsequently put forward (and the correct one in regard to the date of availability of the crematoria) but the second version of mass graves might have some truth in it also, since there had been a typhus epidemic in the summer, at a time when inadequate crematoria facilities existed.

Reitlinger uses the WRB report as a source. This is not entirely justified but, it is not entirely without justification either. One must assume that much of the material in the report is true. As will be elaborated below, there is no question of the competence of the authors of the report. However one must be careful in this regard, obviously, and accept only that which seems corroborated by either common sense or independent evidence. Given the protagonistic and propagandistic role of the report, but recalling that a well organized hoax necessarily contains much valid fact, this is perfectly reasonable.

One can be rather specific about the routes by which information flowed out of the camps. In cases where there was significant industrial activity, the inmates inevitably came into contact with many people who were not camp inmates (company employees, railroad employees, etc.) and these contacts were the basis for an extensive system of clandestine channels of communication. Auschwitz, of course, furnished numerous and excellent opportunities for such contacts and, on account of the communist organization, there were very effective channels to outside underground centers, especially in nearby Cracow. Information about the camp, including, it is claimed, copies of orders received from Berlin or Oranienburg, flowed constantly out of Auschwitz. These channels were also used to send such things as money, medicine and forged papers into the camp. In addition, as discussed in another connection in the next chapter, the Communists in all of the camps were highly organized for illegal radio listening. If they had receivers, they no doubt also had transmitters. There has been witness testimony to possession of radio transmitters by camp inmates, and Reitlinger believes that Auschwitz inmates had transmitters.[41]

In order to grasp completely the nature of the information and propaganda channels that existed, one should take special note of the War Refugee Board and the OSS. The WRB maintained constant contact with events in Hungary even after the German occupation in March 1944. For example, it had its agent, Raoul Wallenberg, in the Swedish diplomatic corps, and there were other links through Jewish organizations. Jewish leaders in Budapest were in constant contact with those in Slovakia, and the Slovakian Jewish leadership was in contact with Polish Jewry, particularly in Cracow.[42]

Possibly more important than the WRB, although its role in the hoax is not nearly as obvious, was the Office of Strategic Services, OSS, the predecessor of the CIA. The OSS was set up early in World War II under the leadership of General William Donovan. Its mission was intelligence of a political nature and related matters (e.g. sabotage, propaganda, guerilla warfare) as distinct from the more conventional forms of military intelligence, to which its operations were related somewhat as the operations of the German SD were related to those of the *Abwehr*, although highly placed Washington observers complained that the OSS seemed to enjoy unlimited funds and knew no bounds on its authority.

With only a few exceptions, the OSS was not staffed by military people but by persons recruited from private life. Thus it included many political types, ranging from Communists to emigré monarchists. On account of their organization, the Communists were naturally a significant force in the OSS, irrespective of their numbers.

The OSS was deeply involved with propaganda. The OWI (Office of War Information), the most prominent U.S. wartime propaganda agency, had been a 1942 split off from the OSS. It had been the propaganda division of the "Office of the Coordinator of Information" (Donovan) when it split off, and the remainder of Donovan's organization was renamed the OSS. Despite this separation, the OSS remained active in the propaganda field, and when the Anglo-American PWB (Psychological Warfare Branch) was set up in Eisenhower's headquarters, it drew its American personnel from both the OWI and the OSS.

Another propaganda operation of the OSS, one which employed a large number of "progressive writers", was the MO (Morale Operations Branch). The mission of MO was "black propaganda", i.e. MO specialized in manufacturing propaganda presented in such a way that it would appear to have come from within the ranks of the enemy. MO thus distributed forged newspapers and military orders among enemy personnel, operated clandestine transmitters that purported to be broadcasting from within enemy territory, and started rumors in the Axis and Axis occupied countries. Its staff included "liberals and communists alike, all dedicated to the idealist interpretation of the fight against fascism".

A particularly relevant facet of the OSS operations was that they had enlisted the cooperation of the Jewish Agency in Palestine (which was really the unofficial Israeli government of the time). The Jewish Agency, on account of extensive and elaborate contacts with Jews in Europe, especially in the Balkans, was able to undertake many important missions for the OSS. Thus the channels to Jews in Hungary, Slovakia and beyond were open.

Finally, it is of interest that the OSS was very significant on the prosecution staff at the IMT trial, especially in the early stages.[43]

The point to be made in this discussion of the WRB report is certainly not that it was invented in the OSS or the WRB. I do not know the identity of the authors and do not believe that the question is of great significance. The main point is that two "internationals", the Communist and the Zionist, played important roles in the intelligence, propaganda and refugee assistance programs of the U.S. The WRB, effectively taking its orders from Harry Dexter White, Henry Morgenthau Jr. and the World Jewish Congress and other Zionists, and the OSS, with its staff of Communists and its Jewish Agency allies, show that the situation was perfectly suitable for the manufacture of a Jewish extermination propaganda lie, built about Auschwitz, which, as a precaution, contained enough real fact to suggest to the unreflective that the allegations were true.

The interior of the Auschwitz camp was not, by any exercise of the imagination, isolated from the Allies. The world's most efficient intelligence organization, the Communist Party, could transmit any information desired to any destination whatever, and the situation was such that the ubiquitous Zionist International was in a position to manufacture and transmit whatever items seemed appropriate for the occasion. Even if the contents of the WRB report were entirely true, an escape by inmates would not have been at all necessary to get the "facts" into the hands of the Allies. Note that we are told that the *entire* contents of the WRB report are due to *three independent* escapes by remarkably well informed inmates. In view of what we know about the channels of communication that existed, this is silly in the extreme.

The authors of the WRB report remained anonymous for quite a bit more than "the time being". The report became a prosecution document at Nuernberg under the number 022-L. The descriptive material accompanying the document, dated 7 August 1945 (the "staff evidence analysis"), seems distressed at the anonymity of the authors. It tells of a certain Dr. Joseph Elias, "Protestant Pastor of Jewish ancestry, organizer of Jewish resistance in Hungary, head of Jo 'Pasztor Bizottsag, who interrogated the first two Slovak Jews after their escape". Then it tells of "Dr. G. Soos — Secretary of Hungarian underground movement MFM, who brought the first report (of the first two Slovak Jews) to Italy". The organization "Jo'Pasztor" was real, but of activities of Elias or Soos in connection with these matters nothing, it seems, is known. Of the origins of the parts of the report attributed to the other three people we are told nothing. It is said that R.D. McClelland, Bern representative of the WRB, forwarded the report to Washington in early July 1944 (the supplemental part was presumably not included).

The WRB report was put into evidence at the IMT, as document 022-L, by Major Walsh on 14 December 1945.[44] There was no defense objection, at the IMT, to the acceptance of the report into evidence. At the Farben trial the prosecution submitted the report (Document Book 89) as evidence but the defense objected and this objection "as to the competence and materiality

94

of each and every document in the book" was sustained by that court. The result of the ensuing legal argument was that the court agreed to taking a certain very ambiguous "judicial notice" of the documents.[45]

Anonymity was maintained for several more years, since the first edition (1953) of Reitlinger's *The Final Solution* considers the authors anonymous. In considering the beginnings of the gassings, reference is made to "the very reliable report of the Birkenau infirmary registrar or *Blockschreiber,* who escaped to Hungary in April 1944" (p. 110). In connection with information about Theresienstadt Jews transported to Auschwitz "we are indebted to a Slovak Jewish doctor, who escaped to Hungary in April, 1944. This man, who was in charge of the Birkenau infirmary records . . . " (pp. 169-170). In discussing the WRB report, Reitlinger told us that "the most important document is that of the anonymous Slovak Jewish doctor who escaped to Hungary in April 1944" (p.540). In all three cases Reitlinger was referring to the author of the first section of the WRB report who, the report says, was the Slovakian Jew who arrived on 13 April 1942 and was given a registration number around 29,000. Reitlinger refers to him as a doctor, but the report actually does not make it clear what he was; it appears that he was supposed to be an "intellectual" or a "clerk".

The next development seems to have been the publication in 1956 in Israel of the book *Im Schatten des Todes,* by J. Oskar Neumann. Neumann had been one of the leaders of the various Jewish councils and resistance organizations in Slovakia. In his account Rabbi Michael Dov Ber Weissmandel (or Weissmandl), originally a Hungarian Jew resident in a part of Hungary that was annexed by Czechoslovakia after World War I, was the leader of Jewish resistance in Slovakia. In Neumann's story the two young Slovakian Jews appear on schedule in Slovakia, as does the Polish major (actually, the WRB report does not say where the Polish major escaped to). Neumann gives the impression that he actually met these people: "Yet here sit eye-witnesses, who have told the whole truth". His account does not mention the two authors of the third, supplementary, section of the WRB report, and he does not tell us the names or tattooed registration numbers of the escapees. Since they were in great danger of being found by the Gestapo, which was looking for them, they "were sent to an outlying mountainous area to rest". Rabbi Weissmandel communicated the report to Budapest, Switzerland, and other destinations, in order to warn other Jews, and to bring help.[46]

Weissmandel emigrated to the United States after the war and set up an orthodox Talmudic seminary in New York State. He died in November 1957. However his war memoirs were published posthumously in 1960, unfortunately, in Hebrew, which I am not able to read. The WRB report is a major subject of his book. I have assumed that his story is essentially similar to Neumann's, since the two authors were similarly situated and had the same connections. However, I could be wrong.[47]

It appears that the next event involved Reitlinger. The anonymity of the authors of the WRB report is a striking and disturbing feature of the first edition of Reitlinger's book, as I am sure he realized. This no doubt bothered him, for it appears that he set out to locate the authors of the report, for he writes in his second edition, published in 1968, that Rudolf Vrba, the author of the "most important" part of the WRB report, i.e., the first section, was "in hospital practice in Cardiff in 1960". Reitlinger's contact with Vrba in 1960, thus, would appear to be the first appearance of an alleged author of the report in any sort of historical record. Vrba was apparently produced as a consequence of Reitlinger's investigations. The town of Cardiff in south Wales is, incidentally, only about 150 miles from Reitlinger's home in Sussex.

Reitlinger does not mention the name of any of the other authors. He considers a stencil book by Silberschein, Riegner's World Jewish Congress colleague in Switzerland, as including the "complete version" of the report.[48]

Both authors of the first two sections of the WRB report (the first two young Slovakian Jews) acquired identities at Eichmann's trial in 1961. Two witnesses testified regarding the report, and it was offered in evidence with the explanation that the first two young Slovakian Jews were Alfred Wetzler (or Weczler) and Rudolf Vrba (ex Rosenberg or Rosenthal, then resident in England). The document was rejected on the grounds that certain contradictions in the figures offered required further explanation. Therefore, late in the trial, the prosecution produced an affidavit by Vrba. The affidavit explains how Vrba arrived at the impressively detailed figures regarding the transports to Auschwitz, which are the main feature of the WRB report. His affidavit gives the impression that, while he got assistance from various people, he was solely responsible for drawing up the figures, and he does not give the name of or even mention his companion who supposedly escaped with him in April 1944. He mentions a Philip Mueller, who helped him somewhat with his figures, because Mueller "is apparently the only survivor alive at present". Vrba's affidavit was rejected by the court on the grounds that there was no excuse for the prosecution not bringing him to Jerusalem to testify.[49]

Vrba appeared again at the Auschwitz trial in Frankfurt in 1964; his book, *I Cannot Forgive* (with Alan Bestic), also appeared in 1964, shortly before his Frankfurt appearance. Vrba's companion in his supposed escape also appeared; Alfred Wetzler was said to have been the other young Slovakian Jew. Wetzler was (in 1964) a 46 year old civil servant in Czechoslovakia, who had arrived at Auschwitz on 13 April 1942 and been given registration number 29,162. He had been a block registrar at Birkenau. Vrba was identified as a 40 year old biochemist living in England, who had arrived at Auschwitz on 30 June 1942 and been given registration number 44,070. He had also been a block registrar at Birkenau. They had, they said, escaped on 7 April 1944 and made their way to Bratislava, Czechoslovakia, where they made their report to the Jewish elders and also to the Papal Nuncio. The report was smuggled to Budapest by Rabbi Weissmandel.[50]

The 1964 story differs, therefore, from that which was told to the authors of the IMT staff evidence analysis in 1945. The most serious apparent contradiction, however, is in the credit for the reporting of the figures related to the transports to Auschwitz. Vrba, in his 1961 affidavit (which did not mention Wetzler), and also in his Frankfurt testimony, presented himself as being primarily responsible for the figures. The WRB report, on the other hand, while it attributes the figures to both men, presents the figures in the first section of the report, whose author is supposed to be Wetzler.

Vrba does not explain, in his 1964 book, why he waited 16 years to talk about his escape from Auschwitz, and his delivery of the statistics which were eventually published by Washington. His book follows, roughly, the story of the WRB report, with a few contradictions of varying degrees of importance. For example, in the book (p. 128) Vrba writes that the girls working in the "Canada" area were in very good health, but in the WRB report (pt.I, p.31) these women were "beaten and brutalized and their mortality was much higher than among the men." Other oddities in his book are his claim to have helped build the crematoria (p. 16, not mentioned in the WRB report), and his description of an Allied air raid on 9 April 1944, of which there is no record (p. 233; he says that he and Wetzler hid in a woodpile for three days at Auschwitz after their 7 April escape. The possibility of an Allied air raid in April is discussed in chapter V.). Wetzler just barely manages to get mentioned in Vrba's book.

Photo: Imperial War Museum

Fig. 9: Yard at Belsen after British capture of the camp.

Vrba says nothing about the Polish major or the two Jews who supposedly escaped later on to supplement the Auschwitz transport figures. In the book the other prisoners refer to him as "Rudi", although his original name, and the name by which he was supposedly known at Auschwitz, is supposed to have been Walter Rosenberg (a point Vrba's book does not bring up but is claimed elsewhere, e.g. in *They Fought Back,* ed. by Yuri Suhl, and in *Fighting Auschwitz,* by Jozef Garlinski). Vrba says nothing about resting in a mountain retreat after escaping.

Just as conclusive, in our evaluation of Vrba's story, as the various contradictions of either the WRB report or known fact, is the general tone of the book and his description of how various people behaved at the camp. Although the book presents utterly incredible material in this connection from beginning to end, the best example is Vrba's description of an alleged visit by Himmler on 17 July 1942 (pp. 9-15, not mentioned in the WRB report). The prisoners were drawn up for inspection, and the orchestra was in readiness to play when Himmler arrived. As they waited, the leader of the orchestra

stood, baton raised, motionless, poised to weave music for the honored guest.
    And then it happened. The catastrophe that every actor dreads. The moment of horror that only great occasions merit. The crisis that seems to dog every moment of truth.
    In the tenth row outside our Block, the Block Senior found Yankel Meisel without his full quota of tunic buttons.
    It took some seconds for the enormity of the crime to sink in. Then he felled him with a blow . . .
    Out of sight, . . . they beat and kicked the life out of him . . .
    . . . Himmler's suite was twenty yards away. The baton moved . . . and the orchestra followed . . . with an excerpt from Aida.
    It was "The Triumph March".
    . . . He lined us up and rapped: "I am the Reichsfuehrer. Let's see how you behave in front of me".
    Slowly he marched down the ranks, a little killer aping a big killer, glaring at each of us in turn. If he found dirty finger nails or wooden shoes not properly blacked, he howled abuse at the offender and thumped him with his heavy bamboo cane. He even inspected us, nursery fashion, behind the ears and then went prowling through the barracks, searching for blankets which had not been folded with precision.

Vrba mentions a second Himmler visit (pp. 15-19; the visit seems to correspond to the March 1943 visit of dignitaries from Berlin to witness a gassing) in January 1943 to witness the gassing of 3,000 Polish Jews. The event was scheduled for 9 A.M. but Himmler took until 11 A.M. to finish breakfast, so the 3,000 Jews had to wait two hours in the gas chamber. Himmler finally witnessed the gassing in a cheerful and relaxed mood, chatting with the commandant and others, occasionally throwing a glance through the peep-hole to observe the Jews being gassed.

The book manages to maintain this utterly incredible tone throughout, as you can verify by reading it, if you can stand it.

Reitlinger does not cite Vrba's book in any connection in the second edition of his book. He writes of Vrba as the author of the "most important" part of the WRB report, the first section, although the data offered shows that this role should be attributed to Wetzler. It does not appear important or relevant to Reitlinger that Vrba was only 18 years old when, he claims, he started collecting the numerical and other data concerning the transports to Auschwitz, with the intention of making this information available to the outside world.

There has been no claimed break, so far as I know, in the anonymity of the Polish major. Erich Kulka, of the Hebrew University in Jerusalem, in an article in Suhl's book, offers names for the two authors of the supplementary section (Czezln Mordowicz who changed his name to Petr Podulka, and Arnost Rosin who changed his name to Jan Rohac), but I know nothing of these people other than that they remained quiet about their heroic exploits for an even greater number of years than Vrba and Wetzler did. Moreover neither Elias, nor Soos, nor Vrba (as Vrba or as Rosenberg), norr Weissmandel appeared as witnesses in any of the Nuernberg trials, despite the sometimes contested role played by document 022-L at those trials.

The records of the International Tracing Service in Arolsen, West Germany, report that two Jews named Wetzler and Rosenberg did escape on 7 April 1944, and this agrees with the *"Kalendarium"* published by the Polish Government in 1964 as no. 7 of *Hefte von Auschwitz,* which also declares that two Jews named Mordowicz and Rosin escaped on 27 May 1944. Since there were many successful escapes from Auschwitz during this period (many many more than Vrba seems to think there were – compare p. 217 of Vrba with Garlinski's remarks about escapes), this data may well be correct, but it still does not authenticate the authorship of the WRB Report, especially since we are told today that after escaping the four Jews adopted aliases for concealment purposes and that three of the four retained these different names after the war rather than reassume their real names.

The details behind the manufacture of the WRB report will probably never be completely uncovered, but it is entirely possible that its creators went to great lengths in simulating a report miraculously smuggled to Slovakia and then to Switzerland. If it was written in Slovakia then it seems clear that Rabbi Weissmandel should be credited with at least coauthorship. It is also possible that, as claimed, the report was given to the Papal Chargé d'affaires in Slovakia, Giuseppe Burzio, and that it was forwarded by him to Rome. It is clear that Burzio was contacted by Jewish propagandists and that he forwarded at least some of their "information" to Rome. Examples which Burzio transmitted to the Vatican were March 1942 claims that the Germans were taking young Jewish women from their families to make them prostitutes for German soldiers on the eastern front (a complete fantasy) and an early 1943 letter from a Bratislava priest claiming that both Jewish and responsible German sources had told him of the soap factories supplied with the bodies of gassed and machine-gunned Jews. Whether Burzio forwarded such material purely as routine procedure or because he gave credence to it is hardly relevant, although the latter appears to be the case. The Vatican received and filed many such reports during the war, but never gave any credence to them. Its present position is that, during the war, neither it nor the "Jewish agencies were aware that the deportations were part of a general mass annihilation operation" (see also Appendix E).[51]

In any case it is obvious that the WRB report is spurious. The data given in the report is not the sort of information that escapees would carry out; the claim that two more Jews escaped later on to supplement this data is more than doubly ridiculous. Instead of coming forward immediately after the war with ostensible authors of the report, in order to lend more support to the lie, it appears that it was assumed that the whole thing was irrelevant until, for some reason (probably Reitlinger's curiosity), an author was produced sixteen years after the event. That person's story is not credible.

Thus was born the Auschwitz legend.

IV
AUSCHWITZ

We now consider the specific Auschwitz "extermination" story that we are offered.

The trials which generated the evidence on which the extermination claims are based took place in a prostrate, starving Germany whose people were in no position to do any but that which the occupying powers wished. This was the political reality of the situation. By the record, it was the "Zionist International" which organized the specific extermination claims that were made, and which were given no credence by high and knowledgeable Washington officials. The leading personality in the setting up of the legal system of the war crimes trials was none other than the American prosecutor at the IMT trial. At that trial the judges had previously expressed themselves on the obvious guilt of the defendants, and the findings of the trial were formal legal constraints on the subsequent trials. The most important of the subsequent trials were those organized by the arch-Zionist Marcus, future hero of Israel and then head of the U.S. War Crimes Branch, an agency which had engaged in torture of witnesses in connection with certain trials. The "honor" of the states conducting the trials was committed to the thesis of extraordinary Nazi brutality. Under such conditions it is difficult to see how one could fail to expect a frame-up; this and the following chapter show that the Auschwitz charges are what one should expect.

It must first be asked; what is the essential attribute, the "trademark" of a hoax on this scale? No sane author of such a thing would present a story which is untrue in every or in most details; ninety nine per cent valid fact can be present in a story whose major claim has no truth whatever to it and recognition of this leads the author of the hoax to the maximally safe approach to his deed: distort the meanings of valid facts.

This is the basic structure of the Auschwitz extermination legend. It is shown here that every real fact contained in the story had (not could have had, but had) a relatively routine significance, having nothing to do with exterminations of people. Thus those who claim extermination must advance a thesis involving a dual interpretation of the facts, but by then the impartial reader, in consideration of what has just been noted, should be on my side; the need for a dual interpretation of fact, the trademark of the hoax, has emerged.

Another trademark, not so obvious at this point, will be suggested by the analysis. Also the facts which contradict the extermination claims will be noted, and for those who still believe the claims these facts are "mysteries". The inconsistencies and implausibilities and obvious lies will appear and finally the crushing blow, a fact contradicting the claims, so huge in significance that there can be no mumbling about "mysteries".

The commandant of Auschwitz from May 1940 to late 1943 was SS Colonel Rudolf Hoess. During the IMT trial he had signed some affidavits for the prosecution, the most noted being signed on 5 April 1946.[1] In accord with a common IMT and NMT practice, he was then called by the Kaltenbrunner defense on 15 April 1946.[2] The major content of his testimony was in his assenting, during cross-examination, to his affidavit of 5 April, and also in certain points of supporting testimony.

Hoess is universally considered the star prosecution witness and, despite the origins of the Auschwitz hoax in the WRB report, the extermination mythologists essentially treat the Hoess affidavit as the Auschwitz extermination story or, more precisely, the framework for the story. All pleaders of the Auschwitz extermination legend present a story which is the Hoess affidavit, with only numerical variations, as supplemented by the IMT, NMT and similar evidence. None of the principal extermination mythologists give prominence to the WRB report, and only Reitlinger seems to perceive a problem of some sort of importance in connection with it.

· Thus it is convenient to allow the Hoess affidavit to act as framework for our analysis also. It is presented in full here and then the individual points are reviewed with due regard for the supplemental and additional evidence. The fateful duality will emerge as an undeniable feature. The contradictions, inconsistencies, wild implausibilities and lies will appear. The analysis will reveal something of the psychological context of the trials.

Due regard is also given to verifiable interpretation of sources, including instances where it is found convenient to reference Hilberg or Reitlinger rather than an original document that the reader is not likely to have convenient access to.

THE HOESS AFFIDAVIT

I, RUDOLF FRANZ FERDINAND HOESS, being first duly sworn, depose and say as follows:

1. I am forty-six years old, and have been a member of the NSDAP since 1922; a member of the SS since 1934; a member of the Waffen-SS since 1939. I was a member from 1 December 1934 of the SS Guard Unit, the so-called Deathshead Formation (*Totenkopf Verband*).

2. I have been constantly associated with the administration of concentration camps since 1934, serving at Dachau until 1938; then as adjutant in Sachsenhausen from 1938 to May 1, 1940, when I was appointed commandant of Auschwitz. I commanded Auschwitz until 1 December 1943, and estimate that at least 2,500,000 victims were executed and exterminated there by gassing and burning, and at least another half million succumbed to starvation and disease, making a total dead of about 3,000,000. This figure represents about 70% or 80% of all persons sent to Auschwitz as prisoners, the remainder having been selected and used for slave labor in the concentration camp industries. Included among the executed and burnt were approximately 20,000 Russian prisoners of war (previously screened out of Prisoner of War cages by the Gestapo) who were delivered at Auschwitz in Wehrmacht transports operated by regular Wehrmacht officers and men. The remainder of the total number of victims included about 100,000 German Jews, and great numbers of citizens, *mostly* Jewish from Holland, France, Belgium, Poland, Hungary, Czechoslovakia, Greece, or other countries. We executed about 400,000 Hungarian Jews alone in the summer of 1944.

3. WVHA (Main Economic and Administrative Office), headed by Obergruppenfuehrer Oswald Pohl, was responsible for all administrative matters such as billeting, feeding and medical care, in the concentration camps. Prior to establishment of the RSHA, Secret State Police Office (Gestapo) and the Reich Office of Criminal Police were responsible for arrests, commitments to concentration camps, punishments and executions therein. After organization of the RSHA, all of these functions were carried out as before, but, pursuant to orders signed by Heydrich as Chief of the RSHA. While Kaltenbrunner was Chief of RSHA, orders for protective custody, commitments, punishment and, individual executions were signed by Kaltenbrunner or by Mueller, Chief of the Gestapo, as Kaltenbrunner's deputy.

4. Mass executions by gassing commenced during the summer 1941 and continued until Fall 1944. I personally supervised executions at Auschwitz until the first of December 1943 and know by reason of my continued duties in the Inspectorate of Concentration Camps WVHA that these mass executions continued as stated above. All mass executions by gassing took place under the direct order, supervision and respon-

sibility of RSHA. I received all orders for carrying out these mass executions directly from RSHA.

5. On 1 December 1943 I became Chief of AMT I in AMT Group D of the WVHA and in that office was responsible for coordinating all matters arising between RSHA and concentration camps under the administration of WVHA. I held this position until the end of the war. Pohl, as Chief of WVHA, and Kaltenbrunner, as Chief of RSHA, often conferred personally and frequently communicated orally and in writing concerning concentration camps. On 5 October 1944, I brought a lengthy report regarding Mauthausen Concentration Camp to Kaltenbrunner at his office at RSHA, Berlin. Kaltenbrunner asked me to give him a short oral digest of this report and said he would reserve any decision until he had had an opportunity to study it in complete detail. This report dealt with the assignment to labor of several hundred prisoners who had been condemned to death . . . so-called "nameless prisoners".

6. The "final solution" of the Jewish question meant the complete extermination of all Jews in Europe. I was ordered to establish extermination facilities at Auschwitz in June 1941. At that time there were already in the general government three other extermination camps; BELZEC, TREBLINKA and WOLZEK. These camps were under the Einsatzkommando of the Security Police and SD. I visited Treblinka to find out how they carried out their exterminations. The Camp Commandant at Treblinka told me that he had liquidated 80,000 in the course of one-half year. He was principally concerned with liquidating all the Jews from the Warsaw Ghetto. He used monoxide gas and I did not think that his methods were very efficient. So when I set up the extermination building at Auschwitz, I used Cyclon B, which was crystallized Prussic Acid which we dropped into the death chamber from a small opening. It took from 3 to 15 minutes to kill the people in the death chamber depending upon climatic conditions. We knew when the people were dead because their screaming stopped. We usually waited about one-half hour before we opened the doors and removed the bodies. After the bodies were removed our special commandos took off the rings and extracted the gold from the teeth of the corpses.

7. Another improvement we made over Treblinka was that we built our gas chambers to accomodate 2,000 people at one time, whereas at Treblinka their 10 gas chambers only accomodated 200 people each. The way we selected our victims was as follows: we had two SS doctors on duty at Auschwitz to examine the incoming transports of prisoners. The prisoners would be marched by one of the doctors who would make spot decisions as they walked by. Those who were fit for work were sent into the Camp. Others were sent immediately to the extermination plants. Children of tender years were invariably exterminated since by reason of their youth they were unable to work. Still another improvement we made over Treblinka was that at Treblinka the victims almost always knew that they were to be exterminated and at Auschwitz we endeavored to fool the victims into thinking that they were to go through a delousing process. Of course, frequently they realized our true intentions and we sometimes had riots and difficulties due to that fact. Very frequently women would hide their children under the clothes but of course when we found them we would send the children in to be exterminated. We were required to carry out these exterminations in secrecy but of course the foul and nauseating stench from the continuous burning of bodies permeated the entire area and all of the people living in the surrounding communities knew that exterminations were going on at Auschwitz.

8. We received from time to time special prisoners from the local Gestapo office. The SS doctors killed such prisoners by injections of benzine. Doctors had orders to write ordinary death certificates and could put down any reason at all for the cause of death.

9. From time to time we conducted medical experiments on women inmates, including sterilization and experiments relating to cancer. Most of the people who died under these experiments had been already condemned to death by the Gestapo.

10. Rudolf Mildner was the chief of the Gestapo at Kattowicz and *as such was head of the political department at Auschwitz which conducted third degree methods of interrogation* from approximately March 1941 until September 1943. As such, he frequently sent prisoners to Auschwitz for incarceration or execution. He visited Auschwitz on several occasions. The Gestapo Court, the SS Standgericht, which tried persons accused of various crimes, such as escaping Prisoners of War, etc., frequently met within Auschwitz, and Mildner often attended the trial of such persons, who usually were executed in Auschwitz following their sentence. I showed Mildner throughout the extermination plant at Auschwitz and he was directly interested in it since he had to send the Jews from his territory for execution at Auschwitz.

I understand English as it is written above. The above statements are true; this declaration is made by me voluntarily and without compulsion; after reading over the statement, I have signed and executed the same at Nuernberg, Germany on the fifth day of April 1946.   *Rudolf Hoess*

By "NSDAP" is meant the Nazi Party, *Nationalsozialistische Deutsche Arbeiterpartei* (National Socialist German Worker's Party).

Some points of information, which have not been included in the affidavit although some might consider them relevant, are that Hoess, as a nationalist brawler in the twenties, had committed a political killing which he served five years in prison for,[3] and that he started in the concentration camps at Dachau as a corporal in 1934. He may seem to have risen unusually quickly since in 1945, during the final weeks of the war, he was a colonel and was negotiating concentration camp matters with the Red Cross and representatives of neutral countries.[4] Most probably, his low rank in 1934 was due to artificial limitations on the size of the SS, imposed for political reasons. His rapid advance was probably the result of the expansion of the SS after the SA-Roehm purge of June 1934 and the greater expansion which took place after the war began.

We now analyze the significant points of the affidavit. The plan of Birkenau is shown in Fig. 29; it is based on information gathered at the "Auschwitz trial" of 1963–1965, but the WRB report presents a similar plan.[5]

Paragraph 2

It would have been helpful in putting things into slightly better focus and perspective if Hoess had briefly indicated what the nature of the "concentration camp industries" at Auschwitz was, and the enormous importance this industry had for the Germans. In the entire transcript of IMT testimony there appears to be only one specific reference to the nature of the industry at Auschwitz. It is in the testimony of political prisoner Vaillant-Couturier where she makes passing reference to an "ammunition factory" (no doubt the Krupp fuse plant) and to a "large Buna factory, but as (she) did not work there (she did) not know what was made there."[6] There may be other references, especially in the documents, but they are buried quite deeply, if they are there.

Not even Hoess clung to the figure of 2,500,000 victims gassed; in private at the time of his testimony and also at his own trial in 1947 in Poland (he was hanged) he used a figure of 1,135,000. The lowest figure to be claimed by those who claim that gassings took place is 750,000.[7] The Russians claimed 4,000,000, including some killed by "injections, ill treatment, etc", but the highest figure claimed seems to be 7,000,000.[8]

The remark about 400,000 Hungarian Jews was in accord with a strange emphasis in the legend on the Hungarian Jews. This emphasis existed well before the Hoess affidavit and it has persisted to this day. It was on 5 May 1944 that Eichmann was supposed to have proposed, through the intermediary Joel Brand, a "trucks for Hungarian Jews" swap with the Western allies.[9] The continued emphasis on the Hungarian Jews seems to be a result of the focus, since 1960, on the activities of Eichmann. For the initial emphasis, the only explanation I can offer is that the problems of the Hungarian Jews started in March 1944 with the German occupation of Hungary, which was simultaneous with the beginnings of the functionings of the War Refugee Board, which had been established in January. Much of the attention of the WRB was thus directed toward Hungary.[10] The problem of the Hungarian Jews is given special attention in the next chapter.

Paragraph 4

Hoess places the commencement of the gassings in the summer of 1941. He gets promoted in December 1943 to the Inspectorate of Concentration Camps at Oranienburg but knows "by reason of (his) continued duties" there that "these mass executions continued". To claim knowledge of significant events at Auschwitz, while with the Inspectorate, seems very reasonable but in his testimony he said that in the summer of 1941 he, Hoess, had been summoned to report directly to Himmler and that during the interview the concentration camp commandant had received directly from the Reichs-fuehrer-SS the order to begin exterminating the Jews, with the stipulation that he should maintain the "strictest secrecy", not allowing even his immediate superior Gluecks to find out what he was doing. "Gluecks was, so to speak, the inspector of concentration camps at that time and he was immediately subordinate to the Reichsfuehrer."[11]

Paragraph 6

It will be seen in a subsequent chapter what the "final solution" of the Jewish question meant. Hoess claims that he "was ordered to establish extermination facilities at Auschwitz in June 1941." Thus he reaffirms the date given in paragraph 4 and his testimony in support of the affidavit reaffirmed this date again; there seems no doubt that Hoess was knowingly and deliberately giving the summer of 1941 as the start and that no slip is involved here. Also Hoess testified that, at the time of the Himmler order, the Inspectorate (Gluecks) was "immediately subordinate" to Himmler. This could only have been true prior to March 1942, at which time Oswald Pohl, chief of the WVHA (paragraph 3), took over the Inspectorate and Gluecks started reporting to Pohl, who reported to Himmler. Prior to March 1942 the Inspectorate seems to have been an orphan organization and may have reported to Himmler, although it had connections with both Heydrich and Juettner's Operational Main Office (*Fuehrungshauptamt*). Hoess, of course, was familiar with these administrative arrangements since in late April 1942 Pohl had held a meeting of all camp commanders and all leaders of the Inspectorate for the specific purpose of discussing them.[12]

Despite all this Reitlinger insists that Hoess meant the summer of 1942, not 1941, for certain reasons that will be seen later and also for other reasons. First, an obvious implicit claim of Hoess' affidavit is that the visit to Treblinka took place after large deportations of Warsaw Jews to that camp. Hoess confirmed this point explicitly in another affidavit. That puts the Treblinka visit in 1942. Second, according to Reitlinger's sources, the first large transports (2,000) of Jews to Birkenau date from March 1942, when "the small gassing installation in the Birkenwald had only started to work."[13] Actually, such arguments only increase the confusion, if we are also told that Hoess received the extermination orders in the summer of 1942.

These are simply the sorts of contradictions that one should expect to emerge from a pack of lies. However for the sake of discussion we should accept that Hoess really meant the summer of 1942 and continue on to other matters. By any interpretation, however, Hoess says that there were three other extermination camps at the time of the Himmler order, that he had visited Treblinka and that this camp had been exterminating for one half year. That puts the beginning of the gas chamber exterminations in early 1942 if we accept Reitlinger's point.

One must agree that gassing with carbon monoxide is inefficient. The source of the carbon monoxide was supposed to have been the exhausts of a diesel engine at Belzec and of captured Russian tanks and trucks at Treblinka![14]

One must also agree that the Cyclon (Zyklon) B was more efficient since it consisted of crystals which, when exposed to air, sublimated into "Prussic acid" (hydrogen cyanide gas). There was no deadlier gas and, in fact, the Zyklon was a well known and widely used insecticide developed by the *Deutsche Gesellschaft fuer Schaedlingsbekaempfung* (DEGESCH), German Pest Control Co.. It had been marketed world-wide before the war as an insecticide;[15] the word Zyklon means "cyclone", i.e. the product was a "cyclone" for pests. It was used throughout the German armed forces and camp system during the war, and it was thus used as an insecticide at Auschwitz. The ordering and receiving of the Zyklon at Auschwitz was done by the so-called *Referat fuer Schaedlingsbekaempfung* (Pest Control Office).[16]

The constant menace of typhus as carried by lice has been noted, and the calamitous results of a complete breakdown of disinfection measures at Belsen have been seen. In view of the particular hospitability of the Auschwitz-Kattowicz operations to the typhus-bearing louse, in view of the fact of epidemics at Auschwitz which actually forced work stoppages, and in view of the tremendous importance of the Auschwitz industry to the German war effort, it is not surprising that the Zyklon was used in liberal quantities at Auschwitz, and in the surrounding region, for its intended purpose. It is this chemical product, known to be an insecticide and known to be used at Auschwitz as an insecticide, which, in the WRB report but starting even earlier, was claimed, and continues to this day to be claimed, as the source of the gas used to exterminate Jews at Auschwitz.

It is not correct to say that the insecticide role of the Zyklon has been concealed; the WRB report mentions the anti-parasite role of the Zyklon and a dual role for the Zyklon at Auschwitz is explicitly claimed in the IMT transcript.[17] We must be careful at this point to note the significance of the legend's Zyklon B allegation. Here we have, on a major point, the main attribute of a hoax as we begin to examine the details of the Auschwitz extermination claims: the fact requiring a dual interpretation. This is not discussed or, apparently, even appreciated in the "final solution" literature. Hilberg merely utters the completely irrelevant assertion that "very little was used for fumigation" and then cites unconvincing authority. Reitlinger does no better.[18]

The most typical use of the Zyklon was in disinfecting rooms and barracks. Everything was sealed and then the necessary amount of Zyklon, which came in green cans (Figs. 27, 28), was emptied in. After the proper time interval it was assumed that all the lice and other insects and pests were dead and then the enclosure was aired out. The Zyklon could be used for disinfecting clothing by employing an "extermination chamber"; such were marketed by the German "extermination" industry, although at that time steam baths were also used for the disinfecting of clothing, especially at permanent installations. The "extermination chambers" were preferred in connection with highly mobile or special conditions. The U.S. Army, which also had insect control problems during the war, had correspondingly similar devices and had devised a "field chamber". Since the U.S. came into the war late, it had time to adopt the newly developed chemical, DDT, for the functions that Zyklon performed for the Germans.[19] Naturally, the Americans employed DDT in their "camps", concentration or otherwise. The DDT, as a more advanced insecticide, was more versatile for various reasons, e.g. it was not nearly as lethal for human beings as Zyklon, which was quite lethal and, in its commercial form contained a "warning stuff", an irritant which was emitted before the cyanide gas was emitted. It is common to leave out frills in military versions of products, and thus the irritant was absent from the Zyklon employed in concentration camps.

The dual role of the Zyklon was asserted at the IMT on 28 January 1946 in the testimony of a witness of French prosecutor DuBost and then on 30 January DuBost had submitted as evidence document 1553-PS, consisting of a number of invoices from DEGESCH, addressed to SS 1st Lieutenant Kurt Gerstein, for various quantities of Zyklon sent to Oranienburg and to

Fig. 10: Mass grave at Belsen.

Photo: Imperial War Museum

106

Auschwitz, plus a lengthy "statement" attributed to Gerstein. After some hesitation over certain legal technicalities both parts of the document were accepted in evidence, the claims of Rassinier and Reitlinger that the "statement" was rejected to the contrary notwithstanding.[20] Two invoices are printed in the IMT volumes and part of the "statement" is printed in one of the NMT volumes.[21] The invoice samples printed in the IMT volumes include one invoice for 195 kg of Zyklon sent to Oranienburg and one for the same sent to Auschwitz. It is probable that the Oranienburg Zyklon was ultimately destined for other camps and that the Zyklon sent to Auschwitz was to be shared with all the smaller camps of the region and possibly also with the coal mines.

The case of Kurt Gerstein shows that there is no limit to the absurdities that intelligent people can attain once they have accepted falsehood as truth. This is the same Gerstein who appears as a major character in Rolf Hochuth's play *The Deputy*.

Gerstein's title in the SS was Chief Disinfection Officer in the Office of the Hygienic Chief of the Waffen-SS,[22] and as such it was his responsibility to supervise the deliveries of disinfection supplies to all the camps administered by the SS. Two versions of what happened to him at the end of the war are offered us. In the one he encountered American interrogators by chance in a hotel in Rottweil, the Black Forest, related that he had obtained a responsible post in the Nazi Party while operating as a secret agent for the sometimes anti-Nazi Rev. Niemoeller, that he had been involved in the operating of gas chambers, and that he was prepared to act as a witness in any court. He then handed them a seven page document, typed in French, together with a note in English and some Zyklon invoices, and then vanished.[23] In the other, he somehow found himself in Cherche-Midi military prison in Paris, composed a document in his own hand, in French, added the Zyklon invoices, and then hanged himself in July 1945.[24] In either case neither he nor his body has ever been found. He vanished allegedly leaving a "statement" and some Zyklon invoices which became document 1553-PS. The former version of the Gerstein story is the one claimed in the descriptive material accompanying the document.

Even if we were not presented with such an obviously fishy story concerning Gerstein, we would doubt the authenticity of the "statement" merely on the grounds of its contents, for it is ridiculous in the story it presents, e.g. that Gerstein took his position in the SS in order to attempt to sabotage the exterminations ("a man who had penetrated hell with the sole intention of bearing witness before the world and aiding the victims"[25]); The text of the "statement", including the part published by the NMT, is included here as Appendix A; the "statement" plays no great role in the analysis but the reader should examine it sometime. It is absolutely insane. It is no marvel that people who can take this story seriously have remarked on the "ambiguity of good" and feel "a certain malaise, an inability to arrive at a full explanation of Gerstein as a person."[26] *The Deputy* opens with "Gerstein" forcing his way into the reception room of the Papal Legation on the Rauchstrasse in Berlin, breathlessly relating the story of his "statement" to the Papal Nuncio!

It is thoroughly unforgivable that Hilberg and Reitlinger use such an obviously spurious "statement" as a source, and without apology. Reitlinger, however, points out that Hitler never visited Lublin, as the "statement" asserts.[27]

DEGESCH was not the only firm involved in the "extermination" business. The firm of Tesch and Stabenow supplied customers with Zyklo

and also with equipment for "extermination chambers" which were of typical volume ten cubic meters and smaller. In Chapter II we saw that there apparently existed such a "gas chamber" at Dachau which was, of course, represented as a murder chamber in the early phases of the propaganda, although today no attempt is made to claim it is anything other than a "disinfection room".

Tesch and Weinbacher, officers of the firm of Tesch and Stabenow, who had sold some "extermination chamber" equipment to the camp at Gross-Rosen, were hanged for their role in the extermination business, their plea that they did not know that their merchandise was to be used for purposes other than disinfection, and their alternate plea that an order of the SS could not be refused, having been rejected by the British military court.[28]

Paragraph 7

According to affidavits given by Hoess and Entress in 1947[29] the first gas chambers, put into operation in the summer of 1942 (now contradicting the affidavit of 1946) were makeshift affairs consisting of two old peasant houses made air tight, with windows sealed up. At the "Auschwitz trial" in 1963–1965 it was held that the "bunker" in Fig. 29 was one of these early gas chambers.[30] The nature of later "gas chambers" is examined below.

This is a good point at which to raise objections regarding lines of responsibility and authority in these operations. Hoess says he received his order directly from Himmler during, we have agreed to pretend, the summer of 1942. This means that Himmler not only bypassed Gluecks, but also Pohl in giving this order directly to the camp commandant, specifying that Gluecks was not to learn what was going on. Himmler reached three levels or more down to give the order and specified that Hoess was to maintain an impossible secrecy. Most irregular.

That is not all. The story we are offered, by the Hoess affidavit and testimony and all other sources is that (except for certain later developments to be discussed) the German Government left the means of killing, and the materials required, a matter for the judgment and ingenuity of the local camp commandant. Hoess decides to convert two old peasant houses. Hoess found the Zyklon kicking around the camp and decided that it offered a more efficient method of solving the Jewish problem than that employed at Treblinka, where they had scrounged up some captured Russian tanks and trucks to use for exterminations. All of this is idiotic and Reitlinger is obviously uncomfortable with the "problem" of the responsibility for the Zyklon decision but gets nowhere with the difficulty except to make it graver by suggesting that Hitler(!) finally decided on the Zyklon "with misgiving".[31]

We are told that those Jews not fit for work were gassed immediately upon arrival (and hence do not appear in any written records, for the most part), but an account directly in conflict with this claim appears even in the WRB report.

According to that report a transport of four or five thousand Jews from Theresienstadt, travelling as families, arrived at Birkenau in September 1943. They kept their baggage and were lodged as families in the camp sector designated in Fig. 29. They were allowed to correspond freely, a school was set up for the children, and the men were not obliged to work. They were considered to be in six months quarantine. It is said that they were gassed on 7 March 1944 and that "the young people went to their deaths singing." The relatives of these Jews got mail from them dated 23 or 25 March, but it is claimed that the mail had been written on March 1 and post-dated, in obedience to German orders.

This procedure was repeated with another group of Jewish families,

5,000 people who arrived from Theresienstadt in December 1943, and whose quarantine was due for expiration in June 1944. Some men were put to work. According to what are said to be surviving records, in May 1944 two thousand were on the employment list, 1,452 were still in quarantine, and 1,575 were considered "in readiness for transport" (*"Vorbereitung zum Transport"*), which Reitlinger considers to mean in reality "waiting for the gas chambers". This was repeated a second time with a group of Theresienstadt families which arrived in May 1944.[32] Since these people were put into "quarantine" it is a certainty that their quarters had been disinfected with the Zyklon just prior to their moving in and perhaps at periods while they were living there. Now we are asked to believe that the Germans planned to kill them with the same chemical product later on!

Essentially the same story was repeated in IMT testimony.[33] The presence of such material in the WRB report is no mystery. Whatever was happening to the Theresienstadt Jews in 1943—1944 was fairly well known in Europe. In October 1943, when 360 Jews were deported from Denmark, they were sent to Theresienstadt, "where the Danish king could be assured of their safety."[34] We noted in the preceding chapter the Red Cross visit of June 1944; the Red Cross involvement with Theresienstadt receives further treatment in the next chapter. In a 1945 visit the Red Cross reported transfers to Auschwitz in 1944, adding no sinister interpretations.

To describe the Theresienstadt Jews as "in readiness for transport" just before their quarantine was to expire was perfectly logical, since it is known that many Theresienstadt Jews were being deported East. A source sponsored by the Israeli government, who had been at Theresienstadt, reports that from 1941 to 1944 the Germans were transporting Theresienstadt Jews to such places as Minsk in Russia and Riga in Latvia. One must have passed by quite a few "extermination camps" to travel from Theresienstadt to those cities. The source also reports that young Theresienstadt Jews were eager to volunteer for transports to Auschwitz as late as August 1944.[35] Rabbi Leo Baeck has claimed that somebody escaped from Auschwitz in August 1943, and made his way back to Theresienstadt, where he told Baeck of gassings. Baeck has explained why he told nobody else of this at the time so that, we will no doubt be told, explains how it was possible that all those people were, in their "ignorance", so eager to go to Auschwitz.[36]

The part of the Auschwitz legend touching on the Theresienstadt Jews is obvious nonsense even without contrary evidence, however. It is not believable that the Germans would quarter for six months at Birkenau each of three distinct groups of people of a category for which there exists an extermination program at Birkenau. The dual role of the Zyklon in this story merely effects passage from the nonsensical to the incomparably ludicrous.

If we examine the other extant source of what is said to be statistical data concerning transports to Auschwitz, we meet the same situation. The data offered in the Netherlands Red Cross reports is more reliable than that offered in the WRB report, although it is rather limited. Nevertheless, as shown in Appendix C, the data shows that virtually all of the male Jews who were deported from the Netherlands to Auschwitz in July and August of 1942 entered Birkenau and were given registration numbers. It is also known that these Dutch Jews wrote letters to acquaintances in the Netherlands in which they described the work at Auschwitz as "hard" but "tolerable", the food "adequate", the sleeping accomodations "good", the hygienic conditions "satisfactory" and the general treatment "correct" (this was reported by the Jewish Council in Amsterdam which claimed, however, that it knew of only 52 such letters). To Reitlinger, these things are "mysteries" for, he says, "at certain periods, entire transports were admitted."[37]

The term "spot decisions" has not been used subsequent to the Hoess affidavit, so far as we know. The common term is "selections"; the story is that "selections" were made on incoming transports on a basis of suitability for work. This, of course, must be essentially true; given the extent and variety of the industrial operations at Auschwitz, selections were required not only on a work *vs.* no work basis but also on, e.g., a light work *vs.* heavy work basis. Other factors which must have figured in this connection were whether a given transport was composed of prisoners, volunteer laborers, Jews being resettled (such as the Theresienstadt Jews) or other. The transports were no doubt also screened for certain key professionals, such as medical personnel, engineers, skilled craftsmen, etc.. The extermination legend merely claims that one category sought in these elaborate sortings and selections was all non-employable Jews, destined for extermination. This claim has already been seriously undermined by the evidence.

Selections on incoming transports are not the only mode of gas chamber selections which have been claimed. A Dutch Jew, Dr. Elie A. Cohen, was arrested in 1943 for attempting to leave the Netherlands without authority. In September he and his family were shipped to Auschwitz and he was separated from his family, which he never saw again. He later wrote a book, *Human Behavior in the Concentration Camp,* based on his experiences as a member of the hospital staff at Auschwitz I. Since Cohen's contact with the people who were being exterminated was of a doctor-patient nature, it was necessary to produce an extraordinary descriptive term for his book, and "objective" was as good a choice as any.

Cohen interprets certain selections in the hospital as selections for the gas chamber:[38]

After the "H.K.B. (camp hospital) administrative room" had given warning that the camp physician was about to make a selection, the whole block became a hive of activity, for everything had to be spic-and-span. . . . while everybody stood at attention, he made his entry with his retinue: S.D.G. (medical service orderly), Blockaelteste and block clerk. The sick Jews were already lined up — as a matter of course, naked. Simultaneously with the presentation of the card with the personal notes concerning each prisoner, to the camp physician, the block physician, in whose ear the diagnosis was being whispered by the room physician, introduced the patient in question to him. . . . in 90 per cent of the cases the card was handed to the S.D.G., which meant death by gassing for the patient, unless the political department gave orders to the contrary, which frequently occurred in the case of "Schutzhaeftlinge" (people charged with ordinary crime).

Not only emaciated prisoners, but also some who looked well fed were sometimes consigned to the gas chamber; and occasionally even members of the H.K.B. staff, who were officially exempt, had to suffer a similar fate. Therefore, especially when one considered the "medical style" of the camp physician, it was generally supposed that it was not only people incapable of work who were scheduled for killing, but that the decisive factor must be that a certain number of persons had to be gassed.

Officially no one knew what the final object actually was, not even the staff of the administrative room, for after the names of the gassed the initials S.B., short for "Sonderbehandlung" (special treatment) were placed.

Cohen does not report having seen any gas chambers; the only evidence which he draws on to support a "gassing" interpretation of such scenes (such interpretation certainly not being evident from the raw facts) consists in the post-war claims of extermination at Auschwitz and also in that there were rumors inside the camp of extermination somewhere at Auschwitz. The existence of such rumors is practically certain since a delegate of the International Red Cross reported their existence among British POW's at Auschwitz III in September 1944.[39] However nothing much can be inferred from the existence of rumors, since rumor spreading is an elementary aspect of psychological warfare, and we have seen that the OSS and, of course, the Communists, engaged in rumor spreading and "black propaganda". In fact, knowledgeable officials of the U.S. Government have admitted the "information" spreading. At the Farben trial, prosecuting attorney Minskoff asked defense witness Muench the following question:[40]

> Now, Mr. Witness, isn't it a fact that, during the time you were at Auschwitz, Allied planes dropped leaflets over Kattowitz and Auschwitz informing the population what was going on in Birkenau?

Muench did not know that. Now Minskoff was knowledgeable in this area, since he had been a foreign operations oriented lawyer in the Treasury Department during the war and was presumably well informed on WRB matters; the WRB had collaborated with the Office of War Information on various leaflet operations. Of course the head of the prosecution staff at the Farben trial was DuBois, who had been general counsel of the WRB, who wrote that in his "office in 1944, (he) knew . . . what was going on at Auschwitz," and who chose in his book to reproduce with general approval the part of the testimony containing the Minskoff question.[41] This is good evidence for an American leaflet operation over Auschwitz, although the method seems somewhat crude. My guess is that if the leaflets were indeed dropped, they were dropped at night, and in moderate quantities.

Actually, a leaflet operation was not necessary to get rumors going in the camps, for the highly organized Communists were very active in this area. Their superior organization, which involved systematic illegal listening to radios, had made the other inmates essentially fully dependent on them for "news".[42] Let us remember that it was a small world, even in 1939–1945, and that, on account of the general ease with which information flowed into and out of the camps (a fact noted in the preceding chapter), the Allied stories about the camps would have ultimately and necessarily penetrated into those camps by various routes.

The Red Cross delegate mentioned above had attempted to visit the Auschwitz camps but apparently got no further than the administrative area of Auschwitz I and the quarters of the British POW's. The latter were all the existing conventions entitled him to visit; with regard to other matters the German officers there were "amiable and reticent". The delegate reported without comment that the British POW's had not been able to obtain confirmation of the rumors by consulting camp inmates. It is claimed that, despite these rumors, the British POW's who were interrogated by the Russians after the capture of the camp "knew nothing at all" of the "crimes".[43]

Subsequent events have, of course, changed the rumors into "knowledge" in many cases. Incoming Jews certainly had no suspicions of gassings.[44]

With the "selections" we are offered another fact for dual interpretation. There is no doubt that the extensive industrial and other activities required "selections" of people for various conventional purposes. We are then asked to add an "extermination" purpose to these activities.

Before leaving Cohen, we should note that there were sick emaciated Jews, as well as others, in the Auschwitz I hospital. He further informs us:[45]

. . . The H.K.B. was housed in five good stone-built blocks. There was one block for surgery, one for infectious diseases, one for internal diseases, one for "Schonung" (less serious cases) and Block 28 (X-ray, specialists' rooms, medical experiments, admissions). The sick lay in three bunks, one above another, on straw mattresses, and were dressed in a shirt (with, later, a pair of drawers added), under two cotton blankets and a sheet. Every week the patients were bathed, and every two weeks they were given "clean" underwear and a "clean" sheet; there were few fleas and no lice. Each berth was seldom occupied by more than two persons. But . . . even patients in a state of high fever had to leave their beds to go to the toilet or to wash in the cold lavatory in the mornings. Because of "organizations" from the SS, there were always medicines, though not in sufficient quantities, including even sulfa drugs; these had been brought in by large transports of Jews from every European country.

He adds that hospital conditions were much worse in other camps (about which he has only read).

The Auschwitz I hospital was obviously no luxury establishment but nevertheless it showed a serious concern, on the part of the Germans, for the recovery of inmates, including Jews, who had fallen ill. This observation also opposes the claim that those not fit for work were killed. Cohen reports certain selections of an incompletely known character, in connection with unknown destinations. It may be that those considered of no further use as labor were sent to Birkenau; this would be very reasonable since it has been shown that the unemployables from the Monowitz hospital were sent to Birkenau.

The term "special treatment", *Sonderbehandlung*, is supposed to have been one of the code words for gassing. When it is said that N Jews in a transport to Auschwitz were gassed, and that this is according to some German record or document, it is the case that the word *"Sonderbehandlung"* is being interpreted as meaning gassing. The documents in question are two in number, and are printed (not reproduced from originals) in a 1946 publication of the Polish Government. Both documents are said to be signed by an SS Lieutenant Schwarz. They state that from several Jewish transports from Breslau and Berlin to Auschwitz in March 1943, a certain fraction of Jews were selected for labor, and that the remainder were *sonderbehandelt*. As far as I know, these documents are not Nuernberg documents; the originals, if they exist (which I am not denying), are in Polish archives.[46]

On account of this relatively well publicized interpretation of the term *"Sonderbehandlung"*, Cohen thinks that he has read "S.B." in the notes made in the Auschwitz I hospital, but it is likely that he misread "N.B.", *nach Birkenau* (to Birkenau).

There exists a document, apparently genuine, from the Gestapo District Headquarters, Duesseldorf, which specifies the manner in which executions of certain offending foreign workers were to be carried out, and which uses the term *"Sonderbehandlung"* as meaning execution. There is also a document, put into evidence at Eichmann's trial, which referred to the execution of three Jews as *Sonderbehandlung*.[47]

Thus it seems correct that, in certain contexts, the term meant execution, but it is at least equally certain that its meaning was no more univocal in the SS than the meaning of "special treatment" is in English speaking countries. There is completely satisfactory evidence of this. At the IMT trial prosecutor Amen led Kaltenbrunner, under cross examination, into conceding that the term might have meant execution as ordered by Himmler. Then, in an attempt to implicate Kaltenbrunner personally in *Sonderbehandlung*, Amen triumphantly produced a document which presents Kaltenbrunner as ordering *Sonderbehandlung* for certain people. Amen wanted Kaltenbrunner to comment on the document without reading it, and there was an angry exchange in this connection, but Kaltenbrunner was finally allowed to read the document, and he then quickly pointed out that the *Sonderbehandlung* referred to in the document was for people at "Winzerstube" and at "Walzertraum", that these two establishments were fashionable hotels which quartered interned notables, and that *Sonderbehandlung* in their cases meant such things as permission to correspond freely and to receive parcels, a bottle of champagne per day, etc..[48]

Poliakov reproduces some documents which show that *Sonderbehandlung* had yet another meaning within the SS. The documents deal with procedures to be followed in the event of pregnancies caused by illegal sexual

112

intercourse involving Polish civilian workers and war prisoners. A racial examination was held to decide between abortion and "germanization" of the baby (adoption by a German family). The term *"Sonderbehandlung"* was a reference either to the germanization or to the abortion. In addition, at Eichmann's trial, some documents were put into evidence which dealt with the treatment of 91 children from Lidice, Bohemia-Moravia. These children had been orphaned by the reprisals which had been carried out at Lidice after Heydrich's assassination. A certain number were picked out for germanization and the remainder were sent to the Displaced Persons Center in Lodz (Litzmannstadt), operated by the RuSHA. The commander of the Center, Krumey, regarded the children as a special case within the Center, to be given *Sonderbehandlung* while at the Center. The term or its equivalent (*eine gesonderte Behandlung*) was also used in the Foreign Office in connection with special categories of prisoners of war, such as priests.[49]

It is only to a person not accustomed to the German language that the term *"Sonderbehandlung"* sounds like it stands for some very special concept. For a German, however, the term is as diverse in possible application as "special treatment" is in English.

Himmler commented somewhat unclearly on *Sonderbehandlung* when he examined the "Korherr report", documents NO-5193 through 5198. Korherr was the chief SS statistician and thus, in late 1942 and early 1943, he prepared a report for Himmler on the situation regarding European Jews. In March 1943 he reported that a total of 1,873,594 Jews of various nationalities had been subjected to a program of "evacuation", with a parenthetical note "including Theresienstadt and including *Sonderbehandlung*". The report also gave numbers of Jews in ghettos in Theresienstadt, Lodz and the General Government, the number in concentration camps, and the number in German cities on account of a special status conferred for economic reasons. It was also remarked that, from 1933 to 31 December 1942, 27,347 Jews had died in German concentration camps.

After Himmler examined the report he informed Korherr, through Brandt, that the term *"Sonderbehandlung"* should not be used in the report, and that transport to the East should be specified. Nevertheless the document, as it has come to us, uses the term in the way indicated. The document gives no hint how the term should be interpreted but, since it occurs in such a way that it is linked with Theresienstadt, it is obviously fair to interpret it in a favorable sense, as a reference to some sort of favored treatment.

Shortly later Himmler wrote, in a document said to be initialed by him, that he regarded the "report as general purpose material for later times, and especially for camouflage purposes." What was to be camouflaged is not indicated in the document but, at his trial, Eichmann testified that after the Stalingrad disaster (January 1943) the German Government quickened the pace of the deportations "for camouflage reasons," i.e., to reassure the German people that everything was OK out there. Himmler specified that the Korrherr report was not to be made public "at the moment," but the camouflage remark could still be interpreted in the sense in which Eichmann suggested (Eichmann's statement was not in connection with the Korherr report.)[50]

Other documents are 003-L, a letter by SS General Katzmann, speaking of 434,329 resettled (*ausgesiedelt*) Jews of southern Poland as having been *sonderbehandelt*, and NO-246, a letter from Artur Greiser to Himmler dated 1 May 1942, asking permission to give *Sonderbehandlung*, specified as getting them "locked up" (*abgeschlossen*), to about 100,000 Jews in the Warthegau (part of annexed Poland). Greiser was sentenced to death by a Polish court on 20 July 1946, despite the intervention of the Pope on his behalf. There is also

Fig. 11: British guard post at entrance to Belsen camp.

Photo: Imperial War Museum

114

a letter by Lohse, which is discussed in Chapter VI.[51]

Summarizing the situation with respect to documents which speak of *Sonderbehandlung*, we may say that, while one can certainly raise questions regarding the authenticity of the relevant documents, it is nevertheless the case that even if all of the relevant documents are assumed authentic, they do not require an "extermination" interpretation of those that apply to Auschwitz. That the term *"Sonderbehandlung"* had more than one meaning within one agency of the German Government is not very peculiar. For example, I understand that, within the Central Intelligence Agency, "termination" can mean execution or assassination in certain contexts. However, the term obviously could also be applied to the dismissal of a typist for absenteeism.

The point in paragraph 7 of the Hoess affidavit about endeavoring "to fool the victims into thinking that they were to go through a delousing process" is, of course, a logical one since anybody on entering a German camp went through a delousing process such as Hoess described in the affidavit and in his testimony — disrobe, shave, shower.[52] Again we are offered a fact for dual interpretation.

The last subject in paragraph 7 is the cremations; it is a big one. According to Hoess and all other accounts of exterminations, Birkenau cremations took place in trenches or pits prior to the availability of the modern crematory facilities there.[53] It is claimed that the new crematoria were intended for extermination of Jews but we have suggested a more routine purpose in the preceding chapter. Let us review their history.

The construction was well into the preliminary stages of planning and ordering early in 1942 and this fact, in itself, makes it difficult, to say the least, to believe that they were related to any extermination program ordered by Himmler in the summer of 1942. The construction plans for four structures containing crematory furnaces are dated 28 January 1942.[54] On 27 February 1942 the head of the construction department of the WVHA, SS Colonel (later Lieutenant General) Dr. Ing. Hans Kammler, an engineer who also supervised the design of the German V-rocket bases and the underground aircraft factories, visited Auschwitz and held a conference at which it was decided to install five, rather than two (as previously planned), crematory furnaces, each having three ovens or doors.[55] This matter, therefore, was not left to the ingenuity of Hoess. In the extermination legend, however, Hoess definitely gets credit for the Zyklon. The fifteen ovens to be installed in one of the structures or buildings were ordered from Topf and Sons, Erfurt, on 3 August 1942.[56] The ovens were of the standard type which Topf (still in business in Wiesbaden in 1962) sold. Fig. 26 is said to be a photograph of one of the crematoria at Auschwitz. Each oven was designed to take one body at a time, as are all standard cremation ovens; there is no evidence for the installation of any non-standard ovens, such as any designed to take more than one body at a time. Topf had also supplied ovens to camps for which exterminations are not claimed, such as Buchenwald.[57]

The plans for the four buildings containing the crematoria, numbered II, III, IV and V (crematorium I seems to have been the ultimately dormant crematorium at Auschwitz I which contained four ovens[58]), show that a large hall or room existed in each. For II and III, these were below ground level and were designated *Leichenkeller* (mortuary cellar — literally corpse cellar — a German word for mortuary is *Leichenhalle*); their dimensions were height 2.4 meters and area 210 square meters and height 2.3 meters and area 400 square meters, respectively. The halls in the buildings containing the crematoria IV and V were at ground level and were designated *Badeanstalten* (bath establishments); they were each of height 2.3 meters and area 580 square meters. According to the information generated at the "Auschwitz trial" of 1963–1965, these four buildings were located as shown in Fig. 29.

The Auschwitz construction department, in erecting the crematoria, was assisted not only by Topf but also by the SS company DAW (*Deutsche Ausruestungswerke*, German Equipment Factory), which helped with miscellaneous constructions. The first ovens installed were in crematorium II and numbered, as we have noted, fifteen: five three-oven units. The construction took considerable time although, as shown by documents, it was carried out with deliberate haste. The NMT volumes offer us the following English translation of document NO-4473; if the reader thinks he sees something in the document which is hostile to my thesis he should withold judgment:[59]

29 January 1943

To the Chief Amtsgruppe C, SS Brigadefuehrer and Brigadier General of the Waffen SS, Dr. Ing. Kammler

Subject: Crematorium II, condition of the building.

The crematorium II has been completed — save for some minor constructional work — by the use of all the forces available, in spite of unspeakable difficulties, the severe cold, and in 24 hour shifts. The fires were started in the ovens in the presence of Senior Engineer Pruefer, representative of the contractors of the firm of Topf and Soehne, Erfurt, and they are working most satisfactorily. The planks from the concrete ceiling of the cellar used as a mortuary (*Leichenkeller*) could not yet be removed on account of the frost. This is, however, not very important, as the gas chamber can be used for that purpose.

The firm of Topf and Soehne was not able to start deliveries of the installation in time for aeration and ventilation as had been requested by the Central Building Management because of restrictions in the use of railroad cars. As soon as the installation for aeration and ventilation arrive, the installing will start so that the complete installation may be expected to be ready for use 20 February 1943.

We enclose a report (not attached to document) of the testing engineer of the firm of Topf and Soehne, Erfurt.

The Chief of the Central Construction Management,
Waffen SS and Police Auschwitz,
SS Hauptsturmfuehrer

Distribution: 1–SS Ustuf. Janisch u. Kirschneck; 1–Filing office (file crematorium); Certified true copy: (Signature illegible) SS Ustuf. (F)

I interpret this as meaning that, although all work for crematorium II was not completed, the ovens could be used in January 1943 for cremations, despite the impossibility of using the *"Leichenkeller"*.

On 12 February 1943 Topf wrote to Auschwitz acknowledging receipt of an order for five three-oven units for crematorium III, the construction to be completed 10 April. I have not seen any documentation indicating installation of any ovens in crematoria IV and V, unless a letter of 21 August 1942 from an SS 2nd Lieutenant at Auschwitz, mentioning a Topf proposal to install two three-oven units near each of the "baths for special purpose", should be interpreted as such.[60] There was, however, carpentry work done on crematoria IV and V.[61]

This brings us to the problem of the number of ovens at Birkenau; it is a problem because it is said that the Germans demolished the crematoria buildings before abandoning Auschwitz.[62] Obviously, we must assume that there were at least thirty available, fifteen in both crematorium II and crematorium III, sometime in 1943. Evidence for ovens installed in IV and V is decent. It consists mainly in the appearance of a labor Kommando assigned to these crematoria in what is said to be the Birkenau employment roster for 11 May 1944 (the same document the Theresienstadt Jews appear in), plus some witness testimony. The Russians and Poles claimed that each of these crematoria had eight ovens, and that the other two had fifteen each: 46 ovens. The WRB report had specified 36 in both II and III and 18 in IV and V: 108 ovens.[63]

116

Reitlinger claims 60 ovens by assuming that each crematorium had fifteen. His only authority for this is the writings attributed to one Miklos Nyiszli, which we should not accept on anything, least of all a number. The Nyiszli account purports to be a record of personal experiences of a Hungarian Jewish doctor deported to Auschwitz in May 1944. It appeared in French in 1951 in the March-April issues of *Les Temps Modernes,* with a preface by translator T. Kremer. Rassinier has reported on his strenuous subsequent efforts to contact Nyiszli and determine whether or not he actually existed; the only person who seemed to unquestionably exist was translator Kremer.[64] An English translation of Richard Seaver, forward by Bruno Bettelheim, was published in New York in 1960 under the title *Auschwitz*. Nyiszli was obviously dead by then since it is specified that the copyright is held by "N. Margareta Nyiszli". As is the usual practice with deceased authors who held doctor's degrees, the title page of a doctoral thesis, by "Nicolaus Nyiszli", Breslau 1930, is reproduced in the 1960 N.Y. edition. The book was republished in French and German editions in 1961.

According to Rassinier, it is difficult enough to reconcile the numbers in the various editions, but it is not even possible to get internal consistency in one edition. In the 1960 edition we read (p. 55) that the 60 ovens could reduce "several thousand" corpses per day. Further on (p. 87) we are told that "when the two (burning pits) were operating simultaneously, their output varied from five to six thousand dead a day, slightly better than the crematoriums", but then later on (p. 92) we learn that crematoria II and III could alone dispose of at least 10,500 per day. This is total confusion.

The writings attributed to Nyiszli also commit what I consider the basic witness-disqualifying act; they claim gratuitous regular beatings of initially healthy prisoners by the SS (e.g. pp. 25, 27, 44, 57); it is known that this was not the case. Aside from possible humanitarian objections to such beatings, the prisoners were a source of income to the SS. Many were the complaints, on the part of the SS, against various forms of alleged Farben mistreatment. On the other hand, for security reasons, the SS discouraged fraternization between guards and prisoners. The SS guard was ordered to maintain "distance" (*Abstand*) from the prisoners, not even talking to them unless absolutely necessary. This regulation was of course difficult to enforce and the regular and very frequent infringements of it produced memoranda from Pohl to the camp commanders ordering appropriate and systematic instruction of the guards.[65]

Despite a certain amount of mention of SS guard brutality as reported by authors of other books, Cohen does not report such experiences at Auschwitz and remarks that the "reception ceremony" for his transport "passed without violence." However, he mentions a specially constructed wooden table used for beating prisoners on the buttocks. This was a formally regulated mode of punishment of prisoners who committed various offenses in the camps; "intensified" beating was defined as whacking on the *naked* buttocks.[66]

When an Auschwitz witness starts claiming regular gratuitous beating, he may be telling the truth on some matters, but one must reject his general credibility.

On the basis of the available evidence, the best assumption is that there were 30 ovens available at Birkenau in the spring of 1943, and 46 a year later. Before leaving the subject of the number of ovens, we should remark that there are certain ambiguities in the documents relating to the crematoria. The most obvious is due to the fact that the WRB report does not seem to be the only source which mistakenly numbers the Birkenau crematoria I–IV rather than II–V; the Germans sometimes did this themselves, or so it would appear from, e.g., NO-4466.[67]

The limit on the rate at which people could have been exterminated in a program of the type alleged is not determined by the rate at which people could have been gassed and the gas chambers ventilated, but by the rate at which the bodies could have been cremated. In estimating the capacity of the crematoria, it is possible for arithmetic to produce some impressive figures. At that time an hour was a very optimistic time to allow for the reduction of one body, and the body's being wasted would not have made much difference.[68] If we allow for one hour of cleaning and miscellaneous operations per day, one oven could reduce perhaps 23 bodies per day so 30 ovens could reduce 690 and 46 ovens could reduce 1058 per day. This could accommodate exterminations at the respectable rate of about 240,000 to 360,000 per year, but of course one must bear in mind that, since the exterminations are supposed to have been halted in the autumn of 1944, Auschwitz could not have had 46 ovens for more than about one year of exterminations.

However the logic leading to such figures as the preceding is rubbish; things do not work that way. People, especially concentration camp inmates, who manned the crematoria, do not work with such efficiency, such equipment cannot be used in such a continuous manner, and equipment needs do not occur with such mathematical regularity in any case. If we allow operations to relax toward something more realistic, take into account downtime for regular and irregular maintenance and allow for usual engineering margins of excess capacity we have figures that are generally in line with anticipated epidemic conditions. It is also possible that, as the WRB report asserts, there was a backlog of buried bodies to dispose of.

It is obvious that, given a policy of cremating dead inmates, a vast operation such as Auschwitz would naturally provide relatively elaborate crematoria facilities for the purpose. Thus we again have a fact for dual interpretation if we are to believe the extermination legend; to the commonplace interpretation of these ovens, unquestionably valid, it is proposed that we also accept as valid a second interpretation of exterminations. Below we will examine specific evidence that the number of ovens was completely compatible with the rate of "normal" deaths.

That is not the last fact for dual interpretation which we are offered in connection with the cremations. Hoess tells us that "all of the people living in the surrounding communities knew that exterminations were going on" on account of the "foul and nauseating stench from the continuous burning of bodies". If I were to select just two points in the extermination tale to hold up as near proof that the whole thing is a hoax, it would be this point and also the alleged role of the Zyklon.

The hydrogenation and other chemical industry which existed at Auschwitz is notorious for creating stenches. Visit the northern part of the New Jersey Turnpike by the Standard Oil (N.J.) refineries, or any other refineries, to see (or smell) this. The only significant difference Auschwitz presented, in terms of a stench, is that the coal the Germans started from is by any relevant measure a "dirtier" source than crude oil. If we are told that 30 to 46 bodies being reduced in modern crematoria could even compete with, much less overwhelm, this stench of industrial origin then we know that what is involved here is not a fact for dual interpretation but an obvious lie. Actually, on account of the furor of phony objections raised by various fanatics in the nineteenth and early twentieth centuries, cremation had been developed so that it was a rather "clean" process.[69] Hoess cannot be believed.

The analysis has revealed a previously unsuspected but nearly inevitable attribute of the great hoax: the excess fact. Following the principle that his story should involve mostly or almost entirely valid fact, the author of the hoax easily slips into the error of including *as much fact as possible* and commits the major blunder we have just seen; the story would obviously have been much better off without *that* "fact". Of course, it is only on account of the passage of time that it has become a major blunder. At the time it was completely effective on account of an hysterical emotional atmosphere that it is impossible to recapture. DuBois wrote in 1952:[70]

On the stand Schneider had said that he never heard of any exterminations, although he recalled going along the main road one day, past a "dormant crematorium". At that time this "dormant" crematorium was burning corpses at the rate of a thousand a day. The flames shot fifteen meters into the air; the stink pervaded the countryside to the north for forty miles until it joined the stink of the Warsaw crematorium; the fumes would pucker the nose of anyone within half a mile, and Schneider – a scientist with a specially acute sense of smell – had passed within a hundred yards of the place.

It does not seem possible that, toward the end of a book which gives (outside of technical literature) the best available description of the chemical industry at Auschwitz, DuBois could write thus, but there it is. It is not explicable in terms of normal errors of judgment; it is explicable only in terms of hysteria.

It would seem that somebody at the trial would have challenged Hoess on this point. There was a challenge, but it was weak and ambiguous. The following exchange occurred near the end of Hoess' testimony (Kauffman was counsel for Kaltenbrunner):[71]

THE PRESIDENT: The last sentence of Paragraph 7 is with reference to the foul and nauseating stench. What is your question about that?

DR. KAUFMAN: Whether the population could gather from these things that an extermination of Jews was taking place.

THE PRESIDENT: That really is too obvious a question, isn't it? They could not possibly know who it was being exterminated.

DR. KAUFMAN: That is enough for me. I have no further questions.

It is possible that there was a language difficulty at the time of this exchange, and that a misunderstanding existed, and that Kaufman really meant "people" rather than "Jews" in his question. In any case this episode suggests the utterly irrational atmosphere which must have pervaded the IMT trial; Hoess was not caught in a clumsy and transparent lie. It is not possible for us to grasp the spirit of these proceedings except to classify them as a form of hysteria. Speer was there, and he could have seen through this lie easily. Was he effectively asleep, resigned to the futility of opposition? Was he or his lawyer merely being careful to avoid becoming entangled in the extermination question? Only he can tell us; we do not know. All that is certain is that the spirit of the trial was such that even a simple truth such as the true source of the stench, exposing with great deftness that the witness was lying, and suggesting the nature of the factual basis for the charges, could not emerge.

The stench was the basis for quite a bit of witness testimony to knowledge of exterminations[72], and its use at one particular point of the Farben trial, to be discussed in a later chapter, was not only rather amusing but also revealing and illustrative of an important point to bear in mind when reading the records of these trials. This is discussed later.

In his booklet, Christophersen considered the problem of the factual basis, if any, for references to a pervasive stench at Auschwitz. The only thing he could recall was a blacksmith establishment at Auschwitz I; when horses were being shod the burning hoofs created a stench which could be perceived in the immediate neighborhood. Christophersen recognizes that this could not account for a stench of the extent claimed in connection with the exterminations.

I communicated with Christophersen on this point, inquiring into the possibility that Christophersen might have forgotten the stench of industrial origin, in searching his memory for some stench that might have approximated the stench of burning flesh. Christophersen recalled no stench of industrial origin. I also communicated with Staeglich, who distinctly recalled only clean and fresh air near Auschwitz.

The recollections of Christophersen and Staeglich are however consistent with the theory that the stench of the hoax is none other than the stench associated with the Farben plant. With reference to Fig. 5, the map of the Auschwitz area, Christophersen was quartered at Raisko during his year at Auschwitz, and had occasional business at Auschwitz I and Birkenau. Staeglich was quartered in the town of Osiek, which is about 6 miles due south of the town of Oswiecim, and mentions that he visited the *"KZ-Lager Auschwitz"* (presumably meaning Auschwitz I) "three or four times". We do not know exactly where the Farben plants were, but we know that the camp called "Monowitz" was either within or immediately next to the town of Monowitz, and that the camp had been placed there so that it would be close to the Farben plants. In consideration of the locations of the rail lines, rivers and roads in the area, it is probable that the Farben plants were either immediately to the east or to the west of the town Monowitz. If the former, they were four or five miles from Auschwitz I and, thus, people at that camp, at Birkenau, and *a fortiori* at Raisko and Osiek would never have smelled the chemical industry (which was very modest in size compared to a typical American cracking plant). If the Farben plants were immediately to the west of the town, it is possible that people at Auschwitz I might have gotten a whiff now and then when peculiar wind conditions prevailed, but that could not qualify as a *pervasive* stench. Thus, close consideration of the point shows that Christophersen and Staeglich should not have experienced the stench of industrial origin to any extent that they would recall thirty years later. Moreover, the trial at which the pervasive stench was a pervasive feature of witness testimony was the Farben trial, at which most of the Auschwitz related defense witnesses and almost all of the prosecution witnesses were people who either lived near or worked at the Farben plant. Thus they did, indeed, experience a stench and testified correctly in this respect, adding only an erroneous interpretation of the stench.

The final subject in paragraph 7 is the gas chambers which, except for Hoess' early sealed up huts, are supposed to have been integrated into the crematoria buildings. Reitlinger and Hilberg take different approaches to making this claim. Reitlinger interprets NO-4473, whose translation as it appears in the NMT volume is presented above (p. 116), as evidence for a gas chamber in crematorium II. This is a result of mistranslation.

The crematoria at Auschwitz are frequently referred to as "gas ovens" but this is hardly informative since, with the exception of electric cremators which enjoyed a brief existence during the Thirties, all modern crematoria consist of "gas ovens"; a fuel-air mixture, which may be considered a "gas", is introduced into the oven to start, control and finish the burning. The fuel used may be "gas"; town gas or some sort of liquefied gas is popular. Such a cremator is termed "gas-fired" on account of the use of gas as a fuel. Other types are "oil-fired" and "coke (or coal) -fired", but all are "gas ovens" since in all three cases it is a fuel-air mixture which is injected, under pressure, into the oven.[73]

The customary German word for the concept in question here is *"Gas-kammer"*, but the word in NO-4473 which was translated "gas chamber" is *"Vergasungskeller"*, which Reitlinger also mistranslates as "gassing cellar".[74]

Now the word *Vergasung* has two meanings. The primary meaning (and the only one in a technical context) is gasification, carburetion or vaporization, i.e., turning something into a gas, not applying a gas to something. A *Vergaser* is a carburetor and, while *Vergasung* always means gasification in a technical context, it usually means, specifically, carburetion in such a context.

There is also a secondary meaning of *Vergasung*, established by military usage in World War I: attacking an enemy with gas. Why the word *Vergasung* was used in this sense is not clear; it may be because the gases used in that war were really dusts and were generated by exploding some chemical into the atmosphere: *Vergasung*.

The translation "gassing cellar" is thus not absolutely incorrect; it is just over-hasty and presumptuous. A "gas oven" requires some sort of gasification or carburetion. In the case of the gas-fired ovens of Utting and Rogers in 1932:[75]

> Burners set in the crown and sole of the furnace are fed by a mixture of air and gas under pressure; the mixture is regulated by fans, housed in a separate building. Separate control of both air and gas provides better regulation of the furnace temperature.

That building is just a big carburetor. Oil-fired crematoria are so similar in design that most gas-fired ovens can be easily adapted for use with oil.

The ovens at Birkenau seem to have been coke or coal-fired,[76] and with this type there is an extra stage of fuel processing due to the initially solid state of the fuel. The two most common methods of producing fuel gases from coal or coke are, first, by passing air through a bed of burning coke to produce "coke oven gas" and second, by passing steam through the coke to produce "water gas".[77] The first coke cremators employed what amounted to coke oven gas.[78] Processes for generating such gases are termed *"Vergasung"* in German, as well as processes of mixing them with air. The coal-fired crematory ovens that W. H. Lawrence saw at the Lublin camp after its capture by the Russians employed equipment, including fans, very similar to that described in the above quotation. Lawrence, incidentally, termed a "gas chamber" what was obviously a steam bath.[79]

In any case it is obvious that the crematoria at Auschwitz required equipment for doing *Vergasung* in order to inject a fuel-air mixture into the ovens and that the translation of NO-4473 should be revised, possibly to "gas generation cellar". I have confirmed this interpretation of the *"Vergasungskeller"* with technically competent sources in Germany. The reasons for installing such equipment in special separate rooms or even buildings are most probably the considerable noise that must be made by the fans and, in coal-fired ovens, the heat of the burning coal.

The primary meaning of the word *Vergasung* is of necessity applicable to document NO-4473. It is written in a technical context; it is a letter from the chief of the Auschwitz construction management to the head of the SS engineering group. It makes reference to a process, *Vergasung,* which is standard with all crematoria, and the wording of the letter is such that it is implied that it would normally be peculiar to find bodies in the *Vergasungskeller,* since bodies are normally stored in what is correctly translated as the "cellar used as a mortuary".

Document NO-4473 tends, in fact, like so many prosecution documents, to rejection of the prosecution's claims when it is properly understood. We see that in crematorium II there were at least two cellars, a *Leichenkeller* and a *Vergasungskeller,* and that neither was a "gas chamber".

Now NO-4473 is included in the NMT volumes in a *selection* of prosecution evidence from Case 4 (trial of concentration camp administration). One must assume that the prosecution has selected well. Yet this is as close as it has gotten to offering documentary evidence that "gas chambers" existed in the crematoria buildings at Birkenau. The three "gas tight *Tuerme*" ordered from DAW in NO-4465[80] are obviously irrelevant.

Hilberg takes a different and even less sound approach. He inexplicably passes over NO-4473 without dealing with the problem it raises; he even quotes from the document without quoting the phrase containing the word *"Vergasungskeller"*. He simply declares that the *Leichenkeller* in crematoria II and III and the *Badeanstalten* in crematoria IV and V were, in reality, gas chambers. Absolutely no evidence is offered for this; the documents cited by Hilberg at this point do not speak of gas chambers.[81] The only "evidence" for intepreting the *Leichenkeller* and *Badeanstalten* in this manner is in the affidavits and testimony (27 and 28 June 1947) in Case 4 of witness (not a defendant) Wolfgang Grosch, an engineer and Waffen-SS major, who "baptised" these as "gas chambers", the existence of the Zyklon at Auschwitz being obvious justification for such baptisms.[82] However, Grosch was a very unsteady witness since in affidavits of 20 February and 5 March 1947, he claimed knowledge of the existence of gas chambers and then on 26 June 1947, the day before he was to testify, he retracted all these statements during interrogation, and denied any knowledge of gas chambers.[83] None of Grosch's testimony is reproduced in the NMT volumes, and Hilberg does not cite his testimony or affidavits.

There is no reason to accept, and every reason to reject, the claims regarding the *Leichenkeller* and *Badeanstalten*. As for the *Leichenkeller*, we have observed that there was nothing peculiar about mortuary facilities existing at Auschwitz, and even document NO-4473 shows that the crematorium II *Leichenkeller* was intended as a mortuary. As for the *Badeanstalten,* we have observed that a shower for incoming inmates was standard procedure at all German camps, so there must have been showers at Birkenau. Now, according to Fig. 29 the "baths" or *Badeanstalten* associated with crematoria IV and V are near "filtration plants" and also near "Canada", where the clothing of incoming inmates was stored.[84] The "steam bath" was no doubt for disinfecting clothes, either prior to storage or after being temporarily taken away from inmates.[85] If it was a sauna for incoming inmates, the inmates would need a cold shower afterwards in any case. The people remove their clothing near "Canada" and then shower. What could be simpler?

No reasonable considerations can make these gas chambers materialize. The claim that the shower baths which are said to have been housed in the same buildings as some of the crematorium ovens were really gas chambers is just as unfounded as was the identical claim concerning the Dachau shower bath which existed in the crematorium building at that camp.

There is, incidentally, a small amount of doubt whether the shower baths were, indeed, in the same buildings as crematoria IV and V, since the camp plan given in the WRB report has the baths in a separate building. However, the point is of no importance.

This completes the analysis of the points raised in paragraph 7 of the Hoess affidavit.

Final Paragraph

This is a minor point. It seems strange that the Hoess affidavit is in English. We are not aware of any evidence that Hoess knew the English language but, in common with many Germans, he might have known something about it.

However a prudent German, signing a document of this importance "voluntarily and without compulsion", would not be satisfied with an ordinary foreign language ability; he would either have considered himself expert at

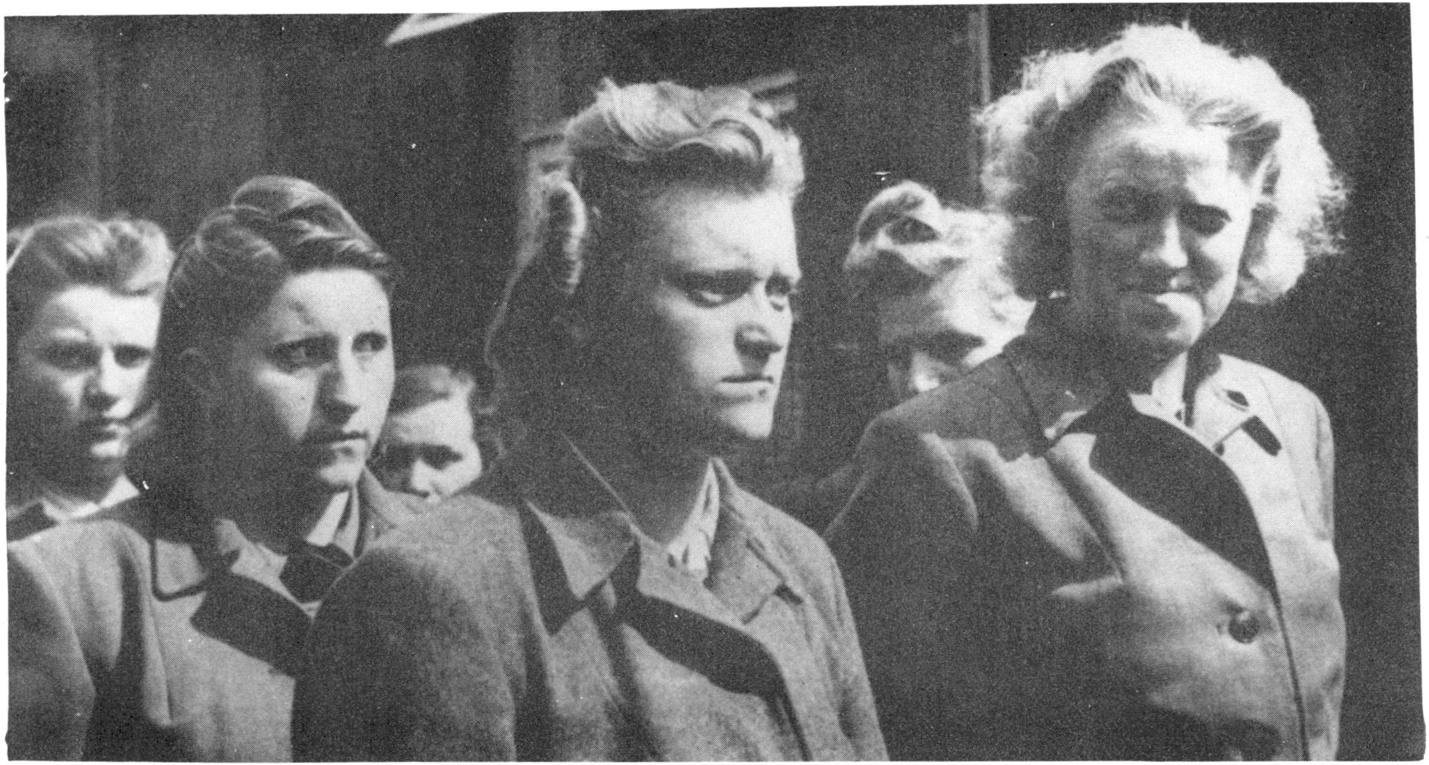

Fig. 12: Women guards at Belsen, lined up after capture of the camp.

123

English or he would have insisted upon a German translation to sign (a request that would necessarily have been honored). Hoess was evidently not in a spirit to insist on anything.

There is no doubt that Hoess hoped to buy his life by cooperating with the IMT prosecution, and it is most probable that a specific offer was made in this connection. However Hoess' reward for his services was to be packed off to Poland about a month after his IMT testimony. In Poland he dutifully wrote out an "autobiography" for his captors, wherein he explained that he was just following orders in the exterminations. His reward on this occasion was final; he was "tried" and killed in April 1947. The "autobiography" was published in Polish translation in 1951 and in German and English in 1959.

The Role of Birkenau

Birkenau, of course, performed the normal functions of a German concentration camp; it quartered inmates for the principal or ultimate aim of exploiting their labor. Thus when we refer to the "role" of Birkenau, we are referring to a theory that Birkenau was the site of certain very special functions which bear particularly strongly on the matters we have been considering.

The theory, which I consider beyond dispute, is simply that Birkenau was designated to accomodate all persons who were in the non-worker category but were, for whatever reason, the responsibility of the Auschwitz SS administration. Thus Birkenau was designated to receive the permanently or semi-permanently ill, the dying, the dead, the underage, the overage, those temporarily unassigned to employment, and those for whom Auschwitz served as a transit camp. These categories could have been received either from other camps (including the many small camps in the Kattowitz region) or from incoming transports. This theory is based on the following considerations.

First, as has been noted, Birkenau was clearly the "principal" camp in terms of inmate accomodating functions. Auschwitz I was the "main" camp in an administrative sense but it was a converted and expanded military barracks while Birkenau had been designed from the beginning as a much larger camp intended for the specific needs of the SS operations in the area.

Second, it has been noted that people discharged from the Monowitz hospital as unfit for work were sent to Birkenau.

Third, family camps existed at Birkenau (the "gipsy" and "Theresienstadt" camps in Fig. 29). It has been seen that these people had been designated as being "in readiness for transport" during their stays of pre-specified limited duration, so that the obvious interpretation of these family camps is that they were transit camps, comparable to those which existed at Belsen and Westerbork. The destination of transport has been suggested and will be discussed further in a later chapter.

Fourth, it was only at Birkenau that unusually extensive facilities for disposal of the dead via cremation were constructed.

Fifth, it was quite normal for a very high proportion of Birkenau inmates to be unemployed. In the two years summer 1942 to summer 1944, as Reitlinger remarks, "only a fraction of the starved and ailing Birkenau population had been employed at all." On 5 April 1944, 15,000 of the 36,000 Birkenau inmates were considered "unable to work", while only about 3,000 of the 31,000 other prisoners of the Auschwitz area were considered in this category. A month later, two-thirds of the 18,000 inmates of the Birkenau male camp were classed as "immobile", "unemployable" and "unassigned" and were quartered in sick and quarantine blocks.[86]

This makes it impossible, of course, to accept the assumption, so often expressed, that to be sick and unemployable and to be sent to Birkenau meant execution. This has been expressed in particular in connection with sick people being sent from Monowitz to Birkenau, the assumption being reinforced by the fact that such inmates' clothing came back to Monowitz. The return of the clothing, of course, was due to their being transferred from the Farben to the SS budget.[87]

Sixth and last, there was an unusually high death rate at Birkenau, although there are some difficulties in estimating the numbers except at particular times. The first major relevant event is the typhus epidemic of the summer of 1942, which resulted in the closing of the Buna factory for two months starting around 1 August. The major evidence of this is the WRB report,[88] but there is confirming evidence. First, there certainly were typhus epidemics at Auschwitz.[89] Second, the data presented by the Dutch Red Cross (Appendix C) shows that the average death rate at the Birkenau men's camp from 16 July to 19 August 1942 was about 186 per day, with the rates towards the end of the period noticeably higher than those toward the beginning. Third, there exists in Amsterdam a single volume of the Birkenau death book (also discussed in the Netherlands Red Cross report). This volume contains death certificates for the five days 28 September to 2 October 1942. The number of deaths is 1,500, and the causes of death that are given are those typical of typhus epidemic conditions, although Reitlinger seems to consider such recorded causes as "weakness of the heart muscles" and others as "invented . . . fanciful diagnoses of internee doctors, who were trying to save their patients from the 'transport list' or the phenol syringe."[90] In fact such causes of death are typical with typhus; under the TYPHUS FEVER listing in the *Encyclopedia Brittanica* (eleventh edition) we read:

> Typhus fever may, however, prove fatal during any stage of its progress and in the early convalescence, either from sudden failure of the heart's action — a condition which is especially apt to arise — from the supervention of some nervous symptoms, such as meningitis or of deepening coma, or from some other complication, such as bronchitis. Further, a fatal result sometimes takes place before the crisis from sheer exhaustion, particularly in the case of those whose physical or nervous energies have been lowered by hard work, inadequate nourishment and sleep, or intemperance.

On account of the policy of sending sick people to Birkenau it appears that the victims of the typhus epidemic got recorded as Birkenau deaths, regardless of where they had been working. The WRB report claims that there were fifteen to twenty thousand deaths at Auschwitz during the two or three months of the epidemic.[91] Despite the unreliability of the source, the claim seems consistent, at least in order of magnitude, with such other information as we have concerning this period at Auschwitz (although there is probably at least some exaggeration). It is also the case, as we shall see below, that the summer of 1942 was by far the worst at Auschwitz.

Incidentally, the "phenol syringe" which Reitlinger mentions comes up in so many places in the literature that it appears to have been real; mortally ill concentration camp inmates were sometimes killed by phenol injections into the heart.[92]

The fact of a very high death rate at Auschwitz during the summer of 1942 is, of course, at best only indirectly material to any "extermination" problem since these were recorded deaths from normal reasons, not exterminations carried out in attempted secrecy. They also have nothing to do with Jews as such, although some of the victims were Jews.

Reitlinger considers the high death rate at Auschwitz and offers an estimate of 160 to 179 deaths per day as a normal rate. However the data he employs is essentially that which applies to the summer of 1942, which was a particularly catastrophic period. In connection with these high death rates we should observe the fact that the extermination mythologists Reitlinger and Hilberg make much over such happenings at Auschwitz, although they recognize the distinction between high death rates and exterminations. It is therefore remarkable, indeed almost incredible, that they do not consider the possibility that the crematoria existed on account of these high death rates. On the contrary, they both treat the crematoria as having been provided primarily to serve in the extermination program.

In establishments that were supposed to be providing desperately needed labor these high death rates were naturally intolerable, so in late 1942 a special campaign got under way to reduce the concentration camp death rate and on 28 December 1942, Himmler ordered that the rate "be reduced at all costs".[93] On 20 January 1943 Gluecks, in a circular letter to all concentration camp commanders, ordered that "every means must be used to lower the death rate." On 15 March 1943 Pohl wrote Himmler that[94]

> the state of health . . . of the prisoners sent in by the administration of Justice is catastrophic. In all camps a loss of between at least 25-30 per cent is to be reckoned with . . . . till now there were 10,191 prisoners . . . of which 7,587 were assigned to . . . Mauthausen-Gusen. From these the deaths totalled 3,853; 3,306 of them died in Mauthausen-Gusen. The reason . . . must presumably be, that the many prisoners . . . who have been in prisons for years are suffering from physical debility owing to the transfer to a different milieu . . .. a great number of tuberculosis patients were also delivered.

On 10 April Pohl requested Himmler's approval of the draft of a letter to the Reich Minister of Justice. The letter, approved and presumably sent, points out that of 12,658 prisoners transferred to concentration camps, 5,935 had died by 1 April. Pohl complained in the letter that these

> shockingly high mortality figures are due to the fact that the prisons transferring them have literally released inmates who are in the worst possible physical condition (and) that in spite of all medical efforts the . . . death of the prisoners cannot be retarded . . .. I do not wish to support a quarantine station in the concentration camps . . ..

What seems involved here is inter-departmental rivalry or, at least, conflict of interest. The prisons of Germany no doubt had their own economic-productive aspects and were not only reluctant to part with their more healthy prisoners but also eager to part with the more sickly ones.

We do not know whether or not Pohl managed to get more cooperation from the prison system. However on 30 September 1943 he was able to report progress, due mainly to hygienic, nutritional, and procedural measures; he presented the Reichsfuehrer-SS the following two tables with a promise that, allowing for the onset of the cold weather, the results achieved were of a permanent nature:[95]

Death Cases in the Concentration Camps, July 1942 to June 1943

Month	Inmates	Deaths	Percent	Month	Inmates	Deaths	Percent
July	98,000	8,329	8.50	Jan	123,000	9,839	8.00
Aug.	115,000	12,217	10.62	Feb.	143,100	11,650	8.14
Sept.	110,000	11,206	10.19	March	154,200	12,112	7.85
Oct.	85,800	8,856	10.32	April	171,000	8,358	4.71
Nov.	83,500	8,095	9.69	May	203,000	5,700	2.80
Dec.	88,000	8,800	10.00	June	199,500	5,650	2.83

Death Cases for the Month of August 1943

Concentration Camp	Inmates	Deaths	Percent (August)	Percent (July)	Percent Change
Dachau	17,300	40	0.23	0.32	−0.09
Sachsenhausen	26,500	194	0.73	0.78	−0.05
Buchenwald	17,600	118	0.67	1.22	−0.55
Mauthausen-Gusen	21,100	290	1.37	1.61	−0.24
Flossenbuerg	4,800	155	3.23	3.27	−0.04
Neuengamme	9,800	150	1.53	2.14	−0.61
Auschwitz (men)	48,000	1,442	3.00	2.96	+0.04
Auschwitz (women)	26,000	938	3.61	5.15	−1.54

Concentration Camp	Inmates	Deaths	Percent (August)	Percent (July)	Percent Change
Gross-Rosen	5,000	76	1.52	2.69	−1.17
Natzweiler	2,200	41	1.87	1.63	+0.24
Bergen-Belsen	3,300	4	0.12	0.39	−0.27
Stutthof (men)	3,800	131	3.45	5.69	−2.24
Stutthof (women)	500	1	0.20	0.00	+0.20
Lublin (men)	11,500	882	7.67	4.62	+3.05
Lublin (women)	3,900	172	4.41	2.01	+2.40
Ravensbrueck (men)	3,100	26	0.84	0.76	+0.08
Ravensbrueck (women)	14,100	38	0.27	0.24	+0.03
Riga	3,000	1	0.03	0.33	−0.30
Herzogenbusch					
Total	224,000	4,699			

Over-all average for August 1943	2.09 percent
Overall average for July 1943	2.23 percent
(Decrease) −0.14 percent	

Thus after more than a half year of a campaign to reduce the death rate in the camps, Auschwitz still had about 80 per day on the average. Since, as has been seen, almost all the "unable to work" were at Birkenau, it is certain that almost all of these deaths occurred there.

Auschwitz also seems to have received some rather bad selections of inmates from other concentration camps.[96]

The Netherlands Red Cross report on Auschwitz (vol. 2) also offers some data on the death rates at Auschwitz for 1942-1943. For the period 30 October 1942 to 25 February 1943 the death rate is specified as about 360 per week on the average, and about 185 per week for the period 26 February to 1 July 1943. It is also said that a total of 124 of the Dutch Jews who entered Birkenau in July-August 1942 (p. 109) died in the period 30 October 1942 to 1 July 1943. However the figures for total deaths seem somewhat low and difficult to reconcile with the data presented above, so there may be some error or misunderstanding here.

It is perfectly obvious that these deaths, however deplorable and whatever the nature and location of the responsibility, had nothing to do with extermination or with Jews as such. From the point of view of the higher SS administration, they were "catastrophic" and efforts were made to bring them under control. It is not at all remarkable that with such death rates, cremation and mortuary facilities anticipating worst period death rates of even hundreds per day existed at Auschwitz.

The Auschwitz death rate improved but slightly during the course of the war. During 1944, when the inmate population of the camp had expanded to 100,000 or more (probably on account of territorial losses in the east which forced evacuations of labor camps), the death rate was 350 to 500 per week at Birkenau (which, as we have seen, accounted for almost the entire Auschwitz death rate).[97]

It is a tragic fact that, even in modern times, "camps" established during wartime have amounted to death traps for many sent to them. The basic causes for such conditions have been similar: people thrown together chaotically in hastily organized camps, with inadequate sanitary measures and an uncertain situation as regards food and other supplies. Thus during the American Civil War, the POW camps in the North such as Rock Island and Camp Douglas experienced death rates of 2%–4% per month. These figures were even exceeded in camps in the South such as Florence, where diarrhoea and scurvy caused 20 to 50 deaths per day, in a prisoner population of about 12,000. Conditions at Andersonville were even worse, and 13,000 of the 50,000 Union POW's who were interned there perished.[98] During the 1899–1902 Boer War in South Africa about 120,000 non-combatant white Boers and 75,000 black Africans were placed in British concentration camps. For about a year, the Boer mortality rate ranged from 120 to 340 deaths per thousand per year (1.1% to 3.4% per month) while the Boer infant mortality rate, due chiefly to epidemics of measles, was as high as 600 per thousand per year (7.35% per month). About 20,000 Boer women and children died in these camps.[99] During World War I the Germans mixed Russian POW's with those of other nationalities, resulting in typhus epidemics in their POW camps; conditions were strikingly similar to those experienced in the World War II concentration camps.[100] We have seen that Russians were used as labor at the concentration camps, especially at Auschwitz, so they were no doubt one of the principal sources of typhus. Since they were not considered regular concentration camp inmates it is not clear whether or not they were included in the camp death figures which were reviewed above. However, it is certain that they contributed to the overall death rates at the camps, and that their bodies were disposed of in the same crematoria, but numbers are not available.

A ridiculous feature of all this, as it strikes the student of the subject, appears in NMT volume 5, which summarizes Case 4, "U.S. *vs.* Pohl". In section B, "The Concentration Camp System", we are presented with documents which show that the camps experienced remarkably high death rates. These have just been summarized above. Then in section E, "The Extermination Program", we are presented with documents showing that the Germans were building crematoria at these camps at the time of the high death rates. Apparently it is believed that nobody would actually read one of these volumes, or maybe the compilers of the volumes did not read them!

Taking into account the different death rates, we can see that the number of ovens at Auschwitz was completely comparable to those which existed at camps where there were no exterminations. In 1942 crematoria were constructed at Dachau and at Sachsenhausen; each contained four ovens. At Dachau, a crematorium consisting of two ovens had existed prior to 1942, and the older crematorium continued to be used after 1942. It is most likely that the same situation with respect to an earlier crematorium held at Sachsenhausen. At Buchenwald, the pre-war cremation facilities were those which existed in the nearby towns of Weimar and Jena. After the war started, crematoria were constructed at the camp, and by the end of 1941 Buchenwald had a six oven crematorium. It appears that the Weimar crematorium continued to be used until the end of the war.[101] It is also possible that concentration camp crematoria, whether at Auschwitz, Dachau or elsewhere, were used to dispose of the bodies of people who had had nothing to do with the camps (e.g. Russian POW's).

This, then, is our view of the "death camp" aspect of the Nazi concentration camps. It is a view which does not harmonize with those of Christophersen and of Staeglich, who saw no high death rates and are not convinced that there existed extensive cremation facilities at Auschwitz. Our view is based on the relevant prosecution documents and comparable material, and their views are based on their observations at Auschwitz in 1944. It may seem that their observations are more to be trusted than the documentary material, but I believe that a careful consideration of the matter resolves the point in favor of our theory, while not denying their observations.

It is true that there exists a possibility of forged documents; indeed, it is more than a possibility. We shall see that there was considerable forgery of

Fig. 13: The building at Dachau which housed the crematorium, which is located under the taller chimney. On the left the door of a disinfection chamber, with its skull and bones warning sign, can be perceived. The shower bath is between the crematorium and the disinfection chamber.

Photo: U.S. National Archives

129

documents at Nuernberg. However it does not appear that the documents dealing with deaths in the camps and with the constructions of crematoria were forged, for the simple reason that there is absolutely nothing about extermination in them, as the reader can verify by consulting the "selections" of documents in NMT volume 5. They speak of a very high death rate, at certain times, in penal institutions (concentration camps), which a relatively small country, fighting against overwhelming odds for its existence, was attempting to exploit for labor. That high death rates might have been one consequence is perfectly plausible.

While the documents we have reviewed say nothing of extermination, they are nevertheless somewhat unsatisfactory in the sense that one does not get a full picture from them in regard to the causes of the death rates and the specific victims involved. The unhealthy prisoners contributed by the Ministry of Justice do not explain everything. The picture must be guessed and inferred, so here we will offer our impressions.

German concentration camps during the Thirties had only punitive and security functions, and no economic function. After the war with Russia got started, the camps underwent rapid expansion and also assumed their economic roles. Thus in 1942 there were three things happening in the camps: (a) the rapid expansion was accompanied by the general chaos, unanticipated problems and organizational difficulties which are common when large new enterprises are put into operation; this is particularly true of Auschwitz, which was a new camp in the process of rapidly expanding into the largest of all the camps; (b) the continued German victories and advances in Russia resulted in hordes of Russian POW's, some of whom were absorbed by the camps; (c) unhealthy prisoners were contributed by the Ministry of Justice. There were probably other problems but these three factors seem to me sufficient to explain a high death rate in late 1942 – early 1943.

By late 1943 the death rate, while still deplorably high, was relatively under control as compared to the previous year, and remained under control until the collapse at the end of the war. The statement of the Birkenau camp commander (Appendix D) indicates that at Auschwitz, by 1944, the deaths occurred primarily among ordinary criminals who had been transferred out of prisons. I have seen no documents, comparable to those we have reviewed, which deal with high death rates for late 1943 or any later period.

Now we are in a position to consider the observations of Christophersen and of Staeglich, which included neither crematoria nor a high death rate at Auschwitz. Very simple considerations support their observations. First, deaths are naturally not things that the Auschwitz camp administration would have advertised; both the deaths and the associated cremations would naturally have been concealed to the extent that such concealment was possible. Thus in mid-1943 Pohl complained to concentration camp commanders that, too commonly, crematorium buildings were situated in excessively public locations where "all kinds of people" could "gaze" at them. In response to Pohl's complaint, Hoess had a belt of trees planted around crematoria II and III. Moreover, it was the policy to carry corpses to the crematorium only in the evening.[102] That Christophersen and Staeglich, who had only slight contacts with Birkenau, were unaware of the existence of a high death rate or of large crematoria, is perfectly understandable.

The role that Birkenau plays in the hoax is very simple. Like any large industrial operation Auschwitz was organized in a systematic manner thought to be of the greatest efficiency. The unemployed were quartered at Birkenau. Thus the transit camps, to be discussed again in a later chapter, were at Birkenau. This explains the existence of the gipsy and Jewish camps there.

Also, the sick and the very sick and the dying and, perhaps, the dead were sent to Birkenau and such concentration of the ill naturally meant that Birkenau was a "death camp", complete with mortuary and cremation facilities, if one chooses to describe things thus. Indeed, of the order of one-half of all of the deaths in the entire German concentration camp system for 1942–1944 occurred at Birkenau. While the whole thing looks quite foolish when examined closely, as we have done in these chapters, the propaganda inventors obviously made a very rational choice in deciding to claim Birkenau as an extermination camp. The death rate in the concentration camp system was very high; it was near its highest at Auschwitz, which was the largest German concentration camp, and the Auschwitz deaths were concentrated at Birkenau.

Summary

In the introduction to this chapter it was promised that the Auschwitz extermination legend would be shown to possess the basic trademark of the great hoax: the need for a dual interpretation of facts. This is true in every significant respect conceivable:

1.   The Zyklon was employed for disinfection and also allegedly for exterminations.
2.   The "selections" were necessary by the nature of the operations at Auschwitz and also allegedly for exterminations.
3.   It would not have been inaccurate (although perhaps somewhat misleading) to call Birkenau a "death camp", especially at certain times (and especially when the Baruch Committee was in existence and immediately thereafter); it was also allegedly an "extermination camp".
4.   Disrobing–showering procedures were followed for delousing and also allegedly for exterminations.
5.   Conventional crematoria existed for accommodating both the death camp role and alleged extermination camp role of Birkenau.
6.   Some *Leichenkeller* were mortuaries while it is alleged that others were, in reality, "gas chambers". The two types of *Leichenkeller* were in proximate locations at Birkenau.
7.   Some *Badeanstalten* were bath establishments while it is alleged that others were, in reality, "gas chambers". The two types of *Badeanstalten* were in proximate locations at Birkenau.
8.   The stench that the people of the area experienced was due not only to the hydrogenation and other chemical processes at Auschwitz but also allegedly to the cremations.

Actually in view of the points made in the analysis it is only charity to say that there are proposed dual interpretations of fact in connection with these eight points. The proposed interpretations of extermination are obvious lies and the last, concerning the stench, is the "excess fact"; the authors of the hoax should never have used the fact of the stench in their story.

The facts in contradiction to the claims, the inconsistencies and the implausibilities have been reviewed. Himmler gives his orders directly to Hoess, but leaves the means to the ingenuity of Hoess. The interview emphatically took place in the summer of 1941; on the other hand it must have taken place in the summer of 1942, so Hoess started improvising half a year after the plans for the four crematoria which were used in the exterminations were formulated. The crematoria were not left to the ingenuity of Hoess. Or something. Jewish families with children reside for months at Birkenau, their quarters having been previously disinfected with the same chemical product that they are supposed to have been killed with on entering, but they will be killed with it later. Or something.

The analysis of Auschwitz is not complete. Although it may seem that the promised "crushing blow" has been delivered, the material of this chapter was not what was being referred to when that expression was used in the introduction to the chapter. Our analysis has, thus far, focused on happenings at Auschwitz and has not considered the fate of any specific nationality group of Jews at Auschwitz. For the sake of thoroughness this must be done, and we can think of no better case for emphasis than that which the bearers of the legend have selected themselves: the Hungarian Jews, whose fate or whatever it should be called will be examined in the next chapter, with special regard for the Auschwitz claims.

V
THE HUNGARIAN JEWS

Since the Germans and their allies allowed the Red Cross, both the International Committee (ICRC) and the various national societies, a not negligible liberty to operate in Axis controlled Europe, it developed that the ICRC was able to report a great deal concerning the European Jews. The reports of such a neutrally situated organization are naturally of great importance in connection with our problem.

We say "neutrally situated" rather than "neutral" since there is no such thing as strict political neutrality; every organization is subject to political pressures. It is a question of degree.

Two ICRC publications are of major interest to us. The first is *Documents sur l'activité du CICR en faveur des civils détenus dans les camps de concentration en Allemagne (1939-1945),* Geneva, 1947. This is a collection of document reprints, the documents being correspondence between the ICRC and various governments and Red Cross societies, and also reports of ICRC delegates to the ICRC itself. Commentary sufficient only to interpret the documents is provided by the Red Cross. The publication is invaluable and has been cited several times in this book. Another 1947 publication was *Inter Arma Caritas,* but this was primarily a public relations effort.

The second important publication is the three volume *Report of the International Committee of the Red Cross on its activities during the Second World War,* Geneva, 1948. This has the form of a historical report; quotations from documents appear only occasionally. In the present chapter is reproduced in full an excerpt from volume 1, namely pages 641-657. I believe that some political pressures are evident in the excerpt of the *Report,* but it will not be necessary for the reader to share my notions regarding the specific manifestations of these pressures in the excerpt in order to accept the major conclusion that I draw from the excerpt. However some obvious urgent questions will arise during the first reading and all that can be said here is that two points should be kept in mind.

First, this *Report* was published in 1948, at a time when the authors could not have failed, especially in view of the politically sensitive nature of the subject matter, to be thoroughly familiar with the Allied claims, exhaustively aired at the war crimes trials and in the press, regarding the fate of European Jews. We expect no careless remarks here.

Second, we are not consulting the ICRC as a general sort of authority. That is to say, we are interested only in the reports which fall within the ICRC area of competence. It had delegations in various European countries which were heavily involved in Jewish affairs and what we want to know is what, insofar as the ICRC was able to observe, happened to these Jews. Our emphasis, in fact, is on the Jews of Slovakia (Eastern Czechoslovakia), Croatia (Northern Yugoslavia) and Hungary. In a way our interest is even more narrow; we are interested in Hungary but the other two lands are contiguous and, to the extent that the Germans controlled things, there was no reason for major differences in Jewish policy.

From a numerical point of view, it might seem that Poland should be selected as the key country in the problem. However the fact remains that Hungary is the key because the creators of the legend chose to emphasize Hungary and not Poland in offering evidence for their claims. They offer no evidence for exterminations of Polish Jews, apart from witness testimony and the general extermination camp claims which the analysis has already demolished. By a happy circumstance, it is possible to consult the reports of the ICRC to learn what happened in Hungary, but this is not the case with Poland. The reason for this is that the Germans did not permit the ICRC to involve itself in Jewish affairs in countries in which they considered themselves sovereign. However the allies of Germany that were considered independent states admitted the ICRC into Jewish affairs. Thus develops the central importance of Hungary in the examination of the legend.

There is a second respect in which the *Report* excerpt is of the greatest importance in our study, but this point is more effectively made in a following chapter.

The *Report* excerpt is reproduced in full here because it is written in such a way that it is difficult to cite on specific points without risking the possibility of being accused of distorting meaning. This will be more clear after the reading.

VI. Special Categories of Civilians
(A). JEWS

Under National Socialism, the Jews had become in truth outcasts, condemned by rigid racial legislation to suffer tyranny, persecution and systematic extermination. No kind of protection shielded them; being neither PW nor civilian internees, they formed a separate category, without the benefit of any Convention. The supervision which the ICRC was empowered to exercise in favour of prisoners and internees did not apply to them. In most cases, they were, in fact, nationals of the State which held them in its power and which, secure in its supreme authority, allowed no intervention in their behalf. These unfortunate citizens shared the same fate as political deportees, were deprived of civil rights, were given less favoured treatment than enemy nationals, who at least had the benefit of a statute. They were penned into concentration camps and ghettos, recruited for forced labour, subjected to grave brutalities and sent to death camps, without anyone being allowed to intervene in those matters which Germany and her allies considered to be exclusively within the bounds of their home policy.

It should be recalled, however, that in Italy the measures taken against the Jews were incomparably less harsh, and that in the countries under the direct influence of Germany, their situation was usually less tragic than in Germany itself.

The Committee could not dissociate themselves from these victims, on whose behalf it received the most insistent appeals, but for whom the means of action seemed especially limited, since in the absence of any basis in law, its activities depended to a very great extent upon the good will of the belligerent States.

The Committee had in fact, through the intermediary of the German Red Cross, asked for information concerning civilian deportees "without distinction of race or religion", which was plainly refused in the following terms: "The responsible authorities decline to give any information concerning non-Aryan deportees". Thus, enquiries as a matter of principle concerning the Jews led to no result, and continual protests would have been resented by the authorities concerned and might have been detrimental both to the Jews themselves and to the whole field of the Committee's activities. In consequence, the Committee, while avoiding useless protest, did its utmost to help the Jews by practical means, and its delegates abroad were instructed on these lines. This policy was proved by the results obtained.

Germany.—Even when the German Wehrmacht was winning, the Committee's activities in behalf of the Jews met with almost insuperable difficulties. Towards the end of 1943, however, the German authorities allowed the Committee to send relief parcels to detainees in concentration camps, many of them Jews, whose names and addresses might be known to it. The Committee was able to collect a few dozen names, and by these slender means the system of individual and then collective relief for political detainees was started, an account of which is given elsewhere in this Report. Each receipt returned bore several names, and these were added to the list of addresses: thus the receipts often gave the first news of missing persons. By the end of the war, the Committee's card index for political detainees (Jewish and non-Jewish) contained over 105,000 names.

During the last year of the War, the Committee's delegates were able to visit the camp of Theresienstadt (Terezin), which was exclusively used for Jews, and was governed by special conditions. From information gathered by the Committee, this camp had been started as an experiment by certain leaders of the Reich, who were apparently less hostile to the Jews than those responsible for the racial policy of the German Government. These men wished to give to Jews the means of setting up a communal life in a town under their own administration and possessing almost complete autonomy. On several occasions, the Committee's delegates were granted authority to visit Theresienstadt, but owing to difficulties raised by the local authorities, the first visit only took place in June 1944. The Jewish elder in charge informed the delegate, in the presence of a representative of the German authorities, that thirty-five thousand Jews resided in the town and that living conditions were bearable. In view of the doubt expressed by the heads of various Jewish organizations as to the accuracy of this statement, the Committee requested the German Government to allow its delegates to make a second visit. After laborious negotiations, much delayed on the German side, two delegates were able to visit the camp on April 6, 1945. They confirmed the favourable impression gained on the first visit, but ascertained that the camp strength now amounted only to 20,000 internees, including 1,100 Hungarians, 11,050 Slovaks, 800 Dutch, 290 Danes, 8000 Germans, 8000 Czechs and 760 stateless persons. They were therefore anxious to know if Theresienstadt was being used as a transit camp and asked when the last departures for the East had taken place. The head of the Security Police of the Protectorate stated that the last transfers to Auschwitz had occurred six months previously, and had comprised 10,000 Jews, to be employed on camp administration and enlargement. This high official assured the delegates that no Jews would be deported from Theresienstadt in future.

Whereas other camps exclusively reserved for Jews were not open to inspections for humanitarian purposes until the end, the Committee's activities were at least effective in several concentration camps containing a minority proportion of Jews. During the final months, the Committee, in urgent circumstances, took on a task of the greatest importance by visiting and giving aid to these internees, providing food, preventing last-minute evacuations as well as summary executions, and even taking charge during the critical hours, sometimes days, which passed between the retreat of the German forces and the arrival of the Allies from the West or the East.

A more detailed account of these various activities is given in the chapters on Political Detainees in this volume and in Vol. III, as well as in special publication entitled *Documents sur l'activité du CICR en faveur des civils détenus dans les camps de concentration en Allemagne, 1939-1945*.

Less is known of the part played by the Committee in countries whose Governments were subject, in varying degrees, to German influence and where special laws concerning Jews had been enacted, similar to those under German legislation.

Through its delegates, particularly in Budapest, Bucharest, Bratislava, Zagreb and Belgrade, the Committee was able to make the best possible use of its moral authority and the well disposed attitude shown to it by a few non-German authorities, who had more or less freedom of action, but who were not so relentlessly bent on carrying out a racial policy as the German Government. In its capacity as a neutral intermediary, the Committee was in a position to transfer and distribute in the form of relief supplies over twenty million Swiss francs collected by Jewish welfare organizations throughout the world, in particular by the American Joint Distribution Committee of New York. Without the help of the ICRC, this concerted effort made by a whole community would have doubtless been vain, as no Jewish organization was allowed to act in countries under German control. A detailed account of this important relief scheme will be found in Vol. III.

The efforts of the Committee were not limited to the activities described above; as time went on, it eventually became in truth a "Protecting Power" for the Jews, by interceding with Governments in their behalf and in some cases exercising a genuine right of protection, by obtaining the benefit of exterritoriality for hospitals, dispensaries and relief organizations, and even by acting as arbitrators in the settlement of disputes. This was its task, especially in Rumania and Hungary, for over a year during the last phase of the war in 1944 and 1945. In countries where the efforts of the Committee were less considerable, they were none the less of great benefit to the Jews. These may be described in a brief summary before reverting to the Committee's activities in Hungary and Rumania.

France. – In November 1940, the Committee obtained permission from the authorities for one of its members to visit camps in the South, where a certain number of Jews were amongst the civilian internees. The camp at Gurs, in particular, contained six thousand Jews from the Bavarian Palatinate. The visit gave a clear idea of the situation

Fig. 14: Delousing Senator Wherry after tour of Dachau.   Photo: U.S. Army

136

inside the camp and the urgent necessity for relief; appropriate steps were taken in the internees' behalf.

The Jews from Poland who, whilst in France, had obtained entrance-permits to the United States were held to be American citizens by the German occupying authorities, who further agreed to recognize the validity of about three thousand passports issued to Jews by the consulates of South American countries. The persons concerned were lodged in camps reserved for Americans at Vittel. In 1942, when Germany and the States in South America began negotiations for the exchange of internees, it was found that the majority of the internees at Vittel held accommodation passports and consequently were in danger of being deported. The ICRC interceded in their behalf through the Berlin Delegation and succeeded in arranging for them to remain at Vittel, only a few being deported.

Greece.—Immediately after the German occupation, the Committee was called upon to deal with the case of 55,000 Jews in Salonica, who were the victims of racial legislation. In July 1942, all men between eighteen and forty-five were registered, and the majority were enrolled in labour detachments. The delegation furnished them with medical and toilet supplies. In May 1943, these workers were sent to Germany, and the delegation in that country insisted on the right to give them food-parcels. This course led to difficulties with the German authorities, who in their resentment demanded that one of the delegates should be replaced.

Slovakia.—Many thousands of Jews had been forced to leave the country and enlist in what was called "labour service", but which in fact seems to have led the greater number to the extermination camps. At the same time, a large proportion of the Jewish minority had permission to stay in the country, and at certain periods Slovakia was even looked upon as a comparative haven of refuge for Jews, especially for those coming from Poland. Those who remained in Slovakia seem to have been in comparative safety until the end of August 1944, when a rising against the German forces took place. While it is true that the law of May 15, 1942, had brought about the internment of several thousand Jews, these people were held in camps where the conditions of food and lodging were tolerable, and where internees were allowed to do paid work on terms almost equal to those of the free labour market. In 1944, the Jewish community had managed to secure an almost complete suspension of forced immigration towards the territories under German control.

At the time of the rising, the interned Jews escaped from the camps; some returned home, and others took to the hills. The measures of repression which followed fell on the Jewish population as a whole. The German military authorities summoned the Slovak Government to make wholesale arrests for the purpose of deporting the Jews to Germany. The order dated November 16, 1944, laid down that all Jews should be mustered in the camp of Sered, and to that end, that Jews living in the capital should previously be assembled, on November 20, in the Town Hall of Bratislava. On the same day, the delegate went to the Town Hall and noted that only about fifty Jews had obeyed the summons. The rest had gone into hiding, as the Slovak authorities had foreseen, either by fleeing to the country or concealing themselves in the town in the so-called "bunkers". In his concern over this situation, the President of the ICRC wrote to the Head of the Slovak Government asking him to put an end to the deportations. Monsignor Tiso received this letter on January 2, 1945, and answered at length on January 10. He recalled the fact that up to that time the Jews had been spared, adding however that in view of the rising, his Government had been forced to yield to the pressure which had been brought to bear upon them. He concluded by saying: "To sum up, it remains wholly true that in the solution of the Jewish question, we have endeavoured to remain faithful to humane principles to the full extent of our powers". Official aid to the fugitives in the "bunkers" was out of the question; the delegation in Bratislava, however, with the help of the Slovak Red Cross and, in the provinces with that of the Catholic Church, succeeded in providing them with funds, which were handed to their spokesmen, and which allowed them to support life during the last months of the war.

The Committee's representative was unable to secure permission to visit the camp of Sered. He was, however, allowed to enter the camp of Marienka, where Jews of alien nationality were interned.

Croatia.—From May 1943 to the end of 1945, the delegation gave aid to the Jewish community of Zagreb, to whom on behalf of the Joint Committee of New York, it paid out an average amount of 20,000 Swiss francs monthly. It also made available to it considerable quantities of food supplies, clothing and medical stores.

In October 1944, the German authorities, on the pattern of measures taken in the neighbouring countries, imprisoned the Jews of Zagreb, and seized their food stores. The delegation at once made representations to the Croat Government, and secured the return of these stores.

Hungary.—As in Slovakia, the Jews were relatively spared, in so far as the local

137

government retained a certain freedom of action. But when German pressure was reasserted, from March 1944 onwards, the position of the Jews became critical. The replacement in October 1944, of Horthy's Government by one in bondage to Germany, provoked a violent crisis; executions, robberies, deportations, forced labour, imprisonments – such was the lot of the Jewish population, which suffered cruelly and lost many killed, especially in the provinces. It was at this point that the Committee, to alleviate these sufferings, took action with vigour and authority. At the same time the aid prompted by the King of Sweden, was given with considerable courage and success by the Swedish Legation in Budapest, helped by some members of the Swedish Red Cross.

Until March 1944, Jews who had the privilege of visas for Palestine were free to leave Hungary. On March 18, 1944, Hitler summoned the Regent, Admiral Horthy, to his headquarters. He expressed his indignation that "in Hungary very nearly a million Jews were able to live in freedom and without restrictions". Even before the Regent had returned to Budapest, German troops had begun the occupation of Hungary in order to prevent her from abandoning her alliance with Germany. This occupation forced upon the Head of the Hungarian State a new government that was far more dependent on German authority than the one preceding it. Emigration of the Jews was straightway suspended, and the persecutions began.

This was a matter of the gravest concern to the ICRC. The President appealed to the Regent, Admiral Horthy: "The matters brought to our knowledge seem to us", he wrote on July 5, 1944, "so utterly contrary to the chivalrous traditions of the great Hungarian people that it is difficult for us to credit even a tithe of the information we are receiving. In the name of the ICRC, I venture to beg Your Highness to give instructions enabling us to reply to these rumours and accusations". The Regent replied, on August 12: "It is unfortunately not within my power to prevent inhuman acts which no one condemns more severely than my people, whose thoughts and feelings are chivalrous. I have instructed the Hungarian Government to take up the settlement of the Jewish question in Budapest. It is to be hoped that this statement will not give rise to serious complications".

In the spirit of this reply, the Hungarian authorities allowed the delegate in Budapest to affix shields on the camps and internment buildings for the Jews, conferring on them the protection of the Red Cross. If the use of these shields (hardly compatible, moreover, with the precise terms of the Geneva Convention) was not more extensive, this was due to the fact that the Jewish Senate of Budapest was of the opinion that the measure would doubtless lose its effectiveness if generally applied.

The Hungarian Government, furthermore, showed themselves willing to favour a resumption of Jewish emigration. The Committee got in touch with the British and United States Governments as a matter of extreme urgency and, during August, obtained a joint statement from these two Governments declaring their desire to give support by every means to the emigration of Jews from Hungary.

To this end, the Committee was requested to transmit the following message to Budapest from the United States Government: "The United States Government has been advised by the ICRC of the Hungarian Government's willingness to permit certain categories of refugees to emigrate from Hungary . . . The Government of the United States, taking into account the humanitarian considerations involved as regards the Jews in Hungary, now specifically repeats its assurance that arrangements will be made by it for the care of all Jews who in the present circumstances are allowed to leave Hungary and who reach the territory of the United Nations or neutral countries, and that it will find for such people temporary havens of refuge where they may live in safety. The Governments of neutral countries have been advised of these assurances and have been requested to permit the entry into their territory of Jews from Hungary who may reach their frontiers".

On October 8, the Hungarian authorities, in conformity with the undertaking given to the Committee, announced the final suspension of deportations and made known that the Kistarcea Camp for Jewish intellectuals, doctors and engineers, had been broken up and the internees released.

The hope raised by this statement was short-lived. A few days later the full tide of the great tribulations of the Hungarian Jews was to set in. In view of the setbacks of the German Army, Admiral Horthy had decided to sever his country's connection with Germany. On October 15, he asked the Allied Powers for an armistice for Hungary. This proclamation had an immense effect amongst the Jews, who were ardent in their demonstrations against the occupying Power. Although the German Army was in retreat both in Eastern and Western Europe, it had still a firm foothold in Hungary. The Regent failed in his plan and was arrested. Hungarian supporters of the Germans seized power and set about a repression, increasing in severity as the fighting zone came nearer, placing Budapest in a state of siege. It is alleged that shots were fired from Jewish houses on the German troops; however that may be, repression was centred on the Jews. It was immediately decided to remove them from Budapest and to confiscate their property. Sixty thousand Jews fit for work were to be sent to Germany, on foot, in parties of one thousand, by way of Vienna. Moreover, among the able-bodied, men between sixteen and sixty, and women between fourteen and forty were commandeered for forced labour in building fortifications in Hungary. The rest of the Jewish population, including the disabled and sick, was confined in four or five ghettos near Budapest. The only Jews to escape evacuation were those in possession of passports with visas for Palestine, Sweden, Switzerland, Portugal or Spain.

These measures were accompanied, at the outset, by brutalities and thefts against which the delegate immediately protested. The Ministry of the Interior, giving heed to this action, issued a decree forbidding pillage as from October 20. Meanwhile, the delegation was giving refuge to the members of the Jewish Senate of Budapest. Since their position was apparently threatened, the delegate renewed his appeals to the German authorities, as to the Hungarian Government and on October 29, the wireless announced that the ICRC buildings were granted exterritoriality, similar to that of the Legations.

His position thus strengthened, the delegate devoted himself with all the more assurance to the relief work he had courageously undertaken in behalf of the Jews. "It is hard", he wrote, "to imagine the difficulty I had in holding out against a gang in whose hands the power lay, and at a time when disorder, murder and aggression were the order of the day, to compel it still to show some restraint and to observe the respect due to the Red Cross emblem . . ."

The fate of children whose parents had been deported to the labour camps was especially tragic. The delegate succeeded, with the help of the "Jo Pasztor" organization, in setting up some twenty homes in which these children, accompanied in some cases by their mothers, could be accommodated. The hospital staff consisted of trained nurses and of Jews, whose employment in these homes ensured them a certificate of protection similar to those which the delegate issued to his fellow workers.

The Committee's representatives also opened soup-kitchens, each able to provide about a hundred hot meals a day. Reception and accommodation centres were set up, as well as hospitals with children's and maternity wards, and a first aid station open to the public "without distinction of race or creed". Furthermore, the delegate issued thirty thousand letters of protection, which although without any legal basis, were respected by the authorities and exempted their holders from compulsory labour.

In November, one hundred thousand Jews poured into Budapest from the provinces. The Government decided to shut them up in a ghetto, and with them the Jews who had remained in Budapest, in particular the children sheltered in the Red Cross homes. "I considered that my main task," wrote the delegate, "lay in ensuring that this ghetto life was at least as bearable as possible. I had incredible difficulty in obtaining from the Hungarian Nazis, in the course of daily bargaining, conditions and concession which would ensure to some degree the means to exist for those in the ghetto. Continual interviews took place with the Jewish Senate on the one hand, and with the town administration on the other, to ensure at least minimum food supplies for the ghetto at a time when all traffic had stopped, owing to the constant bombing, and provisioning was becoming more and more difficult." The delegate secured that the Jews' rations should be fixed at 920 calories, i.e. two thirds of the minimum Hungarian prison fare. Later on it was possible to make a slight increase of this figure, thanks to the issue of relief supplies.

In spite of the delegate's efforts, the children transferred to the ghetto had been put sixty in a room in premises which it had been impossible either to clean or to disinfect. Pleading the danger of epidemics, he succeeded in getting the children inspected by a committee who had authority to make some decision on their situation. This health inspection allowed 500 of the 800 children examined to be sent back to the homes from which they had been removed, and for 300 to be placed in hospitals. The other children did not leave the ghetto, but were taken care of there by relatives or friends. Furthermore, the Delegation sent into the ghetto, with permission of the Government, five persons instructed to furnish regular and detailed reports on each child's need of food and clothing. Finally, on the initiative of the delegate, one thousand orphans selected "without distinction of race or religion" were assembled in the Abbey of Panonalma, a Benedictine monastery placed at the delegate's disposal by the Bishop of Gyor. This refuge, under the protection of the Red Cross, was respected by the German and Hungarian troops in retreat, and also by the Soviet Army.

The devotion and generosity of the Bishop of Gyor were a fruitful help to the delegate in the relief work he had undertaken. His task was to improve the food and shelter of the convoys of Jews who were being deported to labour camps in Germany and compelled to do stages of twenty-five to thirty kilometres a day on foot. The Bishop organized a relief centre en route, which he financed and which was administered by representatives of the Committee. It gave shelter from bad weather, for a few hours at least, to thousands of Jews during their terrible exodus. The "transport groups" of the delegation issued food to them on the road, paid the peasants to carry the weakest, fifteen to twenty at a time, in their carts, gave medical attention to the sick and dispensed medical supplies.

On November 12, a new threat hung over the hospitals protected by the Red Cross emblem, which the police had searched with an order to turn out the Jews. The delegate, on the strength of the authority he had been granted, protested to the Government. As a result, the police authorities were instructed not to proceed with the evictions from the hospitals.

It must be apparent what difficulties and dangers were encountered at every turn by the Committee's representatives in a town subject to the most violent bombardments. They were supported in their courageous work by the untiring devotion to duty of the members of the Jewish Senate, and by the equally generous activity of the representatives of the two main protecting Powers, Switzerland and Sweden.

As soon as Budapest was liberated, the delegate and the local Jewish organizations established, with the funds of the New York Joint Committee stocks of foodstuffs and of the most necessary medical supplies. The Russian military authorities had ordered all foreigners to leave Budapest. When our delegate had to go, a Hungarian minister paid him the tribute of stating that he had, in a time of historic crisis, succeeded in making the capital a "protectorate of Geneva".

Rumania. – The delegate's part was a very important one, owing to the opportunities there were in that country for the purchase of foodstuffs. Financial aid and relief in kind could be sent from Bucharest to Poland and neighbouring countries. The Committee came to an agreement concerning relief in Rumania itself with the National Red Cross there, to whom our delegate handed funds for the purchase of goods. It should be emphasised that wealthy Rumanian Jews contributed in large measure towards assisting their co-religionists in need. From 1943, the Committee's work in Rumania was made easier by the fact that the delegate had been able to inspire the Rumanian Government with trust.

During the period in September 1940, when the "Iron Guard", supported by the Gestapo and the German SS, had seized power, the Jews had been subjected to persecution and deportation to death camps. Later, under the dictatorship of Marshall Antonescu, they met with less severity. Special understanding was shown by the Vice-president of the Council, Mr. Mihai Antonescu, who was entrusted with the settlement of the Jewish question. "The Rumanian Government", he wrote to the delegate in Bucharest, "repudiates any material solution contrary to civilized custom and in defiance of the Christian spirit which dominates the conscience of the Rumanian people".

In December 1943 Mr. Mihai Antonescu had an interview with this delegate which led to making their activities of the Committee in behalf of Jews far easier. This talk bore mainly on the case of Jews deported beyond the Dniester to the Ukraine, who were natives of Bessarabia and the Bukovina. These provinces had been returned to Rumania after the first World War, and came again under Soviet power by the terms of the Soviet-German treaty at the beginning of the Second War. After the reshuffle in 1941, Rumania, who had become Germany's ally against the USSR, reoccupied these two provinces. The Jews, whom the Rumanians considered guilty of having welcomed too easily a return to Russian allegiance, were then deported. The Rumanian Government's plan, drawn up in agreement with Germany, seems to have been to settle these Jews on lands in the region of the Sea of Azov. This could not be carried out, however, unless the USSR were defeated. In the light of the Russian victories, the Rumanian Government decided, towards the close of 1943, to repatriate the survivors of this deplorable migration, the numbers of which had fallen from 200,000 to 78,000. Mr. Mihai Antonescu welcomed the opportunity of the approaches made by the delegate in Bucharest, to entrust him with a mission of enquiry into the means of carrying out this repatriation, and authorized him to tour Transnistria to distribute clothing and relief to these unfortunate people. Furthermore, the delegate succeeded in getting an assurance that the Czernowitz Jews, the only ones still compelled to wear the yellow star, should be exempted, as this badge exposed them to the brutality of German troops passing through. Finally, it was agreed that Red Cross purchases might be freely made at the official rates.

When the delegate saw the Vice-president of the Council again on his return, he drew his attention specially to the plight of the children who had lost their parents and were left abandoned in Transnistria. Mr. Mihai Antonescu promised to allow 150 children to leave each week for Palestine or elsewhere, if the Committee could arrange their journey. Three months later, the Rumanian Government offered two recently-built first-class steamers, the *Transilvania* and the *Bessarabia*, then held in Turkish waters, and suggested the Committee should buy them, reserving to Rumania the option of repurchase, for use as transports for emigrants under the Swiss flag. Switzerland, as the protecting Power for British interests, could in fact be considered as the protecting Power for Jews bound for Palestine, since these Jews were to become on arrival assimilated to British nationals.

Up to that time, the remedy of emigration had been no more than a meagre palliative for the sufferings of the Jews. Bulgaria had shut her frontiers to emigrants travelling on a collective passport, and only Jews under eighteen years of age or over forty-five had been able to reach Turkey, under individual permits. Transport by sea from Rumanian ports would have afforded the best means of emigration. But besides the difficulties met with by the Jews in leaving, account had to be taken of the political problem raised for the British authorities by an influx of Jews, considered as intruders by the majority of the local population of a territory under British mandate. The first vessel, the *Struma*, which left Constanza for Palestine independently of any action by the Committee, at the beginning of 1942, had been detained at Istanbul owing to engine trouble, and was subsequently obliged to sail again for Rumania, as it was impossible to obtain the necessary permits to continue on its route. It was wrecked, and 750 emigrants were drowned. This pioneer expedition, ending so disastrously, was a lesson in the need of prudence.

The Committee was asked to grant the protection of the Red Cross emblem to emigrant transports and would have consented to this, on the basis of a very liberal interpretation of the provisions of the Tenth Hague Convention of 1907, which govern the use of hospital ships, whilst reckoning too that cargo-boats sailing under their control and carrying relief supplies for PW or civilian internees were covered by the Red Cross emblem. However, it would have wished to do this in agreement with all the Powers concerned. Therefore, the Committee made its consent conditional on the following terms. The transport organizations should charter neutral vessels which would be accompanied by the Committee's representative, and would be used exclusively for the transport of emigrants. The ships were not to sail before obtaining safe-conducts from all the belligerents concerned, as well as their agreement as to the route to be followed.

These conditions were unfortunately never obtained. The *Bellacita*, however, was authorized by Rumania to carry out a daily service for the transport of Jewish children from Constanza or Mangalia to Istanbul, and sailed under the protection of the Rumanian Red Cross, the Committee having notified all belligerents of these voyages.

The delegate in Bucharest was faced with a very grave decision when the question arose of embarking Jews for Palestine on two Bulgarian vessels, the *Milka* and the *Maritza*, both chartered by Zionist organizations. There was reason to fear the same fate for them as for those who sailed in the *Struma*. Moreover, the heads of Jewish organizations did not agree as to the names for the list of emigrants, and the Rumanian authorities applied to the Committee to arbitrate. The delegate confined himself to a check of the emigration permits and thus aided their departure. They arrived safely in Istanbul a few days later. In August 1944, the Committee finally agreed that vessels carrying emigrants might display the Red Cross emblem, even in the absence of certain of the conditions which had been laid down.

On August 23, the King of Rumania took advantage of the retreat of the German troops to put an end to the dictatorship of Marshal Antonescu, and to enter into armistice negotiations with the Allies. The racial laws were thereupon abolished in Rumania.

The Committee continued their relief work in behalf of Jews, however, until the close of hostilities.

In its report of December 1944, the delegation in Bucharest stated that, thanks to consignments from the Joint Committee of New York and to collections made on the spot, it had been able to come to the help of 183,000 Rumanian Jews, comprising: 17,000 deportees repatriated from Transnistria; 30,000 men liberated from forced labour with their families (90,000 persons); 20,000 evacuees from small towns and villages; 10,000 evacuees from the war zone; 20,000 homeless persons, as a result of bombardments; 20,000 workmen and officials dismissed from their employment; and 6,000 Hungarians who had succeeded in escaping deportation and were found in Northern Transylvania.

Tribute was paid to this humanitarian work by the President of the American Union of Rumanian Jews. He wrote, in March 1945, to the Committee's delegate in Washington as follows:

"The work of the International Red Cross in helping the Jewish population in Rumania, and the Jews transported to Transnistria has been appreciated at its true worth not only by Dr. Safran, the Chief Rabbi in Rumania and the Jewish Community of Rumania, but also by the many thousands of members of our Union whose own relatives benefitted by that help. The International Red Cross Committee has rendered truly invaluable service to our people in Rumania."

Mr. Joseph C. Hyman, Vice-President of the American Joint Distribution Committee of New York, had already made public the debt of gratitude due to the International Red Cross. In an article published in the journal "News" on February 16,

1945, under the title "The Joint Distribution Committee lands International Red Cross Co-operation," he is quoted as follows: "Thousands of Jews in newly liberated lands and in German concentration camps owe their lives to the sanctuary and the help given them by the International Red Cross. In those parts of the world where J.D.C., major American agency for the rescue and relief of distressed Jews overseas, cannot itself work directly, we know we can count on the International Red Cross . . . to act for us in bringing aid to suffering Jewry."

Volume 3 of the *Report*, particularly pages 73-84, 335-340, 479-481, 505-529, contains additional material which can be cited as needed.

Recall that our objective here is to form a reasonably accurate picture of what happened to the Jews of Slovakia, Croatia and Hungary. However there are some matters raised in the excerpt which deserve at least a few remarks.

There are enough references to "extermination" here to lead the casual reader to the impression that the Red Cross accepted the extermination claims. However, on reflection such an inference is seen as being not so clearly necessary and, even if made, not very relevant. We are told that "the Jews had become . . . condemned by rigid racial legislation to . . . systematic extermination" but there was, as is well known, no such legislation if by "extermination" is meant mass murder. Also "they were . . . sent to death camps", which was true of those who had been conscripted for labor and sent to the concentration camps during the camps' two worst periods (1942 and 1945). It "seems" that "many thousands" of Slovakian Jews went "to the extermination camps". It is anybody's guess what is meant by the "death camps" which some Rumanian Jews were sent to in 1940; whatever is meant, it was not a German measure.

In volume 3 we read (p. 479) that "when military operations spread to Hungarian soil (in early October 1944), the ICRC delegate in Budapest made the utmost exertions to prevent the extermination of the Hungarian Jews". Further on (pp. 513-514) we read that during the war, "threatened with extermination, the Jews were, in the last resort, generally deported in the most inhuman manner, shut up in concentration camps, subjected to forced labor or put to death". The Germans "aimed more or less openly at their extermination".

We can see two possible reasons for the presence of such (ambiguous and/or very general) remarks. The first is that they are there because the authors of the *Report*, or most of them, on the basis of news reports, the war crimes trials, the fact of deportations, the fact of Nazi hostility toward the Jews, and the fact that the Germans wanted the Jews out of Europe, believed the wartime and post-war extermination claims (they obviously did not see any Jews being exterminated). The second possible reason is that the remarks are there for political- public relations reasons. For example, although the Germans and Hungarians had allowed the ICRC to operate in Hungary, and the Russians had expelled it, the *Report* nevertheless finds it expedient to say that Budapest was "liberated" by the Russian capture.

The critical reader will obviously wish that the first explanation for the appearance of these remarks be accepted, at least for purposes of discussion. We should have no objections to this; it makes little difference in the analysis since all we want to know from the *Report* is what happened to the Jews of Slovakia, Croatia and Hungary. The presence of the remarks about "extermination", put into the *Report* at a time when the detailed extermination charges had received the widest publicity, is actually helpful to our case since, whatever the explanation for the remarks, the possibility of extermination of most or many of the Jews of Slovakia, Croatia and Hungary most definitely is part of the proper subject matter of the *Report*. An absence of claims bearing

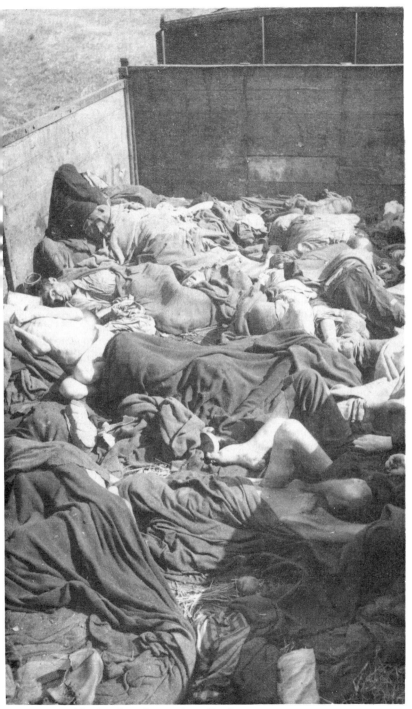

Fig. 15: Dead bodies found on train at Dachau.   Photo: U.S. Army

on extermination should not, thus, be interpreted as meaning that the possibility of extermination is not part of the matters being treated, but that the ICRC did not observe occurrences consistent with the extermination claims.

With these considerations in mind, what does the *Report* say happened to the Jews of Slovakia, Croatia and Hungary? The extent of German influence had differed prior to 1944, and some number of Slovakian Jews had been deported to the East, but the *Report* makes no speculations of extermination here, and obviously accepts that they had merely been deported. By 1944 German influence in the three countries was about uniform and nothing very consequential happened until the autumn of 1944 when the Germans interned, or attempted to intern, many of the Jews for very valid security reasons and also deported a number of Hungarian Jews to Germany for labor.

On the subject of the Hungarian Jews, a certain amount was going on between March and October 1944 but, whatever it was, the events which began in October 1944 after the arrest of Horthy were the most severe. The excerpt is most emphatic on this point in two places and, moreover, to place the critical date in the autumn of 1944 is fully consistent with the identical claim for the contiguous countries of Slovakia and Croatia.

It was after 15 October that "the full tide of the great tribulations of the Hungarian Jews was to set in" on account of the "German pressure (which) was reasserted, from March 1944 onwards", which in October 1944 "provoked a violent crisis; executions, robberies, deportations, forced labor, imprisonments". The Jews "suffered cruelly and lost many killed, especially in the provinces".

To repeat, there was a certain amount going on prior to October 1944, including deportations, but the *Report* asserts unambiguously that the events beginning in October 1944 were the major ones for the Hungarian Jews. The "executions" and "robberies" probably refer to private actions of Hungarians taken, perhaps, with the implicit encouragement or at least unconcern of the new puppet government. The *Report* is fully precise about the "deportations" and "forced labor" measures that were instituted in October 1944. Jews were put to work on fortifications in Hungary and the Germans decided to send 60,000 to Germany for labor (the number actually deported in this action was between 35,000 and 45,000). There being no rail transport available, the Jews had to walk, at least as far as Vienna, but the Red Cross organized aid along the route.[1]

It is not possible that the ICRC delegation in Hungary could have been unaware of anti-Jewish measures, occurring significantly earlier in 1944, which even equalled in severity, much less dwarfed, the events beginning in October 1944. After all, the Jewish Senate of Budapest was being quartered in the Red Cross legation, and was doubtless fully informed on Hungarian Jewish matters. In addition, the later extermination claims should have "reminded" the delegate of far more drastic events earlier in the year, if they had actually occurred, as we shall see shortly.

Before passing on to consider the specific claims of exterminations of Hungarian Jews, we should touch briefly on a few points made in the excerpt in connection with Theresienstadt.

We have had occasion in previous chapters to remark on Theresienstadt in Bohemia-Moravia (Western Czechoslovakia) and our remarks are consistent with those of the excerpt. What is arresting in the Red Cross account is the report that "this camp had been started as an experiment by certain leaders of the Reich, who were apparently less hostile to the Jews than those responsible for the racial policy of the German Government. These men wished to give to Jews the means of setting up a communal life in a town under their own administration and possessing almost complete autonomy".

Jewish policy was administered by Eichmann's office in the RSHA of the SS, and it was Karl Adolf Eichmann, "specialist for all Jewish questions", who had accompanied the head of the Security Police of Bohemia-Moravia, Colonel Erwin Weinemann, in showing the Red Cross delegation around Theresienstadt during the 6 April 1945 visit. During a gathering in the evening Eichmann had explained to the delegates "that Theresienstadt was a creation of Reichsfuehrer-SS Himmler" and had explained the philosophy involved, accurately passed on to us in the *Report* excerpt. Eichmann added that he, "personally, did not entirely approve of these methods but, as a good soldier, he naturally blindly obeyed the orders of the Reichsfuehrer".[2]

It is quite clear, therefore, that Theresienstadt was an operation of the SS, who were the "certain leaders of the Reich" involved here. In addition, it is known that it was RSHA chief Heydrich who made the Theresienstadt decision shortly after he had acquired his secondary role of Deputy Protector of Bohemia-Moravia in September 1941.[3]

What the Red Cross saw at Theresienstadt was part of regular SS policy. It is of some interest that the *Report* tells us, without comment, that the delegate had asked about "departures for the East" and that the ICRC makes no speculations regarding any sinister interpretations to be placed on the "transfers to Auschwitz", despite the notorious and universally known charges in this connection.

In critical evaluation of the Red Cross *Report*, one must obviously be wary in two senses. First, one should reserve some judgments in relation to a *self-serving* aspect of the *Report*. The typical respects in which a charitable organization's publications might be self-serving are in exaggerating the efficacy of measures taken and, in cases where it is evident that no efficacious measures have been taken, in hastily blaming the lack of efficacy on the tight fists of potential contributors (and often there are very solid grounds for such claims). Thus we should not be crushed if it were found that the Hungarian Jewish children or the Jews who walked to Vienna, both of whom were aided by the Red Cross, actually suffered a little bit more than might seem suggested by the *Report* (I am not, of course, making any claim that such was the case).

A second reservation concerns inevitable political bias as a result of external political pressures; the "liberation" of Budapest by the Russians shows this at work in the *Report*. The situation of 1948 clearly implied that when political bias appeared in the *Report* it be anti-German bias. We observe that this exists in the *Report* but, fortunately, if one reads the *Report* with well defined questions in mind, such questions bearing only on matters within the actual sphere of competence of the ICRC and its delegates, this bias is effectively non-existent.

Nevertheless, it should again be stressed that my argument in no way depends upon interpreting the *Report* as meaning other than what it says, or as not really meaning what it says, at those points selected by me. I offer no parallel of the extermination claims, which insist that phrases such as *Leichenkeller, Badeanstalt*, special treatment and "readiness for transport" be attributed meanings consistent with wartime propaganda claims. There is no quarrel with the person who insists on interpreting the *Report* as declaring in a very general way that the Germans were attempting to exterminate the Jews, since all we want to know is what the ICRC delegates were able to witness in their positions in Slovakia, Croatia and Hungary.

We have seen roughly what happened in Hungary and now the extermination claims should be examined. We first review the relevant propaganda during 1944 and then the charges made after the war, constituting the legend of the extermination of the Hungarian Jews. There are both significant differences and significant similarities between the 1944 propaganda and the later claims. Our survey of the former again employs the *N.Y. Times* as source.

In 1944, atrocity and extermination propaganda of a general sort continued:

12 Feb. 1944, p.6

A young Polish Jew who escaped from a mass execution in Poland . . . repeated a story (that at Belzec) . . . Jews were forced naked onto a metal platform operated as a hydraulic elevator which lowered them into a huge vat filled with water . . . They were electrocuted by current through the water.

This claim had also been made in London in November 1942,[4] and we encountered it in Chapter III in the *N.Y. Times* story of 20 December 1942. The emphasis in the propaganda during the spring and summer of 1944 was, however, on the Hungarian Jews. Immediately after the German occupation:

21 Mar. 1944, p.4

The fate of 800,000 Jews in Hungary was one immediate concern of Jewish circles in Stockholm.

Roosevelt involved himself directly with a speech prepared for him by the War Refugee Board:[5]

25 Mar. 1944, p.4

In the meantime in most of Europe and in parts of Asia the systematic torture and murder of civilians — men, women and children — by the Nazis and Japanese continue unabated. In areas subjugated by the aggressors innocent Poles, Czechs, Norwegians, Dutch, Danes, French, Greeks, Russians, Chinese, Filipinos — and many others — are being starved or frozen to death or murdered in cold blood in a campaign of savagery.

The slaughters of Warsaw, Lidice, Kharkov and Nanking — the brutal torture and murder by the Japanese, not only of civilians but of our own gallant American soldiers and fliers — these are startling examples of what goes on day by day, year in and year out, wherever the Nazis and the Japs are in military control — free to follow their barbaric purpose.

In one of the blackest crimes of all history — begun by the Nazis in the day of peace and multiplied by them a hundred times in time of war — the wholesale systematic murder of the Jews of Europe goes on unabated every hour. As a result of the events of the last few days hundreds of thousands of Jews, who while living under persecution have at least found a haven from death in Hungary and the Balkans, are now threatened with annihilation as Hitler's forces descend more heavily upon these lands. That these innocent people, who have already survived a decade of Hitler's fury, should perish on the very eve of triumph over the barbarism which their persecution symbolized, would be a major tragedy.

. . . All who knowingly take part in the deportation of Jews to their death in Poland or Norwegians and French to their death in Germany are equally guilty with the executioner. All who share the guilt shall share the punishment. .

. . . In the meantime, and until the victory that is now assured is won, the United States will persevere in its efforts to rescue the victims of brutality of the Nazis and the Japs. In so far as the necessity of military operations permit this Government will use all means at its command to aid the escape of all intended victims of the Nazi and Jap executioner — regardless of race or religion or color. We call upon the free peoples of Europe and Asia temporarily to open their frontiers to all victims of oppression. We shall find havens of refuge for them, and we shall find the means for their maintenance and support until the tyrant is driven from their homelands and they may return.

In the name of justice and humanity let all freedom loving people rally to this righteous undertaking.

1 April 1944, p.5   HUNGARY ANNOUNCES ANTI-JEWISH DECREES

. . . based on the Nazi Nuremberg laws . . .

whose nature was further specified as:

16 April 1944, p.17

. . . the registration and closing of all Jewish properties . . .

28 April 1944, p.5

. . . recent reports from Hungary said 300,000 Jews had been moved from the eastern and northeastern parts of the country to so-called collection camps.

10 May, 1944, p.5   by Joseph M. Levy

. . . it is a fact that Hungary . . . is now preparing for the annihilation of Hungarian Jews by the most fiendish methods . . . Sztojay's . . . government . . . is about to start the extermination of about 1,000,000 human beings . . . The government in Budapest has decreed the creation in different parts of Hungary of "special baths" for Jews. These baths are in reality huge gas chambers arranged for mass murder, like those inaugurated in Poland in 1941.

18 May, 1944, p.5   by Joseph M. Levy

80,000 Jews of the Carpathian provinces . . . have been sent to murder camps in Poland.

9 June 1944, p.5

300,000 Hungarian Jews have been interned in camps and ghettos (within Hungary) . . .

18 June 1944, p.24

. . . recent statements made by the Hungarian Premier, Doeme Sztojay, that Jews were being exterminated to provide "room for American Hungarians to return to their native country after the war".

20 June 1944, p.5

7,000 Czechoslovak Jews interned in . . . Terezin . . . were dragged to gas chambers in the notorious German concentration camps at Birkenau and Oswiecim. Confirmation of the execution there of uncounted thousands was brought to London recently by a young Pole who had been imprisoned in both camps.

25 June 1944, p.5

(A Polish underground) message said that new mass murders were taking place at the Oswiecim concentration camp. They were carried out by gas in the following order: Jews, war prisoners, whatever their nationality, and invalids. A hundred thousand Jews have already been sent to Oswiecim for execution . . .

27 June 1944, p.6

Hull (called) upon Hungary to halt her mistreatment of Jews (and warned that) those German officers and men . . . who have . . . taken . . . part in the . . . atrocities, massacres and executions will be punished.

2 July 1944, p.12

Hungarian sources in Turkey reported that the 350,000 Jews . . . were being rounded up for deportation to death camps in Poland. By June 17, 400,000 had been sent to Poland; the remaining 350,000 are expected to be put to death by July 24.

On 3 July (p. 3) the "report" that eventually became the WRB report appeared as a report of two relief committees in Switzerland, specifying that since 6 April 400,000 Hungarian Jews had been sent to Auschwitz-Birkenau. The crematoria are reported to contain 50 furnaces each taking 8-10 corpses at a time. On 6 July (p. 6) the story was repeated, Eden endorsed the charges, and the World Jewish

Congress was notified more than two weeks ago that 100,000 Jews recently deported from Hungary to Poland had been gassed in the notorious German death camp at Oswiecim. Between May 15 and 27 sixty two railroad cars laden with Jewish children . . . and six cars laden with Jewish adults passed daily through the Plaszow station near Cracow. Mass deportations have also begun from Theresienstadt, Czechoslovakia, where the Jews have heretofore been unmolested.

13 July 1944, p.3

2,500 Jewish men, women and children . . . will arrive in the Auschwitz and Birkenau camps by this week-end, probably with previous knowledge of their fate.

On 15 July (p. 3) Hull again condemned the alleged killing of Hungarian Jews, and then from the "Polish underground":

4 Aug. 1944, p.5

courier . . . declared that Hungarian Jews were still being sent to Oswiecim, twelve train-loads every twenty-four hours. In their haste . . . the Germans . . . were killing small children with bludgeons. Many bodies were being burned in open fires, he said, because the crematories were over-taxed."

On 11 August (p. 4) is reported a letter by Horthy to the King of

147

Fig. 16: Members of U.S. Congress inspecting the shower bath at Dachau. From left to right, Senator Wherry (Nebraska), Senator Brooks (Illinois), Representative Vorhys (Ohio) and Representative Richards (South Carolina). They are being told that this was the gas chamber.

Photo: U.S. Army

148

Sweden declaring that deportations of Jews had been stopped and that they were being allowed to leave Hungary.

There are too many contradictions in the propaganda for it to equal later charges. However the charges resemble the propaganda somewhat. The present story is that between the middle of May and sometime in early July 1944, approximately 400,000 Hungarian Jews, from districts outside of the capital of Budapest, were deported by rail by the Germans and that almost all of these were killed at Birkenau, the killing having been the primary purpose of the deportations. This operation essentially cleaned out the Hungarian Jews, except for Budapest, where the Jews were left essentially intact. Even Birkenau was not designed for such large numbers of killings so many bodies were disposed of in burning pits, and many were shot rather than gassed. This is the story, despite Reitlinger's unfounded attempt to lower the figure to 200,000 killed. The "evidence" for the extermination of large numbers of Hungarian Jews (reviewed below), if accepted at all, simply does not permit such a wide departure from the 400,000 figure.[6]

It is obvious that no such thing could have happened, and received world-wide publicity during the war and at the later trials, without the ICRC delegation in Budapest learning of it. After all, we are speaking here of the near entirety of non-Budapest Jews and such massive and monstrous events could not have been flippantly forgotten by the persons contributing the "Hungary" section of the excerpt we have examined. The excerpt says emphatically that the major negative events effecting the Hungarian Jews occurred starting in October 1944 after Horthy's arrest. Moreover, the *Report* contains the general remarks about "extermination" which we have noted, so any extermination of Hungarian Jews would, if it were a reality, definitely be mentioned in the *Report*. There is clearly no truth to the claim of exterminations of Hungarian Jews.

At this point it is appropriate to provide some remarks on Hungarian Jewish population in early 1944. The Nazis used a figure of about 700 or 750 thousand.[7] Ruppin's 1940 book reports that the Hungarian Jewish population rose from 440 to 480 thousand in the autumn of 1938, due to the annexation of parts of Slovakia. In the spring of 1939 the Carpatho-Ukraine was annexed so that, in June, 1939, there were about 590,000 Jews in Hungary. It is known that a good number of non-Hungarian Jews, mainly Polish, took refuge in Hungary after 1939, so Ruppin's pre-war figure of 590,000 could easily have swelled to the 700,000 or 750,000 figure that the Nazis used. Ruppin's figure for Budapest's Jewish population is 200,000 in 1930. This figure would not have been supplemented by the annexations, but it would have been supplemented to some degree during the Thirties by German and Austrian Jews and to a greater degree by Polish and other Jews after 1939. It seems reasonable to assume that there were about 300,000 Jews in Budapest in the spring of 1944. Thus we seem to have a fairly good idea of Hungarian and Budapest Jewish population in 1944. Clearly the removal of 400,000 or more non-Budapest Jews in the spring of 1944 would have entailed the removal of essentially all non-Budapest Jews. Not only could this not have failed to be noticed by the Red Cross delegation, it is also difficult to see where the "one hundred thousand Jews" who "poured into Budapest from the provinces" in November could have come from.[8]

There are other arguments against the extermination claims. First, it will be seen that the charges specify that special arrangements were made at a conference in Vienna in early May to provide four trains per day to effect these deportations, and that the trains were in fact provided on schedule. That is, in the crucial few weeks before and after D-Day (6 June), at a time of desperate rail shortages, with both fronts threatening to collapse, the Germans provided an amount of extra rail transportation that would strain the resources of any rail system under the best of circumstances. That is just not believable. It is worth remembering that the rail journey from Budapest to Auschwitz is much more formidable than the map might suggest, on account of the mountains in eastern Czechoslovakia.

A second additional argument against the charges relates to the question, often asked, why did not the Allies attempt to bomb the gas chambers which, by the time of the alleged killings of Hungarian Jews, the whole world "knew" about? The question can be considerably broadened.

On 8 June 1944 the U.S. Fifteenth Air Force, based in southern Italy, was ordered to emphasize oil targets in its bombings, and was given a list of specific oil targets in eastern and southeastern Europe. The principal target, and the one that received the major share of attention, was the Ploesti area in Rumania. However Auschwitz was also one of the targets on the list, was first bombed on 20 August, and was subsequently bombed in September and December.[9]

Now in the Allied bombing operations in World War II it was customary to make extensive use of photographic intelligence. One objective was the assessment of damage done by attacks and another was the planning of attacks: determining whether or not the target was worth attacking and also determining the extent and nature of the defenses in the area of the target.[10] It is a certainty that intelligence had photographed Auschwitz and the surrounding area, rather thoroughly, soon after the 8 June order. In this case the Americans should have been able to provide actual photographs of all these Hungarian Jews being moved into Auschwitz and shot and burned out in the open. They should not even have been obliged to take any special measures to produce for us, either at the time of the alleged killings, or at the later trials, photographic evidence for their claims. Of course, to have been fully convincing, the former time should have been chosen, since the Russians controlled Auschwitz after January 1945.

The photograph of Fig. 7 is claimed to have been taken at Auschwitz in August 1944, but it has already been discussed in proper context. In any case, the number of bodies evident in the photograph roughly corresponds to the rate of ordinary deaths at Auschwitz, especially for 1942.

Despite all the attention the Hungarian Jews and Auschwitz were receiving at the time and despite the Roosevelt promise publicized on 25 March, the Americans did not lift a finger to either interfere with the alleged deportations, by bombing the specific rail lines involved, or with the alleged killings, by bombing the "gas chambers". They not only failed to take the opportunity to provide us with photographic evidence for their claims, they also do not seem to have the evidence despite having taken the photographs.

All of these considerations, the Red Cross *Report*, the wild impracticality of exterminating Hungarian Jews in the spring and summer of 1944, and the non-existence of any relevant consequences of the Allied control of the air, compel the conclusion that nothing resembling or approximating extermination actually happened to the Hungarian Jews.

We will shortly review the evidence for the extermination claim, but first we should provide an aside relative to the problem of the date of the first aid raid at Auschwitz. We remarked in Chapter III that Rudolf Vrba's claim that there was an air raid at Auschwitz on 9 April 1944 undermines his credibility. We have indicated above that Auschwitz was first bombed in August. This view is based mainly on the *Combat Chronology*, edited by Carter and Mueller, that the U.S. Air Force published in 1973, and on the standard and semi-official work by Craven *et. al.*, *The Army Air Forces in World War II*. The latter also treats the activities of the RAF Bomber Command, especially in connection with the oil campaign. The corresponding four volume British work by Webster and Frankland, *The Strategic Air Offensive Against Germany 1939-1945*, bases its account of the oil campaign on that of Craven *et al.*

An attack in early April seems completely out of the question. Auschwitz was of strategic importance only as an oil target. Craven *et. al.* provide an excellent summary of the air force oil campaign. There had been a spectacular raid at Ploesti in 1943, but there was no sustained oil campaign until the spring of 1944, on account of disagreements among Allied leaders regarding target priorities. By May 1944, only 1.1% of Allied bombs had fallen on oil targets. On 17 March 1944 the Fifteenth Air Force was advised to undertake attacks against Ploesti at the first opportunity, but "surreptitiously under the general directive which called for bombing transportation targets supporting German forces that faced the Russians". The first such attack came on 5 April, and there were also attacks on 15 and 24 April, in all three cases directed mainly against the rail centers near Ploesti, with a hope that there would be "incidental" damage to oil refineries. Oil related bombings by England based aircraft did not commence until 19 April, but these were also carried out under cover of an objective other than oil. The Fifteenth Air Force carried out several more raids against Ploesti before the 8 June order, after which the oil campaign got under way officially and extensively.[11]

This being the situation that existed, and in consideration of the confirmation provided by the *Combat Chronology,* it is impossible to believe that Auschwitz was air raided in April, when it was difficult to justify, within the Allied command, raids against even choice targets such as Ploesti. That a relatively minor oil target such as Auschwitz, much smaller than the not distant synthetic oil plants at Blechhammer, was bomed in April, is most unlikely. Even Blechhammer is not mentioned as a target until long after April.

Only the U.S. and British air forces are relevant to the problem of possible air raids at Auschwitz in the period April-September 1944. The Russians did not engage in industrial-strategic boming operations of this nature.

Our conclusions, drawn from the official U.S. Air Force war histories, are confirmed by the recollections of two Germans who were at Auschwitz in 1944. Thies Christophersen, author of the booklet *Die Auschwitz Luege* (mentioned here in Chapter I), wrote that the first aid raid was "in the autumn of 1944". Christophersen seems to be completely unaware that there is any significance in the question of the date of the first aid raid at Auschwitz.

Dr. Wilhelm Staeglich, the Hamburg judge whose statement was published in German journal *Nation Europa* (also mentioned here in Chapter I), did not make any remarks, in his published statement, in connection with air raids but he did write that he was a member of an anti-aircraft unit that was stationed near Auschwitz for a very short time starting in mid-July 1944. In reply to a neutrally worded inquiry by this author, with no reference to the nature of the underlying issue involved, Staeglich replied that there was no air raids while he was there and that he believed there had been none earlier, since he had not been informed of any and had not seen any corresponding destruction.

The August date for the first air raid is confirmed by the Italian Jew Primo Levi, who wrote in his book *Se Questo è un Uomo* (early in the chapter entitled *I fatti dell'estate*) that the first raid was in August, when he had been there five months.

Our analysis of the problem of the first air raid at Auschwitz is also essentially confirmed by the extermination mythologists. Reitlinger does not explicitly take a position on the date of the first raid but remarks (p. 383) on "the failure of the Allies to bomb the passes between Hungary and Auschwitz in May-July, 1944". Hilberg (p. 632) is well off the mark in placing the first raid on 16 December 1944, and this date is accepted by Levin (p. 701). Friedman (p. 78) is relatively on the mark in reporting a raid on 13 September 1944.

Since all evidence rejects a claim that there was an air raid at Auschwitz in April 1944, Vrba's claim that there was such a raid while he was sitting there peeking out from the woodpile is an important factor, in addition to the others mentioned in Chapter III, in demolishing his credibility. Moreover, it would be difficult for Vrba to claim a faulty memory comparable to Staeglich's, since the raid supposedly occurred at a uniquely crucial point in Vrba's life.

Returning to the immediate subject, we now review the evidence which is offered for exterminations of Hungarian Jews. It is mainly documentary.

We will essentially disregard the IMT affidavit (2605-PS) of Kastner, given 13 September 1945. Kastner was a Hungarian Jew who was in contact with Eichmann and associates in Budapest in 1944. His affidavit declares that 475,000 Hungarian Jews had been deported by 27 June 1944. It also gives a general "history" of the entire extermination program, said to be based on things told Kastner by SS Colonel Kurt Becher and SS Captain Dieter Wisliceny. That he enjoyed the confidence of these men is entirely possible, however, since in 1954, as an influential member of Ben-Gurion's Mapai party in Israel, he was accused by another Hungarian Jew of having been a collaborator of Becher, one of Eichmann's superiors in the SS operations in Hungary. The resulting libel actions, with verdicts against Kastner, generated a major political crisis in Israel whose catastrophic consequences were averted by the assassination of Kastner in 1957.[12] Kastner was another victim of the hoax.

Wisliceny, Eichmann's subordinate in Hungary, also gave an affidavit on 29 November 1945 and supporting testimony at the IMT on 3 January 1945.[13] The affidavit is another English language job with, e.g., the obscure (for a German) expression "heads" for people in transports. In Wisliceny's story there were written orders, given in early 1942 by Himmler, to exterminate the Jews. The orders were addressed to, among others, the "Inspector of Concentration Camps" who, according to the later testimony of Hoess, was not intended by Himmler to know anything about the program.

The major evidence is a collection of reputed German Foreign Office documents. In March 1944 one Dr. Veesenmayer of the Foreign Office was sent to Hungary as "plenipotentiary" to act for the German Government, supplementing the activities of special Ambassador Ritter. Veesenmayer communicated a great deal with the Foreign Office in Berlin via telegram. A document, NG-2263, shown in Fig. 30, is typical of those which are said to be one of these telegrams, taken from Foreign Office files. As a telegram received at the Foreign Office, it naturally does not have Veesenmayer's signature. The endorsements consist in the Foreign Office stamps that have been used, and the handwritten notation on the left which says that the document is to be filed under "Hungary" *(Ungarn)* and is initialed by von Thadden and dated: vTh 4/7. It reads:

I.) Transport of Jews out of Zone III concluded with 50,805 according to plan. Total number out of Zones I-III 340,162.

II.) Concentration in Zone IV and transport out of that Zone concluded with 41,499 according to plan. Total number 381,661. Continuation of operations has been

152

separately reported with teletypes no. 279 of 27 June, no. 287 of 29 June and no. 289 of 30 June to Fuschl. Concentration in Zone V (hitherto uncovered region west of the Danube without Budapest) commenced 29 June. Simultaneously smaller actions in the suburbs of Budapest commenced as preparatory measures. A few small transports of political, intellectual and specially skilled Jews, and Jews with many children, are also under way.

It is a collection of such documents which constitutes the evidence for the deportation of over 400,000 Hungarian Jews between 15 May and early July of 1944. In my determination the relevant documents are as summarized below. The nature of the endorsements is indicated in each case. Naturally not all documents dealing with anti-Jewish measures, including deportations during the relevant time period, are involved; only those which might be claimed to compel an interpretation consistent with the extermination claims are listed.

NG-2059 Mimeographed copy of a telegram from Veesenmayer to the Foreign Office, dated 8 May 1944. A certain number of Jews previously scheduled for deportation are to be put to work on military projects in Hungary instead. Application for the 100,000 employable Hungarian Jews requested by Organization Todt (the Speer ministry) must be made to Gluecks of the WVHA, who is in charge of the deportation of Hungarian Jews. The endorsement is Thadden's initials.

NG-2060 In two parts. The second part is a mimeograph copy of a telegram from Veesenmayer to Ribbentrop via Ritter, dated 21 April 1944. It reports that 100,038 Hungarian Jews have been confined to camps as a result of the "Special Operations". The endorsements are a Top Secret stamp and Thadden's initials. The descriptive material accompanying the document (the "staff evidence analysis") indicates that Geiger's initials also appear, but this is not confirmed by examination of the rest of the material (in this case the English translation only).

NG-2061 Mimeographed copy of a telegram from Veesenmayer to the Foreign Office, dated 20 May 1944. It reports arrests of people involved with the anti-Nazi underground, and the interception of "intelligence material concerning the alleged conditions in the German concentration camps in the Government General. In particular the happenings in the Auschwitz camp are described in detail". The endorsements are a Foreign Office stamp and Thadden's initials, although the staff evidence analysis says it is initialed by Geiger.

NG-2190 The first part is a covering note for the second part. Signed by Thadden and Wissberg and initialed by Wagner, and stamped Top Secret. The second part is a report from Thadden to the Foreign Office on anti-Jewish measures in Hungary, dated 26 May 1944. It is reported that the Hungarian Government has agreed to the deportation to the Eastern territories of all Hungarian Jews, with the exception of 80,000 to be retained for labor on military projects. The number of Hungarian Jews is estimated at 900,000 to 1,000,000. Most of the Jews outside Budapest have been concentrated in ghettos. As of 24 May, 116,000 had been deported to the General Government in daily shipments of 14,000. The Jewish Council in Budapest (same as the Jewish Senate of the Red Cross *Report* excerpt) was reassured that these measures were directed only against unassimilated Jews, and that others were to be treated differently. However, the SS expects difficulties with future concentration and deportation measures anyway. Plans for future measures are outlined. Problems stemming from the differing German and Hungarian definitions of a Jew are discussed. It is estimated that about one third of the Hungarian Jews deported to Auschwitz are able to work, and that these are distributed immediately after arrival to Sauckel, Organization Todt, etc. Stamped Top Secret and signed by Thadden. The third part is a covering note for the fourth part, initialed by Wagner and Thadden, with handwritten references to Eichmann. The fourth part is a summary of Thadden's report, with no endorsement.

NG-2230 A copy of a two page letter, dated 24 April 1944, from Thadden to Eichmann relaying the contents of NG-2233 (next to be discussed). Both pages initialed by Thadden. Date stamp and handwritten notations on bottom of page one. Note: the second time I consulted document NG-2230, it was an entirely different document, so there may be some error here.

NG-2233 In two parts. First part is a copy of a telegram from Veesenmayer to Ritter, dated 23 April 1944. It reports on the work of interning Jews from the Carpathians in ghettos. 150,000 Jews have already been rounded up. It is estimated that 300,000 Jews will have been affected when the action is completed. The internment of Jews in other areas is then to follow. From 15 May on, 3,000 Jews are to be shipped daily to Auschwitz and in order not to hold up their transport, the transfer of the 50,000 Jews, demanded for work in the Reich by Veesenmayer, will temporarily be held up. For reasons of security, feeding, and footwear, it is not considered practicable to send them on foot. The endorsement is the stamp of the Foreign Office (Classified Material). The second part of the document is a carbon copy of a letter from Thadden to Eichmann, dated 24 April, repeating the substance of the telegram. Initialed by Thadden.

NG-2235 A carbon copy of a telegram from Wagner to Veesenmayer, dated 21 May 1944. It is reported that Thadden is to visit Budapest shortly to discuss the disposal of the property of German and Hungarian Jews, within the framework of the general European solution of the Jewish question. Initialed by Wagner. There also appear to be initials "VM" on the document, but it does not appear that this is supposed to be Veesenmayer's initials.

NG-2236 A typed memo from Wagner to Steengracht, dated 6 July 1944. Wagner states that it is the Reich policy to prevent Jewish emigration. The War Refugee Board request, through Switzerland, that emigration of Hungarian Jews to Palestine be permitted, must be denied because that would alienate the Arabs. Anyway, the Swiss-American intervention will be too late by the end of the month, for the anti-Jewish action in Hungary will be completed by that time. Stamped Secret and signed by Wagner. Initialed by Thadden and, possibly, by Hencke.

NG-2237 A mimeographed copy of a telegram from Veesenmayer to the Foreign Office, dated 10 June, reporting that the measures for the concentration of Jews located north of Budapest had started, and that deportation of the Jews would start 11 June. The endorsement is a Foreign Office stamp and Thadden's initials.

NG-2238 Typewritten memo by Wagner proposing that negotiations with the Swiss and Swedes on emigration of Hungarian Jews be treated in a dilatory manner until the question of the treatment of the Jews remaining in Hungary has definitely been solved. Dated 16 September 1944. Signed by Wagner, initialed by Thadden and illegible others.

NG-2262 A mimeographed copy of a telegram from Veesenmayer to Ritter, dated 4 May, reporting that evacuation of 310,000 Jews of the Carpathian and Transylvanian regions into Germany ("nach Deutschland") is scheduled to begin in the middle of May. Four daily transports, each holding 3,000, are contemplated. The necessary rail arrangements will be made at a conference in Vienna on 4 May. Foreign Office stamp and Thadden's initials.

NG-2263 A mimeographed copy of a telegram from Veesenmayer to the Foreign Office, dated 30 June, reporting that 381,661 Hungarian Jews had been deported as of 30 June. Round-ups had started west of the Danube, not including Budapest, and also in the suburbs of Budapest. Foreign Office stamp and Thadden's initials.

NG-2424 In two parts. The first part is a typed letter from Foreign Office press chief Schmidt to Foreign Office Secretary of State Steengracht, dated 27 May, suggesting a propaganda campaign ("the discovery of explosives in Jewish clubs and synagogues", etc.) to precede any actions against the Jews of Budapest. The endorsement is initialing by Wagner. The second part is a typed copy of a telegram from Thadden to Budapest, dated 1 June, passing on the suggestion. Initialed by Wagner and Thadden.

NG-2980 In three parts. The first part is a typed copy of a telegram from Wagner to Budapest, dated 21 May, announcing a forthcoming visit to Budapest by Thadden, for negotiations on the Jewish problem. Stamped and initialed by Wagner. The second part is an unsigned carbon copy of a letter from Thadden to Wagner, constituting a covering letter for Thadden's report on his activities in Budapest. Stamped Top Secret. The third part is the typed 5 page report, dated 25 May. It is reported that special referent for Jewish questions at the German Embassy in Budapest von Adamovic, "has no idea of the actual intentions (or) of the practical application of the measures against the Jews". He also reports a visit to Eichmann's office, where he learned that 116,000 Jews had been deported to the Reich and that the deportation of another 200,000 was imminent. Concentration of about 250,000 Jews of the provinces north and northwest of Budapest will begin 7 June. More plans are given. It is estimated that only about 80,000 Jews able to work will remain in Hungary. The entire operation is to be concluded by the end of July. The report is five pages long and the only endorsement is a top secret stamp on the first page.

NG-5510 A typed copy of a telegram from Veesenmayer to the Foreign Office, date 8 May, stating that Count Bethlen and Dr. Schilling do not approve of the Jewish action, and that Veesenmayer will therefore request their dismissal. "Count Bethlen declared that he did not want to become a mass murderer and would rather resign." The endorsements consist of a top secret stamp and a handwritten notation to file under "Hungary".

NG-5532 A typed copy of a telegram from Veesenmayer to Foreign Minister Ribbentrop, dated 9 July, reporting Hungarian Minister of the Interior Jaross' intention to concentrate the Budapest Jews outside of Budapest and then "release them gradually in batches of 30-40,000 Jews for transport to the Reich". No endorsement.

NG-5533 A typed copy of a telegram from Veesenmayer to the Foreign Office, dated 14 June, asserting that numerous Hungarian Jews had been slipping into Slovakia "since we pounced upon them" after 19 March. Stamped with "Hungary" and "State Secretary" handwritten on the bottom.

NG-5565 An original typed copy of a telegram from Thadden to the German Embassy in Pressburg, dated 2 May, announcing that a conference will be held 4-5 May in Vienna for the purpose of organizing rail transport for "a large number of Hungarian Jews for work in the Eastern Territories". Stamped secret and initialed by Thadden.

NG-5567 A mimeographed copy of a telegram from Veesenmayer to the Foreign Office, dated 17 June, giving the total number of Hungarian Jews deported to the Reich as 326,009. Stamped and initialed by Thadden (the staff evidence analysis states that the document is initialed by Wagner and Reichel, but this is not confirmed by the documents I examined).

NG-5568 A mimeographed copy of a telegram from Veesenmayer to the Foreign Office, dated 8 June. "In execution of Jewish measures in Hungary basic principle to be observed is secrecy regarding dates of deportation and of zones which will be cleansed one after the other in order to avoid disquieting of Jewish elements and attempts to emigrate. This applies especially to the city district of Budapest which is to be the last zone and where difficulties in this respect are to be expected." Stamped and blue pencil noted by Thadden.

NG-5569 Several parts. The first and major part is a mimeographed copy of a telegram from Ludin in Pressburg (Slovakia) to the Foreign Office, date 14 June. It is reported that guards had entered the trains deporting Jews from Hungary across Slovakia, and had robbed the Jews of money and jewelry, and had shot some. They had then used the proceeds to get drunk at a nearby restaurant. Stamped. Next four parts are notes discussing the incident. Various stamps; initials of Wagner, Thadden, and Mirbach.

NG-5570 Mimeographed copies of five telegrams. The first is dated 14 October, and reports the plans to deport about 50,000 Jews by foot from Hungary for labor in the Reich. It is added, confidentially, that "Eichmann plans . . . to request 50,000 additional Jews in order to reach the ultimate goal of cleaning of Hungarian space . . . ". Stamped and handwritten notes. Next four parts discuss operations with Budapest Jews and also with the Jews being deported for labor. Stamps and initialings by Wagner and Thadden.

NG-5571 Typewritten telegrams exchanged by Veesenmayer and Altenburg of the Foreign Office, dated 25 and 28 June. In view of the "liquidation of the Jewish problem" in Hungary, the Hungarian Government should reimburse the Reich with the corresponding amounts of food-stuffs. Stamps.

NG-5573 Typed report by Wagner to Ribbentrop, dated 27 October. Of the 900,000 Jews who had been in Hungary, 437,402 had been sent for "labor to the East". A discussion of Hungarian Jews being allowed to emigrate follows. Stamped and initialed by Mirbach.

NG-5576 Typewritten copy of a telegram from Veesenmayer to the Foreign Office, dated 30 June. Horthy objected to measures against the Budapest Jews, but agreed to postponed measures. Thus "assembling in last provincial zone V (so far not covered space west of Danube, with exclusion of Budapest) has started. Simultaneously assembling will be carried out within jurisdiction of first constabulary commando in remoter suburbs of Budapest in order to facilitate drive in capital". Stamped.

NG-5594 Anonymous telegram from Budapest to the Foreign Office, dated 18 April. The "Hungarian population urgently desires a swift, radical solution to the Jewish problem, since fear of Jewish revenge is greater than the fear of Russian brutality". Handwritten notations to file.

NG-5595 Typewritten copy of a telegram from Veesenmayer to the Foreign Office, dated 28 April. "Special operations" in Hungary had resulted in the arrest of 194,000 Jews. Stamped and handwritten notations.

NG-5596 Typewritten copy of a telegram from Veesenmayer to the Foreign Office, dated 28 April, 194,000 Jews arrested by the special operations and Hungarian plans to distribute the Budapest Jews throughout the city on account of the Allied bombing raids. Stamped.

NG-5597 Typewritten copy of a telegram from Veesenmayer to the Foreign Office, dated 30 April. 194,000 Jews arrested by the special operations and discussion of Jews trying to be conscripted for labor in Hungary in order to avoid concentration camps. Stamped and handwritten notations.

NG-5599 Typewritten copy of a telegram from Veesenmayer to the Foreign Office, dated 5 May. 196,700 Jews arrested by the special operations. Stamped and handwritten notations.

NG-5600 Typewritten copy of a telegram from Veesenmayer to the Foreign Office, dated 6 May. Jews are being rounded up, and the Jews think that they are "only going to the special camps temporarily". Stamped.

NG-5602 Typewritten copy of a telegram from Veesenmayer to the Foreign Office, dated 24 May. 110,556 Hungarian Jews have been deported to the Reich. Stamped and handwritten notations.

NG-5603 Typewritten copy of a telegram from Veesenmayer to the Foreign Office, dated 19 May. 51,000 Hungarian Jews had been deported. Stamped, handwritten notations and illegible initials.

NG-5604 Typewritten copy of a telegram from Veesenmayer to the Foreign Office, dated 20 May. 62,644 Hungarian Jews deported. Stamped and handwritten notations.

NG-5605 Typewritten copy of a telegram from Veesenmayer to the Foreign Office, dated 20 May. Same report as NG-2061. Handwritten notations.

NG-5607 Typewritten copy of a telegram from Veesenmayer to the Foreign Office, dated 16 May. The deportation of the 300,000 Jews concentrated in the Carpathian area and in Transylvania had began on 14 May, with four special trains with 3,000 Jews in each leaving daily. Stamped and handwritten notations.

NG-5608 Typewritten copy of a telegram from Veesenmayer to the Foreign Office, dated 25 May. 138,870 Hungarian Jews had been deported to the Reich. Stamped and handwritten notations.

NG-5613 Typewritten copy of a telegram from Veesenmayer to the Foreign Office, dated 20 July. The Hungarian Nazis got the Franciscans to schedule a Thanksgiving mass, to celebrate the deportation of the Jews, but the bishop objected and certain compromises had to be made. Stamped and handwritten notations.

NG-5615 Typewritten copy of a telegram from Veesenmayer to the Foreign Office, dated 11 July. 437,402 Hungarian Jews had been deported. Stamped and handwritten notations.

NG-5616 Typewritten copy of a telegram from Veesenmayer to the Foreign Office, dated 8 July. 422,911 Hungarian Jews had been deported to the Reich. Stamped.

NG-5617 Typewritten copy of a telegram from Veesenmayer to the Foreign Office, dated 17 June. 340,142 Hungarian Jews had been deported to the Reich. Stamped and handwritten notations.

NG-5618 Typewritten copy of a telegram from Veesenmayer to the Foreign Office, dated 17 June. 326,000 Hungarian Jews had been deported to the Reich. Stamped and handwritten notations.

NG-5619 Typewritten copy of a telegram from Veesenmayer to the Foreign Office, dated 13 June. 289,357 Jews had been deported from the Carpathian and Transylvanian regions. Future plans for deportation are outlined. Stamped and handwritten notations.

NG-5620 Typewritten copy of a telegram from Veesenmayer to the Foreign Office, dated 8 June. Document, except for staff evidence analysis, was missing from the collection consulted, but it is apparently similar to those immediately preceding and immediately following.

NG-5621 Typewritten copy of a telegram from Veesenmayer to the Foreign Office, dated 2 June. 247.856 Hungarian Jews had been deported to the Reich. Stamped and handwritten notations.

NG-5622 Typewritten copy of a telegram from Veesenmayer to the Foreign Office, dated 1 June. 236,414 Hungarian Jews had been shipped to the Reich. Stamped.

NG-5623 Typewritten copy of a telegram from Veesenmayer to the Foreign Office, dated 1 June. 217,236 Hungarian Jews had been shipped to the Reich. Stamped and handwritten notations.

NG-5624 Typewritten copy of a telegram from Veesenmayer to the Foreign Office, dated 31 May. 204,312 Hungarian Jews had been shipped to the Reich. Stamped and handwritten notations.

NG-5637 Typed memo from Wagner to Steengracht, dated 21 May 1943. Wagner reports a visit from the Hungarian Ambassador. Difficulties relating to solution of the Jewish problem in Hungary were discussed. The deportations would have to be carried out in stages and, in order not to alarm those left behind, the ones deported should be allowed "a possibility to earn a living, at least for a short period". Stamped and signed by Wagner.

NG-5684 Typewritten copy of a telegram from Veesenmayer to Ribbentrop, dated 6 July. A six page report of a conference with Horthy, who mentioned that "he received

Fig. 17: Representative Vorhys inspects Dachau crematorium, which contained four ovens, three of which are visible here.
Photo: U.S. Army

157

a flood of telegrams every day from all quarters abroad and at home, for instance from the Vatican, from the King of Sweden, from Switzerland, from the Red Cross and other parties" in regard to the Hungarian Jews. He advocated keeping Jewish physicians and also the Jewish labor companies who had been assigned to war related tasks. Veesenmayer told him that "the solution of the Jewish question . . . was carried out by Hungary (but) could never (have been) completed without (SS and SD) support". Initialed by Steengracht.

A few words on the general conditions under which this documents analysis was carried out are in order before proceeding to interpret this evidence. Unless one goes to Washington to examine original documents, what one typically has made available when a specific document is examined may consist of as many as four parts. First, there may be a photostatic copy of the original document. This happens only in a minority of cases. The other three parts are almost always available. First, there is the mimeographed reproduction, in German, of the original document. Thus instead of any handwritten material, there is typewritten material which is indicated as having been handwritten. Second, there is the English translation of this German language document. Third, there is the accompanying descriptive material, the "staff evidence analysis". Among the four parts, quite a few minor contradictions were noted in the course of the study. In addition, a very few documents were missing from the collection examined.

It might be said, with good grounds, that certain of these documents should not be in the list, since they admit of many interpretations other than transport of the majority of Hungarian Jews to the Reich. NG-2424 is of this nature; we have seen that the proposed Budapest action finally took place in October. NG-5533 and NG-5684 admit of many interpretations; with respect to the latter, there is no doubt that some Hungarian Jews were deported to the Reich specifically for labor and the document may be interpreted in that respect.

Nevertheless it is obvious that I must declare, at this point, that a quite considerable amount of forgery was involved in the production of these documents; they were written after the war. That the events the documents speak of, involving over 400,000 Hungarian Jews transported to the Reich (or Poland) in May-July of 1944, did not occur is a certainty, for reasons given. However there are grounds for a certain uneasiness here since forgery does not seem to have been practiced with respect to the parts of the Auschwitz extermination legend which have been examined up to this point. Forgery is a risky business. Thus, although forgery seems a certainty, we should wish for some independent evidence for a charge of forgery.

Forgery is less risky if it does not involve the actual forgery of signatures; if the cooperation of the persons who signed or initialed the forged documents could have been obtained, then it might have seemed that the risk was removed or minimized. Thus we should take a close look at the endorsers of these documents. If NG-5684 is excepted, we have endorsements consisting of initials and/or signatures (or alleged initials and signatures) by Geiger, Wissberg, Hencke, Reichel, Mirbach, Wagner and Thadden, with the great majority of the endorsements coming from the latter two. These seven people have one very interesting thing in common; none were defendants in Case 11 or, apparently, in any other trial. In the cases of the first five, this can be argued to have been reasonable, either on account of the low rank of the person or on account of his peripheral involvement with the alleged crimes. Thus the first five people had only a minor involvement in Case 11; Mirbach appeared as a defense witness and Hencke was a defense affiant.[14]

With Wagner and Thadden, however, the immunity from prosecution is most mysterious if one does not grasp that the apparently safe manufacture of the incriminating Hungary documents required, basically, only their co-operation. We should thus examine their roles in the Foreign Office and their experiences after the war.

Eberhard von Thadden was an official in *"Inland II"* in the Foreign Office. This group's responsibility was liaison with the SS and thus Thadden was, so to speak, the "Jewish expert" of the Foreign Office. Communication with Eichmann relative to the carrying out of Jewish policies, whatever those policies were, was a quite normal part of his duties. NG-2233 and NG-2980 are quite accurate in at least that respect. Horst Wagner was a member of Foreign Minister Ribbentrop's personal staff and, as the head of *Inland II,* was Thadden's superior and, as the documents correctly suggest, he was equally involved in the Jewish policies of the German Government. The Foreign Office had been accused by the various military tribunals of being implicated in the extermination of Jews and at the IMT Ribbentrop had been found guilty in this respect. The main defendants in Case 11 were some officials of the Foreign Office, most of them ordinary diplomats, and implication in Jewish extermination was naturally one of the charges. Both *ex officio* and in consideration of the documents which have been reviewed, both Thadden and Wagner would have seemed, at the start of Case 11, to have been in serious trouble. Moreover, they could not have been considered too obscure in relation to Case 11, the Ministries, or Wilhelmstrasse, Case. For example, the *N. Y. Times* story announcing the opening of Case 11 chose to mention eight prominent "defendants or witnesses", and Thadden was one of those in the list.[15]

It is thus inexplicable, on normal grounds, that they were not even defendants in the trial; they both appeared as prosecution witnesses.[16] Strange occurences continued for several years. With respect to Thadden, German tribunals attempted to correct the glaring omission by prosecuting him. After he was released from American detention in 1949, a German court in Nuernberg charged him in December 1950, but he went to Cologne in the British zone and extradition was denied. Then a Cologne court charged him in May 1952 but the trial never materialized. He signed a prosecution affidavit for Eichmann's trial in 1961. In early 1964 he was arrested again but released after he managed to produce $500,000 bail, but then in November 1964 he was in an automobile accident and died of the injuries received.

Similarly Horst Wagner was arrested by German authorities in 1949, but he managed to flee to Spain and then to Italy. Extradition proceedings commenced in 1953, but failed. In 1958 he returned to Germany to apply for a pension, was arrested, but soon released on $20,000 bond, despite his previous flight to escape prosecution. His case seemed to disappear but a trial was finally scheduled for 20 May 1968, ten years after his return to Germany. However there were several postponements for various stated reasons and finally, in late 1972, his trial was postponed indefinitely. In late 1975 he was living in quiet retirement in a suburb of Duesseldorf.[17]

So much for the documentary evidence supporting the claims of extermination of Hungarian Jews. Wagner and Thadden had joined, as had Hoess and others, the "new *Meistersinger von Nuernberg"* but they evidently did it in an intelligent manner, since they acquired effective immunity from prosecution. In this connection, a detailed study of the documents by some expert person would be, most probably, very worthwhile. One object of analysis should be the language used. For example, the expression *"nach Deutschland"* in NG-2262 sounds as peculiar to me as "to America" would sound in an official State Department document, but I am not the appropriate judge in this matter. In any case, Wagner and Thadden held some cards, merely by virtue of knowledge of the existence of false documents, that others did not hold. For example, Hoess was in a position of dependence only on the gratitude of the Allies.

I have not examined all of the documents in the NG series (there are more than 5,000) and therefore I cannot reject the possibility, or even probability, that a few more exist. It is also possible that one or two might turn up with scribbles, said to be initials, for which I have no immediate answer. However the documents study has been relatively thorough in consideration of the purposes of our study. It went far beyond the documents which happen to have been referenced by Hilberg and by Reitlinger, far enough to satisfy me three times over on the fundamental dependence of this evidence on the post-war cooperation of von Thadden and Wagner.

It is well worth noting that Wagner and Thadden were not the only Germans involved with the Hungarian Jews who were mysteriously excused from prosecution. SS General Otto Winkelmann, Higher SS and Police Leader for Hungary and in command of all SS operations in Hungary, was also a prosecution witness in Case 11. SS Colonel Kurt Becher, representative in Hungary of the SS *Fuehrungshauptamt* (and thus of Himmler), served the prosecution at the IMT. In fact none of the principals unquestionably involved in whatever were the German measures relative to the Hungarian Jews stood trial at Nuernberg or (with the exception of Eichmann) anywhere else. Eichmann was missing at the time of the Nuernberg trials, and the others gave evidence for the prosecution of those whose involvement had been at most peripheral.

Nobody should be surprised to find the most sordid practices behind these trials. We have seen (p. 22-25) that no ethical limitations were respected in the means sometimes employed to produce "evidence". We should, therefore, take a closer look at who was in charge in Case 11. Recall that there was no substantial "indictment" process involving a grand jury, and that, as one may confirm by reading DuBois' book, it was the prosecution in each case that decided who was to be put on trial, and what he was to be charged with.

The Wilhelmstrasse Case was not really commensurate with the other cases tried before the NMT; all of the latter had had special purpose characters, as the chart on page 19 shows. The Ministries or Wilhelmstrasse Case, however, was somewhat like a "little IMT", that is, people from an assortment of German Government ministries were put on trial and the trial had a correspondingly wide scope. Thus it was split into an "economic ministries section" and a "political ministries section", each of which had different prosecution staffs.

The important section from our point of view and, indeed, the most politically important case to come before the NMT, was the political ministries section of Case 11, whose chief prosecutor was Robert M.W. Kempner, who has quite a history. It is very useful to present a short summary here of the "high" points of his career.

Kempner, a Jew, was born in Germany in 1899, studied law, and joined the Prussian Ministry of Interior during the Twenties. In the years 1928-1933 he was a senior counsel for the Prussian State Police (under the Ministry of the Interior) and specialized in investigating the rising Nazi Party. He became an anti-Nazi crusader, in his official capacity, and energetically attempted, without success, to have the party outlawed.

When the Nazis took over the German Government in 1933 he was dismissed from his government position but, although Jewish, he was able to continue his legal practice for a short while as a counselor on international law and Jewish migration problems and also, apparently, as legal counsel for the German taxi drivers' organization. Whether or not he spent any time in a camp or in some other form of detention is not clear. In any case, he moved to Italy in 1935 to take an administrative and teaching (political science) position at a small school in Florence. The Mussolini government closed the school in 1938, so the school and Kempner moved to Nice, France. He did not remain with the school for very long, however, and emigrated to the United States in 1939. His mother already had a research job at the University of Pennsylvania, and this connection seems to have landed him his "research associate" position at that University.[18]

He immediately resumed his anti-Nazi crusading. He had somehow managed to smuggle out of Germany some of the Prussian police papers to which he had contributed, and these became the basis of a book which he published privately in 1943. The book, in stencil form, attempted to show, on the basis of Kempner's past experiences in Germany, what should be done in Germany after the war in order to permanently suppress Nazism. It did not achieve wide circulation but, together with some other books and articles that he wrote, established him as a sort of expert on fighting Nazis. He had also smuggled out some phonograph recordings of Nazi meetings; these had been made by the Prussian police during the years of his service. He contributed them to the University of Pennsylvania. He also did a certain amount of anti-Nazi letter writing to the newspapers. As the war was drawing to a close, he wrote that the Nazi leaders should be tried in the U.S. before regular American courts. In the meantime, he had acquired U.S. citizenship.[19]

During the war he worked for both the U.S. Department of Justice and the OSS. In the latter agency he was charged with drawing up lists of German anti-Nazis who could be trusted with posts in the coming occupation government of Germany. He was one of a large group of German Jews in the OSS (which included, e.g., Herbert Marcuse).

At the end of the war Kempner switched to the War Department and accompanied the U.S. Army back into Germany "on the payroll of the Judge Advocate General". Prior to the opening of the IMT trial, he served in the fairly significant role of prosecution liaison with defense counsel, and later on was in charge of the division which prepared the U.S. trial briefs against individual defendants. During the trial, he was an apparently ordinary member of the prosecution staff, and specialized in the prosecution of the Nazi Minister of the Interior, Frick. He does not appear to have been particularly prominent, although immediately after the trial he contributed a magazine article to the *N.Y. Times* on the great work the trial had done in educating the Germans. The killings of the German military and political leaders had not yet been carried out, so he simultaneously predicted, with great satisfaction, that the doomed Nazis would be buried in unmarked graves, to "avoid fanatical pilgrimages by still ardent Nazis". Actually, the ultimate procedure was even more hysterical, since the bodies of Goering *et. al.* were photographed (in order to be gloated over, shortly later, in the press and in newsreels), disguised in U.S. Army uniforms, taken secretly to Dachau and cremated there, the ashes being sifted into a nearby stream.[20]

As he was taking over his responsibilities in Case 11 in 1947, Kempner was in the news in a related, but nevertheless highly important connection from the point of view of our subject. In 1943 and 1944 there had been held, in the land of the "free press", some "sedition trials" of Americans whose views of the U.S. Government's war policies were considered unwelcome. The U.S. prosecutor was O. John Rogge, an Ohioan who had, in his youth, been expected by family and friends to enter the ministry. He

161

became a lawyer instead, and is said to have turned in a brilliant performance at the Harvard Law School. Attorney General Biddle chose him to prosecute the "sedition" case, replacing William P. Maloney, whose methods had provoked protests from several influential members of Congress. The proceedings, involving 30 defendants, were completely contrary to U.S. constitutional principles, and were fortuitously aborted when the trial judge passed away in November 1944, and a mistrial was declared. While the government was planning to resume the case, the Supreme Court had reversed another sedition conviction, and grave doubt arose within the Justice Department about the wisdom of continuing the spectacle. We hope the reader will abide this long digression on the "sedition" episode, within the present digression on Kempner, for the point to be made is most important.[21]

Rogge lost interest in the sedition case, as such, but he did not lose interest in the general subject of a "Fascist" internal menace in the U.S. In the spring of 1946 he went to Germany on an 11 week "information" gathering expedition, and accumulated some alleged facts which he summarized in a report which he submitted to the Justice Department later in the year. Since there was no immediate reaction from the Justice Department to the material he had submitted, it appears that he got impatient and could not restrain himself. He therefore resorted to going around giving speeches in which he divulged some of the "information" he had been able to gather by interrogating Germans. In a speech to B'nai B'rith in New York in October 1946, he reported in very general language that Fascists are still at large "in the world and in this country . . . Now the Fascists can take a more subtle disguise; they can come forward and simply say 'I am anti-Communist'." A few days later he was much more specific whom he was talking about. John L. Lewis, President of the United Mine Workers, and the late William R. Davis, an oil operator and promoter, had, he declared in a speech at Swarthmore College, conspired with Goering and Ribbentrop to defeat President Roosevelt in the elections of 1936, 1940 and 1944. According to the "evidence" that he had obtained in Germany, other prominent Americans who, in the view of the Nazis, "could be organized against United States participation in the war" included, he said, Senator Burton K. Wheeler, former Vice President John N. Garner, former President Herbert Hoover and Democratic big-wig James A. Farley. Rogge had also given some of his material to Drew Pearson, and it appeared in Pearson's column at about the same time. For such flagrant violation of the rules and standards of the Justice Department and of the legal profession and also, presumably, for stepping on some important political toes, Rogge was immediately dismissed from the Justice Department by Attorney General Clark. Rogge defended his actions, explaining that, after all, he had merely made "a study of international Fascism, for the people under investigation were part of an international movement to destroy democracy both here and abroad". Again he was specific; two of the people posing the Fascist threat were Mr. Douglas MacCollum Stewart and Mr. George T. Eggleston, at the time a member of the staff of the *Reader's Digest.* Rogge said that in Germany he had obtained information about them from former German diplomats who had had official connections with the U.S. before Pearl Harbor. *Pravda* described Rogge's removal as a "scandal".[22]

In the period before Pearl Harbor, Stewart and Eggleston had published the *Scribner's Commentator,* which was dedicated to keeping the U.S. out of World War II. During 1941 Stewart had received a large sum of money, $38,000, and could not explain where it came from. He told the "sedition" grand juries of 1943-1944 that he had found this money in his home. Since, even to an impartial observer, such a story sounds ludicrous, Stewart was assailed by the prosecutor and judge for giving such testimony. His refusal to change it led to his being held in contempt of court and he was sentenced to serve 90 days in jail (he was paroled after 75 days).

In the course of 1946 the Justice Department, including even Rogge, had become convinced that no "sedition" charge could succeed in court, so the case that had been opened in 1943 was finally closed. However there was still the matter of Stewart's testimony, which seemed a good basis for a perjury charge. Thus, in March 1947, Stewart was put on trial for committing perjury in testifying before the wartime grand jury.

The prosecution claimed that Stewart had received $15,000 of the $38,000 from the German Government, and produced two witnesses to support its contention. Baron Herbert von Strempel, former First Secretary of the German Embassy in Washington, testified that he had given Stewart $15,000 in the Hotel Pennsylvania in New York in the fall of 1941. The money had been obtained, he said, from Dr. Hans Thomsen, German Charge d'Affaires. Thomsen then testified in support of von Strempel's story. The testimony of Strempel and Thomsen was, in fact, the direct consequence of Rogge's information gathering expedition in Germany in 1946.

Stewart's defense produced evidence that Stewart had received large sums of money from American sources in 1941. It claimed that some wealthy Americans wished to support the, by then, beleaguered cause of staying out of the war, but anonymously, so they slipped money to Stewart anonymously. Whether this claim was truthful or the truth was that Stewart had, indeed, lied before the wartime grand jury on account of feeling himself obliged not to divulge the identities of his American supporters, is scarcely relevant to our subject. More relevant was the defense cross examination of the prosecution's German witnesses, since the defense was able to discredit the prosecution case by showing that the testimony had been coerced. Baron von Strempel said that he had been arrested in Hamburg by two British agents who, when asked for their warrant, "smiled, drew their guns from their shoulder holsters, and said that was their warrant". He then spent four weeks in an American interrogation center, and then seven months in a detention camp, where he was again subject to continual questioning. During this period, his health was "never so bad". He was questioned by Robert M.W. Kempner, but did not want to talk about this. Judge Laws was obliged to direct von Strempel to reply to defense attorney Magee's questions about this feature of his experiences. He finally said that Kempner had told him that if he "concealed any embassy dealings" he would be court-martialed and sentenced to death. He then told the whole story. Incessant, intensive questioning by interrogators made him feel as if he had been "hypnotized". O. John Rogge became one of von Strempel's interrogators in Germany. During Rogge's interrogation, he said, his necktie and shoelaces were removed, he was kept in solitary confinement, was questioned all day without food, and was "at all times under duress". He admitted that he had signed a statement, but said that this was on account of fear of further solitary confinement. He gave this testimony, so destructive to the prosecution's case, despite the fact that the U.S. was paying him $70 per week, plus hotel expenses, in connection with his appearance as a witness against Stewart. There was also the possibility of U.S. retaliation via some sort of "war crimes" charge. Thomsen was likewise cross examined; he admitted than von Strempel had told him of the death threat, and said that he had been "coached" by Rogge in recalling details. The jury found Stewart innocent during the course of a lunch break. Thus had Kempner appeared in the newspapers even before Case 11 had gotten underway.[23]

163

In examining the sedition affair we have, therefore, encountered the Wilhelmstrasse Case, in the sense that Kempner enters the picture as interrogator and potential prosecutor of incarcerated former officials of the German Foreign Office. The connection with Case 11 is even more substantial since Stewart's attorney in the 1947 trial, Warren E. Magee, was shortly later to become co-counsel for Baron von Weizsaecker, the principal defendant in Case 11. We therefore have the unusual fact that the two sides involved in Case 11 had, almost simultaneously, clashed in a regular U.S. legal proceeding, and that the testimony that had been the result of the interrogation of the captive Germans had been successfully challenged by the defense as coerced. This is an extraordinary and important confirmation of the kind of activity, indicated by the evidence we have already reviewed, which must have transpired behind the scenes at the NMT—carrot and stick tactics of various sorts, including even third degree methods in some cases (but not necessarily in all cases where the evidence could correctly be said to have been "coerced"). Magee's successes along these lines did not, moreover, cease with the Stewart trial. In another extraordinary choice of a person to use as a prosecution witness rather than put on trial, Kempner had used Friedrich Gaus, who had a reputation as "Ribbentrop's evil spirit", as the chief prosecution witness against von Weizsaecker. Magee, evidently by virtue of being an American having access to documents denied the German lawyers, was able to prove in court that Kempner had threatened to hand Gaus over to the Russians if Gaus did not cooperate with the prosecution, a frequent and effective threat which had certain variations. Haefliger, one of the defendants in Case 11, was a Swiss citizen but, according to his trial testimony, he was told by interrogator Sachs that if he stood on his Swiss nationality he would be turned over to the Russians, and Sachs urged him "to note that there were no diplomatic relations between Russia and Switzerland". Much more to the point is the fact that von Thadden, under cross examination by defense attorney Dr. Schmidt-Leichner, admitted that Kempner, in connection with an execution that had supposedly been carried out by German authorities in France,

had made me understand that there were two possibilities for me, either to confess or to be transmitted to the French authorities, before a French tribunal, where the death penalty would be sure for me. A delay of twenty four hours was accorded me, during which I had to decide.

A Swiss journalist wrote at the time that Kempner and colleagues were attempting to misrepresent Nazism as a "concoction of the German upper classes" in order to destroy the pre-Nazi social structure of Germany.[24]

Rogge had a long and interesting career but a thorough summary would carry us too far afield. In fairness to him we should say that his behavior in connection with the "sedition" cases should not lead one to assume that he was insensitive in regard to civil liberties since, when the first postwar steps were being taken to set up an anti-Communist internal security program, Rogge started yelling about "witch hunts" and, in the following years, became Chairman of the N.Y. State (Henry) Wallace for President Committee, a perfectly logical appointment, because Rogge embodied all that was unique in that movement's approach to dealing with the Soviet Union. Characterized by the left wing *Nation* in 1950 as "the lone independent in various Communist-operated congresses, committees, and delegations", he had travelled to Moscow in March to attend the "World Congress of Partisans for Peace". He explained to the Soviets that the cold war was equally the fault of both sides, and stood up in a formal meeting in the Kremlin and quoted Thomas Jefferson, actions that were not appreciated by his Soviet hosts. The *Nation* commented further that[25]

Fig. 18: U.S. Congressmen inspect the crematorium at Buchenwald, which contained six ovens.

Photo: U.S. Army

165

It is easy to put down O. John Rogge as a quixotic busybody, a fuzzy-minded liberal so out of touch with reality that he believes the ills of the world to be merely the result of unfortunate misunderstanding . . . He has shown why the Russian rulers regard with suspicion even their own followers who have had contact with the West.

Rogge also involved himself in the widely publicized "Trenton Six" murder case of 1948-1953, as a lawyer for the "Civil Rights Congress". In December 1949 the judge barred him from the New Jersey trial for

violating the lawyers' canons of ethics by denouncing the conduct of the trial in public, by showing "studied discourtesy and contempt" in the court and by "deliberately distorting the facts". (The judge also charged that) the Civil Rights Congress . . . collected more money from the public than was needed for the trial.

Seven months later, a U.S. court held that Rogge's barring from the trial was wrong, but did not order his restoration.[26] This short discussion of Rogge suffices for our purposes.

To return to Kempner. When the Bonn Government had been newly constituted in 1949, he warned of incipient Nazism there. Such a view did not prevent him from serving, two years later, as Israel's representative to Bonn in negotiations relative to the restitution of Jews who had suffered injury at the hands of the Nazi Government. However, the next month he was attacking the reprieves and reductions of sentences of "war criminals" that had been granted by the U.S.[27]

Kempner next appeared in connection with the 1952 House investigation of the Katyn Forest massacre, a well known Russian atrocity whose handling by the IMT throws full light on the absurdity of that tribunal's claim to respect.

On 13 April 1943 the Germans announced that, in the Katyn Forest near the city of Smolensk in Russia (mid-way between Minsk and Moscow), mass graves of Polish officers who had been captured by the Russians in 1939 had been uncovered. Four days later the minister of defense of the Polish government in exile (in London) announced that he was requesting the International Red Cross to make an inquiry. The Germans supported the proposed inquiry but the Russians opposed it, referring to the London Poles as "Hitler's Polish collaborators", and on 26 April breaking diplomatic relations with that government over the matter.

On account of the Russian opposition, the Red Cross refused to get involved. However, the German Government exhibited the Katyn mass graves to various parties of Poles, to a group of foreign newspaper correspondents, to a group of German journalists, to small parties of British and American POW's, to a technical team of the Polish Red Cross and, most importantly, to an international commission of experts in forensic medicine (specialists in rendering medical opinions in legal proceedings). The commission concluded with a report which demonstrated the certainty that these Polish officers had been murdered by the Russians prior to the outbreak of war between Russia and Germany in June 1941.

When the graves had first been discovered the German propaganda service, not knowing how many bodies were to be found there but knowing the approximate number of Polish officers who could have been involved as victims, used the figures of 10,000 and 12,000 as the number of bodies discovered, and these were the figures which were given the widest publicity during the war. Consequently, at the IMT, the indictment charged the Germans with murdering 11,000 Polish officers at Katyn, although it had been established, later in 1943, that there were only 4,253 bodies to be found. This fact was published by the German Government but naturally, since it contradicted their earlier claims, the Germans did not give the correct figure great publicity.

166

What happened at the IMT with respect to this charge illustrates the foolishness of that tribunal's claim to anything approximating legal jurisdiction. The testimony of members of the forensic commission was naturally of interest so the Russians produced Professor Marko Markov, a citizen and resident of Bulgaria, who had been one of the signers of the commission report. Bulgaria being, by then, under Soviet control, Markov had changed his mind and testified in support of the Russian position, i.e., that the Germans had intimidated him into approving the commission report.[28]

Goering's counsel, on the other hand, applied to have Professor F. Naville, the chairman of the commission, called to testify. On this point one can see the emptiness of the tribunal's effectiveness in getting at the truth, even if it had wished to. Naville was a Swiss citizen, resident in Geneva, and could not be forced to testify and, in fact, he declined to testify. The motivation is obvious. The counsel for Field Marshall Keitel also requested that Naville (who had also been an International Red Cross representative) answer some questions (relative to a different subject) to be put to him in writing, but it appears that this interrogation did not materialize. Thus the IMT tribunal, by its very nature, was prejudiced against the appearance of the most reliable type of witness: the citizen of a country which had been neutral during the war and independent after the war (I am only saying that the IMT could not *compel* testimony from such people; we have seen that Burckhardt, the President of the Red Cross, voluntarily answered, for Kaltenbrunner's defense, written questions put to him in Switzerland). The defense ended up by calling three German soldiers to testify (three witnesses were allowed to each side on this matter).[29]

The tribunal's final disposition of the Katyn issue was a disgrace even independently of the true facts concerning the atrocity: it was quietly dropped and does not appear in the judgment. The Germans were not "found" either guilty or not guilty of this Russian atrocity. The IMT ducked the whole matter.

In 1952 the U.S. House of Representatives investigated the Katyn massacre and naturally made an inquiry into what had happened at the IMT in this respect. The Select Committee set up for this purpose accordingly held some hearings in Frankfurt, Germany in April of that year. The Committee heard, among others, representatives of both the defense and prosecution legal staffs of the IMT. To speak for the German side, the Committee logically called Dr. Otto Stahmer, who had been counsel for the principal defendant Goering, who had also been the defendant who had pressed this particular matter at the IMT. To speak for the American prosecution the Committee, surprisingly, chose Robert M.W. Kempner. Examination of the trial record reveals no reason why Kempner should have been selected for this role. That Kempner appears to have been living in Germany at this time, and that the Committee naturally thought it convenient that he testify at the Frankfurt hearings, does not explain anything. During the course of all of its hearings, the only other member of the prosecution that the Committee heard was Justice Jackson, but his appearance in November in Washington was somewhat ceremonial and added nothing to the record.

According to the record of the public hearing held in Frankfurt, Kempner explained that the Katyn massacre was, according to the understandings among the prosecution staffs, "a clear-cut Russian affair and was handled right from the beginning by the Russians . . . We had no right to interfere in any way". Nevertheless, after the witnesses had been heard the general view, according to Kempner, was that Goering had scored a victory on this point. Thus the failure to mention Katyn in the judgment called into question the integrity of the Nuernberg trials, and a realization of this was implicit in the questions asked by the committee members. Kempner was asked about possible participation by the U.S. prosecution staff in the behind-the-scenes activity in regard to Katyn, and denied that such had taken place. He also, in response to questioning, denied that there had been any "conspiracy or attempt to collude between anybody on the American side and anybody on the Russian side".[30]

The *N.Y. Times* reported that the tone of the Frankfurt hearing was such that "the principles governing the trial procedure in Nuernberg were being questioned. United States officials at the hearing privately expressed concern over the situation".[31] The *Chicago Tribune* reported that, at a secret session the night before the public hearing in Frankfurt, Kempner had admitted that the U.S. prosecution staff at the IMT had possessed the evidence which showed that the Russians had committed the Katyn murders.

The Select Committee on the Katyn Forest massacre concluded that the U.S. Government had suppressed the truth about Katyn both during and immediately after the war. In particular, a report by Lt. Col. John H. Van Vliet, Jr., one of the American POW's who had witnessed the mass graves, "later disappeared from either Army or State Department files". It was also found that the Federal Communications Commission had intimidated radio stations in order to suppress criticism of the Russians.[32]

In the years immediately following 1952 there was little for Kempner to do in relation to Nazis, but with the Eichmann affair he was back in action and served as a "consultant" to the Israeli government in assembling evidence for the trial. From that point on, he was very active. He contributed an article to the *Yad Vashem Studies* on methods of examining Nazis in trials, and he published a book in German, rehashing old propaganda myths. In 1971 he expressed approval of the conviction of Lt. Calley and in December 1972 he endorsed the "evidence" that Ladislas Farago had gathered in connection with Farago's Martin Bormann-is-in-Argentina fiasco of that month. Evidently yearning for the old days, Kempner declared that the "United States and its Allies should reopen the Bormann case within the framework of the International Military Tribunal".[33] Bormann had been tried *in absentia* at the IMT and sentenced to death. He was never found and it is now generally agreed that he died in Berlin.

In regard to Kempner, three principal conclusions may be drawn from this short summary (based entirely on material in the public record) of the man's career. First, he could accurately be characterized as a fanatical anti-Nazi, starting way back in the Twenties, when the Nazis were certainly no more criminal than several other groups on the violent and chaotic German political scene (the Communists and Social Democrats also had private armies). Anti-Nazism is obviously Kempner's consuming vocation. Second, he was an extremely important figure in the trials that the U.S. held in Nuernberg. We have seen that he had critically important responsibilities in connection with the IMT and was also treated, later on, as a particular authority on what had gone on there. At the end of the IMT trial the press described him as "Jackson's expert on German matters" and "chief of investigation and research for . . . Jackson".[34] At the NMT he took over the prosecution of the most important case, the political section of the Wilhelmstrasse Case, and he may very well have been the most important individual on the Nuernberg staff, although further research would be required to clarify the real power relationships that existed on the Nuernberg staff, if such clarification is possible. James M. McHaney headed the division that prepared Cases 1, 4, 7, 8, 9 and 12. Other significant persons at the NMT have been discussed by Taylor.[35] The *Encyclopedia Judaica* describes Kempner as "chief prosecutor" at the NMT trials.

The third conclusion that may be drawn is that there are excellent grounds, based on the public record, for believing that Kempner abused the power he had at the military tribunals, and produced "evidence" by improper methods involving threats and various forms of coercion. The Stewart case makes this conclusion inescapable.

This is the man who held the power of life and death over Eberhard von Thadden and Horst Wagner.

Our digression on Kempner is concluded. We came to the point, in our analysis of Hungary, where irregularities in the production of evidence in Case 11 were clearly indicated. Thus it was necessary to examine two subjects: who was in charge in Case 11 and what was the level of integrity maintained in the operations of the trials at Nuernberg. It was found that the truth in regard to the latter subject was established rather decisively in the course of examining the former; a study of Kempner's career reveals all that one needs to know in order to evaluate the reliability of the evidence generated at the Nuernberg trials.

Clearly, any person who wishes to maintain the authenticity of the Hungary-related documents that imply extermination must produce some tortured story whose structure we cannot begin to imagine.

Another person involved in the documents is Veesenmayer, who was a defendant in the Wilhelmstrasse Case, and who was questioned in connection with some of these documents. The general position taken in his testimony was a reasonable one in view of his objective of gaining acquittal or a light sentence. He had to report everything that went on in Hungary and thus Jewish measures were in his reports. However these measures did not have the importance in his mind at that time that they have in our minds at this time. He testified that he often got twenty assignments a day and in the course of a month would receive mutually contradictory assignments. His reports, he said, were naturally prepared by assistants, hastily scanned by him, and then signed. Shown documents which have him reporting that two transports, each of 2,000 Jews fit for work, were sent to Auschwitz in April 1944, and asked if this were correct, he remarked that he had no specific memory but that it was "quite possible", but that he never knew what Auschwitz was. Shown NG-5567, which has him reporting that up to 17 June, 326,009 Jews had been deported from Hungary, he also remarked "quite possible". In other words, he did not want to involve himself, in any way, in these matters by taking any strong position, either assenting or dissenting, with respect to the alleged facts. If he had said that he clearly recollected, in detail, mass deportations of Jews, in the numbers alleged, in the spring and summer of 1944, then such testimony would have implicated him in the alleged exterminations. On the other hand, if he had denied that such mass deportations had taken place then he would, in effect, have been claiming close involvement in whatever had happened and he would have also, by such testimony, flung down a challenge to the prosecution and court which they could not possibly have ignored. Thus the logic of his testimony. He said that he was concerned with moving the Jews out of Budapest because of the danger of revolt as the Russians approached. Pressed on this matter, he explained that

In practice the question was, will the front hold or won't it? If Budapest revolts, the whole front will be rolled up . . . If I participated in such conversations, which I won't deny is possible, then I participated exclusively from a military point of view. What can I do to hold up the Eastern front as long as possible? Only from that point of view.

Veesenmayer was sentenced to twenty years imprisonment, but he was out by early 1952.[36]

169

This seems to be as good a place as any to point out a fact which seems to be effectively forgotten by many writers on this subject. There was a war going on during World War II. The Germans were thinking about ways of winning it, not about exterminating Jews. The claim of NG-2233, that the extermination program had rail priority over military production, is absolutely ridiculous.

On the subject of what actually happened in Hungary, note that the Red Cross *Report* says that the basic German policy in 1944 was to intern East European Jews, on account of their posing a security menace as the front came nearer. Now, the documents reporting concentration and deportation of large numbers of Hungarian Jews may be correct in regard to concentration alone; this was the policy in neighboring countries. However it seems unlikely that anywhere near 400,000 were concentrated. That would have been quite a huge operation.

It appears possible to get a fairly accurate picture of what happened in Hungary by supplementing the story of the Red Cross with an examination of the documents, rejecting the documents which are obvious forgeries. We are fortunate in having the two volume collection of reproductions of selected original documents, *The Destruction of Hungarian Jewry*, edited by Randolph L. Braham; these volumes offer the normally circumstanced reader a handy substitute for a regular documents collection. Examining the documents included, and rejecting as forgeries those that pertain to alleged deportations of 400,000 Hungarian Jews, a believable story unfolds. On 14 April 1944, Hungary agrees to the deportation of 50,000 employable Jews to Germany for labor (p. 134, NG-1815). On 19 April, Veesenmayer requests freight cars, whose procurement is "encountering greatest difficulties", for the deportation of 10,000 employable Jews delivered by the Hungarians (p. 138, NG-5546). Finally on 27 April Veesenmayer reports on the imminent shipment of 4,000 employable Jews to Auschwitz (p. 361, NG-5535). Also on 27 April, Ritter reports on delays in the deportation of the 50,000 on account of rail shortages (p. 362, NG-2196). Later in the year, 11 July, Veesenmayer reports on the difficulty of carrying out the Jewish policy in Hungary because of the more lenient policies practiced in Rumania and Slovakia (p. 194, NG-5586). On 25 August, Veesenmayer reports Himmler's order to stop deportations from Hungary (p. 481, no document number), and on 18 October Veesenmayer reports on the new Jewish measures in Hungary (p. 226, no document number). A believable story, and one consistent with the Red Cross *Report*. One may also remark that, on Hungary, the authors of the hoax have again attempted to supply a dual interpretation to a perfectly valid fact. There were, indeed, deportations of Hungarian Jews in the spring of 1944 to, among other places, Auschwitz. However the deportations, which were for labor purposes only, were severely limited by the disintegrating European rail system, and do not appear to have been carried out on the approximate schedule originally contemplated or aspired to.

A few words regarding the Joel Brand affair, the proposed swap of Hungarian Jews for trucks and other supplies, are in order.

The pre-war German policy, which was also maintained to some extent early in the war, was to encourage Jewish emigration by all means. However, after the war had developed into a great conflict, the policy changed, and emigration from countries in the German sphere was made very difficult for Jews. The principal reason for this was, of course, that such Jews were manpower that could and would be used against them. There were a variety of lesser reasons, one of the most important being that, in an attempt to drive a wedge between Britain and the Arabs, the Germans supported the Arab side on the question of Jewish immigration into Palestine. Thus, the standard German attitude in the latter half of the war was that Jewish emigration could proceed on an exchange basis, in exchange for Germans held abroad, especially if the Jews were not to go to Palestine. We have seen that Belsen served as a transit camp for Jews who were to be exchanged.

What was involved in the Brand affair was the same sort of thinking on the German side, with a variation regarding the form of the *quid pro quo*. The Germans were willing to let the Jews emigrate in exchange for the trucks and other supplies. Thus there is nothing implausible in the Brand affair, provided one understands that it was not the lives of the Hungarian Jews that were at stake in the matter.

Although the Brand deal was not consummated, there was a trickle of German and Hungarian authorized emigration of Jews from Hungary to, e.g., Sweden, Switzerland and the U.S. A rather larger number slipped into Rumania and Slovakia illegally in 1944 (reversing the earlier direction of movement, which had been into Hungary). The defense documents Steengracht 75, 76, 77 and 87 give a picture of the situation.

The survey of 1944 propaganda which was presented in this chapter shows that Auschwitz (referred to as Oswiecim) finally emerged in the propaganda as an extermination camp in the period immediately after D-Day, when nobody was paying any attention to such stories. Later in the summer of 1944 the emphasis switched to the camp at Lublin, which was captured by the Russians in late July. The expected propaganda nonsense was generated in respect to the cremation ovens (five in number) which were found there, the Zyklon, some bones (presumably human), etc. Lublin remained the propaganda's leading extermination camp well into the autumn of 1944.[37]

This concludes our analysis of the Auschwitz charges. It is impossible to believe them; the allegations are so breathtakingly absurd that they are even difficult to summarize. We are told that the Nazis were carrying out mass exterminations of Jews at the industrial center Auschwitz, employing the widely used insecticide Zyklon B for the killing. The 30 or 46 cremation ovens at Auschwitz, used for disposing of the bodies of the very large numbers of people who died ordinary deaths there, were also used for making the bodies of these exterminated Jews vanish without a trace. As an extermination center, Auschwitz was naturally the place that the Hungarian Jews were shipped to for execution. Shipments of Jews conscripted specifically for desperately needed labor in military production were delayed in order to transport the Hungarian Jews to Auschwitz for execution. The 46 cremation ovens which existed at Auschwitz turned out to be inadequate to dispose of people arriving at the rate of about 10,000 per day, so the bodies were burned out-of-doors in pits. This cleaning out of the Hungarian Jews escaped the notice of the International Red Cross delegation in Budapest, which was deeply involved in Jewish affairs. The evidence for all of this, presented to us by the U.S. Government, consists of documents whose authenticity is proved by the endorsements of Jewish policy specialists Wagner and von Thadden, who are also incriminated by the documents. However, the U.S. Government did not prosecute Wagner and von Thadden in the Wilhelmstrasse Case, where the indictments were in the hands of a lifelong Nazi-hater (Kempner), and where an American lawyer had exposed the evidence as coerced, just as he did in a regular U.S. legal proceeding in Washington where Kempner was involved.

The U.S. Government also failed, despite all of its talk in 1944, to interfere in any way with, or even make photographs of, these alleged events at Auschwitz.

Can anybody believe such a story?

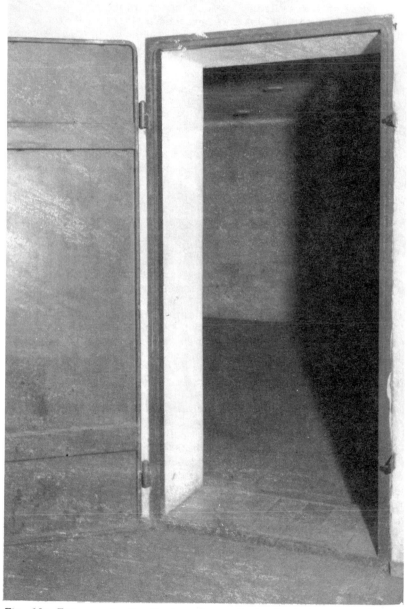

Fig. 19: Entrance to the Dachau shower bath which was baptized "gas chamber"

Photo: U.S. Army

VI
ET CETERA

The extermination claims have been so concentrated on Auschwitz that this book could justifiably end right here; since the central part of the extermination legend is false, there is no reason why the reader should believe any other part of it, even if the evidence might appear relatively decent at first glance. Hundreds of trained staff members were dispatched to Europe and employed there to gather the "evidence" for exterminations and related crimes, and we have seen what kind of story they have presented with respect to Auschwitz; a fabrication constructed of perjury, forgery, distortion of fact and misrepresentation of documents. There is no reason to expect a better case for the less publicized features of the extermination legend. Nevertheless the remainder of the story should be examined, partly for the sake of completeness, partly because the examination can be accomplished rather quickly, and partly because there is a respect in which one feature of the legend may be partially true. It is also convenient to review here a few odd matters that might strike some readers as evidence in support of the extermination claims.

The evidence for exterminations at Belzec, Chelmno, Lublin, Sobibor and Treblinka is fairly close to zero. There is the Hoess affidavit and testimony and the "Gerstein statement". There is a draft of a letter by Dr. Wetzel, another Nazi who became immune from prosecution, speaking of there being "no objections to doing away with those Jews who are unable to work, by means of the Brack remedy" (NO-365). The draft is typewritten and apparently initialed by Wetzel, who had been head of the Race-Political Office of the NSDAP, but was transferred in 1941 to Rosenberg's Ministry for the East, where he served as the expert for Jewish affairs. There is no evidence that the letter, which is addressed to Hinrich Lohse, Reichskommissar for the Ostland (map, Fig. 1), was ever sent. A similar document, bearing a typewritten Wetzel signature, is NG-2325. Wetzel was not called as a witness at any of the Nuernberg trials, and was not threatened with prosecution until 1961, when he was arrested by German authorities in Hannover, but his case seems to have immediately disappeared from the public record, and nothing more was heard of him, except that he is said to have been finally charged in 1966; if such is the case it is odd that he is not listed in the 1965 East German *Brown Book*. However, no trial ever materialized.[1] We will have occasion to comment on Lohse below.

The Viktor Brack of Wetzel's letter was an official of the Fuehrer-Chancellery, involved in the Nazi euthanasia program. The present claim is that the gas chambers in Poland, exclusive of those allegedly used at Auschwitz, "evolved" from the euthanasia program which, it is claimed, employed gas chambers. Despite Brack's testimony, it is difficult to believe that euthanasia was practiced in German hospitals by a method of gassing 20 or 30 persons at a time with carbon monoxide.[2] Auschwitz, of course, must be excluded from this "evolution" from the euthanasia program on account, among other reasons, of the Hoess testimony. Reitlinger and Hilberg do not seem worried over the confusion thus created in the structure of the legend.

173

The euthanasia program came into existence via a Hitler decree of 1 September 1939, authorizing the mercy killing of mortally ill patients. Later the severely insane were included. The program encountered deep hostility in the German population, especially since rumors, of unknown origin, immediately started circulating; the rumors claimed, *inter alia,* mass gassings of the sick and elderly. On 6 November 1940 Cardinal Faulhaber of Munich wrote to the Ministry of Justice, setting forth the Catholic Church's objections, and pointing out[3]

that a great disturbance has arisen in our people today because the mass dying of mentally ill persons is discussed everywhere and unfortunately the most absurd rumors are emerging about the number of deaths, the manner of death, etc.

It did not take long for the euthanasia program to appear in propaganda, and in December 1941 the BBC broadcast an address by author Thomas Mann, in which Mann urged the German people to break with the Nazis. In listing the Nazi crimes, Mann said[4]

In German hospitals the severely wounded, the old and feeble are killed with poison gas – in one single institution, two to three thousand, a German doctor said.

This seems to be the first appearance of gas chambers in the propaganda but, as far as we can see, this claim was not related to the extermination propaganda which started half a year later, and in the course of which no reference, apparently, was made to the euthanasia program. The relating of the euthanasia program to exterminations came much later.

At the IMT, the prosecution did not attempt to relate euthanasia to exterminations. It remained for a defense witness to do this. In the closing days of the IMT, Konrad Morgen appeared as a defense witness for the SS. We have seen that it was Morgen who had exposed the ring of murder and corruption centered around commandant Koch of Buchenwald. Morgen was thus considered a "good" SS man, in contrast to the bloodthirsty scoundrels who had been his colleagues and comrades (he continues to be considered a good guy, although not as good as Gerstein, who has by now achieved beatification in the "holocaust" litany). As a defense witness for the SS under seemingly hopeless circumstances, Morgen presented a story which had an inevitable logic to it and, indeed, the logic of Morgen's testimony has an importance in our analysis which transcends the immediate point we are discussing.

Morgen testified that in the course of his investigations of the camps, carried out in pursuance of his duties as an SS official, he unexpectedly encountered extermination programs at Auschwitz and at Lublin, but that SS involvement was non-existent or minimal. At Lublin the exterminations were being conducted by Wirth of the ordinary criminal police, with the assistance of Jewish labor detachments (who were promised part of the loot). Wirth supervised three additional extermination camps in Poland, according to Morgen. Although the criminal police, the Kripo, was administratively under the RSHA, Morgen was careful to point out that Kriminalkommissar Wirth was not a member of the SS. Morgen claimed that Wirth had been attached to the Fuehrer Chancellery, had been involved in the euthanasia program (which is possibly true), and had later received orders from the Fuehrer Chancellery to extend his exterminating activities to the Jews. Although the only real point of Morgen's testimony was the futile attempt to absolve the SS, the testimony is considered "evidence" by Reitlinger and by Hilberg, who avoid considering the fact that Morgen, in his attempt at excusing the SS, also testified that at Auschwitz the extermination camp was Monowitz, the one of the complex of camps that was administered by Farben. Morgen did not go so far as to claim that Farben had its own company extermination program, but he declared that the only SS involvement consisted of a few Baltic and Ukranian recruits used as guards, and that the "entire technical arrangement was almost exclusively in the hands of the prisoners".[5]

Morgen's ploy obviously inspired the prosecution anew, since it had not occurred to relate exterminations to euthanasia. It was too late to develop the point at the IMT, so it was developed in Case 1 at the NMT (actually the euthanasia program is loosely linked with exterminations in the "Gerstein statement", reproduced here in Appendix A — the Gerstein statement was put into evidence at the IMT long before Morgen's testimony, but nobody paid any attention to its text). To us, this relating of exterminations to euthanasia is just another example of the "excess fact"; the inventors were so concerned with getting some real fact into their story that it did not occur to them that there are some real facts that a good hoax is better off without.

This seems to cover the evidence for gassings at the camps in Poland exclusive of Auschwitz.

We again remark that the logic of Morgen's testimony, as courtroom defense strategy, is of some importance to our study. His side obviously calculated that the court was immovable on the question of the existence of the exterminations and thus Morgen's testimony invited the court to embrace the theory that somebody other than the SS was guilty.

Before passing to consideration of the activities of the *Einsatzgruppen* in Russia, it is convenient to review various statements made or allegedly made by various Nazis, mostly after the war, which explicitly or implicity claim exterminations.

An important category consists of statements made by German witnesses and defendants at the war crimes trials. In evaluating such statements, one must bear in mind the simple fact that the powers which conducted these trials were committed, as an immovable political fact, to the legend of Jewish extermination, especially in regard to Auschwitz. Their leaders had made the relevant charges long before they possessed a scrap of what is today called "evidence". Thus the courts were committed *a priori* to the extermination legend. A finding that exterminations had not occurred was simply not in the realm of political possibility at these trials, in any practical sense. This is an undeniable fact.

On the other hand, with only a tiny handful of exceptions, the courts were not *a priori* committed on questions of personal responsibility of individuals. With respect to individuals the courts were not as greatly constrained, politically speaking. In most cases judgments of absence of personal responsibility were well within the realm of political possibility (as distinct from probability). All defense cases were organized in relation to these undeniably valid observations, and even with those individuals whose cases were hopeless, the lawyers had no choice but to proceed on the assumption that a favorable verdict was within the realm of the possible. In considering the trials from this point of view, it is very helpful to consider them chronologically.

The first relevant trial was not the IMT but the "Belsen trial", conducted by a British military court, of Germans who had been on the staff of the Belsen camp when it was captured. The commandant, SS Captain Josef Kramer (the "Beast of Belsen"), was naturally the principal defendant. The importance of the Belsen trial derives, however, from the fact that Kramer had previously been (during 1944) the Birkenau camp commander. Kramer's trial was conducted in the autumn of 1945, and was concluded in November, just as the IMT trial was beginning. Kramer was hanged in December 1945.

We are fortunate in having the lengthy first statement that Kramer made in reply to British interrogation. The importance of this statement lies in the fact that it was made before any general realization developed among

Germans that the Allied courts were completely serious, and immovable, on the question of the reality of the exterminations (it might have been made within about a month after the capture of Belsen, but this is not certain). There is little courtroom logic playing a role in Kramer's first statement, and for this reason it is reproduced here in Appendix D. Kramer's story was completely in accord with what we have presented here, i.e., there were crematoria in all of the concentration camps, some had rather high death rates, especially Auschwitz which, since it was also a huge camp, required relatively extensive cremation facilities. His statement is quite frank regarding the more unhappy features of the camps, and is as accurate a description of the camps as we are likely to get. In regard to atrocities, he firmly asserted:

> I have heard of the allegations of former prisoners in Auschwitz referring to a gas chamber there, the mass executions and whippings, the cruelty of the guards employed, and that all this took place either in my presence or with my knowledge. All I can say to all this is that it is untrue from beginning to end.

Kramer later retreated from this firm stand and made a second statement, also reproduced in Appendix D, in which he testified to the existence of a gas chamber at Auschwitz, adding that he had no responsibility in this connection, and that the exterminations were under the direct control of the central camp administration at Auschwitz I. At his trial, Kramer offered two reasons for the discrepancy between his two statements:[6]

> The first is that in the first statement I was told that the prisoners alleged that these gas chambers were under my command, and the second and main reason was that Pohl, who spoke to me, took my word of honor that I should be silent and should not tell anybody at all about the existence of the gas chambers. When I made my first statement I felt still bound by this word of honor which I had given. When I made the second statement in prison, in Celle, these persons to whom I felt bound in honor – Adolf Hitler and Reichsfuehrer Himmler – were no longer alive and I thought then that I was no longer bound.

The absurdity of this explanation, that in the early stages of his interrogations, Kramer was attempting to maintain the secrecy of things that his interrogators were repeating to him endlessly, and which by then filled the Allied press, did not deter Kramer and his lawyer from offering it in court. The logic of Kramer's defense was at base identical to that of Morgen's testimony. Kramer was in the position of attempting to present some story absolving himself from implication in mass murder at Birkenau. The truth, that Birkenau was not an extermination camp, had no chance of being accepted by the court. That was a political impossibility. To have taken the truth as his position would have been heroic for Kramer, but also suicidal, since it would have amounted to making no defense at all in connection with his role at the Birkenau camp. Even if he had felt personally heroic, there were powerful arguments against such heroism. His family, like all German families of the time, was desperate and needed him. If, despite all this, he persisted in his heroism, his lawyer would not have cooperated. No lawyer will consciously choose a suicidal strategy when one having some possibility of success is evident. Kramer's defense, therefore, was that he had no personal involvement in the exterminations at Birkenau. Hoess and the RSHA did it. Remember that these proceedings were organized by lawyers seeking favorable verdicts, not by historians seeking the truth about events.

An incidental matter is the claim that Kramer, as commandant at Natzweiler, had had eighty people gassed there for purposes of medical experiments. These people had supposedly been selected at Auschwitz by unknown criteria and then transported to Natzweiler to be killed, since the bodies were needed fresh in nearby Strasbourg. Kramer affirmed this story in his second statement but, since it is (implicitly, but unambiguously) denied in his first statement, I am inclined to believe that it is untrue. However, it is quite possible that some people were executed at Natzweiler when somebody else was commandant, and that the bodies were then used at the anatomical institute in Strasbourg (which certainly possessed bodies for its research purposes). In any case, the matter is not relevant to an extermination program.

The IMT trial is somewhat more complicated to consider, because of the great number of defendants, each one having his own possibilities in regard to excusing himself from any real or imaginary crimes. The trial transcript is not really adequate to study the behavior of the IMT defendants, but the record kept by the Nuernberg prison psychologist, Dr. G.M. Gilbert, and published by him as *Nuremberg Diary*, supplements the transcript to an extent that is adequate for our purposes. Gilbert's book gives an account of the attitudes and reactions of the IMT defendants, not only at the trial but also in the Nuernberg prison. One cannot be absolutely confident in regard to the accuracy of Gilbert's account. Most of the material consists of summaries of conversations the defendants had in the prison, either with each other or with Gilbert. However, Gilbert took no notes on the spot and wrote everything down each day from memory. His manuscript was critically examined by a former employee of the Office of War Information and by the prosecutors Jackson and Taylor. Even with the best will and most impartial disposition, Gilbert could not have captured everything with complete accuracy. His book has a general accuracy, but one must be reserved about its detailed accuracy.

The IMT defendants were arrested shortly after the German capitulation in May 1945, imprisoned separately, and interrogated and propagandized for six months prior to the opening of the IMT trial in November, when they met each other for the first time since the surrender (in some cases, for the first time ever). There are four particularly important observations to make. First, not surprisingly, all except Kaltenbrunner had developed essentially the same defense regarding concentration camp atrocities and exterminations of Jews, whatever the extent to which they might have actually believed such allegations; it was all the fault of Hitler and Himmler's SS. Kaltenbrunner, sitting as a defendant as a substitute for the dead Himmler, was ill when the trial opened, and did not join the other defendants until the trial was a few weeks old. When he appeared the other defendants shunned him, and he said very little to the others during the course of the next ten months.

The second observation is not quite so expected. Indeed, it may be mildly startling; with the exception of Kaltenbrunner and perhaps one or two others, these high ranking German officials did not understand the catastrophic conditions in the camps which accompanied the German collapse, and which were the cause of the scenes which were exploited by the Allied propaganda as "proof" of exterminations. This may appear at first a peculiar claim, but consultation of Gilbert's book shows it to be unquestionably a valid one (the only other possibility is that some merely pretended to misunderstand the situation). The administration of the camps was far removed from the official domains of almost all of the defendants and they had been subjected to the familiar propaganda since the German surrender. To the extent that they accepted, or pretended to accept, that there had been mass murders, for which Hitler and Himmler were responsible, they were basing their view precisely on the scenes found in the German camps at the end of the war, and which they evidently misunderstood or pretended to misunderstand. This is well illustrated by Gilbert's account of an exchange Gilbert had with Goering:[7]

"Those atrocity films!" Goering continued. "Anybody can make an atrocity film if they take corpses out of their graves and then show a tractor shoving them back in again."

Fig. 20: Liberated Dachau inmates abuse an SS guard.

Photo: U.S. Army

178

"You can't brush it off that easily," I replied. "We *did* find your concentration camps fairly *littered* with corpses and mass graves − I saw them myself in Dachau! − and Hadamar!"

"Oh, but not piled up by the thousands like that − "

"Don't tell me what I didn't see! I saw corpses literally by the carload − "

"Oh, that one train − "

" − And piled up like cordwood in the crematorium − and half starved and mutilated prisoners, who told me how the butchery had been going on for years − and Dachau was not the worst by far! You can't shrug off 6,000,000 murders!"

"Well, I doubt if it was 6,000,000," he said despondently, apparently sorry he had started the argument," − but as I've always said, it is sufficient if only 5 per cent of it is true − ." A glum silence followed.

This is only one example; it is clear from Gilbert's book that, when the subject of concentration camp atrocities came up, the defendants were thinking of the scenes found in the German camps at the end of the war. It is probably not possible to decide which defendants genuinely misunderstood the situation (as Goering did) and which merely pretended to misunderstand, on the calculation that, if one was not involved with concentration camps anyway, it was a far safer course to accept the Allied claims than to automatically involve oneself by contesting the Allied claims.

Our third observation is in regard to a calculation that must have figured in the minds of most of the defendants during the trial. It seemed probable, or at least quite possible, to them that the Allies were not completely serious about carrying out executions and long prison sentences. The trial was certainly a novelty, and the defendants were well aware that there was considerable hostility to the war crimes trials in the public opinion of the Allied countries, especially in the U.S. and England. Many must have calculated that their immediate objective should be to say or do whatever seemed necessary to survive the transient wave of post-war hysteria, deferring the setting straight of the record to a not distant future when a non-hysterical examination of the facts would become possible.

Fourth, extermination of Jews was only one of the many accusations involved at Nuernberg. In retrospect it may appear to have been the main charge but, at the time, the principal accusations in the minds of almost everybody concerned responsibilities for "planning, preparation, initiation, or waging of a war of aggression" − so-called "Crimes Against Peace".

With the preceding four observations in mind, we can see that the behavior of the defendants during the trial was about what one would expect from such a diverse collection of dedicated Nazis, technocrats, conservative Prussian officers, and ordinary politicians. In "private", i.e. in prison when court was not in session, the prisoners were just as guarded in their remarks as they were in public and there was an abundance of mutual recrimination, buck passing, and back biting. Frank made the worst ass of himself in this respect, but the practice was rather general. The Nazis were not one big happy family. In regard to trial defense strategy, it will suffice to discuss Speer, Goering and Kaltenbrunner.

Speer's trial strategy was simple, and also relatively successful, since he did not hang. He claimed that his position did not situate him so as to be able to learn of the various alleged atrocities. Even today he is permitted to get away with this nonsense. In fact Speer and his assistants were deeply involved in, e.g. the deportations of employable Hungarian Jews in the spring of 1944, for work in underground aircraft factories at Buchenwald.[8] Any rail transport priority given to Hungarian Jews to be exterminated, as opposed to employable Hungarian Jews, would have become known to them if such had actually happened. If Speer had testified truthfully, he would have declared that he had been so situated that, if an extermination program of the type charged had

had existed, he would have known of it and that, to his knowledge, no such program had existed. However if Speer had testified truthfully, he would have joined his colleagues on the gallows.

In his book, Speer gives only one ridiculous piece of "evidence" that he encountered during the war that he now says he should have interpreted as suggesting the existence of an extermination program, and that was the suggestion of his friend Karl Hanke (who was appointed Himmler's successor as Reichsfuehrer-SS by Hitler in the last days of the war), in the summer of 1944, that Speer never "accept an invitation to inspect a concentration camp in Upper Silesia". Speer also passes along Goering's private remark just before the IMT trial about Jewish "survivors" in Hungary: "So, there are still some there? I thought we had knocked off all of them. Somebody slipped up again".[9] Such a sarcastic crack was understandable under the circumstances since Goering never conceded the reality of any extermination program, and insisted that he had known only of a program of emigration and evacuation of Jews from the German sphere in Europe.

The Introduction to Speer's book, by Eugene Davidson, mentions the fact (noted here in Chapter IV) that many Dutch Jews sent to Birkenau, "within sight of the gas chambers", were unaware of any extermination program. They wrote cheerful letters back to the Netherlands.[10] The remarks about Jewish extermination were not in the original version of Speer's manuscript; they were added at the insistence of the publisher.[11]

Unlike the other defendants, Goering assumed throughout the trial that he was to be sentenced to death, and his testimony appears to be the approximate truth as he saw it. Although he never conceded the existence of a program of extermination of Jews, we have seen that he misunderstood what had happened in the German camps at the end of the war, and assumed that Himmler had, indeed, engaged in mass murder in this connection. However, he never conceded any number of murders approaching six millions.[12]

An incidental remark that should be made in connection with Goering is that he was not, as legend asserts (and as Speer claimed in private on several occasions during the IMT), a drug addict. The Nuernberg prison psychiatrist, Douglas Kelley, has attempted to set the record straight in this regard. Goering was a military man, had been an air ace in World War I, and had been the last commander of the "Flying Circus" of von Richthofen (the "Red Baron"). Refusing to surrender his unit to the Allies at the end of the war, he returned to Germany and found himself a hero without a profession. Eventually joining the Nazi Party, he naturally, as a holder of the *Pour-le-mérite* (Germany's highest military decoration), soon became a leader of the small party. As such, he was a leader of the putsch of 1923, in which he was wounded in the right thigh. The wound developed an infection which caused him to be hospitalized for a long while, during which time he was injected with considerable amounts of morphine. He developed a mild addiction but cured it shortly after being released from the hospital in 1924. Much later, in 1937, Goering developed a condition of aching teeth, and began taking tablets of paracodeine, a very mild morphine derivative which was a common prescription for his condition, and he continued to take the paracodeine throughout the war. His addiction for (or, more exactly, habit of taking) these paracodeine tablets was not severe, since he was taken off them before the IMT by Dr. Kelley, who employed a simple withdrawal method involving daily reductions of the dosage.[13]

To return to the IMT defendants, Kaltenbrunner's position seems to us today to have been somewhat hopeless, and it is probable that his lawyer felt the same way, but he nevertheless had to present some sort of defense, and his defense on the matters that we are interested in rested on two main points.

The first point was that he was head of the RSHA, which was charged with security, and not the head of the WVHA, which administered the concentration camps. He thus claimed that he had had almost nothing to do with the camps. The only known instance of Kaltenbrunner involvement with the internal operation of the camps was in his order of March 1945, concerning permission for the Red Cross to establish itself in the camps (how he assumed authority for giving this order we do not know). He made a great deal of this matter in his defense and, rather than setting the record straight in regard to the catastrophic conditions in the camps at the end of the war, he inflated his action in connection with the Red Cross to make it appear to be an act against concentration camps as such, which, of course, he had always deplored anyway, he said.

Kaltenbrunner's second point was that, as everybody would agree, it was his predecessor Heydrich, and not he, who had organized the details of the Jewish policy, whatever that policy was. He took over the RSHA in 1943 with a directive from Himmler to build up the intelligence service of the SD, a fact which he distorted in claiming that, under the new arrangement in which Himmler was not going to allow anybody to grow to the stature that Heydrich had attained, Kaltenbrunner was to concern himself only with intelligence, and not to have any control over the police and security functions of the RSHA, in particular, the Gestapo, which sent political prisoners to the camps and also, through Eichmann's office, administered the Jewish deportations. Thus, according to Kaltenbrunner, there was no respect in which Kaltenbrunner could be held responsible for exterminations of Jews which, he conceded, had taken place just as the Allies charged (except that they had started, according to Kaltenbrunner, in 1940). Indeed, according to him, it was not until the summer of 1943 that he learned of the extermination program that Eichmann of his department was conducting. He learned from the foreign press and the enemy radio. He got Himmler to admit it early in 1944 and then protested, first to Hitler, then to Himmler. The extermination program was stopped in October 1944, "chiefly due to (his) intervention".[14] The manner in which Kaltenbrunner claimed to have learned of the exterminations, while nonsense, is nevertheless consistent with the extreme secrecy that is always said to have been maintained in connection with the extermination program.

Kaltenbrunner's story was complete nonsense, but this fact should not blind us to the serious character of this testimony as defense strategy. Suppose that Kaltenbrunner had testified that no extermination program had existed. In such a case, any leniency shown by the court in the judgment would have been tantamount to that court's conceding the untruth, or possible untruth, of the extermination claim, a political impossibility. By claiming that, while the extermination program had existed, Kaltenbrunner had had no responsibility, and had even opposed it, the defense was making it politically possible for the court to be lenient in some sense, or was at least making a serious attempt along this line. A few seconds' reflection reveals that this was the only possible strategy for Kaltenbrunner on the extermination charge. Obviously the trial was going to end with some death sentences, some acquittals, and some in between dispositions of cases; this was necessary in order to give it the semblance of a real trial. Thus, on analysis, we see that there was perfectly sound lawyer's logic operating in Kaltenbrunner's defense. That the specific story presented was nonsense was not very important from this point of view; the manner in which facts have been treated in connection with these matters has been endless nonsense anyway. The case of

181

Speer shows that a nonsensical story not only had a chance of being accepted by the IMT, but also by general opinion much later, when there should have been adequate opportunity to see matters clearly.

The ordinary person, and even the informed critic, can easily fail to understand the significance of such things as the Kaltenbrunner testimony, because he so easily fails to grasp the perspective of the defendants, who did not have the historical interests in these trials that we have. Their necks were at stake, and they regarded the trials, quite correctly, as a manifestation of hysteria. Attempting to save their necks meant devising trial strategies to suit the prevailing conditions, and no optimum trial strategy seeks to move the court on matters the court is immovable on. This also happens in ordinary legal proceedings. Once something has been decided, it has been decided, and the lawyers organize their cases accordingly.

Of course it is deplorable that Nazis or anyone else should lie in order to promote their personal interests. I have seen scholars tell lies almost as big just to pick up an extra bit of summer salary, and that too is deplorable.

At Kramer's trial and at the IMT the courts were effectively committed *a priori* to the conclusion that Nazi Germany had had a program of exterminating Jews. At the later NMT trials the courts were committed *a priori* as a formal matter, on account of the legal constraint previously noted (p. 25), that statements made in the IMT judgment constituted "proof of the facts stated". The IMT judgment had said that millions had been exterminated in German concentration camps, particularly at Auschwitz, which was "set aside for this main purpose"; specifically, 400,000 Hungarian Jews were said to have been murdered there.[15] Thus defendants and witnesses at the NMT faced a situation similar to that faced by earlier defendants and witnesses, except that it was formalized. Prosecutors were known to redirect the attentions of judges to this legal constraint, when there seemed a chance of its being overlooked.[16]

Here we will take special note of only two cases. Defendant Pohl, of course, did not deny the extermination program; in denying personal involvement in the exterminations, he took advantage of the fact that the Allied charges had naturally been directed at the Gestapo and the SD functions of the SS, which were not in Pohl's domain as head of the WVHA.[17] Even the Hoess affidavit and testimony explicitly support him in this position. After all, who ever heard of the *Wirtschafts-Verwaltungshauptamt?* Nevertheless, Pohl was hanged.

The testimony of Muench, a doctor at Auschwitz, is of some interest. He appeared as a defense witness at the Farben trial, having previously been acquitted by a Polish court. This is the witness whom prosecution lawyer Minskoff asked about the leaflets dropped at Auschwitz by Allied planes (p. 111). Muench testified that while he had known about the exterminations while he was at Auschwitz, and had even witnessed a gassing, people outside the Auschwitz area, that is those in Germany, did not know. Also, the whole thing was arranged "masterfully" so that "someone who visited a plant in Auschwitz twice or three times a year for a period of one or two days" would not learn of the exterminations. Almost all of the defendants, of course, were in the category of those who could not have known, according to Muench, but he did not stop there. He also asserted that, while all of the SS men and prisoners knew of the exterminations, they did not talk to civilians about them, for fear of punishment. For example, Farben engineer Faust, whom Muench knew very well as Auschwitz, did not know about the exterminations. Muench also remarked several times that all one could perceive of the exterminations was the odor, "perceptible everywhere", of the cremations. Nobody at this trial of chemical engineering experts bothered to point out that the chemical industry of the area also created a bit of an odor. An odd feature of Muench's testimony is his placing of the crematoria and the gas chambers "one or one and a half kilometers southwest of the Birkenau camp camouflaged in a small woods".[18]

The Muench testimony is merely another illustration of the manner in which defense cases were formulated. The strategy was to not contest things that the courts were already decided on but to present stories exonerating defendants of personal responsibility. Thus it was invariably claimed that the extermination program had features which happened to excuse the relevant defendants but, obviously, to claim that the features of the program existed it was necessary to claim also that the program itself existed.

The next trial that is worth examination is the Eichmann trial. It will be recalled that Adolf Eichmann was illegally abducted from Buenos Aires in May 1960 by Israeli agents, who sent him to Israel to become the victim of a "trial" that was to break all records for illegality, since the state conducting the trial had not even existed at the time of the alleged crimes. The illegal courtroom proceedings opened in Jerusalem on 11 April 1961, the Jewish court pronounced the death sentence on 15 December 1961, and the murder was carried out on 31 May 1962.

In order to understand Eichmann's defense strategy, consider his situation prior to the trial as a lawyer would have seen it. It was basically a political situation involving an Israeli determination to stage a show trial. In capturing Eichmann Israel had spat on Argentine sovereignty and, from a lawyer's point of view the only hope of securing a favorable verdict (a prison sentence to be later commuted) depended upon world opinion developing so as to encourage Israel to temper its arrogance somewhat with a magnanimous gesture. However the possibility of such an outcome depended upon presenting a defense whose fundamental acceptance by the Jerusalem court would have been within the realm of political possibility. Thus, just as with the Nuernberg defendants, a denial that the extermination program had existed was out of the question as defense strategy, and thus, also as with the Nuernberg defendants, Eichmann's only possible defense under the circumstances was to deny personal responsibility.

Eichmann conceded the existence of an extermination program, and the first edition of Reitlinger's book was accepted by both sides as approximately descriptive of what had happened. Eichmann's fundamental defense, thus, was that he had merely organized the transports of Jews, in obedience to orders which could not be disobeyed. In one respect, his defense was partially successful, for his (accurate) picture of himself as a mere "cog in a machine" has been more or less universally accepted by those who have studied and written about his trial (e.g. Hannah Arendt's book).

Actually, Eichmann inflated himself a bit beyond "cog" status, for a secondary feature of his testimony is that he claimed that he, Eichmann, had done whatever a person as lowly as he could do in order to sabotage the extermination program, and his interpretations of the meanings of many of the documents used in the trial were obviously strained in this respect. A good example was Eichmann's comments on two particular documents. The first document was a complaint by the commander of the Lodz resettlement camp, dated 24 September 1941, complaining of overcrowding at the camp due to tremendous transports of Jews that were pouring in — "And now they face me with a *fait accompli,* as it were, that I have to absorb 20,000 Jews into the ghetto within the shortest possible period of time, but further that I have to absorb 5,000 gypsies". The letter is addressed to the local head of government. The second document is a letter by that local head, dated 9 October 1941, passing on the complaint to Berlin, and adding that Eichmann had acted like a "horse dealer" in sending the Jewish transport to Lodz for, contrary to Eichmann's claim, the transport had not been approved. Eichmann's Jerusalem testimony in regard to these documents was that the complaints were justified since he had, indeed, shipped the Jews to Lodz without authorization. His motivation, he claimed, had its source in the fact that there were only two places he could have shipped the Jews to, the East (where he was supposed to send them, he said) or Lodz. However, according to him, there were exterminations in the East at that time, but none at Lodz. Being in strong disapproval of the exterminations, and doing everything that his low office permitted to thwart them, he shipped the Jews to Lodz despite the inadequate preparations there.[19]

This feature of Eichmann's defense strategy is also illustrated by his testimony regarding the "trucks for Hungarian Jews" proposals of 1944. He naturally attempted to represent efforts on the German side to conclude the deal as being due in no small measure to the force of his initiative, motivated, again, by Eichmann's desire to save Jews.[20]

It is worth mentioning that the major thrust of the prosecution's cross examination of Eichmann did not treat wartime events directly. The prosecution's chief effort was to hold Eichmann, in court, to whatever he was supposed to have said to Israeli interrogators during his year of imprisonment prior to the trial, and also to what he was supposed to have said to one Sassen in the Argentine in 1957. According to Eichmann's testimony, he encountered Sassen, an ex-SS man, in Buenos Aires in 1955. At this time Eichmann was, except within tiny circles, a very much forgotten man. The Eichmann-Sassen relationship eventually led to a project to write a book on the persecutions of the Jews during the war. The book, to be completed and promoted by Sassen, was to be based on tape recorded question-answer sessions with Eichmann, but according to Eichmann's testimony the original form of these sessions could not be retained:

when these questions were put to me, I had to reply from time to time, that I did not remember and did not know; but, obviously, this was not the way to write a book ... and then it was agreed that it did not really matter what I remembered – the main thing was to describe the events as they had happened; then we spoke about poetic license, about license for journalists and authors, which would entitle us to describe the events – even if I did not remember certain details, the essence which would remain would be a description of the events as they had taken place and this is really what was eventually taken down.

(Sassen) told me to say something about every point, so that the necessary quantity be obtained.

... it was also agreed that he Sassen would then formulate everything in the form of a book and we would be co-authors in this book.

Sassen's material eventually appeared, in the autumn of 1960, in *Life* magazine, so it is clear that Sassen's sessions with Eichmann were designed for the primary purpose of producing a marketable, as distinct from historical, book. Eichmann, obviously, planned to acquire a share of the profits, but his testimony does not shed any light onto the specific financial expectations that Eichmann and Sassen had.

Sassen transcribed some of the tape recorded material into typewritten form, and Eichmann added comments and corrections in the margins of some of the pages in his own hand. He also composed 83 full pages of handwritten comments. After the appearance of the *Life* articles, the prosecution obtained material from Sassen, namely, a photostat of a 300 page typewritten document with marginal comments, apparently in Eichmann's hand, purporting to be a transcript of 62 of 67 tape recorded sessions, and also a photostat of

Photo: U.S. Army

Fig. 21: Liberation day at Dachau.

what was said to be the 83 page document in Eichmann's hand. Original documents were evidently not procured, thus raising the possibility of tampering and editing, especially in the case of the 300 page document. In regard to the original tapes, the prosecution commented

We do not know about the tapes themselves – I don't know whether the people who took part in this conversation kept the tape or whether the tape was erased and re-used for other recordings.

The defense challenged the accuracy of the documents, claimed that the majority of marginal corrections were not included in the document, and further claimed that if Sassen himself could be brought to court to testify, it could be proved that

he changed and distorted what was said by the accused, to suit his own aims. He wanted to produce a propaganda book; this can be proved, how the words were distorted.

However, the prosecution assured the court that if Sassen were to come to Israel, he would be put on trial for his SS membership.

The court decided to admit the photostats of the 83 pages in Eichmann's hand, but the prosecution, finding during the course of the rest of the trial that there was virtually nothing in the 83 pages that it could use, made another bid very late in the trial, and finally managed to get accepted into evidence the excerpts of the typewritten document which carried handwritten corrections. *Life* magazine, which apparently received the same material from Sassen, treated all of it as unquestionably authentic.[21]

We close this short discussion of the Eichmann trial by reporting Eichmann's reaction to the allegation, widely publicized, that at the end of the war he had declared that he would "jump gladly into the grave" with the knowledge that five or six million Jews had been killed. Eichmann testified that he had, indeed, made a bitter remark such as this to his staff at the end of the war, but that the five million killed were not "Jews" but "enemies of the Reich", i.e. enemy soldiers, principally Russians. While his defense strategy entailed not contesting the general reality of the extermination program, he insisted that he was in no position to know even the approximate number of Jews killed, and that all remarks attributed to him in this connection (e.g. Hoettl's affidavit) are falsely attributed.[22]

The trials held in West Germany during the Sixties are barely worth mentioning and, moreover, rather difficult to study, on account of the obscurity of the defendants involved. The most publicized, of course, was the "Auschwitz trial" of 1963-1965, and a few words are perhaps in order.

The group of war crimes trials, of which the Auschwitz trial was the most prominent, was held for political reasons in the aftermath of the hysterical publicity surrounding the capture of Adolf Eichmann. One of the first victims was Richard Baer, successor to Hoess and last commandant of Auschwitz, who was arrested on 20 December 1960 near Hamburg, where he was working as a lumberjack. He was imprisoned and interrogated in prison, and insisted that the Auschwitz gas chambers were a myth. Unfortunately he did not live to take this position in court, since he died in prison on 17 June 1963, at the age of 51, apparently from a circulatory ailment, although his wife considered his death rather mysterious.[23]

When the trial finally opened in Frankfurt in December 1963, the principal defendant was one Robert K.L. Mulka, an ex-SS Captain who had served briefly as adjutant to Hoess at Auschwitz. Mulka had been tried and sentenced, by a German chamber, immediately after the war, in connection with his role at Auschwitz, and quite a few of the other 21 defendants at the Auschwitz trial were standing trial for the second time on basically the same charges.

The court, of course, did not ignore legal matters entirely, and it took the trouble to explain that the Bonn Government considers itself the legal successor to the Third Reich, and thus it was competent to try persons for infringing laws which were in force in Germany during the war. Killing Jews, of course, had been illegal in Nazi Germany, and thus the majority of the defendants were charged in that respect. In regard to the reasonableness of such a trial, one can do no better than to quote from the opinion of the Frankfurt court itself:[24]

This determination of guilt has however confronted the court with extraordinarily difficult problems.

Except for a few not very valuable documents, almost exclusively only witness testimonies were available to the court for the reconstruction of the deeds of the defendants. It is an experience of criminology that witness testimony is not among the best of evidence. This is even more the case if the testimony of the witness refers to an incident which had been observed twenty years or more ago under conditions of unspeakable grief and anguish. Even the ideal witness, who only wishes to tell the truth and takes pains to explore his memory, is prone to have many memory gaps after twenty years. He risks the danger of projecting onto other persons things which he actually has experienced himself and of assuming as his own experiences things which were related to him by others in this terrible milieu. In this way he risks the danger of confusing the times and places of his experiences.

It has certainly been for the witnesses an unreasonable demand for us to question them today concerning all details of their experiences. It is asking too much of the witnesses if we today, after twenty years, still wish to know when, where and how, in detail, who did what. On this basis astonishment was repeatedly expressed by the witnesses, that we asked them for such a precise reconstruction of the past occurrences. It was obviously the duty of the defense to ask about those details. And it is unjust to impute to the defense that it wished to make these witnesses appear ridiculous. On the contrary, we must call to mind only once what endless detail work is performed in a murder trial in our days — how out of small mosaic-like pieces the picture of the true occurrences at the moment of the murder is put together. There is available for the court's deliberations above all the corpse, the record of the post-mortem examination, the expert opinions of specialists on the causes of death and the day on which the deed must have occurred, and the manner in which the death occurred. There is available the murder weapon and finger prints to identify the perpetrator; there are footprints he left behind as he entered the house of the slain, and many more details at hand which provide absolute proof to the court that this person was done to death by a definite perpetrator of the deed.

All this was missing in this trial. We have no absolute evidence for the individual killings; we have only the witness testimonies. However sometimes these testimonies were not as exact and precise as is necessary in a murder trial. If therefore the witnesses were asked, in which year or month an event happened, it was entirely necessary for the determination of the truth. And these dates sometimes presented to the court the only evidence for the purpose of determining whether the event related by the witness did in fact happen as the witness related it, or whether the witness had committed an error or confused victims. The court was naturally aware that it was an extraordinary burden for the witnesses, in view of the camp conditions, where no calendars, clocks or even primitive means of keeping records were available, to be asked to relate in all details what they experienced at the time. Nevertheless the court had to be able to determine whether an individual defendant did in fact commit a real murder, and when and where. That is required by the penal code.

This was an ordinary criminal trial, whatever its background. The court could only judge according to the laws it is sworn to uphold, and these laws require the precise determination of the concrete guilt of an accused on both the objective and subjective sides. The overburdening of the witnesses shows how endlessly difficult it is to ascertain and portray concrete events after twenty years. We have heard witnesses who at first appeared so reliable to the court that we even issued arrest warrants on their declarations. However in exhaustive examination of the witness declarations in hours long deliberations it was found that these declarations were not absolutely sound and did not absolutely correspond to objective truth. For this purpose certain times had to be ascertained and documents reexamined — whether the accused, who was charged by a witness, was at the camp Auschwitz at all at the time in question, whether he could have committed the deed there, or whether the witness perhaps projected the deed onto the wrong person.

In view of this weakness of witness testimony — and I speak now only of the sworn witnesses whose desire for the truth, the subjective and objective truth, the court was thoroughly confident of — the court especially had to examine the witness testimonies. Only a few weeks ago we read in the newspapers that a member of the Buchenwald concentration camp staff had been convicted of murdering an inmate who, it is clear today, is alive and was certainly not murdered. Such examples should make us think. These cases of miscarriages of justice do not serve to strengthen the respect for the law. On these grounds also the court has avoided whatever could even in the most remote sense suggest a summary verdict. The court had examined every single declaration of each of the witnesses with great care and all earnestness and consequently is unable to arrive at verdicts of guilty on a whole list of charges, since secure grounds could not be found for such verdicts. The possibilities of verifying the witness declarations were very limited. All traces of deeds were destroyed. Documents which could have given the court important assistance had been burned . . .

Although these admissions on the part of the Frankfurt court should be conclusive in forming one's opinion of such trials, we must add that the court understated the facts of the situation. The great majority of the witnesses were citizens of Soviet bloc countries, with all that such a fact implies regarding their testimonies. The court complained that "this witness testimony was not so accurate and precise as is desirable", but one should observe that it was certainly attempted to organize the memories of the witnesses suitably, for the "Comité International d'Auschwitz" had set up its headquarters in Frankfurt and from there had issued "information sheets" on the terrible things that had happened at Auschwitz. These "information sheets" had been made available to, and had been read by, the witnesses before they testified. There was also a "Comité des Camps" in circulation, and other persons, e.g. the mayor of Frankfurt, made suggestions to the witnesses of varying degrees of directness and subtlety.[25]

The farce extended also into the matters that the court considered in the course of the long trial, and the sentences that were imposed. Mulka, found guilty of being second man in the administration of the great extermination camp, of having ordered the Zyklon B on at least one occasion, of having been in charge of the motor pool, which transported the condemned, of having handled some of the paperwork dealing with transports, and of having been involved in the construction of the crematoria, was sentenced to 14 years at hard labor, but was released less than four months later on grounds of ill health. Defendant Franz Hofmann, ex-SS Captain who had been in charge of Auschwitz I, received a life sentence for the simple reason that, although found guilty in connection witl. exterminations, he had really been tried on a charge of having thrown a bottle at a prisoner, who later died from the head injury received. This incident evidently had a greater impact on the court than mass exterminations, which is not surprising, since the bottle episode could clearly be recognized as the sort of thing that happens in penal institutions. Hofmann was sentenced to life imprisonment, but shortly later released anyway on the grounds of his previous detention.[26]

In searching the history books for proceedings comparable to the "war crimes trials", it is not suitable to fasten on prior politically motivated trials for precedents. Such trials, e.g. the trial of Mary, Queen of Scots, lack the hysterical atmosphere of the war crimes trials. Another feature of the usual political trial is that there is generally only one, or at any rate only a few, victims, and the proceedings are not spread over more than two decades. Even the trial of Joan of Arc, which had aspects of hysteria, is not really comparable to the war crimes trials because only a single person, and not an entire state, was on trial.

In determining precedents for the war crimes trials, only the witchcraft trials of Europe's younger days offer satisfactory comparisons. A most important similarity lies in the fact that the accused in witchcraft trials frequently found it expedient, in the contexts in which they found themselves, to go along with the charges to some extent. In fact in many cases a partial confession offered the only possible trial strategy. One could not deny the very existence of the sorts of Sabbaths that the popular imagination had decided must have existed. When the sentences of the condemned were carried out, one had scenes:[27]

> On one scaffold stood the condemned Sorceresses, a scanty band, and on another the crowd of the reprieved. The repentant heroine, whose confession was read out, stuck at nothing, however wild and improbable. At the Sabbaths they ate children, hashed; and as a second course dead wizards dug up from their graves. Toads dance, talk, complain amorously of their mistresses' unkindnesses, and get the Devil to scold them. This latter sees the witches home with great politeness, lighting the way with the blazing arm of an unbaptised infant, etc., etc.

The situation was such that one had to feed the fantasies and passions of the judges and the population, and there were even ways of getting ahead by claiming to be a witch, and thus informed on the activities of certain other witches, knowledgeable on ways of exposing them, etc.

The comparison of the war crimes trials with the witchcraft trials is almost perfect. Both involve large numbers of potential victims, and the possibilities for mutual recrimination are boundless. Most important, both take place in an atmosphere of unreality and hysteria. The person who will not disbelieve those who claim that a modern state was exterminating masses of human beings at a center of chemical industry, employing an insecticide, and that the pervasive stench at that site was due to the associated cremations, is the complete twentieth century equivalent of the person who, in earlier centuries, believed those who claimed that misfortunes were caused by people who conversed with toads, had intercourse with the Devil, etc.

Another important relation between witchcraft trials and the war crimes trials is that torture of witnesses and defendants played roles in both. Invented testimony at witchcraft trials is usually explained in terms of torture (although our reference employed above points out that mass hysteria also provides a completely effective motivation). We know that some people were tortured in connection with the war crimes trials, and we should therefore consider the problem of the extent to which torture might have accounted for testimony, especially defendant testimony, in support of exterminations.

Available evidence indicates that torture was frequently employed in the war crimes trials. We have noted at length, in Chapter I, the tortures inflicted on German defendants in the Dachau trials. Very similar scenes took place, under British sponsorship, in connection with the Belsen trial, and Josef Kramer and other defendants were tortured, sometimes to the point where they pleaded to be put to death.[28] On the other hand, it appears that defendants at the IMT were too prominent to torture, although Julius Streicher was an exception, and it is even said that he was forced to eat excrement. (Streicher complained at the IMT that he had been beaten up by Negro soldiers after his arrest. On the motion of prosecutor Jackson, this testimony was stricken from the record since otherwise "the court would have had to conduct an investigation." Streicher was the editor and publisher of a very disreputable and quasi-pornographic magazine *Der Stuermer,* which attacked not only Jews, Freemasons and clerics but on occasion even top Nazis. Streicher once claimed in *Der Stuermer* that Goering's daughter had not been fathered by Goering but by artificial insemination. *Der Stuermer* was considered offensive by nearly all political leaders in Germany but Streicher had the protection of Hitler, out of gratitude for Streicher's having delivered Nuernberg to the Nazi Party. In 1940, Goering arranged for Streicher to be put partially out of action; although *Der Stuermer* was not suppressed,

Streicher was deprived of his Party position of *Gauleiter* of Nuernberg. Streicher never held a position in the German Government, before or during the war, and his inclusion in the first row of "defendants" at the IMT was ludicrous.)[29]

There was never any general or massive expose of torture of witnesses and defendants at the NMT trials, but we believe that the fact, noted in the previous chapter, that the Nuernberg prosecution did not hesitate to torture witnesses even in connection with a regular U.S. legal proceeding, is strong support for our assumption that torture was employed rather commonly at Nuernberg or, more precisely, employed on witnesses and defendants who played roles in the trials at Nuernberg.

We are inclined to believe that Adolf Eichmann was not tortured by his Israeli captors, at least not for the purpose of forcing him to give specific trial testimony. This view is based on the simple fact that he did not complain, in his trial testimony, that he had been tortured thus, although he did complain, early in his trial testimony, that he had suffered rather rough treatment during the few days immediately after his capture, particularly when his captors forced him to sign a declaration that he had come to Israel voluntarily (and which the prosecution had the audacity to put into evidence at the trial). However the extreme secrecy that surrounded Eichmann's imprisonment in Israel allows the possibility that he was tortured in some sense, but that he had tactical or other reasons for not charging torture in his testimony.[30]

In considering the problem of torture, it is important to observe that the efficacy of torture in producing testimony having a desired content is rather questionable. We cannot believe that the prosecuting authorities at Nuernberg had any moral compunctions about using torture, but they most probably made the rather obvious observation that, no matter how much you torture a man, you still cannot be absolutely sure what he will say on the witness stand. Exceptions to this statement are provided by the "Moscow trials" of the Thirties, and other trials staged by Communists, but the defendants is such cases are always "brainwashed" to the extent that they utterly prostrate themselves before the court when on trial, and denounce themselves as the foulest beings on earth.[31] No such attitude is perceptible in the Nuernberg defendants who, despite much untruthful testimony damaging to the Nazi regime in general, always argued their personal innocence.

In examining the torture problem, we must be careful regarding what questions one might ask, and what inferences may be drawn from the answers. Obviously, there is the question of whether or not a man was tortured. Second, there is the question of whether or not he testified to the reality of exterminations. Assuming that affirmative answers apply to both questions, it is a *non sequitur* to infer that the former accounts for the latter. This is illustrated by the case of Kramer who, despite torture, spoke the truth in his first statement, and evidently only changed his story when his lawyer explained to him the logical implications of insisting on a story that the court could not possibly accept. On the other hand, if a witness has been tortured, we may infer that the authorities in charge are not to be trusted.

Moreover, one must not make assumptions too quickly in regard to the probably motivations that the Nuernberg jailers might have had for employing torture; the motivation need not have been to produce specific testimony, and may have been either more or less thoughtfully conceived. First, torture might have been employed purely to produce pleasure; the Jews in charge hated their German victims. Second, torture may have been employed merely on the basis of the passing observation that, while it was not guaranteed to be helpful, it also could not hurt matters as long as the proceedings were kept

Fig. 22: The door of a disinfection chamber at Dachau. The inscriptions on the door specify that the chamber is used from 7.30 to 10 in the morning. The warning reads "Caution! Gas! Life danger! Do not open!" The U.S. Army caption for this photograph declares that "Gas chambers, conveniently located to the crematory, are examined by a soldier of the U.S. Seventh Army. These chambers were used by Nazi guards for killing prisoners of the infamous Dachau concentration camp."   *Photo: U.S. Army*

suitably confidential.

A third possible motivation, a far more intelligent one, could have been that torture, while not of much use in producing specific pieces of testimony, could be of assistance in a less specific and more general sense. If my interrogator threatens that he will take steps against my family if I do not cooperate, I may doubt him on the basis that I see no evidence that he either has the necessary power, or the necessary cruelty, or both. However, if he imprisons me for a year or more, torturing at will, I will eventually believe that he is both powerful and cruel. Thus we see that torture, while indeed inadequate in itself to produce the sort of testimony that was produced at Nuernberg, might very well have been employed to achieve a general "softening up" of witnesses and defendants that would help the process of coercion and intimidation at other points.

A few complications are also worth mentioning. First, physical torture is not such a very well defined thing. One could argue that extended imprisonment under unhealthy, or even merely uncomfortable, conditions, with daily interrogation, is a form of torture. Another complication is that there are modes of torture, mainly sexual in nature or related to sex, that one could never learn about because the victims simply will not talk about them. Finally we should observe that almost none of us, certainly not this author, has ever experienced torture at the hands of professionals bent on a specific goal, and thus we might suspect, to put it quite directly, that we simply do not know what we are talking about when we discuss the possibilities of torture.

Our basic conclusion in respect to the torture problem is that there is something of an imponderable involved. We believe it likely that torture was employed to achieve a general softening up of the victims, so that their testimonies would more predictably take courses that were motivated by considerations other than torture, and we have analyzed witness and defendant testimony, in preceding pages of this chapter, on this basis; the effects of and fear of torture do not, in themselves, explain testimony in support of exterminations. We thus tend to disagree with much of the existing literature in this area which, it seems, places too much weight on the singular efficacy of torture at Nuernberg, although we concede that our analysis of this hard subject is not conclusive. We have similar suspicions that writers on witchcraft trials have also leaped to invalid conclusions on the basis of the two indisputably valid facts that, first, victims in witchcraft trials were tortured and, second, many of these people later testified to impossible happenings. The former does not really account for the latter, but it can be a contributing factor when its effects are added to the more weighty motivations for delivering certain kinds of false testimony.

We will return to some statements made at trials in due course. There are a few remarks, allegedly made by top Nazis, that should be mentioned. On 17 April 1943 Hitler met Admiral Horthy at Klessheim Castle. Hitler was critical of Horthy's lenient Jewish policy and, it is said, explained to Horthy that things were different in Poland:

> If the Jews there did not want to work, they were shot. If they could not work, they had to be treated like tuberculosis bacilli, with which a healthy body may become infected. This was not cruel if one remembers that even innocent creatures of nature, such as hares and deer, which are infected, have to be killed so that no harm is caused by them.

The evidence that Hitler said this is the alleged minutes of the meeting and the supporting IMT testimony of Dr. Paul Otto Schmidt, Hitler's interpreter, who normally sat in on such conferences and prepared the minutes. Schmidt testified that he was present at the meeting, and that the minutes were genuine and prepared by him. However, in his later book he wrote that he was not present, since Horthy had insisted on his leaving the room![32]

There is also a statement in Hitler's political testament:

I also made it quite plain that, if the peoples of Europe were again to be regarded merely as pawns in a game played by the international conspiracy of money and finance, they, the Jews, the race that is the real guilty party in this murderous struggle, would be saddled with the responsibility for it.

I left no one in doubt that this time not only would millions of grown men meet their death and not only would hundreds of thousands of women and children be burned and bombed to death in cities, but this time the real culprits would have to pay for their guilt even though by more humane means than war.

This statement is frequently interpreted as an admission of extermina-tions, but its meaning is at least ambiguous. After all, the payment spoken of was by "more humane means than war". The Jews who had been in Hitler's domain had lost property and position in Europe, and that fact may offer the correct interpretation. Loss of property and position might seem a woefully inadequate payment for the events charged to the Jews, but it is well known that all politicians, before leaving the public scene, like to exaggerate the significance of their works.

There also exists a possibility that the text of the testament was tam-pered with, since its discovery by British and American authorities was not announced until 29 December 1945, and since only the last page is signed. Only the typewriter and stationery Hitler's secretary used would have been required to make an undetectable alteration.[33]

There is a speech allegedly given by Himmler in Posen in October 1943. The translation of the relevant part, as it appears in the NMT volumes, is as follows, with the original German given in some cases:[34]

I also want to talk to you, quite frankly, on a very grave matter. Among our-selves it should be mentioned quite frankly, and yet we will never speak of it publicly. Just as we did not hesitate on 30 June 1934 to do the duty we were bidden and stand comrades who had lapsed up against the wall and shoot them, so we have never spoken about it and will never speak of it . . .

I mean the evacuation of the Jews *(die Judenevakuierung)*, the extermination *(Ausrottung)* of the Jewish race. It's one of those things it is easy to talk about, "The Jewish race is being exterminated *(ausgerottet)*," says one Party Member, "that's quite clear, it's in our program – elimination *(Ausschaltung)* of the Jews and we're doing it, extermination *(Ausrottung)* is what we're doing." And then they come, 80 million worthy Germans, and each one has his decent Jew. Of course the others are vermin, but this one is an A-1 Jew. Not one of all those who talk this way has watched it, not one of them has gone through it. Most of *you* must know what it means when 100 corpses are lying side by side, or 500, or 1,000. To have stuck it out and at the same time – apart from exceptions caused by human weakness – to have remained decent fellows, that is what has made us hard. This is a page of glory in our history which has never been written and is never to be written, for we know how difficult we should have made it for ourselves, if with the bombing raids, the burdens and the deprivations of war we still had Jews today in every town as secret saboteurs, agitators, and trouble-mongers. We would now probably have reached the 1916-1917 stage when the Jews were still in the German national body.

We have taken from them what wealth they had. I have issued a strict order, which *SS Obergruppenfuehrer* Pohl has carried out, that this wealth should, as a matter of course, be handed over to the Reich without reserve. We have taken none of it for ourselves . . . We had the moral right, we had the duty to our people, to destroy this people *(dieses Volk umzubringen)* which wanted to destroy us. But we have not the right to enrich ourselves with so much as a fur, a watch, a mark, or a cigarette, or any-thing else. Because we exterminated *(ausrotteten)* a germ, we do not want in the end to be infected by the germ and die of it . . . Wherever it may form, we will cauterize it.

The evidence that Himmler actually made these remarks is very weak. The alleged text of the Posen speech is part of document 1919-PS and covers 63 pages in the IMT volumes. The quoted portion occurs in a section of 1½ pages length which stands about mid-way in the text under the heading "Jewish evacuation". The manuscript of the speech, which bears no signature or other endorsement, is said (in the descriptive material accompanying the trial document) to have been found in Rosenberg's files. It was put into evidence at the IMT as part of document 1919-PS but it was not stated, during the IMT proceedings, where the document was supposed to have been found, and nobody questioned Rosenberg in connection with it. On the other hand Rosenberg was questioned in regard to 3428-PS, another document said to have been found in his files (which is discussed briefly below), and he denied that it could have been part of his files.[35] It is further claimed that during Case 11 "the Rosenberg files were rescreened and 44 records were discovered to be a phonographic recording of Himmler's Poznan speech of 4 October 1943".[36] The records are supposed to be document NO-5909, and were put into evidence during the testimony of defendant Gottlob Berger, SS General, former head of the SS administrative department, Himmler's personal liaison with Rosenberg's Ministry for the Occupied East, and chief of POW affairs toward the end of the war. In his direct examination Berger had testified that he had known nothing of any extermination program and also that Himmler had, indeed, delivered an "interminable" speech at Posen in 1943, to an audience of higher SS leaders which included himself. However he denied that document 1919-PS was an accurate transcript of the speech since he recalled that part of the speech had dealt with certain Belgian and Dutch SS leaders who were present at the meeting, and[37]

That is not contained in the transcript. I can say with certainty that he did not speak about the *Ausrottung* of the Jews, because the reason for this meeting was to equalize and adjust these tremendous tensions between the Waffen SS and the Police.

In the cross examination prosecutor Petersen played a phonograph recording of somebody speaking the first lines of the alleged speech, but Berger at first denied that the voice was Himmler's and then, after a second playing of the same lines, he said that it "might be Heinrich Himmler's voice". The records were then offered in evidence and more excerpts, including the one dealing with Jewish evacuation which is quoted above, were played in court. Berger was not questioned further, however, on the authenticity of the voice, and was excused immediately after the playing of the records. It was only with some reluctance that the court accepted these records in evidence:

JUDGE POWERS, Presiding: Well, I think that there is enough evidence here, *prima facie,* that the voice is the voice of Himmler to justify receiving the document in evidence. There is no evidence. however, that it was delivered at Poznan or any other particular place. The discs will be received in evidence as an indication of Himmler's general attitude.

The only *"prima facie"* evidence for the authenticity of the voice (at only one point in the speech), as far as I can see, was the Berger statement at one point that the voice "might be Heinrich Himmler's".

In our judgment the prosecution did not submit one bit of evidence that the voice was that of Himmler or even that the Posen speech, which everyone would agree dwelled on sensitive subjects, was recorded phonographically. Thus the authenticity of these phonograph recordings has not even been argued, much less demonstrated.

It may be that no recording purporting to be Himmler's remarks on "Jewish evacuation" still exists. No such recording, so far as I know, surfaced in public during the avalanche of propaganda that accompanied the Eichmann affair. Reitlinger remarks that a "partial gramophone recording" of the Posen speech exists, but he does not say what part still exists.[38] I have not pursued the question any further, since I would not be qualified to evaluate such recordings if they were produced.

Note that these recordings, claimed to have been belatedly discovered in a dead man's files, were put into evidence at the same "trial", Kempner's circus, which the analysis has already conclusively discredited on independent grounds. In addition, it seems quite peculiar that Himmler would have allowed the recording of a speech containing material that he "will never speak of . . . publicly" and then, despite his control of the Gestapo, have seen these recordings fall into the hands of his political rival Rosenberg. On the basis of these considerations, and also on account of the fact that it is very difficult to believe that Himmler would have wasted the time of so many high SS leaders by delivering the supposed text in document 1919-PS (a most general discussion of the war), one can be sure that we have another forgery here. However, parts of the alleged speech may be authentic, and some parts may have been delivered during the Posen speech or on other occasions.

It is true that Pohl testified in Case 4 that he was present at the Posen speech (probably true) and that Himmler did deliver the remarks concerning extermination of the Jews. However, Pohl's real point was a ludicrous one. We have noted that Pohl's basic trial strategy was to attempt to exploit the fact that the extermination charges had been thrown specifically at the Gestapo and the RSHA, and he was quick to pounce on such things as the Hoess affidavit as absolving him in regard to exterminations. His defense strategy had the same basic logic as the strategies of all defendants we have examined, except for Goering. Thus Pohl's testimony concerning the Posen speech came in the context of his declaration that the speech was his first information about the exterminations! In other words, the exterminations were allegedly so far removed from his official responsibilities that it required a declaration by Himmler for him to learn of them. He naturally further testified that he shortly later protested to Himmler, but was told that it was "none of your business". Thus was expressed merely Pohl's defense strategy of putting self-serving interpretations on that which was passing as fact in court.[39]

A lesser point should be made before we leave the subject of the Posen speech. It is possible to argue that the text may be genuine at this point but that by *"Ausrottung"* Himmler merely meant "uprooting" or some form of elimination less drastic than killing. The principal basis for such an argument would be that *Ausrottung* is indeed explicitly equated in the text with *Judenevakuierung* and with *Ausschaltung*. The corpses referred to could easily be interpreted as German corpses produced by the Allied air raids, which the Nazis often claimed the Jews were ultimately responsible for. On the other hand it can be noted that if the remarks are authentic then Himmler regarded it as a right and a duty *dieses Volk umzubringen*, and the comparison with the bloody purge of 1934 at the outset of the remarks seems to justify taking *"Ausrottung"* in its primary sense of extermination. Thus, while such an argument could be made, it would not be very solid.

The conclusive point is that in being asked to believe that the text is genuine we are, in effect, being asked to believe Kempner.

Finally, there are a number of remarks in *The Goebbels Diaries* but, as the "Publisher's Note" explains, the "diaries were typed on fine water-marked paper" and then "passed through several hands, and eventually came into the possession of Mr. Frank E. Mason". Thus the authenticity of the complete manuscript is very much open to question, even if the authenticity of much of the material can be demonstrated somehow. Interpolation with a typewriter is simple. The original clothbound edition of the *"Diaries"* even contains a U.S. Government statement that it "neither warrants nor disclaims the authenticity of the manuscript".

Wilfred von Oven, who was an official in the Goebbels Ministry and became, after the war, the editor of the right wing German language Buenos Aires journal *La Plata*, has come forward with a curiously eager endorsement

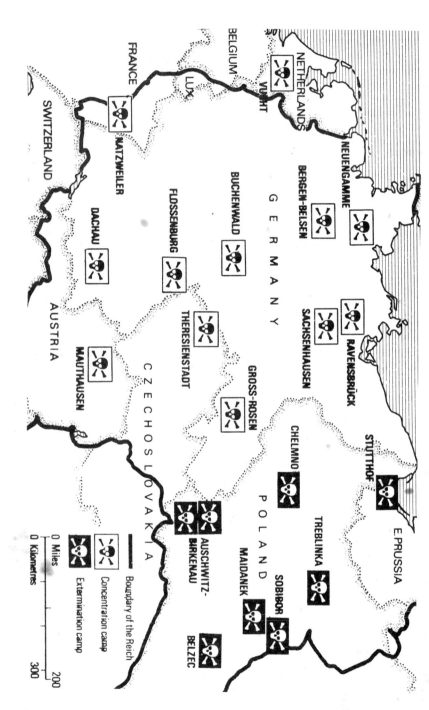

Fig. 23: Some of the principal German camps. Theresienstadt was not really a camp, but a ghetto or village, as you wish.

196

of the authenticity of *The Goebbels Diaries*. However the net effect of his comments is in the reverse direction for he tells us that (a) the diaries were dictated from handwritten notes (which were subsequently destroyed) by Goebbels to *Regierungsrat* Otte, who typed them using the special typewriter, having characters of almost 1 cm height, that was used for typing the texts that Goebbels used when he gave speeches (!) and (b) Oven "often observed" Otte, at Goebbels orders, "carefully and precisely as ever" burning these pages toward the end of the war after having made microfilms of them. The point of the latter operation, as Goebbels is said to have explained to Oven in the 18 April 1945 entry in the latter's diary (which was published in 1948/1949 in Buenos Aires), was that Goebbels "had for months taken care that his treasure, his great secret, result and accumulation of a more than twenty year political career, his diary, will remain preserved for posterity but not fall into unauthorized hands".

· This strange story of Oven's at least throws some light on the reference to an unusual typewriter in Louis P. Lochner's Introduction to the *Diaries*. If Oven's account is true, then it is possible that persons unknown obtained the special typewriter or a facsimile and a set of the microfilms, and manufactured an edited and interpolated text. However it is next to impossible to believe that Goebbels' diaries were indeed transcribed as Oven has described.[40]

The remaining part of the extermination legend is that the *Einsatzgruppen* exterminated Russian Jews in gasmobiles and by mass shootings. This is the only part of the legend which contains a particle of truth.

At the time of the German invasion of Russia in June 1941, there was a Fuehrer order declaring, in anticipation of an identical Soviet policy, that the war with Russia was not to be fought on the basis of the traditional "rules of warfare". Necessary measures were to be taken to counter partisan activity, and Himmler was given the power to "act independently upon his own responsibility". Everybody knew that that meant executions of partisans and persons collaborating with partisans. The dirty task was assigned to four *Einsatzgruppen* of the SD, which had a total strength of about 3,000 men (i.e. of the order of 500 to 1,000 men per group). Knowledgeable authorities, incidentally, have accepted that such anti-partisan operations were necessary in the Russian theater, where the enemy had no regard for the "rules".[41]

We have had occasion to note in several instances that Jews did, in fact, pose a security menace to the German rear in the war. The Red Cross excerpt makes this quite clear. The task of the *Einsatzgruppen* was to deal with such dangers by all necessary means, so we need not be told much more to surmise that the *Einsatzgruppen* must have shot many Jews, although we do not know whether "many" means 5,000, 25,000 or 100,000. Naturally, many non-Jews were also executed.

However the claim goes beyond this, and asserts a *dual* role for the *Einsatzgruppen;* they were charged not only with keeping the partisan problem under control but also with exterminating all Jews (and gipsies). Common sense alone should reject the notion that the *Einsatzgruppen*, which had a total strength of about 3,000 men, as a matter of general policy, spent their time and effort pursuing objectives unrelated to military considerations. We are again offered a fact for dual interpretation.

The story is that there was no written order to exterminate the Jews, but that the *Einsatzgruppen* commanders got their orders orally, and at different times. Ohlendorf commanded Group D in southern Russia and he got his orders orally from Streckenbach in June 1941. Rasch of Group C, operating to the immediate north of Ohlendorf, did not get his orders until August. Groups A and B operated around the Baltic states and to the south-east of the

Baltic States, respectively, and were commanded by Stahlecker and Nebe respectively.[42]

The main evidence for exterminations is a huge amount of documentary evidence which is simply funny. There is the celebrated document 501-PS which the Russians possessed at a show "trial" that they staged in December 1943 (sic).[43] One part is said to be a letter to Rauff in Berlin, written by an SS 2nd Lieutenant Becker. This is apparently the only document claimed to be signed by Becker, who is said to have been dead at the time of the IMT trial. It reads:[44]

The overhauling of the *Wagen* by groups D and C is finished. While the *Wagen* in the first series can also be put into action if the weather is not too bad, the *Wagen* of the second series (Saurer) stop completely in rainy weather ... I ordered the *Wagen* of group D to be camouflaged as housetrailers ... the driver presses the accelerator to the fullest extent. By doing that the persons to be executed suffer death from suffocation and not death by dozing off as was planned.

The text of the document is as spurious sounding as one should expect the text of such a document to be; it was allegedly written by an obscure 2nd Lieutenant and fortuitously fell into the hands of the Russians in 1943! Aleksandr I. Solzhenitsyn, in *The Gulag Archipelago*, mentions the case of the Bavarian Jupp Aschenbrenner, whom the Russians persuaded to sign a similar declaration that he had worked on wartime gas vans, but Aschenbrenner was later able to prove that, at the time he had supposedly been working on the vans, he was actually in Munich studying to become an electric welder.[45]

The most frequently cited evidence is a collection of documents purporting to be daily and other reports of the *Einsatzgruppen* to Himmler and Heydrich for the period June 1941 to May 1942. Document numbers are 180-L (said to be a report of Stahlecker found in Himmler's files),[46] 2273-PS (said to be another Stahlecker report on actions up to January 31, 1942, "captured by Russians in Riga"; Stahlecker was killed in March 1942),[47] 119-USSR and many others, too numerous to list, most having numbers around NO-3000. Besides telling of regular anti-partisan activities, the reports tell of individual actions of mass executions of Jews, with numbers of victims usually running in the thousands. It is indicated, in most cases, that many copies, sometimes as many as a hundred, were distributed. They are mimeographed and signatures are most rare and, when they occur, appear on non-incriminating pages. Document NO-3159, for example, has a signature, R.R. Strauch, but only on a covering page giving the locations of various units of the *Einsatzgruppen*. There is also NO-1128, allegedly from Himmler to Hitler reporting, among other things, the execution of 363,211 Russian Jews in August-November 1942. This claim occurs on page 4 of NO-1128, while initials said to be Himmler's occur on the irrelevant page 1. Moreover, Himmler's initials were easy to forge: three vertical lines with a horizontal line drawn through them.[48]

In connection with these matters, the reader should be informed that when examining printed reproductions of documents in the IMT and NMT volumes a handwritten signature should not be assumed unless it is specifically stated that the signature is handwritten; "signed" generally means only a typewritten signature. Document 180-L, for example, is reproduced in German in the IMT volumes and excerpts in English are reproduced in the NMT volumes. In both cases signatures are indicated but the actual document merely has *"gez. Dr. Stahlecker"* (signed Dr. Stahlecker) typewritten in two places.[49]

There are two documents said to have been authored by Hinrich Lohse, Reichskommissar for the Ostland, who was also the person to whom Wetzel's "Brack remedy" letter was addressed (p. 173). One of the documents deals with *Sonderbehandlung* and was alluded to in Chapter IV (p. 115). Like

Wetzel, Lohse was never called as a witness at Nuernberg. Unlike Wetzel, however, Lohse stood trial before a German court and was sentenced in 1948 to ten years imprisonment. However, he was released in 1951 on grounds of ill health and awarded a pension which was shortly later disallowed on account of public protest. As for the documents attributed to him, Reitlinger remarks that they "saved him from the Allied Military Courts and perhaps the gallows" for, while they speak of atrocities, they are so worded as to put the author of the documents in opposition to the crimes. The document dealing with *Sonderbehandlung* is a letter from Lohse to Rosenberg dated 18 June 1943. The actual document, 135-R, seems to be claimed to be an unsigned carbon copy of the correspondence, found in SS files. The relevant passage reads:[50]

That Jews are *sonderbehandelt* requires no further discussion. But that things proceed as is explained in the report of the Generalkommissar of 1 June 1943 seems scarcely believable. What is Katyn compared to that? . . .

Three unsigned reports supposedly received from the Generalkommissar (Wilhelm Kube, Generalkommissar for White Russia) are attached to the document.

The second Lohse document is 3663-PS, and is one of several documents bearing the major irregularity of having been processed by the Yivo (Yiddish Scientific Institute) of New York before being submitted as Nuernberg trial documents. There are about 70 such documents said to have been found in the Rosenberg Ministry in September 1945 by Sergeant Szajko Frydman of the U.S. 82nd Airborne Division. Frydman, however, was a staff member of the Yivo both before and after his service in the Army (indeed the Yivo was so active in producing documents supposedly found in the Rosenberg Ministry that it may very well have some enlightening information on the origins of the supposed text of Himmler's Posen speech). The first part of the document is written on the stationery of the Ministry. It is a letter to Lohse, dated 31 October 1941, with a typewritten signature by Dr. Leibbrandt and an illegible handwritten endorsement by somebody else. It reads:

The RSHA has complained that the Reichskommissar for the Ostland has forbidden executions of Jews in Libau. I request a report in regard to this matter by return mail.

The second part of the document is the reply, handwritten on the reverse side of the first part, supposedly in the hand of Trampedach, and initialed by Lohse (with a letter "L" about 1½ inches high). It reads:

I have forbidden the wild executions of Jews in Libau because they were not justifiable in the manner in which they were carried out.

I should like to be informed whether your inquiry of 31 October is to be regarded as a directive to liquidate all Jews in the East? Shall this take place without regard to age and sex and economic interests (of the Wehrmacht, for instance, in specialists in the armament industry)? Of course, the cleansing of the East of Jews is a necessary task; its solution, however, must be harmonized with the necessities of war production.

So far I have not been able to find such a directive either in the regulations regarding the Jewish question in the "Brown Portfolio" or in other decrees.

Obviously, Lohse could not have any conceivable reason to contest the authenticity of these documents since, though they suggest exterminations, they emphatically excuse him.

Another document from the Yivo is 3428-PS, supposedly a letter from Kube to Lohse, reporting shipments of German, Polish and other Jews to the Minsk area and the liquidation of some of them. From the mimeographed summary examined, it is not clear whether or not the document is supposed to have a handwritten signature. Wilhelm Kube was assassinated in September 1943.[51]

Other documents that are relevant are numbered 3660-PS through 3669-PS (excepting 3663-PS). The documents are attributed to various people, e.g. Kube and Gewecke, and in every case the descriptive material accompanying the document specifies that the location of the original is unknown, and that only a photostat is available. With only a couple of exceptions, there are no handwritten signatures.

Even Reitlinger seems puzzled by the existence of these reports and other documents since he remarks:[52]

It is not easy to see why the murderers left such an abundant testimony behind them, for in spite of their wide circulation list, Knobloch's (the Gestapo official who edited the reports) reports seem to have been designed primarily to appeal to Himmler and Heydrich. Thus, in addition to much juggling with the daily death bills in order to produce an impressive total, there are some rather amateur essays in political intelligence work.

It is the "amateur essays" that convince one of forgery here; the contents of these reports are ridiculous in the selection of things reported. To give a few examples from excerpts reproduced in NMT volume 4:[53]

The tactics, to put terror against terror, succeeded marvelously. From fear of reprisals, the peasants came a distance of 20 kilometers and more to the headquarters of the *Teilkommando* of *Einsatzgruppe A* on foot or on horseback in order to bring news about partisans, news which was accurate in most of the cases . . .

In this connection a single case may be mentioned, which proves the correctness of the principle "terror against terror". In the village of Yachnova it was ascertained on the basis of a report made by the peasant Yemelyanov and after further interrogations and other searches that partisans had been fed in the house of Anna Prokovieva. The house was burned down on 8 August 1941 at about 21 hours, and its inhabitants arrested. Shortly after midnight partisans set light to the house of the informer Yemelyanov. A detachment sent to Jachnowa on the following day ascertained that the peasant woman Ossipova had told the partisans that Yemelyanov had made the report which had caused our action.

Ossipova was shot and her house burned down. Further, two 16-year-old youths from the village were shot because, according to their own confession, they had rendered information and courier service to the partisans . . .

. . . Several Jews who had not been searched thoroughly enough by the Lithuanian guards drew knives and pistols and uttering cries like "Long live Stalin!" and "Down with Hitler!" they rushed upon the police force of whom 7 were wounded. Resistance was broken at once. After 150 Jews had been shot on the spot, the transport of the remaining Jews to the place of execution was carried through without further incident.

In the course of the greater action against Jews, 3,412 Jews were shot in Minsk, 302 in Vileika, and 2,007 in Baranovichi.

The population welcomed these actions, when they found out, while inspecting the apartments, that the Jews still had great stocks of food at their disposal, whereas their own supplies were extremely low.

Jews appear again and again, especially in the sphere of the black market. In the Minsk canteen which serves the population with food and is operated by the city administration, 2 Jews had committed large-scale embezzlements and briberies. The food which was obtained in this way was sold on the black market.

It is not difficult to see why these documents exist; without them the authors of the lie would have no evidence for their claims except testimony. We have seen that with Auschwitz there was an abundance of material facts to work with and whose meanings could be distorted: shipments of Jews to Auschwitz, many of whom did not return to their original nomes, large shipments of a source of hydrogen cyanide gas, elaborate cremation facilities, selections, the stench. The situation with the *Einsatzgruppen* was different; there was only one fact, the executions. Standing alone, this fact does not appear impressive as evidence, and this consideration was no doubt the motivation for manufacturing these documents on such a large scale. This is in contrast to the Auschwitz hoax, for which forgery of documents is not nearly so prominent, and where the forgeries were accomplished with more care. With Auschwitz we are dealing with a lie manufactured by Washington, but with the *Einsatzgruppen* we are dealing with one manufactured by Moscow,

Photo: U.S. National Archives

Fig. 24: Russian soap "evidence" at the IMT

201

and the hand is correspondingly heavier.

It is worth mentioning that the "gasmobiles" were not charged in Soviet propaganda until the middle of the war. Massacres of Jews were claimed, of course, early in the development of the propaganda, and the *N.Y. Times* story of 6 April 1942 which appeared in our survey in Chapter III is an example. The massacres are not claimed to have taken place via gasmobiles. A contemporary Soviet propaganda production was a book, *We Shall Not Forgive!* (Foreign Languages Publishing House, Moscow, 1942). The book opens with a summary, presented by Molotov on 27 April 1942, of the crimes that the Germans had supposedly committed in their invasion of Russia. The remainder of the book elaborates the charges with commentaries and photographs, with quite a few obvious phonies in the collection. Since the Germans are charged with virtually every crime imaginable, they are naturally charged with pogroms and massacres of Jews, but gasmobiles do not appear in the charges. As far as we can see, the first claims of gasmobile exterminations on Russian territory (as distinct from claims of gasmobiles at Chelmno in Poland) came in July 1943, during a Soviet trial of 11 Russians accused of having collaborated with the Germans at Krasnodar. This suggests that the Russian gasmobile claims may have been inspired by the gas chamber propaganda that had started in the West late in 1942. In any case, the late appearance of the gasmobile charges, just as in the case of the Auschwitz propaganda, is further proof that the charges are inventions.[54]

There is also a certain amount of testimony that should be mentioned. At the risk of belaboring a perfectly simple point, let us again observe what has been pointed out here from many different angles; that a witness testifies in court to the truth of X, under conditions where the court is already committed to the truth of X, is historical evidence of absolutely nothing.

The most frequently referred to testimony is that of Ohlendorf, an SS Lieutenant General and an economist who had had some differences with Himmler and consequently found himself assigned to command group D for one year, summer 1941 to summer 1942, in southern Russia. Ohlendorf was the most literate of the people involved in this matter.

At the IMT, when other people were on trial, Ohlendorf had appeared as a prosecution witness and had testified in agreement with the extermination claims.[55] He testified that he had received oral orders to add extermination of Jews to his activities, that gasmobiles were used to exterminate women and children, that document 501-PS was authentic (Becker's letter), and that the Wehrmacht was implicated in these things. Thus this charge regarding the *Einsatzgruppen* was part of the IMT judgment, which even stated that Ohlendorf exterminated Jews with group D.[56] As we have seen, these statements in the judgment constituted "proof of the facts stated" when Ohlendorf, no doubt contrary to his expectations, was put on trial as the principal defendant in Case 9. In view of the legal constraints involved here, nobody's position could have been more hopeless than Ohlendorf's at his own trial.

Ohlendorf's NMT testimony was simply contradictory; he was stuck with his IMT testimony, which the prosecution was mindful of holding him to, but he tried to squirm out anyway and the result was a story having no coherency whatever.[57] He retracted his earlier statement that there had been specific extermination orders, but under cross examination he said that he was killing all Jews and gipsies anyway, but that this was just an anti-partisan operation, not part of a program to exterminate all Jews and gipsies on racial or religious grounds". However, the total number of persons of all categories executed by group D during his year in Russia was only 40,000, and not the 90,000 that he had testified to at the IMT and which the NMT prosecutor attempted to hold him to. Either figure, of course, especially the former, makes some sense if the executions were only in connection with anti-partisan measures, but make no sense at all if one is supposed to be executing all Jews and gipsies, including women and children, at the same time.

Ohlendorf's NMT testimony is thus hopelessly contradictory, as it was bound to be in the hopeless circumstances in which he found himself. One should note, however, that Ohlendorf did not testify to the reality of any executions which his court was not formally committed, *a priori*, to accepting as factual anyway. The only part of Ohlendorf's testimony that may be of value is his attack on the *Einsatzgruppen* reports as "edited".

Ohlendorf's testimony contrasts with that of Haensch, an SS Lieutenant Colonel who was in command of a *Sonderkommando* in group C for about seven weeks. The fact that Haensch had not testified previously, when others were on trial, and the fact that his lower rank made the *a priori* constraints on Case 9 of lesser effect in his case, gave him a freedom which Ohlendorf did not enjoy. He testified that absolutely nobody, in giving him his orders, had ever mentioned Jews, as such, in connection with executive activities of the *Einsatzgruppen*, and that his *Sonderkommando* had not, as a matter of fact, had a policy of executing Jews as such. He estimated that his *Sonderkommando* executed about sixty people during his period of service. All of these claims were completely in conflict with what are said to be the reports of the *Einsatzgruppen*, as the court pointed out in detail in the judgment, concluding that in connection with Haensch[58]

one can only dismiss as fantastic the declaration of the defendant that his predecessor who had admittedly executed thousands of Jews under the Fuehrer Order, and whose program Haensch was to continue, said nothing to Haensch about that program. And when Haensch boldly uttered that the first time he ever had any inkling of the Fuehrer Order was when he arrived in Nuernberg six years later, he entered into a category of incredulousness which defies characterization.

Ohlendorf and Haensch were both sentenced to hang. Ohlendorf's sentence was carried out in 1951, but Haensch's sentence was commuted to fifteen years. Presumably, he was out sometime during the Fifties.

Of course, the basic plea of all defendants in Case 9, as well as in almost all other cases, was that whatever they did was done in obedience to orders that could be disobeyed only under circumstances that would have resulted in the execution of the disobedient person. Incidentally, in my opinion this is a perfectly valid, defense, and it may have been this consideration that played a role in whatever inducements were offered to Germans to become prosecution witnesses at the IMT trial; it did not imply his guilt or, at least, it logically did not, if it was done in obedience to orders. In fact, this was the case in the German military law that the German witnesses were familiar with. Disobedience of even an illegal order was a serious and punishable offense. People such as Hoess and Ohlendorf had, no doubt, reasoned that their testimony at the IMT had incriminated them only in the sense of perjury, an offense that they knew the Allied tribunals would never charge them with. Ohlendorf's attempts to ingratiate himself with the U.S. prosecutors did not, moreover, end with the IMT for he was also used, after his own trial and while he was under sentence of death, as a prosecution witness against Wehrmacht generals in Case 12.

Personal guilt, obviously, is not involved if the actions demanded or suggested by the accusers would have led to the clearly inevitable death of the accused. I suspect that every accuser of the *Einsatzgruppen* would have obeyed orders to participate in the air raids on Hamburg, Dresden, Hiroshima and Nagasaki (none of which, incidentally, had credible military motivations).

However I do not want to create an impression that I am denying that the *Einsatzgruppen* executed apparent civilians, including women and children, in connection with their activities in Russia. All experience with anti-partisan warfare, whether conducted by the British, the French or the Americans suggests, quite independently of the tainted (to put it mildly) evidence of the trials at Nuernberg, that such things happened. In the Viet Nam war, the Americans did much of this with napalm, and then made a big fuss over the fact that one obscure Lieutenant had been caught doing it with bullets.

Neither am I trying to create an impression that, actually, everybody is very brutal, but a thorough discussion of the problems involved would carry us far afield, so it will not be attempted; only the essentials can be outlined here.

It is an unhappy fact that partisan, irregular or guerilla warfare, together with the measures taken to suppress such operations, is not only the dirtiest business in existence but has also been a regular feature of twentieth century history. It is dirty business even when the two sides are highly civilized and culturally similar. A good example is the British campaign against the Irish rebellion of 1916-1921, where both sides acted with remarkable brutality.

If, to the fact of guerilla warfare, one adds that at least one side is drawn from a primitive population, uncivilized or semi-civilized, then one has a situation that it is most difficult for an ordinary civilized person to grasp if he has no direct experience of it. It is too easy for us, sitting in the warmth of our living rooms, to generate moral indignation over operations which involve the killing of "apparent civilians, including women and children". The typical West European or American has lived in a culture in which certain standards of charity, kindness and honor have been taken for granted, and it is difficult for him to understand that certain fundamental assumptions about other people would not hold in a context such as guerilla warfare in Asia or Russia; the viciousness involved exceeds the imagination. To give just one example drawn from Viet Nam experience: what do you do, dear reader, if a child, despite signalled warnings to stay away, is obstinately approaching you asking for food or candy and it is known that there is a good chance that there is a grenade attached to him?

Of course, many needless brutalities always occur in such circumstances, but one should attempt to understand the situation.

What I am denying with respect to the *Einsatzgruppen* is that one can give any credence to the story told by the trials evidence which, while it is somewhat variable on some points, has the basic feature of asserting that the *Einsatzgruppen*, which had a total strength of about 3,000 for the anti-partisan operations for all of occupied Russia, regularly and as a matter of policy pursued a second set of objectives not related to military considerations, those objectives (exterminations) requiring substantial means for their attainment. We can, especially in view of the obvious forgery and perjury which has been practiced in connection with making this claim, dismiss all of that as propaganda. What did in fact happen can only, most probably, be approximately grasped, on account of the scantiness of reliable evidence. Unfortunately, it would appear that the events in Russia will never be established with exactitude, and that these episodes will remain partially in darkness.

VII
THE FINAL SOLUTION

/ PREFACE

We have shown that the exterminations are a propaganda hoax, i.e., we have shown what did not happen to the Jews. To complete our study, we should show what did, in fact, happen to the Jews.

The problem of what happened to the European Jews is a fairly easy one if one wishes only a general answer, and a very difficult, indeed probably impossible, problem if one demands statistical accuracy. To answer the question in general, all one need do is consult the relevant German documents. What the German leaders were saying to each other about their policy is obviously the first authority that one should consult.

The general nature of German Jewish policy is very simple to discover; it is all set out in NMT volume 13. The U.S. prosecution in the Wilhelmstrasse Case presented a document, NG-2586, which consists of several parts, each part being some document important in the development of German Jewish policy. One part, NG-2586-J, in fact, is a summary of the other parts and, thus, a handy summary of the policy. One can do no better than simply reproduce the text, a memo by Martin Luther (Horst Wagner's predecessor), dated 21 August 1942:[1]

1. The principle of the German Jewish policy after the seizure of power consisted in promoting with all means the Jewish emigration. For this purpose in 1939 Field Marshall Goering in his capacity as Plenipotentiary for the Four Year Plan established a Reich Central Office for Jewish Emigration and the direction was given to SS Lieutenant General Heydrich in his capacity as chief of the Security Police. The Foreign Office is represented in the committee of the Reich Central Office. The draft of a letter to this effect to the Chief of the Security Police was approved by the Reich Foreign Minister as 83/24 B in February 1939.

2. The present war gives Germany the opportunity and also the duty of solving the Jewish problem in Europe. In consideration of the favorable course of the war against France, D III (department Germany III) proposed in July 1940 as a solution – the removal of all Jews from Europe and the demanding of the Island of Madagascar from France as a territory for the reception of the Jews. The Reich Foreign Minister has basically agreed to the beginning of the preliminary work for the deportation of the Jews from Europe. This should be done in close cooperation with the offices of the Reichsfuehrer-SS (compare D III 200/40).

The Madagascar plan was enthusiastically accepted by the RSHA which in the opinion of the Foreign Office is the agency which alone is in the position technically and by experience to carry out a Jewish evacuation on a large scale and to guarantee the supervision of the people evacuated, the competent agency of the RSHA thereupon worked out a plan going into detail for the evacuation of the Jews to Madagascar and for their settlement there. This plan was approved by the Reichsfuehrer-SS. SS Lieutenant General Heydrich submitted this plan directly to the Reich Foreign Minister in August 1940 (compare D III 2171). The Madagascar plan in fact had been outdated as the result of the political development.

The fact that the Fuehrer intends to evacuate all Jews from Europe was communicated to me as early as August 1940 by Ambassador Abetz after an interview with the Fuehrer (compare D III 2298).

Hence the basic instruction of the Reich Foreign Minister, to promote the evacuation of the Jews in closest cooperation with the agencies of the Reichsfuehrer-SS, is still in force and will therefore be observed by D III.

3. The administration of the occupied territories brought with it the problem of

the treatment of Jews living in these territories. First, the military commander in France saw himself compelled as the first one to issue on 27 September 1940 a decree on the treatment of the Jews in occupied France. The decree was issued with the agreement of the German Embassy in Paris. The pertinent instruction was issued directly by the Reich Foreign Minister to Ambassador Abetz on the occasion of a verbal report.

After the pattern of the Paris decree similar decrees have been issued in the Netherlands and Belgium. As these decrees, in the same way as German laws concerning Jews, formally embrace all Jews independent of their citizenship, objections were made by foreign powers, among others protest notes by the Embassy of the United States of America, although the military commander in France through internal regulation had ordered that the Jewish measures should not be applied to the citizens of neutral countries.

The Reich Foreign Minister has decided in the case of the American protests that he does not consider it right to have military regulations issued for making an exception of the American Jews. It would be a mistake to reject objections of friendly states (Spain and Hungary) and on the other hand to show weakness toward the Americans. The Reich Foreign Minister considers it necessary to make these instructions to the field commanders retroactive (compare D III 5449).

In accordance with this direction the Jewish measures have been given general application.

4. In his letter of 24 June 1940 – Pol XII 136 – SS Lieutenant General Heydrich informed the Reich Foreign Minister that the whole problem of the approximately three and a quarter million Jews in the areas under German control can no longer be solved by emigration – a territorial final solution would be necessary.

In recognition of this Reich Marshall Goering on 31 July 1941 commissioned SS Lieutenant General Heydrich to make, in conjunction with the interested German Control agencies, all necessary preparations for a total solution of the Jewish problem in the German sphere of influence in Europe (compare D III 709 secret). On the basis of this instruction, SS Lieutenant General Heydrich arranged a conference of all the interested German agencies for 20 January 1942, at which the State Secretaries were present from the other ministries and I myself from the Foreign Office. In the conference General Heyrich explained that Reich Marshall Goering's assignment to him had been made on the Fuehrer's instruction and that the Fuehrer instead of the emigration had now authorized the evacuation of the Jews to the East as the solution (compare page 5 of the enclosure to D III 29/42 Secret). State Secretary Weizsaecker had been informed on the conference; for the time being the Reich Foreign Minister had not been informed on the conference, because SS Lieutenant General Heydrich agreed to holding a new conference in the near future in which more details of the total solution should be discussed. This conference has never taken place due to Lieutenant General Heydrich's appointment as acting Reich Protector of Bohemia and Moravia and due to his death.

In the conference on 20 January 1942 I demanded that all questions concerned with countries outside Germany must first have the agreement of the Foreign Office, a demand to which SS Lieutenant General Heydrich agreed and also has faithfully complied with, as in fact, the office of the RSHA handling Jewish matters has from the beginning carried out all measures in frictionless cooperation with the Foreign Office. The RSHA has in this matter proceeded indeed almost over cautiously.

5. On the basis of the Fuehrer's instruction mentioned under 4 (above), the evacuation of the Jews from Germany was begun. It was urged that at the same time these Jews should also be taken who were nationals of the countries which had also undertaken Jewish measures. The RSHA accordingly made an inquiry of the Foreign Office. For reasons of courtesy, inquiry was made by way of the German legations in Bratislava (Slovakia), Zagreb (Croatia), and Bucharest (Rumania) to the governments there as to whether they wanted to recall their Jews from Germany in due time or to agree to their deportation to the ghettos in the East. To the issuance of this instruction agreement was given before dispatch by the State Secretary, the Under State Secretary in Charge of the Political Division, the Director of the Division for Economic Policy and the Director of the Legal Division (compare D III 336 Secret).

The German Legation in Bucharest reports with reference to D III 602 Secret, that the Rumanian Government would leave it to the Reich Government to deport their Jews along with the German Jews to the ghettos in the East. They are not interested in having the Rumanian Jews return to Rumania.

The Legation in Zagreb has informed us that the Croat Government expresses gratitude for the gesture of the German Government; but it would appreciate the deportation of its Jews to the East (compare D III 624 Secret).

The Legation in Bratislava reported with reference to D III 661 Secret that the Slovak Government is fundamentally in agreement with the deportation to the eastern ghettos. But the Slovak claims to the property of these Jews should not be endangered.

DOCUMENT 022-L

EXCERPT FROM A REPORT OF THE WAR REFUGEE BOARD, WASHINGTON, D. C., NOVEMBER 1944, ON GERMAN EXTERMINATION CAMPS — AUSCHWITZ AND BIRKENAU — GIVING AN ESTIMATE OF THE NUMBER OF JEWS GASSED IN BIRKENAU BETWEEN APRIL 1942 AND APRIL 1944 (EXHIBIT USA-294)

EXPLANATORY NOTE:

Offset printed copy; orig. in archives of U. S. State Dept; report consists of two accounts of escaped concentration camp inmates—two young Slovakian Jews and a Polish major

Executive Office of the President
War Refugee Board
Washington, D. C.

German Extermination Camps —
Auschwitz and Birkenau.
(page 33)

Careful estimate of the number of Jews gassed
in BIRKENAU between April, 1942 and April, 1944
(according to countries of origin).

Poland (transported by truck)	approximately	300,000
,, ,, ,, train)	,,	600,000
Holland	,,	100,000
Greece	,,	45,000
France	,,	150,000
Belgium	,,	50,000
Germany	,,	60,000
Yugoslavia, Italy and Norway	,,	50,000
Lithuania	,,	50,000
Bohemia, Moravia and Austria	,,	30,000
Slovakia	,,	30,000
Various camps for foreign Jews in Poland	,,	300,000
	approximately	1,765,000

Fig. 25: A page from document 022-L, as reproduced in the 42 volume record of the International Military Tribunal.

The wire reports have also been submitted, as customary, to the Reich Foreign Minister's Bureau.

, On the basis of the reports of the Ministers I have informed the RSHA with reference to D III 661 Secret that the Jews of Rumanian, Croat, and Slovak nationality could also be deported; their property should be blocked. The Director of the Political Division, Section IV of the Political Division, Section IX of the Legal Division and Section IV of the Division for the Economic Policy have cosigned the document. Accordingly, the deportations of the Jews from the occupied territories was undertaken.

6. The number of Jews deported in this way to the East did not suffice to cover the labor needs there. The RSHA therefore, acting on the instruction of the Reichsfuehrer-SS, approached the Foreign Office to ask the Slovak Government to make 20,000 young, strong Slovak Jews from Slovakia available for deportation to the East. The German Legation in Bratislava was provided, by D III 874, with proper instruction. The instruction was signed by the State Secretary, the Under State Secretary in charge of the Political Division, and Section IV of the Political Division.

The Legation in Bratislava reported re D III 1002 that the Slovak Government has taken up the suggestion eagerly; the preparatory work could be begun.

Following up this pleased concurrence of the Slovak Government, the Reichsfuehrer-SS proposed that the rest of the Slovak Jews also be deported to the East and Slovakia thereby be made free of Jews. The Legation was, re D III 1559 Ang. II, provided with proper instruction. The draft of the instruction was signed by the State Secretary; after its dispatch it was submitted for their information to the bureau of the Reich Foreign Minister and the Under State Secretary in charge of the Political Division.

As the Slovak Episcopacy meanwhile raised objections to the deportation of the Jews before the Slovak Government, the instruction carries the express statement that in no case must there develop internal political difficulties on account of the evacuation of the Jews in Slovakia. By the telegraphic report, re D III 2006, the Legation reported that the Slovak Government, without any German pressure, has declared itself agreeable to the deportation of all Jews and that the State President agreed personally to the deportation. The telegraphic report was submitted to the bureau of the Reich Foreign Minister. The Slovak Government has furthermore agreed that it will pay as a contribution to the cost entailed RM 500 for every evacuated Jew.

In the meantime 52,000 Jews have been removed from Slovakia. Due to church influences and the corruption of individual officials 35,000 Jews have received a special legitimation. However, Minister President Tuka wants the Jewish removal continued and therefore has asked for support through diplomatic pressure by the Reich (compare D III 3865). The Ambassador is authorized to give this diplomatic help in that he may state to State President Dr. Tiso that the exclusion of the 35,000 Jews is a surprise in Germany, the more so since the cooperation of Slovakia up to now in the Jewish problem has been highly appreciated here. This instruction has been cosigned by the Under State Secretary in charge of the Political Division, and the State Secretary.

7. The Croat Government is likewise fundamentally agreeable to the removal of the Jews from Croatia. It especially considers the deportation of the four to five thousand Jews from the Italian occupied Second Zone (centered around Dubrovnik and Mostar) to be important, as they represent a political burden and their elimination would serve the general pacification. The removal can of course take place only with German aid, as difficulties are to be expected from the Italian side. There have been practical examples of resistance to the Croat measures by Italian officials on behalf of well-to-do Jews. Furthermore, the Italian Chief of Staff in Mostar has said that he cannot approve the removal since all the people living in Mostar have been assured of the same treatment.

Since meanwhile according to a telephone communication from Zagreb, the Croat Government has given its written approval of the proposed measure, Minister Kasche thinks it right to begin with the removal, and in fact to begin for the whole country. One could therefore take the risk of having difficulties develop in the course of the action, so far as concerns the zone occupied by Italians.

A report for the Reich Foreign Minister to this effect (D III 562 Secret) has been held up by State Secretary von Weizsaecker since he considered an inquiry should first be made at the Embassy in Rome. The answer has not been received.

The problem of the Italian Jews has come up in the same way in connection with the evacuation of the Jews in France.

Ambassador Abetz points out in connection with the deportation in preparation from the Occupied French Territory that there was an urgent political interest to take the foreign Jews first in the evacuation measures. Since these Jews were regarded as foreign bodies they were already especially hated and passing them over and giving them thereby a quasi privileging would cause bad feeling, the more so since among them were to be found responsible instigators of Jewish terror and sabotage acts. It was regrettable that the Axis appeared exactly in this point to pursue no uniform policy.

If the evacuation of the foreign Jews were not immediately possible, the Italian Government should be for the time being asked to repatriate their Jews from France.

On the Italian side economic interests appear to play a decisive role. The safeguarding of these interests however is entirely possible, so that on this point there needs to be no obstacle to the planned solution.

On this question of the Italian Jews in France a conference record of 24 July, re D III 562 Secret, has been submitted to the Reich Foreign Minister.

8. On the occasion of a reception by the Reich Foreign Minister on 26 November 1941 the Bulgarian Foreign Minister Popoff touched on the problem of according like treatment to the Jews of European nationalities and pointed out the difficulties that the Bulgarians had in the application of their Jewish laws to Jews of foreign nationality.

The Reich Foreign Minister answered that he thought this question brought up by Mr. Popoff not uninteresting. Even now he could say one thing to him, that at the end of this war all Jews would have to leave Europe. This was an unalterable decision of the Fuehrer and also the only way to master this problem, as only a global and comprehensive solution could be applied and individual measures would not help very much. Furthermore, one should not attribute too much worth to the protests on behalf of the Jews of foreign nationality. At any rate, we would not let ourselves be taken in any further by such protests from the American side. He — the Reich Foreign Minister — would have the problem described by Mr. Popoff investigated by the Foreign Office.

The Reich Foreign Minister commissioned me to undertake the investigation promised (compare D III 660g) (document NG-4669).

I should like to make reference to my basic conference memorandum of 4 December 1941, re D III 660 Secret, which I am dispatching, together with the proper files. This conference memorandum was held up by the State Secretary, because he considered a further examination by the Legal Division first necessary. In their opinion the German-Bulgarian trade and shipping pact was not in agreement with the German-Bulgarian arrangements proposed by me. I therefore notified the German Legation in Sofia, re D III 497 Secret, under date of 19 June, in reference to the suggestion of the Bulgarian Foreign Minister Popoff at his reception to contact the Bulgarian Government and find out whether it was prepared to come to an agreement in the Jewish problem that there should be no rights from the trade and shipping pact given effect in favor of the Jews in the promise of reciprocality.

If the question is put from the Bulgarian side as to whether Germany is ready to deport Jews from Bulgaria to the East, the question should be answered in the affirmative, but in respect to the time of the deporting should be answered evasively. This decree was cosigned by the State Secretary, the Under State Secretary, the Director of the Political Division, the Director of the Division for Economic Policy, Section IV of the Political Division, Section IV of the Division for Economic Policy, and also by Ribbentrop. The Legation exchanged notes with the Bulgarian Government and reported that the Bulgarian Government is fundamentally prepared in the problem of the evacuation to sign an agreement with us. Thereby the basis is given to include the Bulgarian Jews in the Jewish measures. (D III 559 Secret and 569 Secret).

9. The Hungarian Government has not yet been approached with respect to the Jewish removal, because the status of the Hungarian legislation up to the present does not promise a sufficient success.

10. In accordance with the agreement of the Rumanian Government mentioned under 8 the evacuation of the Rumanian Jews from Germany and the occupied territories was begun, whereupon various Rumanian consulates and the Rumanian Minister in Berlin, who had no instructions from their Government, intervened. Ambassador von Killinger was therefore asked for clarification. The Legation seems to have made use of the Jewish advisor assigned to it, Richter, for this purpose. He is a person to whom the Rumanian Government confirmed its earlier agreement to the inclusion of the Rumanian Jews in the German measures and to whom the Deputy Ministry President Mihai Antonescu informed of the request of the Marshall that the German agencies should also carry out the removal from Rumania itself and should be then immediately with the transport of the Jews from the areas Arad, Timisoara and Turda.

For details may I refer to my conference memorandum of 17 August ad D III 649.

11. At the request of the governments concerned, the legations in Bratislava, Zagreb and Bucharest have been assigned advisors for Jewish affairs. They have been made available at the request of the Foreign Office by the RSHA. Their assignment is for a limited time. It ends as soon as the Jewish problem in the country concerned can be regarded as solved in the German sense. Originally it was regarded as solved as soon as the country concerned had issued Jewish laws similar to the German ones.

Accordingly Richter was recalled from Rumania last year by the RSHA.

At the urgent request of the legation in Bucharest, Richter was again assigned to the legation despite the objection of the RSHA. This was done with the express intention of having him remain there until the actual final solution in Rumania (D III 1703 Secret and 1893 Secret).

Since all negotiations with the Rumanian Government went through the Foreign Office, the report of SS First Lieutenant Richter submitted by the Reichsfuehrer-SS should be considered only as an internal work report to the RSHA. The unusual procedure of having the confirmation of a final conference in the handwriting of the Deputy Minister President was sharply objected to immediately through the directive of the 17th of this month; the official handling of the affair must be carried out immediately. The files have been submitted there already under D III 3 Secret.

The intended deportations are a further step forward on the way of the total solution and are in respect to other countries (Hungary) very important. The deportation to the Government General is a temporary measure. The Jews will be moved on further to the occupied Eastern Territories as soon as the technical conditions for it are given.

I therefore request approval for the continuation of the negotiations and measures under these terms and according to the arrangement made.

Signed: LUTHER

The material starting with the words "If the question is put from the Bulgarian side . . . " and ending with the words "The files have been submitted there already under D III 659 Secret", is deleted in NMT volume 13. In section 4 the date of 24 June 1940 for document Pol XII 136 appears, from the context, to be in error; it should be 1941.

This is not a solitary document; not only is it a summary of a certain number of documents spelling out the Jewish policies of the German Government, but all documents bearing on Jewish policies, except for those we have identified as forgeries, fall within the scheme implied by it. The "final solution" meant the expulsion of all Jews from the German sphere of influence in Europe. After the invasion of Russia, its specific meaning was the resettlement of these Jews in the East. The German documents at every level (among those that have survived) express this unambiguously, a fact which is conceded even by the bearers of the extermination legend, who are forced to declare that this must just be code terminology for extermination.[2]

Actually, in the discussions prior to this chapter we have had several occasions to refer to this program of resettlement to the East. Its most important expression has been in the Red Cross excerpt which, despite its ambiguous remarks about "extermination", presents a picture in rather close accord with the story told by NG-2586-J. At Theresienstadt the Red Cross wondered if the place "was being used as a transit camp and asked when the last departures for the East had taken place". In Slovakia the Jews had been subject to "forced immigration towards the territories under German control". A large number of Rumanian Jews had been resettled in the East, but things did not work out and many returned, although there had been adequate opportunity to exterminate them if such had been the policy. Despite the several vague and ambiguous remarks about "extermination" which we noted in Chapter V, the undeniable effect of the Red Cross *Report* is to confirm that the Germans were doing what their documents say they were doing.

The German documents are not only confirmed by neutral authority; we have seen that they are even confirmed by hostile sources. In Chapter IV we discussed the Theresienstadt Jews sent to Auschwitz, as related by the WRB Report. The manner of their treatment makes sense only if Birkenau was serving as a transit camp for them. Moreover, the Israeli source cited in Chapter IV reported that Theresienstadt Jews were, indeed, being sent to the East (p. 109). Thus even hostile sources report that the Germans were doing what their documents say they were doing.

What is described in NG-2586-J is the program as it existed starting in early 1939. Actually, on account of the pressures against the Jews between 1933 and 1939 the great majority of German-Austrian Jews had emigrated before the outbreak of the war. The Germans had not cared very much where the Jews emigrated to. Palestine seemed a good possibility on account of the British Balfour Declaration of 1917, but negotiations with the British on this did not go very well because the British wished to maintain good relations with the Arabs who, at that time, constituted the bulk of the population of Palestine. Nevertheless there was some steady Jewish emigration from Europe to Palestine, but this was finally cut to a trickle by the policy announced by the British White Paper of May 1939.[3]

The Madagascar project, fantastic as it seems today, was taken quite seriously by the Germans, although nothing ever came of it. The war with Russia which started in June 1941 opened up obvious new resettlement possibilities, and this resulted in Goering's famous letter to Heydrich regarding the "final solution of the Jewish question", dated 31 July 1941:[4]

As supplement to the task that was entrusted to you in the decree dated 24 January 1939, namely to solve the Jewish question by emigration and evacuation in a way which is the most favorable in connection with the conditions prevailing at the time, I herewith commission you to carry out all preparations with regard to organizational, factual, and financial viewpoints for a total solution of the Jewish question in those territories in Europe under German influence.

If the competency of other central organizations is touched in this connection, these organizations are to participate.

I further commission you to submit to me as soon as possible a draft showing the organizational, factual, and financial measures already taken for the execution of the intended final solution of the Jewish question.

It is customary to quote this letter with deletion of the reference to "emigration and evacuation".[5] The planned Jewish emigration to the Eastern territories of not only the German Jews but also the Jews in the "territories in Europe under German influence" was a relatively extensive project and so, in accord with Goering's reference to the "competency of other central organizations", Heydrich called a special conference, the "Wannsee Conference", which was finally held on 20 January 1942. Representatives of several branches of the German Government attended the conference. Eichmann was the next to lowest ranked person at the conference. The minutes of the conference, NG-2586-G, are lengthy but the heart of the project was expressed as follows:[6]

Meanwhile, in view of the dangers of an emigration during the war and in view of the possibilities in the East, the Reichsfuehrer-SS and the Chief of the German Police had forbidden the emigrating of the Jews.

The emigration program has now been replaced by the evacuation of the Jews to the East as a further solution possibility, in accordance with previous authorization by the Fuehrer.

These actions are of course to be regarded only as a temporary substitute; nonetheless here already the solution of the Jewish problem is of great importance.

* * * * *

Under proper direction the Jews should now in the course of the final solution, be brought to the East in a suitable way for use as labor. In big labor gangs, with separation of the sexes, the Jews capable of work are brought to these areas and employed in road-building, in which task undoubtedly a great part will fall out through natural diminution.

The remnant that finally is able to survive all this — since this is undoubtedly the part with the strongest resistance — must be given treatment accordingly, since these people, representing a natural selection, are to be regarded as the germ cell of a new Jewish development, if they are allowed to go free. (See the experience of history.)

In the program of the practical execution of the final solution, Europe is combed through from the West to the East. The Reich area, including the Protectorate of Bohemia and Moravia, will have to be taken in advance, alone for reasons of the housing problem and other social-political necessities.

The evacuated Jews are brought first group by group into the so-called transit ghettos, in order from there out to be transported farther to the East.

An important provision for the whole execution of the evacuation, so SS General

Heydrich explained further, is the exact establishment of the category of persons who are to be included.

It is intended not to evacuate Jews over 65 years of age, but to remove them to a ghetto for the aged — Theresienstadt is under consideration.

Along with these old-age classes — of the perhaps 280,000 Jews who on 31/10/1941 were in the Old Reich and in Austria, perhaps 30% are over 65 years old — there will also be taken to the ghettos for the aged the Jews who are serious war-wounded cases and Jews with war decorations (Iron Cross, First Class). With this appropriate solution the many potentials for exceptions will be eliminated with one blow.

* * * * *

In connection with the problem of the effect of the Jewish evacuation on the economic life, State Secretary Neumann stated that the Jews employed in war-important industries could not be evacuated for the present, as long as there were no replacements available.

SS General Heydrich pointed out that these Jews, in accordance with the directives approved by him for the execution of the current evacuations, would not be evacuated.

State Secretary Dr. Buehler states that the Government General would welcome the initiation of the final solution of this problem in the Government General, because here for once the transport problem plays no out-of-the-ordinary role, and here labor commitment considerations would not hinder the course of this action . . . Furthermore, of the approximately two and one half million Jews here in question the majority of cases were unfit for work . . . He had only one request, that the Jewish problem in this territory be solved as quickly as possible. *evacuation = not an.*

Here is unambiguous documentary evidence that no extermination program existed; the German policy was to evacuate the Jews to the East. It did not, moreover, require the capture of German documents to expose this fact. It was well known during the war and, during the resettlement program's early stages, it was reported and commented on countless times in the Allied press. In the case of Vienna Jews deported to Poland in early 1941, the *N.Y. Times* even remarked that they "found their new homes much more comfortable than they expected or even dare hope". Later reports on the resettlement program did not describe it so favorably, but the press at least reported approximately what was going on.[7]

Rothe, incidentally, has taken the position that the Wannsee Conference is itself a propaganda myth. His principal reason for this is his belief, for which he presents respectable evidence, that Heydrich was in Prague on 20 January 1942. However the date attributed to the conference, and the document said to be the minutes of the conference, are so consistent with everything else that is known about the German policy that we believe that Rothe is mistaken on this point.[8]

The only factual aspect of the program of evacuation to the East which is generally consistent with the extermination claims is that many Jews sent to the camps in Poland did not return, at least not to their former homes. This, apparently, has been the reason why many people with more or less first hand information about certain individuals have accepted the extermination claims. However, the situation is basically simple. These camps were obviously serving as transit camps for the program of evacuation to the East. We have observed that at Birkenau there was a special compound that served as a transit camp for Theresienstadt Jews, and that Dutch Jews also passed through Auschwitz (pp. 108-109). The concentration camp at Lublin also played this incidental role on occasion.[9] Treblinka, which was a labor camp but does not appear to have been administered by the WVHA, clearly served also as a transit camp, especially for Warsaw Jews. As with Auschwitz, Reitlinger finds the alleged facts put forward concerning gassings at Treblinka difficult to reconcile with one another. Sobibor was explicitly called a transit camp.[10]

It may astonish the reader that the documents we have reviewed, which constitute very strong evidence that no extermination program existed, are

212

Photo: Panstwowe Museum, Oswiecim

Fig. 26: *This is said to be a photograph of one of the crematoria at Auschwitz.*

213

not passed over in silence by the bearers of the extermination legend, but are thrust boldly into our faces as evidence that an extermination program *did* exist. Not only is this the implicit idea conveyed by the collection of documents in NMT volume 13; Reitlinger and Hilberg are quite serious in considering these documents relevant to an extermination program. Thus the "evacuation to the East" is claimed as a code term for extermination.

On account of the fact that a fixed feature of the extermination legend is that one of the tasks of the *Einsatzgruppen* in Russia was the extermination of the Jews, the bearers of the legend are committed to the view that the policy of extermination had been settled on by the summer of 1941. Thus although Goering's letter of 31 July 1941 to Heydrich specifically states that the "final solution" is a program of emigration and evacuation, and although it makes specific reference to the program which existed from 1939, which both Reitlinger and Hilberg concede was an emigration program, both authors must and do take the position that this was really an extermination order. They are apparently not bothered by the fact, noted by them, that deportations of Reich Jews to Russia and the Baltic states had started in the autumn of 1941.[11]

Continuing to keep faith with their fundamental commitment, the Wannsee Conference of January 1942 is also interpreted as a veiled discussion of extermination, although the evacuation program of which the minutes of the Conference speak was in fact in progress. Both authors lay stress on the reference to the "remnant that finally is able to survive all this" and are to be "given treatment accordingly". This passage could mean any number of things. The version of the Wannsee Conference minutes that is printed in NMT volume 13, incidentally, has the phrase "if they are allowed to go free" deleted by the editors. This suggests that the editors may have interpreted the passage as a recommendation that the "remnant" should be "allowed to go free". In commenting on the Wannsee Conference minutes, Reitlinger remarks that "Heydrich was discreet enough not to mention the rest", and that "the drafting of circumspect minutes was one of the major arts of Hitler's Reich". Hilberg resolves the lack of clarity of meaning of some of the passages (from his point of view) by remarking that "we know from the language of the *Einsatzgruppen* reports that he meant killing".[12] This amounts to making the extraordinary claim that Hitler's Reich was "circumspect" regarding the language used in the minutes of secret conferences, but not circumspect regarding the language used in the widely distributed *Einsatzgruppen* reports. In any case, these passages in what is said to be the minutes of the Wannsee Conference are the only passages in the documents describing German Jewish policy for which a sinister interpretation is possible, although many interpretations are possible.

The excessively strained interpretations of these documents are factors, added to the several mentioned in Chapter IV, which force Reitlinger to declare that Hoess must have really meant the summer of 1942 as the date of receiving his extermination orders from Himmler. Reitlinger and Hilberg both assume that the deportations to the East were for the purpose of killing the Jews there, in one way or another, and that the gas chambers in Poland were established in mid-1942 as a change in the method of killing. We have seen that this theory does not harmonize with the dates associated with the planning of and preliminary work on the Auschwitz crematoria that are supposed to have been designed for the exterminations. Thus the claim that the documents should be interpreted as meaning other than what they say leads one into irresolvable contradictions and difficulties, but such would be the result if comparable practices were applied to the interpretation of recipes, road signs, mathematical formulae, etc.

yet he does earue !

There is no point in discussing further these efforts to make these documents mean other than what they say. The German policy, the "final solution", was to resettle Jews in the occupied territories in the East. This is what their documents say and the program spoken of in these documents is confirmed by neutral sources and even, to a significant extent, by hostile sources. By way of additional confirmation, it is worth mentioning passages by Grayzel in his *History*. In one paragraph he says that the Germans were doing what their documents say they were doing:

> They followed this up with wholesale deportations. They set aside a number of places in Eastern Europe in which they concentrated Jews from other lands, in line with the avowed Nazi policy of "freeing" all of Europe from Jewish influence.

In the next paragraph Grayzel contradicts this statement by saying that the Germans were doing what the Allied propaganda said they were doing: exterminations, gas chambers, etc. Grayzel makes no attempt to resolve the contradiction.[13]

It may be wondered why the authors of the hoax have presented us with the documents which describe, in very general terms, what the German policy was. The hoaxers were confronted with (a) the fact that Europeans were told by the Germans, at the time of the deportations, that the Jews were to be resettled and (b) the fact that the resettlement program had been reported in the Allied press and (c) the fact that, in regard to the documents, it was necessary to make a choice among three possibilities: presenting no high level documents dealing with the Jewish policy, presenting forged high level documents dealing with the policy, and presenting selected high level documents dealing with the policy. Under the circumstances, the third of the three possibilities was obviously to be preferred. It was clearly better to present a genuine document, signed by Goering and speaking of the "final solution" of the Jewish question, than to present a forged document or no document. Although the final solution is specified as "emigration and evacuation", it was considered not possible to avoid the fact that the Nazis described their program in such terms. Thus today the bearers of the extermination legend merely claim that all of this was code terminology.

One must not pass over the important work of R.L. Koehl, who is that strange bird, a professional academic historian writing in or near a field completely dominated by non-historians. The main value of Koehl's work is in putting Poland into proper focus and perspective.

During the war years Germany undertook to change the composition of the populations near its eastern borders. The main instrument of this program was the RuSHA (Race and Settlement Main Office) of the SS. The basic policy was to move selected Reich Germans and ethnic German communities of Eastern Europe *(Volksdeutsche)* into the conquered territories contiguous to Germany. Jews and Poles were expelled from these areas and sent to various places, in some cases to the farms the ethnic Germans had vacated, to special Eastern ghettos, and also to certain special "Z villages" in Poland.

Koehl explicitly endorses the reality of the extermination program, but his account of it is most peculiar:[14]

> The official version insisted that the Jews were going to be moved further east into conquered Soviet territory to remove them more effectively from the German sphere of life. Like many other German pronouncements this one contained several grains of truth: (1) train-loads of Jews from the Reich were sent as far east as possible for liquidation, often at the hands of non-Germans such as the Ukranians or the Baltic peoples. (2) The Poles were, in Rosenberg's early plans as Minister for the East, to be considered for resettlement in the Soviet area (Smolensk), thus freeing the General Government for German settlement.

Koehl does not provide any evidence for the killings by Ukranians or the Baltic peoples; the sources cited at this point make no such claims. Then in referring to the extermination camps:[15]

In the fall and winter of 1941-1942 the last 240,000 Jews of the annexed provinces were removed to the newly constructed extermination camps at Kolo, Belzec, Majdanek, and Sobibor.

The list excludes Auschwitz, which comes up in Koehl's book only in a remark about some Germans sent there for punishment, in connection with "Action Reinhardt" (to be explained below), and also in the following:[16]

(Dr. Klukowski) stated that of 691 villages in the county of Zamosc, 297 were wholly or partly evacuated by July 1943. He estimated that 110,000 Poles and Jews were removed from the area, males and females of working age going to forced labor in the Auschwitz Hydrogenation Plant, the rest going to the other 394 ("Z") villages.

One may draw one's own conclusions. Koehl's book is recommended to the reader who wishes a detailed view of Nazi population policies, especially in their relations to German nationalism, Nazi racial ideology, and internal Nazi party politics.

Many European Jews were deported East and we should now take a closer look at this program of deportations. There are several obvious questions: who was deported, how many, to where, what was life like where they were sent, and what happened to them. To some extent only partial or provisional answers are possible here.

First we should consider the numbers and origins of the Jews involved in this resettlement program. Here we run into the problems discussed in Chapter I; counting Jews can be difficult. However it is not statistical accuracy we seek here but order of magnitude or approximate figures that can be used to show that, on the basis of verifiable data, the Jews who were deported could easily have survived after all. It will thus be satisfactory to merely accept certain figures offered by Reitlinger and by Hilberg for the purposes of discussion, although one can pick quarrels with them (as one can with Rassinier's study). The figures are estimates of numbers *killed;* it is understood that here we assume that these people had merely been resettled in the East. In the case of Reitlinger we employ his higher estimate:[17]

	Reitlinger	Hilberg
Germany	180,000	160,000
Austria	60,000	53,000
Czechoslovakia	251,000	271,000
Denmark		1,000
France	65,000	70,000
Belgium	28,000	50,000
Luxembourg	3,000	2,000
Norway	700	1,000
Holland	102,700	120,000
Italy	8,000	17,000
Yugoslavia	58,000	63,000
Greece	60,000	62,000
Totals	816,400	870,000

To some extent these figures are based on German documents, notably the "Korherr report", documents NO-5193-8; to some extent neutral sources are involved, such as the Dutch Red Cross with the Holland figures. There is also a certain amount of demographic speculation involved. However I believe that at least the totals given are of the correct order.

We do not admit Hungary into the list, since those said by both Reitlinger and Hilberg to have been exterminated are pure invention; they were not even deported East. Somewhat less than 100,000 were sent to Germany for labor toward the end of the war; quite a few of these must have perished in the chaotic conditions of the last months but the number is essentially impossible to arrive at.

Rumania is also supposed to have lost 200,000 – 370,000 Jews via extermination but, as Reitlinger remarks, such figures are "conjectural" on account of "the lack of reliable information". Conceded to be in the same category are the largest groups of allegedly exterminated Jews: 2,350,000 – 3,300,000 from Poland and 400,000 – 700,000 from the U.S.S.R. These figures are pure demographic speculation, with absolutely no supporting data other than the declarations of post-war Communist governments.

These figures will be considered further below. At this point we merely recall that the Jews deported from France and Belgium were not French or Belgian Jews, but that those deported from Holland were almost all Dutch Jews (pp. 79, 82). The reason for this appears to have been a mere legal technicality. France and Belgium had formally surrendered to the Germans and formal armistice terms were agreed to. In Holland the King had merely fled to England and thus the Germans viewed Holland as being without an independent state.[18] German rights in Holland were correspondingly more extensive. Of course, the Germans intended to eventually expel all Jews from Europe, but they naturally started with the ones for which the minimum of legal difficulties existed.

The excerpt of the Red Cross *Report*, which we examined in Chapter V, is certainly in conflict with the extermination claims in the case of the Rumanian Jews. It is reasonable to assume that the bulk of the Jews in Soviet controlled territory that was occupied by the Germans after 22 June 1941 escaped into the interior before the arrival of the latter, a belief that is also held by Reitlinger (p. 241). In any case, there is no evidence that the Germans did more than adopt, toward the Jews who remained, the sort of guarded and hostile attitude that was implied by the partisan menaces discussed in the preceding chapter. The Polish Jews constituted the majority of the Jews moved around by the Germans and present, on account of their location and circumstances, the greatest difficulties to any detailed analysis of the matter. We can only reconstruct in general outline what happened to them.

We first remark that, while it is convenient here to distinguish between Russian and Polish Jews, the real distinction is most slight, if it could be said to exist at all. Before World War I, both sets of Jews were subjects of the Russian Empire.

The first relevant events involving Polish Jews were due to Russian, rather than German, measures. Germany and Russia partitioned Poland in 1939, the eastern half and thus a large portion of the Polish Jews thereby coming under Soviet rule. These Jews were the objects of a Russian resettlement program whose broad features have been described by Korzen in an article published by the Israeli Government. Korzen's article is of some importance to the matters treated in this chapter.[19]

Briefly, what happened is that "hundreds of thousands" of these Jews were dispersed throughout the Soviet Union in an evacuation program which commenced in June 1940. At first, many were sent to labor camps but, after September 1941, a serious effort was made "to convert the refugees into Soviet citizens and prevent their leaving the Soviet Union". The dispersion was as far as Central Asia and even to the Far East. Details are difficult to develop and Korzen pleads for more interest in research into the matter. Many became Soviet citizens, some trekked back to Poland after the war and,

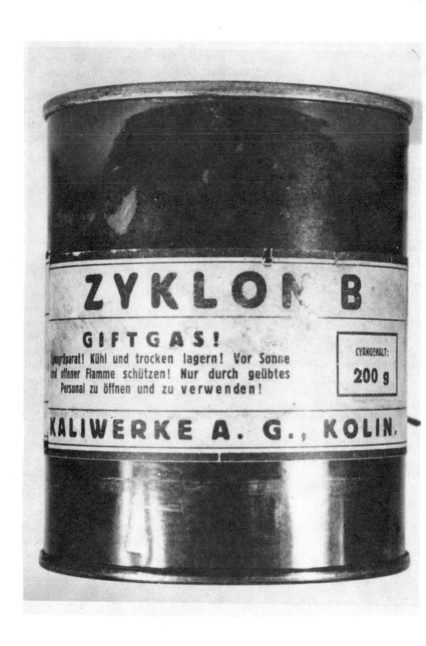

Fig. 27: A can of Zyklon B. The label says "POISON GAS! Cyanide! Store in a cool and dry place! Protect from the sun and open flames! To be opened and employed only by trained personnel!"   Photo: U.S. National Archives

218

in many cases, proceeded on to Israel (Korzen remarks that the Jews who remained in Poland as leaders of the new Communist regime were put under pressure "to change their names to purely Polish-sounding ones, as well as to keep their Jewish origin secret"). Some eventually arrived at places such as Persia and India via Shanghai. The Joint Distribution Committee of New York maintained contact with the refugees in the Soviet Union during the war, and assisted their movements after the war.

It is also known that a large number of Jews, given by one source as 300,000, fled from western to eastern Poland in 1939 when the Nazis invaded the former.[20] Thus a significant fraction, perhaps as many as a third, of the Polish Jews had been moved beyond reach of the Germans before the outbreak of war between Russia and Germany in June 1941.

Although there had been a limited German resettlement program earlier, notably for Vienna Jews, the Nazi resettlement program began with earnestness in the autumn of 1941. If Polish Jews are excluded but Rumanian Jews included in our immediate considerations, we see that the Germans moved at most a million Jews to settlements or ghettos in the occupied East. From the locations that have been mentioned we can get a fairly good idea of where these settlements were located: Riga — Minsk — Ukraine — Sea of Azov (north of the Black Sea) forms a connected and plausible line on a map.

While we have a good idea of where these settlements were, we know little else about them other than that they existed. As one should naturally expect, the Allied occupation destroyed the relevant German records and documents, so that only scraps survive that deal with the resettlement program in terms more specific than, say, the Luther memorandum (NG-2586-J, pp. 205-210). Indeed, Steengracht's defense made a serious effort to produce such documents at Nuernberg, but the best it could do, relative to the eastern camps, was to submit two documents into evidence. The first, Steengracht 64,[21] is a letter from Eichmann, dated 5 June 1943, to the Foreign Office for the attention of Thadden. It concerns the Jewish camps in the East and some articles which had appeared in various European magazines concerning them. It appears that "fantastic rumors" in Slovakia concerning these camps were being given credence by some people there and Eichmann remarked that, in addition to citing the magazine articles,

> to counteract the fantastic rumors circulating in Slovakia about the fate of the evacuated Jews, attention should be drawn to the postal communications of these Jews with Slovakia . . . which for instance amounted to more than 1,000 letters and postcards for February – March this year. Concerning the information apparently desired by Prime Minister Dr. Tuka about the conditions in Jewish camps, no objections would be raised by this office against any possible scrutinizing of the correspondence before it is forwarded to the addressees.

The second Steengracht document, Steengracht 65 (also going under the number NO-1624), is somewhat more effective in giving a picture of the situation of the Jews in the occupied East. It is an order, dated 20 August 1943, by the chief of the RuSHA (Race and Settlement Main Office), SS General Hildebrandt, relative to associations between Germans and Jews in the occupied East, and to the permissible ways in which the latter could be employed. It reads:

> It has been pointed out to me by various sources, that the behaviour of German offices in the occupied Eastern territories towards Jews has developed in such a way in the past months as to give rise to misgivings. In particular, Jews are being employed in jobs and services which, in consideration of maintaining secrecy should only be assigned to absolutely reliable persons, who should appear to be the confidential representatives of the German offices in the eyes of the indigenous population. Unfortunately, in addition to this, there is allegedly personal association of Reich Germans with Jewesses which exceeds the limits that must be strictly observed for ideological and racial reasons. It is

said to concern native Jews as well as Jews and Jewesses who have been deported from the Old Reich to the occupied Eastern territories. This state of affairs has already led to the fact that Jews are exploiting their apparently confidential positions in exchange for the supply of preferential rations by the indigenous population. It is said that recently, when apprehensions were expressed in the East about a German retreat, indigenous persons endeavored to ingratiate themselves particularly with those Jews employed in German offices, in order to ensure better treatment at the hands of the Bolshevists. The decent section of the indigenous population viewed these events with great disapproval, because it saw in them the contradiction between National Socialist principles and the actual attitude of the Germans.

Owing to improper labor assignment of Jews, the esteem of the Greater German Reich, and the position of its representatives are being harmed, and the necessity for effective police security of the occupied Eastern territories prejudiced. Grave dangers could arise particularly from the fact that the Jews are utilizing the jobs assigned to them for espionage and propaganda in the service of our enemies.

I therefore request that the subordinate offices in the occupied Eastern territories be given the following instructions:

1) Jews and persons of a similar status may only be employed in manual labor. It is prohibited to employ them in office work (such as book-keeping, typewriting, card indexing, registration). Strict attention must be paid to the fact that they will not be given work which would permit them to draw conclusions on matters that are to be kept secret.

2) It is forbidden to employ Jews for general or personal service, for the discharging of orders, for the negotiation of business deals, or for the procuring of goods.

3) Private association with Jews, Jewesses and persons of a similar status is prohibited, as well as any relations beyond those officially necessary.

The "persons of a similar status" referred to were probably mainly gipsies. We assume that Steengracht's counsel made a thorough search of the documents which had been allowed to survive at Nuernberg. Hildebrandt's order to the RuSHA merely repeated, verbatim, a Kaltenbrunner order of 13 August 1943, to all German offices in the occupied eastern areas (document NO-1247). The failure of Steengracht to use NO-1247 was probably due to its being nearly identical to NO-1624.[21]

Such documents are only a pathetic scrap from what must have been extensive written records dealing with the Jewish settlements in the East. The first was probably allowed to survive because it speaks of "fantastic rumors" in circulation in Slovakia. The other two probably just slipped through because their implications were not sufficiently obvious.

In Boehm's book *We Survived*, Jeanette Wolff, a German Jewess who was a leader of the German Social Democratic Party, has contributed an article on her experiences after being deported to Riga in Latvia. Her tale of gratuitous beatings by the SS, sex orgies and drunkenness is not believable. Her article is worth noting, however, because it shows that there was a large system of settlements, ghettos and camps for Jews in the vicinity of Riga. These settlements quartered not only Latvian Jews, but also large numbers of Jews deported from Germany and other European countries. Of course, in Chapter IV (p. 109) we noted the Theresienstadt source who reported that the Nazis were deporting Jews to Riga and other places throughout the course of the war. Nazi documents dealing with the Riga settlement have not survived.

One can see, in general outline, what happened to the Polish (and Latvian and Lithuanian) Jews by consulting the "holocaust" literature which has been contributed by "survivors". In the larger towns and in the cities, the Jews within Poland were quartered in ghettos which existed throughout the war. In Poland, there were particularly large ghettos at Lodz (Litzmannstadt), Warsaw, Bialystok, Lwow and Grodno; in Lithuania, at Vilna and Kovno; in Latvia, as we noted above, at Riga. Although the "survivor" literature offers endless raving about exterminations (frequently of a sort not reconcilable with the legend, e.g., gas chambers in Cracow in December 1939), it also offers enough information for one to grasp approximately how things were.

In each ghetto, there was a Jewish Council, *Judenrat*, which was the internal government of the ghetto. The ghetto police were Jewish and responsible to the *Judenrat*. The *Judenrat* usually counselled cooperation with the Germans since, under the circumstances, it saw no other plausible course. The Germans made frequent demands for labor details drawn from the ghetto, and the *Judenrat* then drew up the lists of people to be thus conscripted. There were also resistance organizations in the larger ghettos, usually well armed, whose members often viewed the *Judenrat* as composed of German stooges.[22]

Dawidowicz' book devotes several chapters to conditions in the Polish ghettos. Although the initial policy of the Germans, immediately after occupying Poland, had been to forbid Jewish schools, this policy was soon abandoned and Jewish children received an essentially regular education in schools operated either privately or under the authority of the *Judenraete*. Cultural activities for adults — literary, theatrical, musical — helped alleviate the otherwise unhappy features of ghetto life. The Jewish social welfare agency was the ZSS (dissolved in mid-1942 by the Germans but shortly later reconstituted as the JUS), which drew supplies of food, clothing and medicine from the German civil administration and which also maintained contact, through the German Red Cross, with foreign organizations which provided money and supplies. Before the U.S. entry into the war, the bulk of such external funds came from the Joint Distribution Committee in New York, but after December 1941 this was no longer legally possible.

Despite the protected status of the ZSS-JUS, it sometimes provided cover for illegal political activities. The various political organizations — Socialist, Communist, Zionist, Agudist — were connected with the resistance organizations, whose activities ranged from active sabotage to propaganda and, on occasion, to armed resistance. Extermination propaganda started in underground publications slightly earlier than it started being generated by the World Jewish Congress (see Appendix E) but it was not believed by the Jewish population since nothing in their experiences supported it; letters received from Jews deported East reassured friends and relatives. As Dawidowicz writes in her introductory chapter on the problems posed by the "holocaust" for historical research:

> One impediment was the inadequacy of Jewish documentation, despite its enormous quantity . . . The absence of vital subjects from the records may be explained by the predicament of terror and censorship; yet, lacking evidence to corroborate or disprove, the historian will never know with certainty whether that absence is a consequence of an institutional decision not to deal with such matters or whether it was merely a consequence of prudential policy not to mention such matters. The terror was so great that even private personal diaries, composed in Yiddish or Hebrew, were written circumspectly, with recourse to Scripture and the Talmud as a form of esoteric expression and self-imposed reticence.

As is clear from all studies of German population policies in Poland, e.g. those of Dawidowicz and of Koehl, there was a constant moving about of Jews, in accordance with the general German policy of concentrating them as far east as practicable. According to the "Korherr report" of March 1943, 1,449,692 Jews had been transported "out of the East provinces to the Russian East". It is further specified that 90% of these had passed through camps in the General Government, and the others had passed through camps in the Warthegau (presumably meaning mainly Lodz). The huge ghetto of Warsaw was liquidated in the spring of 1943 and most of the Jews were sent further east, with Treblinka serving as a transit camp for this resettlement. This was only accomplished, however, after fierce Jewish resistance and a battle that received world publicity while it was raging. The resettlement, however, was not complete, since there were always at least some Jews at the site of the ghetto and, as remarked above, all of the larger ghettos existed in some degree throughout the war.

When a resettlement was announced to a ghetto, it was the duty of the *Judenrat* to draw up the lists of those to be resettled. With only rare exceptions, the Jews being resettled went along peacefully, since it was well known that the "resettlement" was just that.

It appears that epidemics were common in the ghettos. The Germans attributed them to "a lack of discipline" on the part of the Jews. They took what countermeasures they could and, as the *N.Y. Times* reported on at least one occasion, "many ambulances were sent to Warsaw to disinfect the ghetto".[23]

While the general eastward movement of these Jews is an established fact, the data to reconstruct exactly what numbers were sent where does not exist. The important point to note, however, was that it is almost certain that the greater number of Polish Jews were completely cleared out of all of pre-war Poland except the most eastern part. Since the territory of post-war Poland is made up of what had been eastern Germany and western and central Poland (Russia acquiring what had been eastern Poland), this means that most Jews had, indeed, been removed from what is today referred to as Poland. In connection with the large ghettos which are mentioned above, it is worth noting that Lwow, Grodno, Vilna, Kovno and Riga were all absorbed into the Soviet Union after the war, and that Bialystok is now at the extreme eastern side of Poland. If there were about three million Jews in Poland before the war then, when one takes into account the numbers which fled to the Soviet Union in 1939, those who were deported by the Russians in 1940, those who managed to slip into such countries as Slovakia or Hungary, and those who might have perished in epidemics, we see that there were at most two million Polish Jews in scattered ghettos in German controlled territory, and that the greater number of these people had been sent to territory considered Soviet after the war.

Thus we see, in general outline sufficient for our purposes, the actual nature of the so-called "final solution of the Jewish problem". It is not necessary here to attempt to fill in much more detail and the ultimate prospects for providing great detail are questionable in any case. That this "solution" was really in no sense "final", and that the Jews would have returned with a change in the political climate, is not so extraordinary. Twentieth century governments invariably give their projects bold and unrealistic labels: Peace Corps, Alliance for Progress, Head Start, war to end wars, etc.

It remains to consider what happened to all of these people. Here again we have a situation in which there exists much less data than one would hope for. However we have enough information to reconstruct, to an extent suitable for our purposes, what happened. Actually, we must consider several possibilities in this respect. The following are the reasonable possibilities.

1. The Germans liquidated many while in retreat, since these people could be considered manpower to be employed against the Germans. It is necessary to consider this as a reasonable possibility since we have noted that the Germans had, indeed, considered this aspect of the matter seriously enough to make it difficult for Jews to emigrate from Europe.

However there are two things working strongly against the possibility that the Germans liquidated on a significant scale while in retreat. First, the most able workers, who were also of military age, had already been picked out for labor and were being employed by the Germans in various ways. Second, and most importantly and simply, if the Germans had carried out such liquidations on a large scale the Allies would have charged them with it.

The Allies would have had material for legitimate extermination charges rather than the "gas chamber" nonsense.

While the evidence indicates that the German authorities did not carry out large scale liquidations of Jews while in retreat, common sense and a feel for the conditions that existed should cause us to assume that there were numerous massacres of Jews carried out by individuals and small groups acting on their own. Some German, Hungarian or Rumanian troops, and some East European civilians, their anti-Jewish feelings amplified by the disastrous course of the war, no doubt made attacks on Jews at the time of the German retreats. It is known that earlier in the war, when East Europeans had attempted to start pogroms, the German authorities had restrained and suppressed them.[24] However, under conditions of chaotic retreat, the Germans were probably much less concerned with anti-Jewish pogroms.

2. The Russians liquidated many. We list this only because Russia is such an enigma and its actions in the populations area often seem very arbitrary. However, there is no evidence for liquidations at the hands of the Russians and one should doubt this possibility.

3. Many perished on account of conditions in the camps or ghettos. This is a most serious possibility. We have seen that health conditions can be very unstable in camps and that the situation can be very sensitive to any sort of chaos or shortage of necessities. Moreover, we have observed that the ghetto conditions, whether the Germans were at fault or (as the Germans claimed) the Jews were responsible, were favorable to epidemics even early in the war when the Germans had the general situation under control in other respects. Therefore there is a good possibility that many Jews in ghettos perished in the chaotic conditions that accompanied the German retreats. Also, Korzen believes that many of the 1940 exiles to Russia died in the Russian camps they were sent to, so it is possible that many ghetto Jews perished on account of Soviet ways of administering the ghettos after they fell into Russian hands.

4. Many were dispersed throughout the Soviet Union and integrated into Soviet life somewhere. This is a most likely possibility because it is well established that the Soviet Union encouraged the absorption of Jews during and immediately after the war. For example, we have noted that this was the policy exercised toward the 1940 deportees. Another example is what happened with respect to the Carpatho-Ukraine, before the war a province of Czechoslovakia, and annexed by the Soviet Union after the war. Ten thousand Jews, former residents of the Carpatho-Ukraine, had the status of refugees in Czechoslovakia in the spring of 1946. Russia insisted that these Jews be repatriated to the Soviet Union. Although such a step was contrary to the existing agreements on refugees, the Soviet pressure on President Benes was great enough to force him to yield.[25]

One should also note the existence, within the Soviet Union, of the specifically Jewish "autonomous state" of Birobidzhan, which is in the Soviet Far East, on the Amur river on the border of Manchira. Birobidzhan had been established by the Soviets in 1928 as a Jewish state. Immediately after the war there existed in New York the "Einstein Fund of Ambijan" (acronym for American Birobidzhan Committee), whose purpose was "to help refugee colonization of Birobidzhan". There were other operations in New York which aided Jews resettled in Birobidzhan immediately after World War II.

There were also Jewish organizations, such as the Joint Distribution Committee, which aided Jews in other parts of the Soviet Union, and there also existed in New York the Committee for Aid to Minsk and Neighboring Towns. There also existed UNRRA programs in White Russia (Byelorussia)

Fig. 28: Several cans of Zyklon B.   *Photo: U.S. National Archives*

and the Ukraine, which will be commented on below. These efforts to aid Jewish refugees in the Soviet Union had the public support of prominent Jews, e.g. Albert Einstein expressed appreciation to the Soviet Government for helping "hundreds of thousands of Jewish people" by giving them a home in the U.S.S.R.[26]

While the Soviet Union encouraged the absorption of Jews, it also made a specific agreement with the Communist government of Poland for the repatriation of those who had been Polish citizens on 17 September 1939. The agreement, made in July 1945, specifically included those resident on territory annexed by the Soviet Union and those who had been deported to the interior of the Soviet Union in 1940, and provided that such people could either elect Soviet citizenship or Polish citizenship. With respect to Jews, it was eventually decided that the deadline for making the choice was 30 June 1946.

As we noted in Chapter I, Reitlinger concedes that the post-war Jewish population of the Soviet Union might very well have exceeded the pre-war figure, on account of the addition of Polish (and Baltic and other) Jews. He regards the *Jewish Observer* estimate of 500,000 Polish Jews who elected to remain in the Soviet Union as "very conservative", and concedes huge and insuperable uncertainties in this connection. Thus, although the Russians were willing to let Polish Jews leave before the 30 June 1946 deadline, they nevertheless encouraged their absorption into the Soviet Union. This could account for an enormous number of the Jews who had been resettled to the East by the Germans. It is pointless, however, to try to infer anything from alleged population statistics offered by the Russians or by Jewish organizations.[27]

5. Many of the uprooted Jews might have returned to their original homes, or at least to their original homelands, in Europe. We have seen that the Russians were willing to allow Polish Jews to leave the Soviet Union, and we should assume that a similar policy was practised toward Jews of other nationalities. It is only possible, and not probable, that the Soviet Union absorbed all of the Jews who had been deported East, by the Germans, from Germany, the Netherlands, etc.

At first thought it might appear that the clearly logical course after the war, for any uprooted Jew, would have been to return to his original country of residence. This is not the case, however, for various reasons. For one thing, in perhaps the majority of cases there was nothing to return to. The main reason for this was the German program called "Action Reinhardt" in which Jews deported to the East were deprived of almost all of their property; their furniture, any livestock, business property, their jewelry, any clothing they could not carry as luggage, and all but about $25 of any ordinary currency they had were simply confiscated in the course of resettlement (some of the business property might have been resettled with them). The camps at Lublin and Auschwitz were principal gathering and processing points for much of this property, wherever it had actually been confiscated.[28] Thus many Jews, having neither property nor relatives at their original homes, had no very compelling reasons for returning to them. The German program had truly been one of uprooting.

Another aspect of the situation was that, in late 1945 and in 1946, there was much talk about anti-Jewish pogroms allegedly occurring with great frequency in Poland and other East European countries. If these reports were true, then the pogroms were a powerful inducement to the Jews to leave. If these reports were merely Zionist propaganda having little, if any, basis in fact, then one can infer that the Zionists were engaging in operations designed to move Jews out of eastern Europe. Thus, whether the reports of pogroms were true or false, they suggest a movement of Jews out of eastern Europe.

At the Yalta meeting in 1945, Churchill, Roosevelt and Stalin had agreed that "it would be impossible for Jewish refugees to return to Poland and be reintegrated into its normal life".[29] While it is certain that many Jews returned to their homelands, there were solid facts and also, apparently, much propaganda discouraging them from doing so. If this is true, and if it is also true that a significant number of Polish Jews left Soviet territory, then many of them must have proceeded through Poland to other destinations. This is the case. The Zionist political leadership had other destinations in mind for them.

6. Many of the Jews eventually resettled neither in the Soviet Union nor in their original countries but elsewhere, mainly in the U.S. and Palestine. We all know this to be true but there is some uncertainty in the numbers involved, principally in the case of the U.S. immigrants. Until November 1943 the U.S. Immigration and Naturalization Service recognized a category "Hebrew" among "races and peoples", but in that month this practice was stopped, and no official records of Jewish immigration have been kept since then.[30]

Another problem in accounting in detail for Jewish movements around the time of the end of the war is that we run right into the War Refugee Board and the UNRRA (United Nations Relief and Rehabilitation Administration) in attempting to examine this subject. It will be recalled that the WRB was set up in early 1944 as an apparently joint venture of the U.S. State, Treasury and War Departments but that it was, in fact, under the control of Secretary of the Treasury Morgenthau. The Board was granted the extraordinary power of appointing special attachés with diplomatic status. Another very irregular feature was that the WRB worked very closely with private organizations. Collaboration with the Joint Distribution Committee and the World Jewish Congress and several other Jewish and Zionist organizations was extensive. Some non-Jewish organizations were also involved, notably the American Friends Service Committee. The WRB and the three U.S. Government Departments involved with the WRB were specifically "authorized to accept the services or contributions of private persons of organizations".[31] We therefore have a rather slippery entity involved here, engaged in both propaganda and relief work, with the rights of a government operation when an official status seemed convenient, and the rights of a private organization when a private status was advantageous.

Relief activities were carried on by the WRB from about mid-1944 to mid-1945, at which time the operations of an international character fell almost entirely into the hands of the UNRRA. This organization had been set up in November 1943, and had operated until March 1949. Its first Director, appointed by Roosevelt, was Herbert Lehman, ex-Governor of New York State and a leading New Deal Democrat. Roosevelt's reported logic for choosing Lehman was that "It would be a fine object lesson in tolerance and human brotherhood to have a Jew head up this operation, and I think Herbert would be fine".[32] Lehman was succeeded in early 1946 by Fiorello La-Guardia, ex-Mayor of New York City. Although LaGuardia's father was not Jewish and he naturally found it profitable to court the huge New York Italian vote, LaGuardia really counts as a Jewish-Zionist politician and is essentially treated as such by the *Encyclopedia Judaica*. Thus we can be sure that the crowd involved here is basically the same as with the WRB. Also, we again have a slippery entity, this time because it is a so-called international organization. For example when, in September 1945, Congress demanded that the General Accounting Office be allowed to examine the UNRRA operations (the U.S. was said to be paying about two-thirds of the costs of UNRRA, but the fraction was probably somewhat higher), Lehman told it to mind its own business.[33]

The UNRRA operations were far-flung. Most of the UNRRA aid went to Eastern Europe, and the amount sent to Poland was second only to that sent to China. Aid was also sent to White Russia and the Ukraine.[34]

By mid-1944 the WRB and the UNRRA were operating a large system of refugee camps in North Africa, Italy and Palestine. These camps were almost exclusively for Jews. Starting in 1944 extensive evacuations of Jews from Europe to these camps were in progress. Many were evacuated from the Balkans via Istanbul, and there was also a Black Sea route through Istanbul. Entry into the U.S. or countries of South America was sought and obtained for many of these people while the war was still in progress. It was in this context that the camp at Oswego, N.Y., right next to the Canadian border, was established. In addition, many who had not initially been put into one of the camps in Palestine managed to reach that destination anyway.[35]

After Germany collapsed the UNRRA administered DP (displaced persons) camps, mainly in the British and American zones of occupation in Germany and Austria. Of course, there were many non-Jews in these camps, but the Jews had a privileged position and, in many cases, were quartered in houses or hotels which had been requisitioned for them.[36]

The UNRRA operations in Germany were one of the scandals of the occupation era. Notorious were the raids on German homes for purposes of "rescuing" children. It had been the Nazi policy in Eastern Europe, when orphans fell into their hands, to conduct a racial examination in order to select the Aryan orphans for adoption by German families. These children were being raised exactly as German children were, and became the innocent victims of the UNRRA terror. It is not known what happened to them.[37]

The behavior of the DP's in the UNRRA camps was abysmal. As the most prominent historian of the U.S. military government in Germany wrote:[38]

They not only consumed large quantities of food, but they exhibited many of the psychoneurotic traits which must be expected from people who have undergone the tribulations that many of the displaced persons suffered. It was commonplace for them to allege that they were not receiving the consideration that they deserved from the Allied authorities. They often objected to the camps in which they were living, maintaining that it reflected on their position to be lodged in camps. Some urged that the best German houses be cleared of their occupants and placed at the disposal of the displaced persons, especially the Jews. They refused to assist in some instances in keeping their quarters reasonably habitable, taking the position that it was not their responsibility to make any effort to help themselves. During this period the actual care of the displaced persons was handled for some months by UNRRA, but final responsibility remained with military government and it had to give attention to the charges made in the press as to inadequate treatment.

Moreover, the displaced persons continued their underground war with the German population, despite all their promises and the efforts exerted by UNRRA and the American Army personnel. Forages into the countryside never ceased; some displaced persons took advantage of every opportunity to pick a quarrel with the Germans. With German property looted, German lives lost, and German women raped almost every day by the displaced persons, widespread resentment developed among the populace, especially when they could not defend themselves against the fire-arms which the displaced persons managed to obtain.

In one well publicized incident Jewish and Polish DP's, with the assistance of some U.S. Army personnel, forced German townspeople to dig up recently buried bodies and, while beating and kicking the Germans, forced them to remove decayed flesh and clean the bones.[39]

We are interested, however, in the political role that these DP camps

227

played, and the simple fact of the matter is that the Jewish DP camps and other living quarters served as transit and military training camps for the invasion of Palestine.

The world had an opportunity to learn this fact as early as January 1946. As happens on occasion in "international organizations", the nominal head of the UNRRA operations in Germany, British General Sir Frederick E. Morgan, was his own man and no Zionist stooge. While he had real control only over a part of the UNRRA German operations, he knew most of what was going on, and made a public issue of it. At a press conference in Frankfurt he charged that an organized Jewish group was sponsoring an exodus of Jews from Poland into the U.S. zone in Germany. He ridiculed "all the talk about pogroms within Poland", pointing out that Jews arriving in trainloads in Berlin were well fed, well dressed and had plenty of money: "They certainly do not look like a persecuted people. I believe that they have got a plan, a positive plan, to get out of Europe". Morgan added that their money was to a great extent occupation marks, printed by the Russians. It may be recalled by the reader that one of the most spectacular acts of Soviet agent Harry Dexter White, whom we encountered in Chapter III as the boss of the U.S. Treasury's international operations, was his transmission to the Russians of the plates of the U.S. occupation currency.

Chaim Weizmann denounced Morgan's statement as "palpably anti-semitic" and Rabbi Wise declared that it savoured of Nazism at its worst and was reminiscent of the forged Protocols of Zion. UNRRA headquarters in the U.S. announced that Morgan had been dismissed, but Morgan denied this. Wise, Henry Monsky, president of B'nai B'rith, and other prominent Jews then huddled with Lehman and "assured Governor Lehman that it was unwise under the circumstances to press the case against Morgan", since Morgan apparently had enough evidence to support his statement.

Later in 1946, there was an inquiry into the Jewish problem by an Anglo-American committee, which determined that Morgan had under-estimated the situation. In the Jewish DP camps "faces changed from day to day and new persons answered to old names on the nominal roles as the Zionist Organization moved Jews ever nearer to Palestine". The Jews, mainly Polish, were pouring into western Germany from the East and passing through the UNRRA operated camps. In these camps many of them received military instruction, for the invasion of Palestine, from uniformed non-commissioned officers of the British and U.S. armies. Although it was the case that almost none actually wanted to go to Palestine but to the U.S., every means of forcing immigration to Palestine was employed. Summing up his association with UNRRA, General Morgan wrote in his memoirs (*Peace and War*, 1961): "To serve such an outfit is beyond description".

Years later, Zionist authors conceded Morgan's charges in laudatory accounts of the organized exodus of Jews from Europe.[40]

In August 1946 LaGuardia fired Morgan for charging that UNRRA served as "an umbrella covering Russian secret agents and criminal elements engaged in wholesale dope-peddling and smuggling". Morgan was replaced by Meyer Cohen of the Washington office of UNRRA. This action was taken at a time when there was a great deal of well-publicized conflict between UNRRA and military authorities in Germany. LaGuardia had come to Germany at the time, in order to deal with various problems, Morgan being one of them. At a news conference held immediately after he fired Morgan, LaGuardia had an angry exchange with Hal Foust of the *Chicago Tribune,* whom we encountered in Chapter I. Foust had asked how much money nations other than the U.S. had contributed to UNRRA. LaGuardia, however, would answer none of

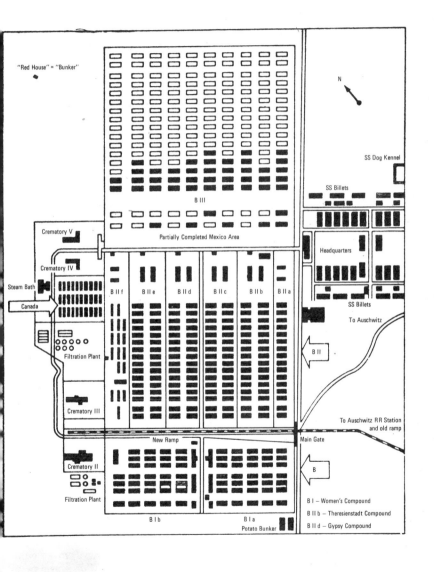

Fig. 29: *Plan of Birkenau.*

229

Foust's questions, on the grounds that Foust's "dirty, lousy paper would not print it anyway". To Foust's repeated requests for the information, LaGuardia shrieked "Shut up!"[41]

Morgan had not been the first high ranking Allied officer to collide with the Zionists. In the summer of 1945 the "Harrison report" to the White House had asserted that Jews in the U.S. zone in Germany were treated almost as badly as they had been under the Nazis. Although many Jews in the camps publicly ridiculed these claims, General Eisenhower, the Supreme Allied Commander, visited General George S. Patton, Jr. (U.S. Third Army commander and military governor of Bavaria) and "read the riot act to him and astounded him by saying that he meant it when he said that Germans were to be ousted from their homes, if necessary, to make their victims comfortable". Shortly later, Eisenhower relieved Patton of his duties, allegedly because Patton had said in public that too much fuss was being made about ousting Nazis from key positions, that the distinction between Nazis and non-Nazis was similar to the distinction between Republicans and Democrats, and that the key to a successful occupation of Germany lay in showing the Germans "what grand fellows we are". This was just the most publicized instance of the widespread "reluctance of occupation authorities on the operational level to act as tough as the policies enunciated by the heads of state in Berlin and by General Eisenhower himself". Patton was assigned to command a group writing a military history, but he was in an automobile accident in December 1945 and died two weeks later from complications.[42]

Eisenhower's attitude toward Zionists had always been most friendly. Shortly before the end of the war the Zionist organizer, Ruth Klieger, a native of Rumania who had emigrated to Palestine before the war, had visited Eisenhower's SHAEF headquarters in Paris in order to explain to Judge Rifkind, Eisenhower's adviser on DP matters, her mission of organizing transports of Jews to Palestine from Germany. She was made a U.S. Army colonel on the spot and given the papers necessary for her mission in Germany. Eisenhower's services did not end there, since the troop transport ship *Ascania*, owned by SHAEF and manned under orders from Eisenhower's Command, was then put at the disposal of the Zionists and 2,400 Jews were taken to Palestine in it. The British met it on arrival but did not want complications with SHAEF so they allowed the passengers to enter Palestine. Eisenhower later became President of the United States.[43]

As suggested above, the Jews who left the Soviet Union for Poland did not, for the most part, remain in that country very long. Supported by the Joint Distribution Committee and related Jewish organizations (the contributions to which were tax-free in the U.S.),[44] the Jews moved on to Germany and, in some instances, Czechoslovakia, spurred on by Zionist propaganda of all sorts. There was the talk, which we have noted, of pogroms, and there was also, no doubt, a widespread idea among the Jews that all were bound for the U.S. From Germany many did, indeed, eventually depart for the U.S. but many others moved on to Italy, where there were also UNRRA camps for them, or to France which, at that time, earned a reputation for marked friendliness to the Zionist cause. From Czechoslovakia the Jews moved on to Italy or to Vienna, and from Vienna to ports in Italy or Yugoslavia or to Budapest, Belgrade and points nearer Palestine. In all this hectic illegal movement there was, of course, no respect paid to such things as legitimate passports or identity papers. Greek identity papers were manufactured on a large scale and many Jews posed as Greeks returning home from Poland. When the Greek Government learned of this, they sent an official to investigate, but the official was an active Zionist himself, and merely informed the Zionist Organization that he could cover up the past illegalities, but that the "Greek" angle would have to be discarded. It had, however, served so well that in Czechoslovakia, border guards who thought that they had learned from the large number of "Greeks" that they had processed, what members of that nationality looked like, got suspicious and made arrests when real Greeks appeared.[45]

In the beginning of the mass movements the Zionist Organization had found that the Jews were too undisciplined and demoralized to serve as members of an effective movement. They therefore settled on the method of the propaganda of hatred to boost the fighting morale of the Jews in the various camps; they began "to instil into these Jews a deep dislike and hatred for the German and, indeed, for their entire non-Jewish environment, for the *goyim* around them". In the winter of 1946, the Anglo-American investigation committee visited the Jewish camps in Germany, and was "overwhelmed by this *anti-goyism* among the camp inmates, by the impossibility of maintaining any contact between the displaced Jews and the British and American peoples".[46]

The U.S. occupation authorities in Germany were naturally very concerned about the fact that so many people, so tenuously classified as "refugees", were pouring into their area of responsibility, but were reluctant to speak out too loudly or bluntly for fear of the sort of abuse that had been heaped on Patton and Morgan. However, the constant increase in the "refugee" population was creating problems that could not be ignored. In June 1946 a group of U.S. editors and newspaper executives arrived in Frankfurt as the first stop in a tour of Germany, and were told by "high United States officers" that Jews were flooding into the U.S. zone at the rate of 10,000 per month, thereby creating a "grave problem". It was said that "many of them are coming from Russia and if they join those in Poland in an apparent mass movement toward Palestine, we may have to look after 3,000,000 of them". Of particular interest in this statement is where "many" of the Jews were coming from, and the fact that the U.S. Army authorities felt it plausible to use a figure of 3,000,000 (not a misprint). They were, of course, exaggerating the situation in order to provoke some sort of relevant action, for there was never any possibility that 3 million Jews would enter the U.S. zone in Germany. Nevertheless, their use of such a figure, and their specifying that "many" of the Jews were "coming from Russia", are worth noting.[47]

The problem got so much attention that in early August 1946 the American military governor, General McNarney, announced that "the United States border patrol will not permit Jewish refugees from Poland to enter the United States zone in organized truckloads and trainloads". McNarney added, however, that "if persecutees come across the borders individually, of course, it is a different matter, and we will accept them". It may have surprised many observers that this seemingly unimportant qualification was so satisfactory for the Zionists that, shortly later, Rabbi Wise and other prominent Zionists publicly lauded "the attitude of Gen. Joseph T. McNarney . . . toward the entire problem". The puzzle was resolved the following November, when it was reported that a record 35,000 Jews entered West Germany from Poland (the greater part of them to the U.S. zone) in September, and that the "trickle" that existed in November amounted to "150 to 200 persons daily."[48]

In the news stories of this period, it was frequently the case that the Jews "returning" from Russia to Poland were described as consisting mainly of the 1940 deportees to the Soviet Union. Such a press treatment was to be expected, since the others were supposed to be dead, but such interpretations may be disregarded although, as Korzen remarks, this group included 1940 deportees.

During 1946, the U.S. Senate War Investigating Committee sent its chief

231

counsel, George Meader, to Germany to investigate the U.S. occupation policies. Meader's report, which charged, *inter alia,* widespread immorality and racketeering in the Army, was suppressed as a result of "tremendous pressure by the White House, State and War Departments, and Senator Arthur Vandenberg" and a threat of resignation by General Clay, but the contents eventually were made public anyway. The report was very critical of the entire practice of accomodating the Jews who were pouring in from Poland, since they were not really refugees (in the sense of having been stranded in Germany at the end of the war) but part of a mass movement of people that was being sponsored by private groups on behalf of a specific political cause, Zionism. The U.S., therefore, was "financing a political program" by receiving these Jews in the German DP camps, although that program had never been submitted to the Congress for consideration. In the U.S., therefore, there was concern with and opposition to the substantial support that U.S. "refugee" policy was giving to the Zionist cause, but it was too late and too little to have any significant influence on events.

In his report, Meader complained of the difficulty of getting the Jewish (as distinct from non-Jewish) DP's to do any work or even help fix up their own dwellings. Nevertheless they constantly complained that things were not being done as well as they thought they could be done. Meader also pointed out that illegal activities and crimes of violence by DP's were numerous. He remarked that the U.S. had agreed to accept as immigrants 2,250,000 refugees from Europe.[49]

It is of only slight value to report here the figures that were being given for the number of Jewish DP's. In the autumn of 1946 is was said that there were 185,000 Jewish DP's in camps in West Germany. When one adds those in Austria, the figure would exceed 200,000. It is also said that there were over 400,000 Jewish refugees in Western Europe on 1 July 1947.[50] However such figures do not say very much because the camps for Jews and other refugees really served as transit camps and, in the case of the Jews, there was the constant movement toward the U.S. and Palestine, largely illegal or "unofficial" in the case of the latter destination and also, possibly, in the case of the former destination as well.

The principle, but not sole, destinations of the Jews who left Europe were Palestine and the U.S., so we should attempt to estimate the numbers involved. Palestine population figures kept by the British authorities are probably accurate up to some point in 1946:[51]

	Moslems	Jews	Christians	Others
1924	532,636	94,945	74,094	8,263
1929	634,811	156,481	81,776	9,443
1934	747,826	282,975	102,407	10,793
1939	860,580	445,457	116,958	12,150
1944	994,724	528,702	135,547	14,098

In late 1946 there were supposed to be 608,000 Jews and 1,237,000 Moslems, Christians and "Others". Past this point accurate British figures do not exist, on account of the large extent of illegal immigration as the British gradually lost control of the situation. In any event, by the time some of the dust had settled in July 1949, the Israeli Government reported that there were 925,000 Jews in Israel. These were predominantly Jews of European origins, the large scale immigration of Jews from North Africa and Asia having been a subsequent development promoted by the Israeli Government. By 1957, there were about 1,868,000 Jews in Israel, and 868,000 Arabs had fled to neighboring countries since the Jewish takeover.[52]

It is worth pausing here to remark that many people have a very mistaken picture of Zionism and Israel. It is now widely assumed that Zionism was born at the end of World War II, when large numbers of European Jews, having decided that they could no longer live in Europe, invaded a previously all-Arab Palestine and drove the Arab inhabitants out. In fact Zionism, the movement for the establishment of a Jewish state in Palestine, has a history that starts in the late nineteenth century. By 1917 Zionism was such a potent political force that Britain, locked in bloody struggle with Imperial Germany, made the "Balfour Declaration", effectively promising Palestine to the Jews, in return for Jewish support in the war. Since Britain also had certain agreements with the Arabs, Palestine became the "too often promised land".

Zionist organizations promoted the movement of Jews to Palestine after World War I, and during the Thirties, as the population figures above suggest, Palestine had become perhaps the biggest headache of British foreign policy, which faced the impossible task of reconciling the Jewish and Arab claims to Palestine. It was during the late Thirties that Zionism found itself actively cooperating with the Gestapo, which met regularly with Zionist representatives and even helped in the provision of farms and facilities to set up training centers in Germany and Austria for Jewish emigrants. The Zionists and the Gestapo had the same objective of getting Jews out of Europe.[53]

The consequence of World War II did not create Zionism as an effective political movement; they merely gave Zionism the world political victory it needed for the final stage of the takeover of Palestine. All world power had fallen to the U.S. and the Soviet Union, both of which were most friendly to the Zionist cause at the time. Under the circumstances the Arab position was hopeless, since it depended on the firmness and political independence of a Britain that was almost prostrate politically and economically.

While it is possible to get a presumably fair idea of the extent of Jewish immigration into Palestine, one encounters what amounts to a stone wall in attempting to determine this for the U.S. We have seen that the policy of classifying immigrants as "Hebrews" was dropped in the same month of 1943 that the U.S. Government went into the business of processing DP's on a large scale through the creation of UNRRA. Immediately after the war, there was naturally much Jewish pressure for the admission of great numbers of Jewish immigrants, and in December 1945 President Truman announced that there would be an acceleration in the immigration process in order to allow a higher rate of admission. While Truman regretted that the unused quotas from the war years were not cumulative and could not be applied to future admissions, he pledged that all outstanding immigration quotas and regulations would be respected.[54] If they were, indeed, respected then the effect on Jewish admissions would nevertheless have been secondary since they entered under the categories of the various nationalities: German, Austrian, Dutch, Polish, etc. However the existing regulations did not permit the admission of as many persons as was desired so, shortly after the war, there was special legislation relating to the admission of DP's, in which "existing barriers were set aside". The legislation also set up a "Displaced Persons Commission" to assist in the resettlement of the immigrants and, according to the account of the Commission, over 400,000 such persons were resettled in the U.S. in the period 1948-1952 (the period specified in the legislation). The official account goes on to claim that only 16% of these 400,000 were Jewish, but that is just the official account of a Government which had taken specific steps to assure that the relevant data would not exist.[55]

For what it is worth, we summarize here the more relevant parts of the immigration data that the U.S. Government has published:[56]

233

B u d a p e s t, den 30. Juni 1944 –
Ankunft: 3. Juli 1944 – 11.05 Uhr

1347 g

Nr. 1838 v. 30. VI. Im Anschluß an Drahtbericht – Nr.1657 +
+) bei Anl. II V.S. /1. . . / vom 13. Juni.

        I.) Abtransport Juden aus Zone III
planmäßig mit 50.805 abgeschlossen. Gesamtziffer aus Zonen I – III 340.162.

        II.) Konzentrierung in Zone IV und Ab-
transport mit 41.499 planmäßig abgeschlossen
Gesamtziffer 381.661 Fortgang der Aktion
ist gesondert mit Fernschreiber – Nr. 279 –
vom 27. Juni Nr. 287 vom 29. Juni und –
Nr. 289 vom 30. Juni nach Fuschl berichtet
worden. Konzentrierung in Zone V (bisher
nicht erfaßter Raum westlich der Donau ohne
Budapest) hat 29. Juni begonnen. Gleich-
zeitig hat kleinere Sonderaktion in Vor-
städten von Budapest als Vorbereitungsmaß-
nahme begonnen. Ferner laufen noch einige
kleine Sondertransporte mit politischen,
intellektuellen, kinderreichen und Fach-
arbeiter-Juden.

                    Veesenmayer.

St. b. Knopler
. . . Std
. . . Her O . .
. . . . . G.
. . . .
. . . . .
. . . . P.
. . . . ssa
. . . . . undh.
C . . . . . .
Lg. P. . . . .
G . . Le . . er Inf. I
G . Leiter Inf. II . . . . .
A . b.-Expl. bel . . . . .

Botsch. v. Rintelen
Ges. Schnurre
  „ Frohwein
  „ v. Grundherr
Dr. Megerle
VLR Ripken
  „ Melchers
LR v. Grote

K213896

487144

Fig. 30: *Reproduced from Braham,* The Destruction of Hungarian Jewry,
Ch. 5. Document NG-2263.

Fig. 31: The crematorium at the Lublin camp. There were five ovens.
Photo: U.S. National Archives

Area	Regular Immigration		DP's	Total
	1941-1950	1951-1960	1948-1952	from Area
Austria	24,860	67,106	8,956	100,922
Belgium	12,189	18,575	951	31,715
Czechoslovakia	8,347	918	12,638	21,903
Denmark	5,393	10,984	62	16,439
Estonia	212	185	10,427	10,824
France	38,809	51,121	799	90,729
Germany	226,578	477,765	62,123	766,466
Greece	8,973	47,608	10,277	66,858
Hungary	3,469	36,637	16,627	56,733
Italy	57,661	185,491	2,268	245,420
Latvia	361	352	36,014	36,727
Lithuania	683	242	24,698	25,623
Netherlands	14,860	52,277	64	67,201
Poland	7,571	9,985	135,302	152,858
Rumania	1,076	1,039	10,618	12,733
U.S.S.R.	548	584	35,747	36,879
Yugoslavia	1,576	8,225	33,367	43,168

We have only given the numbers for selected European countries, i.e. those countries that may have contributed many *uprooted* Jews, although there is a difficulty involved here, as we shall see shortly. The total for Hungary 1951-1960 does not seem to include those who entered on account of special legislation passed in connection with the refugees from the Hungarian rebellion in 1956, about 45,000 of whom were admitted to the U.S. It is worth mentioning that 285,415 persons entered the U.S. from Europe in the years 1954-1971 under various other provisions for refugees.

For reasons that will be clear when we attempt to interpret this data we note the immigration totals from the various continents:

Area	Regular Immigration		DP's	Total
	1941-1950	1951-1960	1948-1952	from Area
Europe	621,704	1,328,293	405,234	2,355,231
Asia	31,780	147,453	4,016	183,249
N. & S. America	354,804	996,944	307	1,352,055
Africa	7,367	14,092	107	21,566
Pacific	19,242	16,204	10	35,456
Totals:	1,034,897	2,502,986	409,674	3,947,557

An important point in interpreting this data is that, in the case of regular immigration in the years 1941-1950 and 1951-1960, the country of origin is defined as the country of last permanent residence, while in the case of the DP's who entered the U.S. in 1948-1952, the country of origin is the country of birth.

That nationality was the country of last permanent residence in the case of regular immigration makes these figures particularly difficult to interpret. This is well illustrated by the total 766,466 who entered the U.S. from Germany, more than 90% on the regular quota basis. If we imagine a German Jew as a Jew who actually was raised in Germany and had possessed German citizenship, then only a fraction of the 766,466 could have been Jews, for the simple reason that the greater number of the estimated 500 or 600 thousand German Jews had emigrated before the war. In order to get some idea of the number of German Jews who might have immigrated into the U.S. after the war, recall that the Jews deported East by the Germans from France and Belgium were almost all German Jews who had emigrated from Germany before the war. Thus if we accept Reitlinger's figures the total German Jews deported to the East might have been around 250,000. If, say, half went to Palestine after the war, then it would appear that no more than about 125,000 of the "Germans" who entered the U.S. could have been Jews. However this calculation is upset by the simple observation that the status of "permanent resident" might have been conferred on many of the Jews of several nationalities who were quartered under various conditions in Germany immediately after the war. The period was not noted for strict adherence to legalities, so it is safe to assume that somewhat more than 125,000 of these "Germans" were Jews. Likewise with the figures for Italy.

The haziness of the concept of "permanent resident" is also the reason for the inclusion of immigration figures from such places as North and South America and Asia. We should not expect that the uprooted Jews were particularly scrupulous in regard to legal credentials, and we have seen this illustrated in the case of the "Greeks" who passed through Czechoslovakia. It should not have been difficult to arrange for the creation of credentials which declared Jews to have been permanent residents of various South American countries, and possibly also of Canada. A side trip to the country in question while en route to the U.S. might have been necessary, but such a trip would have been scenic anyway. South American countries would probably have been happy to cooperate, since the Jews were not in the process of settling with them, and there was no doubt bribe money as well.

For these reasons I believe that one is perfectly safe in assuming that at least 500,000 uprooted Jews entered the U.S., and the correct figure is probably higher. Since the area of New York City is the home of millions of Jews, a few hundred thousand could have moved there alone, and nobody would have observed more than the fact that he, personally, was aware of a few Jews who came to New York from Europe after the war.

In this analysis we have assumed, of course, that the great masses of Jews who resettled after the war were uprooted Jews and did not include statistically significant portions of, say, French Jews, who had no more reason to leave France than Jews in the U.S. have to leave that country. The net result of the Nazi Jewish resettlement policies was that a great number of Jews, uprooted from their homes, came into the power of Zionist controlled refugee relief organizations, which were able to direct these masses of Jews to destinations chosen for political reasons.

This is as far as the demographic analysis need be carried here and it is probably essentially as far as it could be carried in any case. If we assume that at the end of the war there were about three million uprooted Jews whose situations had to be disposed of somehow by the Allies, then it is possible that one-half million emigrated to the U.S., one-half million went to Palestine, one million were absorbed by the Soviet Union, 750,000 settled in Eastern Europe excluding the Soviet Union, and 250,000 settled in Western Europe. On the other hand, the correct figures, including those offered here as data, may very well be somewhat different. The treatment presented here is guaranteed to be valid in a general way, but statistical accuracy cannot be attained.

If we attempt to estimate the number who perished, on account of the chaotic conditions in the camps as the Germans retreated, on account of epidemics in the ghettos during more normal periods, on account of pogroms or massacres that might have taken place especially while the Germans were retreating, on account of *Einsatzgruppen* executions, and on account of unhealthy conditions in the concentration camps in Germany, especially at the very end of the war (which affected only Jewish political prisoners and ordinary criminals and the young adult Jews who had been conscripted for labor and

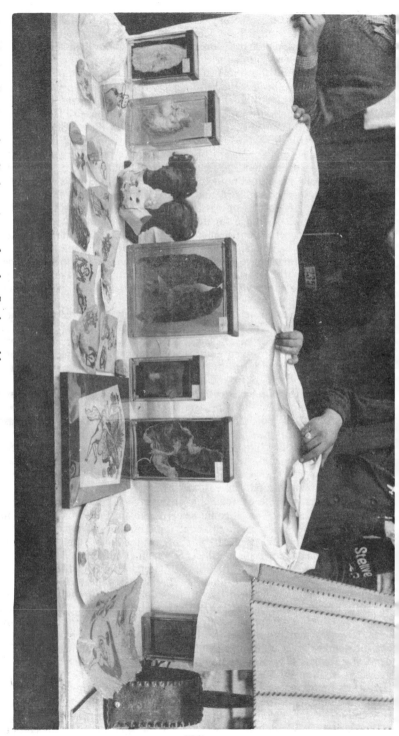

Fig. 32: A collection of medical specimens found at Buchenwald.

Photo: U.S. Army

238

sent to the concentration camps), we again have an impossible, in my opinion, problem on our hands. Rassinier's estimate is about a million Jewish dead, but one can take very many exceptions to his arguments. A figure of a million Jewish dead, while possible, seems rather high to me. However, given the vast uncertainties involved, I really have no taste for arguing the matter one way or another.

One should feel no need to apologize for such confessions of statistical ignorance. Korzen, in his study of the Polish Jews dispersed by the Russian deportations of 1940, confesses large and important areas of ignorance in his study, especially in regard to numbers, and he had the friendly offices of the Israeli Government to help with his research. A study such as the present one necessarily labors under severe handicaps regarding relevant statistics. Indeed, I was surprised that it was possible to reconstruct statistical and quantitative aspects even to the incomplete extent presented here. The most powerful groups on earth have sought to distort the record of what actually happened to the Jews of Europe during the Second World War.

In his memoirs, J.G. Burg (Josef Ginsburg) has presented a story completely consistent with the historical record. At the outbreak of war in September 1939 he was resident in Lemberg, Poland. He immediately fled with his family to Czernowitz, Rumania, in the province of Bukovina, which the Red Army occupied in June 1940. A year later the German attack on Russia drives the Red Army out, and Ukranian bands start conducting pogroms, which are halted by German and Rumanian troops. Later Ginsburg and his family are deported east to Transnistria, where life is at least bearable. A Mr. Kolb of the Swiss and International Red Cross visits their settlement in early 1943.

After the German defeats mount, there is growing tension between the Germans and Rumanians and many Rumanians attempt to befriend the Jews. The German-Rumanian front starts to collapse in mid-1944 and Ginsburg and family return to Czernowitz. Everywhere there is chaos, starvation and the Russian terror. Even after the end of the war conditions are not very good so, in 1946, Ginsburg and family moved on to Breslau and then proceeded to an UNRRA DP camp near Munich in the U.S. occupation zone of Germany. In the camp almost all Jews are naturally very interested in the possibility of proceeding to the U.S., since they know that many Jews are doing just that. However the Zionist leadership attempts by all means to divert their interest from the U.S. to Palestine. To the question "Can one emigrate to the U.S. and remain a Zionist?", a Professor Spiktor replies: "Whoever emigrates to the U.S. in this hour of destiny, can not only be no Zionist, he also thereby forsakes his own Jewish people". Six months later Professor Spiktor emigrates to the U.S. Ginsburg and his family go to Palestine with many of the other Jews from the camp.

We are now very close to the end of our study. The thesis of this book has been proved conclusively. The Jews of Europe were not exterminated and there was no German attempt to exterminate them. The Germans resettled a certain number and these people were ultimately resettled again in accordance with Allied programs. Although various statistical details are missing from our analysis, it was possible to reconstruct quantitative aspects of the problem to a satisfactory degree.

The Jews of Europe suffered during the war by being deported to the East, by having had much of their property confiscated and, more importantly, by suffering cruelly in the circumstances surrounding Germany's defeat. They may even have lost a million dead.

Everybody in Europe suffered during the war, especially the people of central and eastern Europe. The people who suffered most were the losers, the Germans (and Austrians), who lost 10 million dead due to military casualties, Allied bombings, the Russian terror at the end of the war, Russian and French labor conscriptions of POW's after the war, Polish and other expulsions from their homelands, under the most brutal conditions, and the vengeful occupation policies of 1945-1948.[57]

The "gas chambers" were wartime propaganda fantasies completely comparable to the garbage that was shoveled out by Lord Bryce and associates in World War I. The factual basis for these ridiculous charges was nailed with perfect accuracy by Heinrich Himmler, in an interview with a representative of the World Jewish Congress just a few weeks before the end of the war:[58]

In order to put a stop to the epidemics, we were forced to burn the bodies of incalculable numbers of people who had been destroyed by disease. We were therefore forced to build crematoria, and on this account they are knotting a noose for us.

It is most unfortunate that Himmler was a "suicide" while in British captivity since, had he been a defendant at the IMT, his situation would have been such that he would have told the true story (being fully informed and not in a position to shift responsibility to somebody else) and books such as the present book would not be necessary since the major material could be read in the IMT trial transcript. But then, you see, it was not within the bounds of political possibility that Himmler live to talk at the IMT.

That Himmler's assessment of the gas chamber accusations is the accurate one should be perfectly obvious to anybody who spends any time with this subject, as we have seen especially in Chapter IV. In particular, Hilberg and Reitlinger should have been able to see this before completing even fractions of their thick books, which are monumental foolishness.

VIII
REMARKS

We close this work with a few miscellaneous remarks, most of which deal with some objections that may arise in certain situations.

An objection that one highly intelligent critic actually expressed was that he thought that my story was similar to ones he had read about "flying saucers" and "divining rods". The reaction was startling but it was at least understandable. Years of propaganda have so associated Nazi Germany with the six million legend that, for many people, denial of the legend seems at first almost as preposterous as denying that World War II happened at all. Nevertheless the objection is not one that can be answered, except by pointing out that our account does not involve the supernatural or extra-terrestrial or, indeed, anything more unusual than people lying about their political enemies. With this critic, one can only ask that he attempt to say something intelligent.

The most consequential objection to this work will be that I have employed the "holocaust" literature, in particular the books by Reitlinger and Hilberg, as sources although I have also denounced such books as "monumental foolishness". This objection is a serious one since I would be the first to hold that, once the extermination legend has been buried, these books will become significant only as supreme examples of total delusion and foolishness, and will be referenced only in connection with the great hoaxes of history. However our task here is precisely to bury the legend and the only way to do that is by considering the story that has been advanced, and this amounts to analysing the cases put forward by Reitlinger and Hilberg. The only practical way of exposing the hoax is by considering the claims that have been put forward by the extermination mythologists. ~~doing more than that if us~~ *mg*

There was a second reason for employing Reitlinger and Hilberg as sources. In this work great weight has been placed on providing documentation that a reader with access to a large library can confirm on his own. Unfortunately this desire could not be entirely satisfied, since a good part of the analysis relies on documents and publications that are not readily available without going through complicated borrowing procedures. In order to partially overcome this difficulty I have used Reitlinger and Hilberg as sources on many such points, but I have only done this in cases where I have been able to confirm their remarks. I have not adopted the practice of assuming that anything that Reitlinger or Hilberg says that helps my case must be true. For example, in connection with our discussion in Chapter V concerning the date of the first Allied air raid at Auschwitz, I gave reasons for the conclusion that the first raid did not occur before August 1944. It would have been dishonest to merely reference Hilberg on this point, since Hilberg believes that the first raid occurred in December 1944, and is obviously confused on this point.[1]

Another reason for the frequent referencing of Reitlinger and Hilberg is my sincere wish that the reader would take a look at such books; it is only then that the reader can become completely convinced that the hoax is a hoax. In this connection one can recommend a typical procedure that the

benefit other s.

reader may go through to confirm the matter in a general way. First get a copy of Hilberg's book. On pages 567-571 Hilberg presents a magnificent discussion of the alleged role of the Zyklon B in the exterminations, and on page 619 or 621 he points out that the German documents speak only of a program of deportations to the East and associated operations. It is also useful to read his discussion of what the Nuernberg trial documents say happened in Hungary, 509-554, and to note the document numbers he cites in this connection. Next find, if possible, a copy of Reitlinger's book, first or second edition. On pages 158-159 (150 in the first edition), he reproduces the text of document NO-4473, in which he notes that the "gas chamber" that allegedly existed in the building which contained Crematorium II at Auschwitz was described as a *"Vergasungskeller"* in the original German. On pages 118, 121 and 182 (112, 114-115 and 169 in the first edition) Reitlinger remarks on the "mystery" that "at certain periods, entire transports (of Jews) were admitted" into Auschwitz. Reitlinger also briefly mentions the chemical industry at Auschwitz, pages 109 and 492 (105 and 452 in the first edition). Hopefully, the reader will undertake a more thoroughgoing confirmation, but the above would be a good start.

Some people may assume, fallaciously, that opinions expressed by Jews and Germans on the subject of the "Final Solution" carry nearly authoritative weight.

Under circumstances where the subject of this book is being discussed by a group of people a seemingly potent argument, because it is so laden with emotion and can upset the decorum of the group, may be offered by a Jew who claims to have lost some relative or close acquaintance in the "holocaust", and he may even have knowledge that the supposedly missing relative had been sent to Auschwitz, Treblinka or some such place.

There are several ways to react to such a point. An obvious possibility is that the man is lying. However it is more probable that he is telling the truth as he knows it. Assuming that his story is valid, there is only one sense in which it can be valid. That is, all he can claim is that he or his family lost contact with some relative in Europe during the war and never heard from that person again. Obviously, such data does not imply the existence of a Nazi extermination program.

That contact was lost during the war was almost inevitable, either because it was difficult for Jews deported to the East to communicate with people in Allied countries, or because it was difficult or impossible to communicate from the East to points farther west during the chaotic last year of the war. Thus the only point of interest in such a case is the claim that contact was not reestablished after the war.

The simplest explanation is that the relative did, indeed, along with an indeterminate number of other persons of Central and East European nationalities, perish somewhere in Europe during the war, or in a concentration camp, from causes that have been covered in this book.

The second possibility is that the relative survived the war, but did not reestablish contact with his prewar relations. One possible, although not very likely motivation for such a failure to reestablish contact could have been some prohibition on such correspondence imposed by the Soviet Government on those Jews who had been absorbed into the Soviet Union.

A more important and more plausible motivation for failing to reestablish contact held when a separation of husband and wife was involved. A very large number of marriages are held together by purely social and economic constraints; such constraints did not exist for a great number of the Jews uprooted by the German policies and wartime and postwar conditions.

In many cases deported Jewish families were broken up for what was undoubtedly intended by the Germans to be a period of limited duration. This was particularly the case when the husband seemed a good labor conscript; just as German men were conscripted for hazardous military service, Jews were conscripted for unpleasant labor tasks. Under such conditions it is reasonable to expect that many of these lonely wives and husbands would have, during or at the end of the war, established other relations that seemed more valuable than the previous relationships. In such cases, then, there would have been a strong motivation not to reestablish contact with the legal spouse. Moreover none of the "social and economic constraints" which we noted above were present, and Jews were in a position to choose numerous destinations in the resettlement programs that the Allies sponsored after the war. This possibility could account for a surprisingly large number of "missing" Jews. For example suppose that a man and wife with two small children were deported, with the man being sent to a labor camp and the wife and children being sent to a resettlement camp in the East. Let us suppose that the wife failed to reestablish contact with her husband. We thus seem to have four people reported dead or missing; the husband says his wife and children are presumably dead and the wife says her husband was lost. However, this one separation of husband and wife could account for even more missing Jews, for it is likely that the parents and other relatives of the wife, on the one hand, and the parents and other relatives of the husband, on the other, would also have lost touch with each other. Thus one has some number of people on the husband's side claiming that some number of people on the wife's side are missing, and vice versa. Obviously, the possibilities of accounting for missing Jews in this way are practically boundless.

It is said that the *Yad Vashem* archives in Jerusalem now have the names of between 2.5 and 3 million Jewish "dead from the Nazi holocaust". The data has supposedly been "collected on one page testimony sheets filled in by relatives or witnesses or friends". Of course, it is in no way possible to satisfactorily substantiate this production of the Israeli Government, which certainly cannot be claimed to be a disinterested party in the question of the number of Jews who perished. There is no doubt that many Jews died during the war, so we should expect that a part of the *Yad Vashem* claim is valid, but it is also the case that there is no possible way to distinguish, in this data, between Jews who actually died during the war and Jews with whom the signers of the "testimony sheets" have merely lost contact. The data is particularly meaningless when it is a "friend" who has contributed a declaration; I have lost contact with a great many former friends and acquaintances, but I assume that nearly all are still alive. Indeed, the use of the testimony of "friends" for the purpose of gathering the *Yad Vashem* data shows that the data is mostly meaningless; such "friends" have no more basis for declaring their missing acquaintances dead than I do.[2]

I have no idea what is meant by the "witnesses" who signed the testimony sheets. There is also a better than negligible possibility that some signers of these declarations invented missing friends and relatives for any of a number of possible motivations, and it is even possible that some of the signers never existed.

To summarize our reaction to the claims of Jews regarding persons said to be victims of the "holocaust", such claims are no doubt valid to some extent, since many Jews died, but the hard data possessed by Jews who report such losses, when they are reporting truthfully, is not conclusive in regard to the deaths of the persons involved, and certainly in no way implies the existence of a Nazi extermination program.

243

One must be careful in interpreting the fact that Germans, themselves, seem to believe in the exterminations. Certainly, most individual Germans seem to concede the myth, and not all do so in order to stay out of trouble. However it is clear that the German people were no better situated to see the truth than anybody else. Many might, indeed, have observed local Jews being deported, not to return after the war, and this may have given some an even more vivid conviction in support of the extermination hoax than that which holds generally. The basic observation to make relative to the views of individual Germans is that the standard sort of "information" on this subject has been available to them, and they are thus just as innocently deluded as other nationalities.

The West German Government which, by interminable war crimes trials, now being held thirty or more years after the alleged crimes, by instruction in the schools, and now by means of naked terror, as shown in the Staeglich episode, does everything possible to keep the lie propped up and to prevent open discussion, is a different matter because the cause for its behavior is not innocent misunderstanding. The basic fact is that the claim of the Bonn Government to be a German Government is somewhat tenuous. The fact is that the entire political structure of West Germany was established by the U.S. Government. This includes the control of the newspapers and other media, the control of the schools, and the constitution of the *Bundesrepublik*. As a puppet creation this "German"-political establishment necessarily has an interest in the lies of the conquerors, and behaves accordingly. That is very simple, and this situation is perfectly illustrated by the career of the man who was Chancellor of West Germany during the greater part of the time when this book was being written: Herr Willy Brandt (an alias — Brandt's real name is Herbert Ernst Karl Frahm — Frahm was his mother's maiden name and he never knew who his father was).

Marxist Brandt left Germany after the Hitler takeover and acquired Norwegian citizenship. After the German invasion of Norway in 1940, he slipped into neutral Sweden and eventually was given a position in the press corps there. It was none other than Willy Brandt who, during the war, was transmitting the concocted propaganda stories that had supposedly originated in Stockholm and ended up on the pages of the *N.Y. Times*.[3]

After the defeat of Germany Brandt naturally decided that the atmosphere back home had improved so he returned to Germany, resumed German citizenship, and entered West Berlin politics as a Social Democrat. He eventually became Mayor of West Berlin and acquired a press aide, Hans Hirschfeld, a German Jew who, along with Kempner, Marcuse, *et. al.*, had been employed in the OSS during the war. During the 1961 espionage trial in the U.S. of R.A. Soblen, which resulted in Soblen being sentenced to life imprisonment, a government witness, Mrs. J.K. Beker, who had been a courier in a Soviet espionage ring during the war but had turned FBI informer later, testified that she had carried information from Hirschfeld to Soblen for transmission to Moscow. Mrs. Beker was the principal government witness, so the obvious answer of the defense should have been to produce Hirschfeld. Indeed, Soblen's defense counsel said that he had attempted to convince Hirschfeld to come to the U.S. to testify, but Hirschfeld declined, at first on the grounds that the publicity associated with his appearance as a witness could hurt Brandt, who was engaged in an election campaign. Hirschfeld was also concerned about the possibility that he might be charged with some sort of offense if he journeyed to the U.S. Brandt, in New York during the controversy involving Hirschfeld, naturally defended his former close associate, who had by that time been living in retirement in Germany.

In order to give the defense every opportunity to make a case for Soblen, the government offered Hirschfeld immunity against prosecution for "any past acts or transactions" if he would come to the U.S. to testify, adding only that Hirschfeld could be prosecuted for any perjury committed in a retrial of Soblen. Hirschfeld nevertheless declined to appear in Soblen's defense.[4]

Brandt eventually became Chancellor of West Germany and won the Nobel Peace Prize for 1971 for his efforts to build friendlier relations with the eastern bloc, his *"Ostpolitik"*. Brandt seemed to be riding high but by 1974 various Brandt policies, including his *Ostpolitik*, had brought his Social Democratic Party to a new low in popular esteem, and even S.P.D. politicians in long term S.P.D. strongholds expressed the belief that they were going to lose their next elections. Fortuitously for the S.P.D., the Guenter Guillaume scandal erupted in late April with Guillaume's arrest as an East German espionage agent. Although it had been known that Guillaume had been a member of an East Berlin espionage organization, he had been cleared by the Brandt government for a high post in the inner circle of Brandt's associates and advisers. The scandal brought Willy Brandt's downfall with his resignation on 7 May 1974. Brandt was succeeded by Helmut Schmidt, whose leadership terminated the decline of the S.P.D.[5]

Clearly, a career such as Brandt's postwar career is possible only in a country in which treason has become a normal part of political life, so it is not in the least surprising that the Bonn Government is a defender of the hoax.

An interesting objection is the claim that nobody would dare invent such a tale as the six million legend; nobody has the extraordinary imagination required and, even if he did, the obvious risks in telling such gigantic lies should dissuade him. The argument amounts to the claim that the mere existence of the legend implies the truth of its essentials, so I suppose we can classify it as the hoaxers' ontological argument.

What is interesting about this objection is its superficially logical quality. Indeed I imagine that this calculation accounts in good measure for the widespread acceptance of the legend; people assume that nobody would be so brazen as to invent such lies. Nevertheless the logic is not sound, for history affords us numerous examples of popular acceptance of gigantic lies, and in this connection we can again cite witchcraft hysteria as precedent for the psychological essentials of the six million hoax.

It is ironic that Hitler anticipated the psychology of the "big lie" in his remarks on the subject in Chapter X of *Mein Kampf*. It is also ironic that the most mind boggling invented accounts of exterminations appear in the Jewish Talmudic literature in connection with the last two of the three great Jewish revolts against Rome, the Diaspora revolt of 115-117 A.D. and the Palestine revolt of 132-135 A.D. In connection with the Palestine revolt of 66-70 A.D. the Talmudic writings do nothing more than bewail the loss of the Temple in Jerusalem and discuss the implications of the loss for Jewish law. A good discussion of the three revolts is given in Michael Grant's *The Jews in the Roman World*.

According to the ancient accounts (mainly Cassius Dio, who wrote around 200 A.D., and Eusebius, the early fourth century Bishop of Caesarea) the Disapora revolt started in Cyrenaica(northeast Libya) at a time when the Emperor Trajan had, for the purpose of annexing Parthia and its valuable Mesopotamian territory, constituted a huge eastern army at the price of withdrawing many small contingents which had served to keep order in various parts of the Empire. The Jews attacked the Greek and Roman civilian populations and it is said they killed 220,000 in Cyrenaica, amusing themselves in various gruesome ways. The revolt then spread to Egypt, where the Jews killed an unknown number, and to Cyprus, where they are said to have killed 240,000. In Alexandria, however, the predominantly Greek population gained control of events and are said to have massacred the Jews of that city. Recent archaeological evidence indicates that the ancient accounts are not exaggerated.[6]

The Talmud says almost nothing about this revolt, except to give the number of Jews killed in Alexandria as "sixty myriads on sixty myriads, twice as many as went forth from Egypt", i.e. 1,200,000 on the assumption that addition and not multiplication is intended. The killings are blamed on "the Emperor Hadrian", which may be due to the fact that Hadrian was at the time the commander of Trajan's eastern army and succeeded Trajan as Emperor when Trajan died in 117, possibly before the final suppression of the revolt.

The figure given for the number of Jewish victims is obviously exaggerated for, while it is usually difficult to be more than approximately correct in estimating the populations of ancient cities, Alexandria of the period had a population of 500,000 or more, with an upper bound of one million a reasonable one to assume because that was the approximate population of the city of Rome, a figure concerning which there is also some uncertainty, but if Rome ever attained a population significantly greater than one million, it never got near two million.[7] The 1,200,000 martyred Jews may seem a brazen invention, but you haven't seen anything yet.

The next great revolt was in Palestine in 132-135 and was a serious attempt by its leader, Bar-Kokhba, to set up a Jewish state with himself as king, although he eventually claimed to be the Messiah. During the revolt he made laws, issued money, and performed the other regular functions of government.

Bar-Kokhba's end came in 135. Jerusalem not being suitable to withstand a siege, he led the remnant of his army to the village of Bethar (the present Bittir), which is located on high ground about 10 miles southwest of Jerusalem, 25 miles from the Dead Sea and 35 miles from the Mediterranean. The dimensions of the ancient town were roughly rectanglar, with a north-south length of about 600 meters and an east-west width of about 200 meters. The south half of the town was fortified.[8] These dimensions plus the fact that the estimates for the Jewish population of Palestine of the time range from a low of 500,000 to a high of 2.5 million make it unlikely that Bar-Kokhba's Bethar army numbered as many as 50,000 men.[9]

The Romans laid siege to Bethar in the summer of 135 and Bar-Kokhba's resistance collapsed in August. The Romans broke into the fortress and Bar-Kokhba was killed in that final battle.

For general reasons it seems unlikely that the Romans carried out a massacre of the Jewish population of Bethar. The only "evidence" for a general massacre occurs in the Talmudic literature (including in this context the *Midrash Rabbah*) which for reasons unknown comments extensively on the siege of Bethar and its supposed aftermath. Except where noted, the Talmudic passages are reproduced in the Appendix to the book *Bar-Kokhba* by the archaeologist Yigael Yadin. The size of Bar-Kokhba's Bethar army is given as 200,000 men. Bar-Kokhba is said to have been so tough that, when the Romans catapulted missiles into his fort, he would intercept the missiles with his knee with such force that he would knock them back into the faces of the astonished Romans, killing many. The *Talmud* goes on to claim that the number of Jews killed by the Romans after the fortress fell was 4 billion "or as some say" 40 million, while the *Midrash Rabbah* reports 800 million martyred Jews. In order to reassure us that these figures are given in earnest, the necessarily accompanying events are set forth. The blood of the slain Jews reached to the nostrils of the Romans' horses and then, like a tidal wave, plunged a distance of one mile or four miles to the sea, carrying large boulders along with it, and staining the sea a distance of four miles out.

The Jewish school children of Bethar, according to the Talmudic literature, were of course not spared by the Romans, who are said to have wrapped each of them in his scroll, and then burned all of them, the number of these school children having been either 64 million or at least 150,000 (the approximate present public school population of Washington, D.C.).

The Romans matched the Germans in efficiency, for the bodies of the slain Jews were used to build a fence around Hadrian's vineyard, which is said to have been eighteen miles square, and blood saved over from the tidal wave was used to fertilize Roman vineyards for seven years. Shades of soap, glue and fertilizer factories!

It is also claimed that Bar-Kokhba (usually referred to in the Talmudic literature as Bar-Koziba – it is still not clear what his real name was) was killed by rabbis for falsely claiming to be the Messiah.[10]

The Talmudic literature was not intended for general circulation so its authors could exercise more freedom than the inventors of the six million hoax, who had to assess the gullibility of a possibly skeptical gentile audience. However the spirit of the Talmudic accounts, in the above instances, seems remarkably similar to the spirit of our century's hoax. In this connection it may be noted that it is not really anomalous that a Talmudic scholar such as Rabbi Weissmandel plays a possibly significant role in the hoax. Also, since Rabbi Wise translated a good deal of ancient and medieval Jewish literature and also founded a Jewish seminary, he may also have some claim to being a Talmudic scholar. One suspects that such scholars might have been exactly the type required to give birth to the hoax.

A remaining objection could raise the question of my credentials for writing such a book. This is a good point for it is true that my formal training has been in engineering and applied mathematics and not history.

It is not unprecedented for investigators to make contributions in fields apparently remote from their specialties, but I will concede that the point should not be waved aside lightly. Normally, we expect developments in historical investigation to come from historians, just as developments in engineering come from engineers. Exceptions to this rule can be admitted, but some justification for the exception should be expected.

My justification is the obvious one: default on the part of regular professional historians. No such person has come forward with a critical study of the question or with any work actually arguing any particular side of the extermination question and presenting the evidence which supports the thesis. The closest thing to such a work is the book by Reitlinger, who is at least willing to take explicit note of some of the anomalies that develop in presenting the story of the "holocaust", but Reitlinger is not a historian but an artist and art collector. He has written several books, the most significant being his three volume study of the history of dealings in objects of art, *The Economics of Taste*. After Reitlinger, Hilberg manages a tiny bit of a critical attitude, but Hilberg is a professor of political science (at the University of Vermont) and his doctorate is in public law and government.

The books by Reitlinger and Hilberg recognize, to a very inadequate but nevertheless perceptible degree, a responsibility to convince the skeptic. The other extermination mythologists do not make any effort whatever to show that the exterminations happened; they just assume we all know it happened and then they take it from there. This is the case with the remaining three of the five leading extermination mythologists – Nora Levin, Leon Poliakov and Lucy S. Dawidowicz. Levin was a research librarian while writing her book and now teaches history at Gratz College, a small Jewish school in Philadelphia. Poliakov is research director of the *Centre Mondiale de Documentation Juive Contemporaine* in Paris, and thus a professional Jewish propagandist. Dawidowicz is the only regular professional historian in the group and occupies the Leah Lewis Chair in Holocaust Studies at the Yeshiva University in New York. All five of the leading extermination mythologists are Jews.

In books and articles on subjects that are other than, but touch on, the "holocaust", professional historians invariably give some sort of endorsement to the lie, but the extent to which contrary hints are found in their writings is considerable. No professional historian has published a book arguing, and presenting evidence, either for or against the reality of the exterminations. The motivations are obvious. No established historian has been willing to damage his reputation by writing a scholarly-sounding work supporting the extermination allegations, solemnly referencing documents and testimonies produced at illegal trials held under hysterical conditions and seriously setting forth, without apology, obvious idiotic nonsense such as the alleged dual role of the Zyklon. At least, no inducement to produce such a work seems to have come along. On the other hand, the pressure of intellectual conformity (to put it mildly) in academia has evidently terrorized historians into silence in the opposite regard. This being the case, it is both justified and expected that works such as the present one be produced by engineers and whatever.

As promised early in this book, we have dealt here at depth with only one propaganda myth and have in no sense attempted to cover the general field of World War II revisionism. There is no point in repeating here what has been ably said by other authors who have contributed to demolishing lingering mythology relating to the war, but a few words, intended mainly to direct the reader to the appropriate literature, are in order.

The myth of Germany's solitary responsibility for the outbreak of war in 1939 has been demolished by the American historian David L. Hoggan. His book has appeared, however, only in German – *Der erzwungene Krieg.* A.J.P. Taylor's *The Origins of the Second World War* is not as extensive, but it has achieved a much greater circulation and has been available in paperback for some time. Taylor's well deserved reputation as a Germanophobe has made his book a notable addition to the revisionist literature.

The myth of extraordinary Nazi brutality, as compared to the brutalities of the Western democracies, has been exploded by a number of books, of which the best is F.J.P. Veale's *Advance to Barbarism,* of which a new and expanded edition appeared in 1968. Other noteworthy books are *Unconditional Hatred* by Captain Russell Grenfell, R.N., *America's Second Crusade* by William Henry Chamberlin, and Freda Utley's *The High Cost of Vengeance.* However these authors ignore one of the greatest crimes of the Western democracies, the forcible repatriation of Soviet citizens to the Soviet Union after the war ("Operation Keelhaul"). Most of what we know of this shameful episode is due to the efforts of Julius Epstein, a Jew who left Germany during the Thirties for the usual reasons, but started his crusades for truth during the war with his investigations into the Katyn Forest massacre and has spent the greater part of the postwar period investigating Operation Keelhaul. His book on the subject was published in 1973. Solzhenitsyn's *The Gulag Archipelago* offers a long discussion of Operation Keelhaul which, since it is written from a Russian point of view, supplements Epstein's treatment notably. Nicholas Bethell's *The Last Secret* explores the political background of the forced repatriations.

For a reader interested in a more thoroughgoing discussion of the revisionist literature, the best seems to appear in the testimonial volume *Harry Elmer Barnes*, edited by Arthur Goddard. The pamphlet by Barnes, *Blasting the Historical Blackout*, is a more intensive analysis of the status of World War II revisionism, and is still available.

None of the above named publications touch the gas chamber myth or deal in a serious way with whatever was supposed to have happened in the German concentration camps. Here we have treated the camps almost entirely from a single point of view and have not deeply investigated the factual basis of other allegations of brutalities of a more random and less systematic nature. However the Ilse Koch case, which was discussed in Chapter II, should be sufficiently instructive in distinguishing between fact and fiction, and the methods used at Dachau by the U.S. authorities to produce "evidence" of extraordinary brutalities should be conclusive.

The scandal of the continued imprisonment of Rudolf Hess, now over 81 years old, has been treated by a number of recent books, notably *Prisoner No. 7: Rudolf Hess*, by Eugene K. Bird, one of the U.S. commanders at Berlin's Spandau prison, who broke regulations by not only talking to Hess but also interviewing him in depth. Two other books are *Motive for a Mission*, by James Douglas-Hamilton, and *Hess: The Man and His Mission*, by J. Bernard Hutton.

In this book we have necessarily restricted ourselves to the demolition of only one myth, and have not attempted to treat the very broad subject of the general behavior of Nazi Germany as compared to the Allies, except by recommending the above publications. If they are read they will help support the major implication of this work; the media in the Western democracies are exposed as constituting a lie machine of vaster extent than even many of the more independent minded have perceived.

A second implication of this work naturally relates to Palestine. The "justification" that Zionists invariably give for driving the Arabs out of Palestine always involves the six million legend to a great extent. Of course there is more than one *non sequitur* involved; Palestine was not invaded by six million dead Jews or, indeed, by any dead Jews and, in any case, it is not just or reasonable to make the Arabs pay for whatever the Germans are supposed to have done to Jews in Europe during the Second World War. Moreover Israel is not a land that welcomes all persons who suffered in some way at the hands of the Nazis, but all Jews, regardless of whether they or their relatives had ever had any contact with the Nazis.

Today the United States supplies enough aid to Israel to assure that Israel is able to retain, by armed occupation, lands which the United States itself declares to be rightfully Arab (the territories seized in the 1967 war). Although it is hard to see why the six million legend should motivate such a policy, such a motivation or justification is very often advanced. When, in November 1975, an overwhelming majority at the United Nations, in a burst of intellectual clarity rare for that organization, endorsed a resolution declaring Zionism to be a form of racism (a truth as inescapable as 2+2=4) the U.S. representative, Daniel Patrick Moynihan, an otherwise impressive intellect, was reduced in astonishingly short order to hysterical yapping about the six million. As was shown by the aftermath of the "Yom Kippur War" of 1973, this support of Israel is completely contrary to the interests of the West. The obvious fact that this support is immoral in terms of the moralizing that has become a pervasive feature of Western foreign policies makes it doubly mad.

Another country that has extended considerable material aid to Israel is West Germany. As of 1975, the Bonn Government had paid Jews about $2 billion worth of restitutions and indemnifications of various sorts (calculated mainly in terms of dollars of the late Fifties and early Sixties), and was still making commitments for new payments.[11] The largest single such program was defined in the 1952 Luxembourg Treaty between the Federal Republic and Israel; Bonn committed itself to paying Israel $750 million, primarily in the form of German industrial products and oil shipments from Britain. The program, referred to in Israel as the *Shilumin* program, was completed in 1966. The text of the Luxembourg Treaty opens with the words[12]

Whereas
unspeakable criminal acts were perpetrated against the Jewish people during the National Socialist regime of terror
and whereas
by a declaration of the Bundestag on 27 September 1951, the Government of the Federal Republic of Germany made known their determination, within the limits of their capacity, to make good the material damage caused by these acts . . .

The Bonn Government has undertaken additional programs of indemnification which have been similarly motivated. Since this work has shown that the "unspeakable criminal acts", in the sense in which that expression is used in the Luxembourg Treaty, are largely a hoax and, specifically, a Zionist hoax, it then develops that Israel owes Germany a lot of money, since the proposed justification for the reparations has been invalidated.

APPENDIX A
THE "GERSTEIN STATEMENT"

The principal part of the statement is the document which was typewritten in French and whose English translation, as provided by the Nuernberg staff, is presented below (except for minor corrections):
Graduate engineer for Mine surveying
(Bergassessor Diplomingenieur)

Kurt Gerstein   Rottweil, 26 April 1945
　　　　　Personal particulars: Gerstein, Kurt, Mine Surveyor, expelled from State service in 1936 as an anti-Nazi; certified engineer. Born on 11 August 1905, at Muenster, Westphalia. Partner of the factory De Limon Fluhme & Company, automatic greasing of locomotives, brakes Westinghouse, Knorr, etc. Duesseldorf, Industriestrasse 1 – 17.
　　　　　Father: Ludwig Gerstein, President of the District Court (Landgerichtspraesident) at Hagen, Westphalia, retired.
　　　　　Mother: Clara Gerstein, nee Schmemann, died 1931.
　　　　　Married since 2 May 1937, to Elfriede nee Bensch at Tuebingen, Gartenstrasse 24, 3 children: Arnulf, 5 years old; Adelheid 3½ years old; Claf, 2 years old. Life: 1905 to 1911 Muenster, 1911 to 1919 Sarrebruck, 1919 to 1921 Halberstadt, 1921 to 1925 Neuruppin near Berlin, graduated from high school in 1925. – Studies 1925 to 1931, Marburg on the Lahn, Aachen, Berlin-Charlottenburg Universities and technical colleges, 1931, certified engineer's examination. Since 1925, active member of the Protestant youth organization the Y.M.C.A., and above all, of the Higher Christian Youth, called the "Bible Circle" (Bk, Bibelkreis). Political career: follower of Stresemann and Bruening, active on their behalf; since June 1933, persecuted by the Gestapo for Christian activities against the Nazi State. 2nd of May 1933, joined the NSDAP; 2 October 1936, expelled from the NSDAP because of activities against Party and State.
　　　　　30 January 1935, public protest in the theater of the town of Hagen in Westphalia, against the anti-Christian drama "Wittekind". Beaten and wounded by the Nazis. 27 November 1935, mining surveyor's examination (Bergassessor). Then employed by the State at Sarrebruck. On 27 September 1936, imprisoned by the Gestapo for "activities against the State" because of having sent 8,500 anti-Nazi pamphlets to high officials of the State. Imprisoned until the end of October 1936, released, was expelled from civil service. From December 1936 till the beginning of the war, medical studies at the Institute for the Protestant Medical Mission in the tropics, at Tuebingen. One-third – approximately – of income, that is one-third of 18,000 Reichsmarks per year, I donated since 1931 for my ideal religious goals. At my own expense, I had printed and mailed about 230,000 religious anti-Nazi pamphlets.
　　　　　14 July to 28 August 1938, second imprisonment, in the Welzheim concentration camp. Hearing of the massacres of idiots and insane people at Grafeneck, Hadamar, etc., shocked and deeply wounded, having such a case in my family, I had but one desire, to see, to gain an insight of this whole machine and then to shout about it to the whole world! With the help of two references written by the two Gestapo employees who had dealt with my case, it was not difficult for me to enter the Waffen SS. 10 March to 2 June 1941, elementary instruction as a soldier at Hamburg-Langehorn, Arnhem and Oranienburg, together with forty doctors. Because of my twin studies – technology and medicine – I was ordered to enter the medical-technology branch of the SS-Fuehrungshauptamt (SS Operational Main Office) – Medical Branch of the Waffen SS – Amtsgruppe D (Division D), Hygiene Department. Within this branch, I chose for myself the job of immediately constructing disinfecting apparati and filters for drinking water for the troops, the prison camps and the concentration camps. My close knowledge of the industry caused me to succeed quickly where my predecessors had failed. Thus,

251

it was possible to decrease considerably the death toll of prisoners. On account of my successes, I very soon became a Lieutenant. In December 1941, the tribunal which had decreed my exclusion from the NSDAP obtained knowledge of my having entered the Waffen SS. Considerable efforts were made in order to remove and persecute me. But due to my successes, I was declared sincere and indispensable. In January 1942, I was appointed Chief of the Technical Branch of Disinfection, which also included the branch for strong poison gases for disinfection. On 8 June 1942, the SS Sturmbannfuehrer Guenther of the RSHA entered my office. He was in plain clothes and I did not know him. He ordered me to get a hundred kilograms of prussic acid and to accompany him to a place which was only known to the driver of the truck. We left for the potassium factory near Colling (Prague). Once the truck was loaded, we left for Lublin (Poland). We took with us Professor Pfannenstiel MD., Ordinary Professor for Hygiene at the University of Marburg on the Lahn. At Lublin, we were received by SS Gruppenfuehrer Globocnik. He told us: this is one of the most secret matters there are, even the most secret. Whoever talks of this shall be shot immediately. Yesterday, two talkative ones died. Then he explained to us: at the present moment – 17 August 1942 – there are three installations:

1. Belcec, on the Lublin-Lemberg road, in the sector of the Russian demarcation line. Maximum 15,000 persons a day. (Seen!)
2. Sobibor, I do not know exactly where it is located. Not seen. 20,000 persons per day.
3. Treblinka, 120 km NNE of Warsaw. 25,000 persons per day. Seen!
4. Maidanek, near Lublin. Seen in the state of preparation.

Globocnik then said: You will have to handle the sterilization of very huge quantities of clothes, 10 or 20 times the result of the clothes and textile collection (Spinnstoffsammlung) which is only arranged in order to conceal the source of these Jewish, Polish, Czech and other clothes. Your other duties will be to change the method of our gas chambers (which are run at the present time with the exhaust gases of an old Diesel engine), employing more poisonous material, having a quicker effect, prussic acid. But the Fuehrer and Himmler, who were here on 15 August – the day before yesterday – ordered that I accompany personally all those who are to see the installations. Then Professor Pfannenstiel asked: "What does the Fuehrer say?" Then Globocnik, now Chief of Police and SS for the Adriatic Riviera to Trieste, answered: "Quicker, quicker, carry out the whole program!" he said. And then Dr. Herbert Lindner, Ministerialdirektor in the Ministry of the Interior said: "But would it not be better to burn the bodies instead of burying them? A coming generation might think differently of these matters!" And then Globocnik replied: "But, gentlemen, if ever, after us such a cowardly and rotten generation should arise that they do not understand our so good and necessary work, then, gentlemen, all National Socialism will have been for nothing. On the contrary, bronze plates should be buried with the inscription that it was we, who had the courage to achieve this gigantic task". And Hitler said: "Yes, my good Globocnik, that is the word, that is my opinion, too".

The next day we left for Belcek. A small special station of two platforms leans against a hill of yellow sand, immediately to the north of the road and railways: Lublin-Lemberg. To the South, near the road, some service houses with a signboard: "Belcek, service center of the Waffen SS". Globocnik introduced me to SS Hauptsturmfuehrer Overmayer from Pirmasens, who with great restraint showed me the installations. That day no dead were to be seen, but the smell of the whole region, even from the large road, was pestilential. Next to the small station there was a large barrack marked "Cloakroom" and a door marked "Valuables". Next a chamber with a hundred "barber" chairs. Then came a corridor, 150 meters long, in the open air and with barbed wire on both sides. There was a signboard: "To the bath and inhalations". Before us we saw a house like a bath house with concrete troughs to the right and left containing geraniums or other flowers. After climbing a small staircase, 3 garage-like rooms on each side, 4 x 5 meters large and 1.90 meters high. At the back, invisible wooden doors. On the roof a Star of David made out of copper. At the entrance to the building, the inscription: Heckenholt Foundation. That was all I noticed on that particular afternoon.

Next morning, a few minutes before 7, I was informed: In 10 minutes the first train will arrive. And instead, a few minutes later the first train came in from Lemberg. 45 cars, containing 6,700 persons, 1,450 of whom were already dead on their arrival. Behind the little barbed wire opening, children, yellow, scared half to death, women, men. The train arrives: 200 Ukranians, forced to do this work, open the doors, and drive all of the people out of the coaches with leather whips

Then, through a huge loudspeaker instructions are given: to undress completely, also to give up false teeth and glasses – some in the barracks, others right in the open air, to tie one's shoes together with a little piece of string handed everyone by a small Jewish boy of 4 years of age, hand in all valuables and money at the window marked "Valuables", without bond, without receipt. Then the women and girls go to the hairdresser, who cuts off their hair in one or two strokes, after which it vanishes into huge potatobags "to be used for special submarine equipment, door mats, etc.", as the SS Unterscharfuehrer on duty told me. Then the march begins: Right and left, barbed wire, behind, two dozen Ukranians with guns. Led by a young girl of striking beauty they approach. With police Captain Wirth, I stand right before the death chambers. Completely naked they march by, men, women, girls, babies, even one-legged persons, all of them naked. In one corner a strong SS man tells the poor devils, in a strong deep voice: "Nothing whatever will happen to you. All you have to do is to breathe deeply, it strengthens the lungs; this inhalation is a necessary measure against contagious diseases, it is a very good disinfectant!" Asked what was to become of them, he answered: "Well, of course, the men will have to work, building streets and houses. But the women do not have to. If they wish to, they can help in house or kitchen". Once more, a little bit of hope for some of these poor people, enough to make them march on without resistance to the death chambers. Most of them, though, know everything, the odor has given them a clear indication of their fate. And then they walk up the little staircase – and see the truth!

Mothers, nurse-maids, with babies at their breasts, naked, lots of children of all ages, naked too; they hesitate, but they enter the gas chambers, most of them without a word, pushed by the others behind them, chased by the whips of the SS men. A Jewess of about 40 years of age, with eyes like torches, calls down the blood of her children on the heads of their murderers. Five lashes into her face, dealt by the whip of Police Captain Wirth himself, chase her into the gas chamber. Many of them say their prayers, others ask: "Who will give us the water for our death?" (Jewish rite?). Within the chambers, the SS press the people closely together, Captain Wirth had ordered: "Fill them up full". Naked men stand on the feet of the others. 7-800 crushed together on 25 square meters, in 45 cubic meters! The doors are closed. Meanwhile the rest of the transport, all naked, wait. Somebody says to me: "Naked in winter! But they can die that way!" The answer was: "Well, that's just what they are here for!" And at that moment I understood why it was called "Heckenholt Foundation". Heckenholt was the man in charge of the Diesel engine, the exhaust gases of which were to kill these poor devils. SS Unterscharfuehrer Heckenholt tries to set the Diesel engine moving. But it does not start! Captain Wirth comes along. It is plain that he is afraid because I am a witness to this breakdown. Yes, indeed, I see everything and wait. Everything is registered by my stopwatch. 50 minutes, 70 minutes – the Diesel engine does not start! The people wait in their gas chambers. In vain. One can hear them cry. "Same as in a synagogue", says SS Sturmfuehrer Professor Dr. Pfannenstiel, Professor for Public Health at the University of Marburg/Lahn, holding his ear close to the wooden door. Captain Wirth, furious, deals the Ukranian who is helping Heckenholt 11 or 12 lashes in the face with his whip. After 2 hours and 49 minutes, as registered by my stopwatch, the Diesel engine starts. Up to that moment the people in the four already filled chambers were alive, 4 times 750 persons in 4 times 45 cubic meters. Another 25 minutes go by. Many of the people, it is true, are dead at that point. One can see this through the little window through which the electric lamp reveals, for a moment, the inside of the chamber. After 28 minutes only a few are living. After 32 minutes, finally, all are dead! From the other side, Jewish workers open the wooden doors. In return for their terrible job, they have been promised their freedom and a small percentage of the valuables and the money found. Like stone statues, the dead are still standing, there having been no room to fall or bend over. Though dead, the families can still be recognized, their hands still clasped. It is difficult to separate them in order to clear the chamber for the next load. The bodies are thrown out, blue, wet with sweat and urine, the legs covered with excrement and menstrual blood. Everywhere among the others, the bodies of babies and children. But there is not time! Two dozen workers are engaged in checking the mouths, opening them by means of iron hooks: "Gold to the left, without gold to the right!" Others check anus and genitals to look for money, diamonds, gold, etc. Dentists with chisels tear out the gold teeth, bridges or caps. In the center of everything, Captain Wirth. He is on familiar ground here. He hands me a large tin full of teeth and says: "Estimate for yourself the weight of gold. This is only from yesterday and the day before yesterday! And you would not believe what we find here every day!

Dollars, diamonds, gold! But look for yourself!" Then he led me to a jeweler who was in charge of all these valuables. After that they took me to one of the managers of the big Store of the West (Kaufhaus im Westen), in Berlin, and to a little man whom they made play the violin, both chiefs of the Jewish worker commands. "He is a captain of the royal and imperial (K.u.K.) Austrian Army, who held the German Iron Cross 1st Class", I was told by Hauptsturmfuehrer Obermeyer. The bodies were then thrown into large ditches of about 100 x 20 x 12 meters, located near the gas chambers. After a few days the bodies would swell up and the whole contents of the ditch would rise 2-3 meters high because of the gases that developed in the bodies. After a few more days swelling would stop and the bodies would collapse. The next day the ditches were filled again and covered with 10 centimeters of sand. A little later, I heard, they constructed grills out of rails and burned the bodies on them with Diesel oil and gasoline in order to make them disappear. At Belcek and Treblinka nobody bothered to take anything approaching an exact count of the persons killed. The figures announced by the BBC are inaccurate. Actually, about 25,000,000 persons were killed; not only Jews, however, but especially Poles and Czechoslovakians, too, who were, in the opinion of the Nazis, of bad stock. Most of them died anonymously. Commissions of so-called doctors, actually nothing but young SS men in white coats, rode in limousines through the towns and villages of Poland and Czechoslovakia to select the old, tubercular and sick people and to cause them to disappear shortly afterwards, in the gas chambers. They were the Poles and Czechs of (category) No. III, who did not deserve to live because they were unable to work. The Police Captain, Wirth, asked me not to propose any other kind of gas chamber in Berlin, to leave everything the way it was. I lied – as I did in each case all the time – that the prussic acid had already deteriorated in shipping and had become very dangerous, that I was therefore obliged to bury it. This was done right away.

The next day, Captain Wirth's car took us to Treblinka, about 75 miles NNE of Warsaw. The installations of this death center differed scarcely from those at Belcek, but they were still larger. There were 8 gas chambers and whole mountains of clothes and underwear about 35 – 40 meters high. Then, in our "Honor" a banquet was given, attended by all of the employees of the institution. The Obersturmbannfuehrer, Professor Pfannenstiel MD., Professor of Hygiene at the University of Marburg/Lahn, made a speech: "Your task is a great duty, a duty so useful and so necessary". To me alone he talked of this institution in terms of "beauty of the task, humane cause", and to all of them: "Looking at the bodies of these Jews one understands the greatness of your good work!" The dinner in itself was rather simple, but by order of Himmler the employees of this branch received as much as they wanted as far as butter, meat, alcohol, etc. were concerned. When we left we were offered several kilograms of butter and a large number of bottles of liqueur. I made the effort of lying, saying that I had enough of everything from our own farm, so Pfannenstiel took my portion, too.

We left for Warsaw by car. While I waited in vain for a vacant berth I met Baron von Otter, Secretary of the Swedish Legation. As all the beds were occupied we spent the night in the corridor of the sleeper. There, with the facts still fresh in my memory, I told him everything, asking him to report it to his government and to all the Allies. As he asked for a reference with regard to myself I gave him, as such, the address of the Superintendant General, Dr. Otto Dibelius, Berlin-Lichterfelde West, Bruederweg 2, a friend of Martin Niemoeller and chief of the Protestant resistance against Nazism. Some weeks later I met Baron von Otter twice again. He told me that he had sent a report to the Swedish Government, a report which, according to him, had a strong influence on the relations between Sweden and Germany. I was not very successful in my attempt to report everything to the chief of the Vatican Legation. I was asked whether I was a soldier, and then was refused an interview. I then sent a detailed report to Dr. Winter, secretary of the Berlin Episcopate, in order to have him pass it on to the bishop of Berlin and through him to the Vatican Legation. When I came out of the Vatican Legation in the Rauchstrasse in Berlin I had a very dangerous encounter with a police agent who followed me. However, after some very unpleasant moments I succeeded in giving him the slip.

I have to add, furthermore, that in the beginning of 1944, SS Sturmbann-fuehrer Guenther of the RSHA asked me for very large supplies of prussic acid for obscure use. The acid was to be delivered to his business office in Berlin, Kurfuerstenstrasse. I succeeded in making him believe that this was impossible because there was too much danger involved. It was a question of several carloads of poisonous acid, enough to kill a large number of persons, actually millions! He had told me he was not sure whether, when, for what kind of persons, how and where this poison was needed. I do not know exactly what were the intentions of the RSHA and the SD. But later on, I thought of the words of Goebbels of "slamming the door behind them" should Nazism never succeed. Maybe they wanted to kill a large part of the German people, maybe the foreign workers, maybe the prisoners of war – I do not know! Anyhow, I caused the poison to disappear for disinfection purposes, as soon as it came in. There was some danger for me in this, but if I had been asked where the poisonous acid was, I would have answered that it was already in a state of dangerous deterioration and that therefore I had to use it up as disinfectant! I am sure that Guenther, the son of the Guenther of the Racial Theory, had, according to his own words, orders to secure the acid for the – eventual – extermination of millions of human beings, perhaps also in concentration camps. I have here bills for 2,175 kgs, but, actually about 8,500 kgs are involved; enough to kill 8 million people. I had the bills sent to me in my name; I said this was for reasons of secrecy; however, I did this in order to be somewhat free in my decisions and to have a better possibility of making the poisonous acid disappear. I never paid for these shipments in order to avoid refunding, which would have reminded the SD of these stocks. The director of Degesch, who had made these shipments, told me that he had shipped prussic acid in ampules for the purpose of killing human beings. On another occasion Guenther consulted me about the possibility of killing a large number of Jews in the open air in the fortification trenches of Maria-Theresienstadt. In order to prevent the execution of this diabolic proposal, I declared that this method was impracticable. Some time later I heard that the SD had secured, through other channels, the prussic acid to kill these unfortunate people at Therensienstadt. The most disgusting camps were not Oranienburg, Dachau, or Belsen, but Auschwitz (Oswice) and Mauthausen-Gusen near Linz/Danube. These are the places in which millions of people disappeared in gas chambers or gas chamber-like cars. The method of killing the children was to hold a tampon with prussic acid under their nose.

I myself witnessed experiments on living persons in concentration camps being continued until the victim died. Thus, in the concentration camp for women, Ravensbrueck near Fuerstenberg-Mecklenburg, SS Hautpsturmfuehrer Grundlach MD. made such experiments. In my ffice, I read many reports of experiments made at Buchenwald, such as the administration of up to 100 tablets of Pervitine per day. Other experiments – every time on about 100 – 200 persons – were made with serums and lymph, etc., till the death of the person. Himmler personally had reserved for himself the granting of permission to conduct these experiments.

At Oranienburg, I saw how all the prisoners who were there for being perverts (homosexuals) disappeared in one single day.

I avoided frequent visits to the concentration camps because it was customary, especially at Mauthausen-Gusen near Linz-Danube, to hang one or two prisoners in honor of the visitors. At Mauthausen it was customary to make Jewish workers work in a quarry at great altitude. After a while the SS on duty would say: "Pay attention, in a couple of minutes there will be an accident". And, indeed, one or two minutes later, some Jews were thrown from the cliff and fell dead at our feet. "Work accident" was written in the files of the dead. Dr. Fritz Krantz, an anti-Nazi SS Hauptsturmfuehrer, often told me of such events. He condemned them severely and often published facts about them. The crimes discovered at Belsen, Oranienburg, etc., are not considerable in comparison with the others committed at Auschwitz and Mauthausen. I plan to write a book about my adventures with the Nazis. I am ready to swear to the absolute truth of all my statements.

(signed by hand:) Kurt Gerstein

It is difficult to believe that anybody intended that this "statement" be taken seriously. A few specific points are examined here but, on the whole, I leave the reader to marvel at it. The part printed in the NMT volumes starts as "Hearing of the massacres . . . " and ends at "one understands the greatness of your good work!" However the remark about the BBC and the 25 million gas chamber victims is deleted. The version used by Eichmann's Jerusalem tribunal was far more drastically edited.[1]

In this book it has been the practice not to give SS ranks since these would not be understood by most readers; an *Oberscharfuehrer* sounds just as important as an *Obergruppenfuehrer*. Approximate U.S. Army equivalents have been used instead. However in presenting the Gerstein statement this practice has not been adhered to on account of the confusion in the rank of Prof. Pfannenstiel (another Nazi who acquired a mysterious immunity from prosecution), who is identified at one point as an "Obersturmbannfuehrer" (Lieutenant Colonel) and at another as a "Sturmfuehrer"

(Lieutenant; the ranks of *Untersturmfuehrer* and *Obersturmfuehrer* were equivalent to the U.S. Army ranks of Second and First Lieutenant, respectively; SS ranks are explained in Appendix B). It is scarcely likely that Gerstein would have made such an error if he had written out this "statement" voluntarily.

Another obvious internal contradiction, illustrating the carelessness with which this document was composed, is in referring to events which took place in August as having taken place "in winter". It also may seem impossible to squeeze 700 or 800 people into a chamber 20 or 25 meters square and 1.9 meters high, but it is feasible if one uses a scrap press, but in that case the victims would be literally, just as the document asserts, "crushed" and gassing would be quite superfluous.

The reference to leaving for Warsaw by car and then meeting Baron von Otter on the train is reproduced here just as it is in the document, of course. No confirmation of the Gerstein-Otter meetings came from any Swedish source during the war, i.e., before the document was created, and it is not clear whether or not one came after the war.[2]

As Rassinier has put it, if it is not true that Hitler ever visited Lublin, if it is not true that 700 to 800 people can be contained in a gas chamber of 25 square meters, if it is not true that August occurs in winter in Europe, and if it is not true that the Germans gassed 25 million people then, since the document contains little else, we should ask what does it contain that is true?

What was presented above is what would normally be considered the "Gerstein statement" but the statements allegedly (according to document 1553-PS) deposited by Gerstein in various languages in the spring of 1945 actually continue:

Kurt Gerstein, additional statement.

In my flat in Berlin W 35, Buelowstrasse 47, second floor, left, I was surrounded by a circle of anti-Nazis. Here are some of their names:
Major Lutz Reis, now at Hamburg, Glasurit-Works.
Dr. Felix Buss, chief legal counsel to Telefunken, Berlin, SW 11, Hallesches Ufer 30.
Director Alex Menne, Hamburg, Glasurit-Works.
Pastor Buchholz, chaplain of the Pleetzensee prison, who accompanied the officers of July 20, 1944 to the scaffold. These officers as well as my good friend, Pastor Martin Niemoeller, smoked the cigarettes and cigars I got into the prison for them.
Pastor Mochalsky, who replaced Pastor Martin Niemoeller at the Annon Church at Dahlem.
Dorothea Schulz, secretary of Pastor Niemoeller.
Mrs. Arndt, secretary of Pastor Martin Niemoeller at Dachau.
Emil Nieuwenhuizen and his friend Hendrik, from Phillips-Eyndhoven,
deportees whom I had met at Church and who, for a long time already were my guests twice or three times a week. They had meals at my place, and listened to the wireless.
Director Haueisen, Berlin NW 7, Mittelstrasse, Francke printing works.
Herbert Scharkowsky, editor, Scherl-press.
Captain Nebelthau and his wife, now at Kirchentellinsfurth-Wuerttemberg.
Dr. Hermann Ehlers, trustee of the Niemoeller anti-Nazi resistance Church.
Dr. Ebbe Elss, same as Dr. Ehlers.
Other references: General Superintendant Dr. Otto Dibelius, chief of the Church resistance against Nazism.
Pastor Rehling, Hagen-Westphalia, active in the Westphalia Church anti-Nazi resistance movement.
Praeses Dr. Koch, anti-Nazi professor of the University of Tuebingen.
Bernhard J. Goedecker, producer, Munich, Tizianstrasse, anti-Nazi.
Director Franz Baeuerle, Munich, Siemensstrasse 17, anti-Nazi.
The Catholic Priest, Valpertz, Hagen-Westphalia.
Pastor Otto Wehr, Sarrebruck.
Pastors Schlaeger and Bittkau, Neuruppin near Berlin.
August Franz and his entire family, great anti-Nazi, Sarrebruck, now at Thalheim-Wuerttemberg.
Doctor Straub, Metzingen-Wuerttemberg, and family.

(unsigned)

I have no idea what connection, if any, Gerstein actually had with this document. He might have, at the command of his captors, cooperated in its manufacture, or he may have had nothing to do with it. It may be possible to decide on the basis of the (presumably handwritten) signature in the first part and the handwritten statement reproduced below, but the question scarcely seems worth investigation.

A German version of the "Gerstein statement", of essentially the same content, was produced about a year after Gerstein's disappearance. His wife said that Gerstein had,

nknown to her at the time, deposited it among their belongings at the Hotel Mohren in
.ottweil. Frau Gerstein's discovery of such a document in the dark days of 1946
naturally buttressed her status as the wife of Saint Gerstein rather than the wife of
rdinary SS officer Gerstein, an enviable position for a German at the time.

The German version of the "Gerstein statement" is typewritten and unsigned, but
nere is said to be a handwritten postscript of unspecified content. For reasons unex-
lained, Gerstein is said to have included in the German version ten pages of "statements
rom hearsay" that were not included in the material he originally supposedly handed
ver to the U.S. investigators before he disappeared.

Several years later Otto Dibelius, Lutheran Bishop of Berlin, declared that
erstein and Baron von Otter had indeed communicated with him on these matters.
lthough Dibelius had been a leading member of Hugenberg's Nazi linked DNVP before
933, he became associated with the Niemoeller led church opposition to the Nazis after
933. Niemoeller was incarcerated in 1935, but Dibelius was allowed to go free and then
e vanished into the obscurity of a minor post in a church welfare organization, being
nade Bishop after the war ended in 1945. It is not correct to characterize Dibelius as an
ctive member of the wartime resistance, as the "Gerstein statement" and the above
upplement do, thereby inflating his significance well beyond what the facts warrant.[3]

As for the other names on "Gerstein's" list of "anti-Nazis", with the exception of
liemoeller I recognize none in connection with any known wartime activities, anti-Nazi
r otherwise. Only one I recognize in any connection: Dr. Hermann Ehlers, who became
leading CDU politician after the war, and who died in 1954. It may be that the person
lentified as "Praeses Dr. Koch" is supposed to be Dr. Karl Koch, a Protestant theo-
ogian who was a member, along with Dibelius, of the DNVP in the Weimar days, and
rho died in 1951.

In the relevant reports of Cesare Orsenigo, the Papal Nuncio in Berlin, that have
een published by the Vatican, there is of course no reference to Gerstein. See Appendix

The next part of document 1553-PS is a letter to Gerstein from DEGESCH regard-
ng the preservability of the Zyklon and the possibilities for future shipments in the face
f bombing attacks which had destroyed a plant. The letter would be worth reproducing
ere only if it, too, were in French (it is in German). The next part of the document is a
nort handwritten note:

According to the annexed notes, the prussic acid was requested by the RSHA,
Berlin W 35, Kurfuerstendamm, by order of SS Sturmbannfuehrer Guenther. I
was in charge of this particular job and I performed my duties very faithfully, so
that once the acid had arrived at Oranienburg and Auschwitz, I could have the
boxes disappear into the disinfection rooms. Thus it was possible to prevent a mis-
use of the acid. In order to avoid drawing the attention of the RSHA to the
presence – or, as I should say, to the absence – of these stocks, I never paid for
these shipments, the bills for which went to the same address, that is, my own. In
this manner, it was possible to have the acid disappear as soon as it had arrived. If
the absence of the acid had been noticed I would have answered: It is a mistake
made by the local disinfection office which did not know, and should not have
known, either, the real destination; or I would have said: The acid had become
putrefied and it was impossible to keep it any longer.

(signed:) Gerstein

The final part of the statement is the note in English:

Bergassessor a.D.   Domicil permanent:
Kurt Gerstein   Tuebingen/Neckar, Gartenstr. 24
Diplomingenieur   26 April 1945
My report is intressant for Secret Service. The Things, I have seen, no more than
4–5 others have seen, and these others were Nazies. Many of responsables of
Belsen, Buchenwald, Maidoneck, Oscrice, Mauthausen, Dachau, etc. were men of
my service, daily I have seen them in my double position.
1) SS Fuehrungs-Hauptamt, D, Sanitary-service and
2) Reichsarzt SS and Polizei, Berlin.
I am in a situation to say the names and crimes of in reality responsables of this
things, and I am ready to give the material for this accusation in World-Tribunal.
Myself, cordial friend of reverend Martin Niemoeller and his family (now at
Leoni/Starnberger See/Bavaria) I was after two prisons and concentration-camp
agent of "confessional-church", SS-Obersturmfueurer and compartment-chief in
SS-Fuehrungshauptamt and of Reicharzt SS and Polizei, a dangerous position!
The things I have seen nobody has seen. 1942 August, I have made my reports for
Svenska legation in Berlin, I am ready and in situation to say all my observations
to your Secret-Service.
The secretary of Svenska legation Berlin, now at Stockholm Baron von Otter is

ready to be wittnes of my relation of 1942 of all this coneltys — I propose demand for me this informations.

Reference: Msr. Niemoeller

(reverend Martin Niemoeller's woman
Leoni/Starnberger See/Muenchen Bavaria
(signed:) Gerstei

Nota: Your army has not find
Mr. Niemoeller
Mr. Stalin junior
Mr. Schuschnigg
    at Dachau.

They are deported, nobody know, who they are. Please do not publish my repo bevore exactement now: Niemoeller is liberated or dead.

Gerstei

The remainder of document 1553-PS is the collection of Zyklon invoices. Through out the "Gerstein statement" I have made minor corrections, except that the last par the note in "English", is reproduced exactly as it stands, for obvious reasons; clearly, i was composed by a person who knew something of the French language. "Mr. Stali junior" is no doubt a reference to Stalin's son, who was a POW in Germany. Schuschnig was the Austrian Chancellor at the time of the *Anschluss*; he and Niemoeller had bee detained at Dachau for some time. Rassinier has provided an interesting discussion o Niemoeller.[4]

APPENDIX B
SS RANKS

The SS ranks and their approximate U.S. Army equivalents are as follows:

U.S. Army	SS
Private	SS Mann
Private First Class	Sturmmann
Corporal	Rottenfuehrer
Sergeant	Unterscharfuehrer
Staff Sergeant	Scharfuehrer
Technical Sergeant	Oberscharfuehrer
Master Sergeant	Hauptscharfuehrer
First Sergeant	Sturmscharfuehrer
Second Lieutenant	Untersturmfuehrer
First Lieutenant	Obersturmfuehrer
Captain	Hauptsturmfuehrer
Major	Sturmbannfuehrer
Lieutenant Colonel	Obersturmbannfuehrer
Colonel	Standartenfuehrer
Colonel	Oberfuehrer
Brigadier General	Brigadefuehrer
Leiutenant General	Gruppenfuehrer
General	Obergruppenfuehrer
General of the Army	Oberstgruppenfuehrer

One can exercise a certain amount of choice on this subject. The three grades of *Gruppenfuehrer* are sometimes equated with Major General, Lieutenant General and General, respectively. An *Oberfuehrer* is sometimes described as a "Senior Colonel" or a Brigadier General; in the latter case a *Brigadefuehrer* is equated with a Major General.

These ranks had their origin in the early days when the SS was something of an offshoot of the SA, which had similar ranks.

APPENDIX C
DEPORTATION OF JEWS

The six booklets which are the Netherlands Red Cross report entitled *Auschwitz* are actually about the approximately 100 transports of Jews which left the Netherlands, the first leaving on 15 July 1942 and the last on 13 September 1944. Auschwitz was the immediate destination of about two-thirds of the deported Jews, although large numbers were also sent to Sobibor, and some were sent to Theresienstadt, Bergen-Belsen and Ravensbrueck.The Netherlands Red Cross (NRC) data is exhaustive in regard to all matters pertaining to the transports while they were in the Netherlands; the dates of departure, the destinations of the transports, and the numbers of people in each transport, with breakdowns of the numbers according to sex and age. The authors assume that all Jews whom they are unable to account for, after the Jews reached their immediate destination, were gassed or perished in some other manner. Thus they conclude that a majority of the approximately 100,000 Jews deported from the Netherlands perished, since, obviously, their study is very short on data regarding what happened at the camps when these people reached them. There are, however, exceptions to this statement; there is data regarding the evacuation of Auschwitz in 1945 and there are other bits, e.g., data from the Monowitz hospital. The most significant data, however, is what is said to be the registration and death record from the Birkenau men's camp for the period 16 July to 19 August 1942, which is presented in volume two of the report. Since the NRC also provides detailed data regarding the Jewish transports from Westerbork (transit camp in the Netherlands) during this period, a comparison can be made, and the comparison (as Reitlinger admits) contradicts the claim that a majority, or even a significant number, of the Jews were immediately gassed on arrival at Auschwitz. There were thirteen transports from Westerbork in July and August, 1942, and they were composed as follows:

Date of deportation	Total deported	Total men	Men 0–12 years	Men 13–15 years	Men 16–17 years	Men 18–35 years	Men 36–50 years	Men 51–60 years	Men 61+ years
15.7	1135	663	41	9	85	356	157	11	4
16.7	895	640	32	7	41	285	193	62	20
21.7	931	511	62	14	54	317	61	2	1
24.7	1000	573	51	6	83	340	75	11	7
27.7	1010	542	60	17	90	315	55	4	1
31.7	1007	540	47	13	93	326	56	5	
3.8	1013	520	72	21	31	255	139	1	1
7.8	987	510	67	28	21	172	168	48	6
10.8	559	288	18	8	19	93	97	45	8
14.8	505	238	43	14	5	36	68	72	
17.8	506	364	36	8	11	247	60	2	
21.8	1008	493	56	12	49	269	97	9	1
24.8	519	351	26	5	19	192	78	23	8
Total	11075	6233	611	162	601	3203	1304	295	57

Total women	Women 0–12 years	Women 13–15 years	Women 16–17 years	Women 18–35 years	Women 36–50 years	Women 51–60 years	Women 61+ years	Women with children to 15 years
472	36	3	38	318	74	3		63
255	28	6	27	161	32		1	42
420	53	8	36	268	54	1		83
427	52	3	42	273	51	6		75
468	55	13	50	291	55	4		85
467	65	10	51	296	44	1		81
493	85	17	29	232	129	1		104
477	74	21	26	167	175	13	1	96
271	19	8	12	99	109	23	1	35
267	53	19	3	43	100	49		52
142	18	6	12	49	53	4		26
515	58	16	36	253	132	19	1	85
168	26	8	6	63	39	18	8	39
4842	622	138	368	2513	1047	142	12	866

The data said to be from the Birkenau men's camp is now presented, in order to be compared with the preceding Westerbork data. Column 1, below, gives the dates and times (morning, M, and evening, E) of the roll-calls at Birkenau, column 2 gives the total number counted in the roll call, column 3 gives the number who died between roll-calls, column 4 gives the number of new arrivals registered between roll-calls, and column 5 gives the number lost between roll-calls on account of release or escape. In column 6 are comments on the origins of the various transports to the camps, and the transports from Westerbork are indicated. Pithiviers, Drancy and Beaune la Rolande were assembly points in France for Jewish transports and Mechelen had the same function in Belgium. The transports from Slovakia were probably Jewish transports, but the composition of those from Poland is rather problematical. Where "various nationalities" (var. nat.) are indicated, the transports were most probably composed predominantly of political prisoners and ordinary criminals. Column 7 gives registration numbers assigned to the people indicated in column 4.

(1)	(2)	(3)	(4)	(5)	(6)	(7)
		40	22			
M 16.7.42	16246					
		100	131			
E 16.7.42	16277					
		30	601		Westerbork 15.7.42	47087-47687
M 17.7.42	16848					
		83	185		var. nat.	47688-47842
E 17.7.42	16950					
		25	977		Westerbork 16.7.42	47843-48493
					Slovakia	48494-48819
M 18.7.42	17902					
		101	46	1]	var. nat.	48820-48901
E 18.7.42	17846					
		18	24	]		
M 19.7.42	17852					
		82				
E 19.7.42	17770					
		53	809		Pithiviers 17.7.42	48902-49670
M 20.7.42	18526					
		122	74]			
E 20.7.42	18478					
		28	]		var. nat.	49671-49795
M 21.7.42	18450					
		110	21]			
E 21.7.42	18361					
		18	620]		Pithiviers 19.7.42	49796-50270
M 22.7.42	18963				var. nat.	50271-50405
		125	9]			
E 22.7.42	18847					
		14	479		Westerbork 21.7.42	50406-50884
M 23.7.42	19312					
		127	134		Poland	50885-51002
E 23.7.42	19319					
		13	411		Drancy 20.7.42	51003-51413
M 24.7.42	19717					
		173	91		Poland etc., etc.	51414-51503
E 24.7.42	19635					
		11	791		Drancy 22.7.42	51504-52102
					var. nat.	52103-52115
M 25.7.42	20415					
		208	73	2	Slovakia	52116-52332
					var. nat.	52333-52367
E 25.7.42	20278					
		26	515		Westerbork 24.7.42	52368-52882
M 26.7.42	20767					
		71				
E 26.7.42	20696					
		28	370		Pithiviers 24.7.42	52883-53252
M 27.7.42	21038					
		167	69	1]		
E 27.7.42	20939					
		24		1]	var. nat.	53253-53325
M 28.7.42	20914					
		205	4	]		
E 28.7.42	20713					

(1)	(2)	(3)	(4)	(5)	(6)	(7)
		23	473		--- Westerbork 27.7.42	53326-53790
M 29.7.42	21163					
		100		31 <--- var. nat.	53791-53829
E 29.7.42	21094					
		16	249		Pithiviers 27.7.42	53830-54078
M 30.7.42	21327					
		91				
E 30.7.42	21236					
		16				
M 31.7.42	21220					
		113		76	var. nat.	54079-54154
E 31.7.42	21183					
		32	270		Pithiviers 29.7.42	54155-54424
M 1.8.42	21421					
		98		166	Slovakia	54425-54590
E 1.8.42	21489					
		31	495		Westerbork 31.7.42	54591-55071
					var. nat.	55072-55085
M 2.8.42	21953					
		71				
E 2.8.42	21882					
		41	693		Pithiviers 31.7.42	55086-55778
M 3.8.42	22534					
		107		51]		
E 3.8.42	22478					
		35		]	var. nat.	55779-55840
M 4.8.42	22443					
		100		11]		
E 4.8.42	22354					
		38	480		var. nat.	55841-55907
					Westerbork 3.8.42	55908-56334
		82		67	var. nat.	56335-56387
M 5.8.42	22796					
E 5.8.42	22781					
		44		22	var. nat.	56388-56409
M 6.8.42	22759					
		78	446		Mechelen 4.8.42	56410-56855
E 6.8.42	23127					
		48				
M 7.8.42	23079					
		93		79 <--- var. nat.	56856-56991
E 7.8.42	23065					
		55	373		---> Beaune la Rolande 5.8.42	56992-57308
M 8.8.42	23383					
		121		91	var. nat.?	57309-57399
E 8.8.42	23353					
		70	315		Westerbork 7.8.42	57400-57714
M 9.8.42	23598					
		98				
E 9.8.42	23500					
		80		63	var. nat.	57715-57777
M 10.8.42	23483					
		219		128	Pithiviers 7.8.42	57778-57905
E 10.8.42	23392					
		56				
M 11.8.42	23336					
		232		5	var. nat.	57906-57910
E 11.8.42	23109					
		69		164	Westerbork 10.8.42	57911-58074
M 12.8.42	23204					
		205		11	var. nat.	58075-58085
E 12.8.42	23010					
		44		140	Drancy 10.8.42?	58086-58225
M 13.8.42	23106					
		213		306	Mechelen 11.8.42?	58226-58531
E 13.8.42	23199					
		111				

262

	(1)	(2)	(3)	(4)	(5)	(6)	(7)
M	14.8.42	23088					
			206	102		????	58532-58633
E	14.8.42	22984					
			63	152		Drancy 12.8.42	58634-58785
M	15.8.42	23073					
			177	270		????	58786-59055
E	15.8.42	23166					
			109	165		Westerbork 14.8.42	59056-59220
M	16.8.42	23222					
			134	9		var. nat.	59221-59229
E	16.8.42	23097					
			127	115		Drancy 14.8.42?	59230-59344
M	17.8.42	23085					
			157	255		Mechelen 15.8.42	59345-59599
E	17.8.42	23183					
			92	5		var. nat.	59600-59604
M	18.8.42	23096					
			390	87		var. nat.	59605-59691
E	18.8.42	23112			319		Westerbork 17.8.42	59692-60010
M	19.8.42	23112					
			220	33		var. nat.	60011-60043
E	19.8.42	22925					
Totals			6507	13173	5		

To give an example of interpretation of these figures, we see that between the evening of 16 July and the morning of 17 July 1942, the Westerbork transport of 15 July arrived at Auschwitz, and that 601 men from this transport were registered in the Birkenau men's camp and assigned registration numbers 47087-47687. During this period 30 men also died in the camp, so the net change in the roll-call figure is 601-30 = 16848-16277 = 571. Note that the 601 men from the Westerbork transport of 15 July are approximately the total men that started out on that transport if one subtracts boys through 15 years of age. Since the table of Westerbork deportations has a separate column for "Women with children to 15 years", it is most probable that such children went with the women.

We have taken the liberty of making two corrections of obvious errors in the Birkenau men's camp data. The NRC report specifies that 43 died between the evening of 5 August and 6 August, but a figure of 44 deaths brings agreement with the roll-call figures and the total of column 3. Also, the NRC report specifies that the Mechelen transport of 15 August received registration numbers 59345-59699, an obvious error which has been corrected.

The increments in registration numbers in column 7 do not agree in all cases with the numbers reported in column 4. Indeed, this is the case with the majority of transports which arrived between 17 July and 24 July, and it is also true of the transports which received registration numbers 56856-57308. However, in all other cases the registration numbers in column 7 agree with the figures in column 4.

When boys through 15 years of age are subtracted from the total of men in the various deportations from Westerbork, the resulting figures are in good general agreement with the numbers reported registered in the Birkenau men's camp although, for reasons that one can probably guess, the agreement is not perfect. There were probably small numbers who either joined the incoming transports, and are not listed as such, and also numbers who were not accepted into Birkenau for various reasons and sent to another destination. The largest unaccounted differences are in connection with the Westerbork transports of 7 August and 10 August, where about 100 men are missing in each case in the registration at Birkenau.

This data, plus the one volume of the Birkenau Death Book (which is also discussed in vol. 1 of the NRC reports, except that it is referred to as the Auschwitz Death Book there), confirm the WRB report claim that there was a great epidemic at Auschwitz in the summer of 1942, forcing work there to stop. We know of no data covering a substantially later period which reports comparably high death rates at Auschwitz although, as explained in the text, the death rate there was always deplorably high from 1942 on.

APPENDIX D
THE BELSEN TRIAL

Josef Kramer's two statements as they appear in Fyfe, ed., *The Belsen Trial*

STATEMENT OF JOSEF KRAMER

I was born on 10th November, 1906, at Munich. I am married and have three children. I volunteered for the S.S. in 1932; I had no training whatsoever and was detailed for duty in a concentration camp. I did not volunteer for this specific kind of duty. When war broke out the S.S. was taken over by the Army and I volunteered for active service, as I would have preferred a fighting job, but I was told that I would have to do the job for which I was detailed. My first rank was Unterscharführer and my promotion to Scharführer and Oberscharführer was in 1934 and 1935. I cannot remember the dates.

Dachau. In 1936 I was in the office of the concentration camp at Dachau. The Kommandant of that camp was Standartenführer Loritz. There were only German prisoners in the camp. I cannot be absolutely certain, but as far as I can remember, they were all German. The S.S. Unit was Wachttruppe, Ober-Bayern. There were only political prisoners, criminals and anti-socials in this camp. Anti-socials are people like beggars and gypsies and people who do not want to work. No death sentences were carried out in the camp. The only cases in which people were killed was when they were trying to escape, in which case the guard had orders to shoot. In the case of any shootings, whilst prisoners were trying to escape, investigations were made by the Police. I left this camp at the beginning of June, 1937.

Sachsenhausen. From Dachau I went to Sachsenhausen Concentration Camp. I had been promoted to commissioned rank, outside the establishment, to Untersturmführer. When I went to Sachsenhausen I was on the establishment there. The prisoners at Sachsenhausen consisted of the same three types as at the previous camp. The Kommandant of the camp was Standartenführer Baranowsky. There were no death sentences carried out in this camp. I was in charge of the mail department and therefore did not know everything that was going on, but have heard occasionally that people have been shot while trying to escape.

Mauthausen. My next concentration camp was Mauthausen in Austria. This camp was just being built when I arrived. The Kommandant was Standartenführer Ziereis. Here I had the same rank as before. Whilst in this camp I was promoted to Obersturmführer. I think this was in January, 1939. I was a sort of adjutant in charge of the office and at the disposal of the Kommandant. The prisoners were all Germans and of the same three types as I have described before. The last type, *i.e.* rogues and vagabonds, were mainly Austrians, as there seemed to have been many when Austria was taken over by Germany. There were between 1500 and 2000 prisoners and they were all men. This includes Jewish prisoners. There was sufficient room in the camp for all prisoners when I was there. None of the prisoners knew at the time they arrived when they were going to leave. There were only a few who had a sentence like three months or six months, and the biggest part of the prisoners were there for an undefined period. Solitary confinement and solitary confinement with bread and water, or extra work on Sundays, were the sentences awarded for breaches of discipline. The prisoners were never beaten, nor do I know of any case of shooting. There were prison-breaks, but I was never present when somebody tried to escape. I was in the office and the telephone would ring and one of the guards would report that one of the prisoners had tried to escape. It was my duty then to go out and see where the prisoner worked and how it was possible for him to escape. We then notified the police and gave particulars of the person who had escaped. The instructions were that no prisoners had to go beyond a certain border-line. If a prisoner did, the guard had to challenge him three times with the words, "Halt, or I shoot", then first fire a shot in the air and only the second shot to kill. It is difficult to say how many shootings of this kind took place whilst I was at the camp because it is such a long time ago. I think that 10 to 15 people were shot, but I cannot say exactly. Every case of shooting had to be reported to the authorities at Mauthausen and at Linz. The nearest big town carried out an investigation. If someone was shot at, or shot whilst escaping, the guard was immediately put under a sort of open arrest, but none was ever convicted of wrongful shooting. Most of the people who were shot in this manner were criminals or vagabonds, the reason being that the larger part of the inmates of the camp belonged to that category.

The deaths that occurred were mostly from natural causes. When somebody died his relatives and the authorities, who had sent him to the concentration camp, had to be notified. There was one very severe winter when the deaths rose, but otherwise there were very few deaths. The prisoners were kept in wooden huts with three-tier beds, 250 to 300 in a hut. Whilst I was at this camp, Obergruppenführer Eike, who was in charge of all concentration camps, visited the camp three or four times, but I cannot remember the dates. There were no war prisoners in this camp. A few more political prisoners came in, but there were no great increases. Their nationality was mostly Austrian. There was no member of the former Austrian Government or of Schusnigg's Party either in Dachau or Mauthausen. I was in charge of the office and I dealt with the incoming and the outgoing mail on behalf of the Kommandant. I would read the mail to him and he would give me his orders, which I would pass on to the various sub-commanders. The powers of the Kommandant, with regard to punishment of prisoners, were not exactly laid down, but I think he could give up to 21 days. He was the only one who had disciplinary powers. I do not know the number of prisoners when I left in 1940, but the camp was full. The strength was recorded every day, but I cannot remember now what the number was. Some of the prisoners were sent away to other camps. These transfers were made not according to the type of prisoners but according to the type of work we wanted done, and according to their trades. Whilst I was there, some people were released back to freedom. I cannot remember whether they were political prisoners or others, but I remember that on Hitler's birthday, 20th April, 1940, I saw 50 prisoners in the courtyard who were going to be released.

Auschwitz. I went to Auschwitz in May, 1940. I lived outside the camp in a village with my family. I had an office in the camp where I worked during the day. The Kommandant of the camp was Obersturmführer Hoess. I was adjutant. I do not know what the number of the staff was when I came. The biggest part of the prisoners at Auschwitz were political prisoners of Polish nationality. There was very little there when I arrived, as the camp had just been built. All that was there when I left, four months after my arrival, were stone buildings which had been built by the Poles. There had been men, women and cattle living in the wooden buildings. The stone buildings were empty. The former inhabitants of the wooden buildings were shifted. When I first started, the camp staff consisted of only myself and one clerk, and there was only one S.S. Company for guard there. I cannot remember the name of the company, but they were referred to as "Guards Company Concentration Camp, Auschwitz". This company had no "Feldposte" number. The highest ranking officer was the camp Kommandant, after him came the Kommandant of the Guards Company, Obersturmführer Plorin. There were no officers, apart from the company commander. The platoons were commanded by warrant officers. There were three platoons per company and between 30 and 40 men in a platoon. This varied as required. Besides the camp Kommandant, myself, the clerk and the S.S. Company, there was nobody there. A second clerk came later. There were 40 or 50 S.S. men who did not belong to the Guards Company, who had administrative duties in the camp, such as in charge of the kitchen and of the barracks, etc.

I do not know the number of prisoners in that camp. It may have been between 3000 and 4000, but I would not like to commit myself. Untersturmführer Meyer was in charge of administration. I cannot remember his Christian name as I always kept well away from the others. The reason for that was that I had my family there. There was a doctor there and I think his name was Potau. He came from Upper Silesia. He died later on, but I cannot recollect this very well. There was another Untersturmführer, by the name of Meier (or Meyer), who was in charge of the prisoners. I think his Christian name was Franz. The Kommandant issued orders to the S.S. officer in charge of the guard. His orders came from the next highest S.S. formation. This formation was S.S. Wirtschaftsverwaltungshauptamt, Berlin, Amtsgruppe D, Berlin, Oranienburg.

When prisoners arrived we were notified by the Gestapo in Katowice. There were cases when prisoners came in who were brought by ordinary policemen, and they also brought files relating to them. They came mostly in batches. They arrived by train at Auschwitz station and were collected by car from there. The prisoners were all men. There were no questionings by the Gestapo in the camp. All the questioning was done before the prisoners arrived. There was one official of the police on the camp staff who dealt with criminals against whom proceedings had been taken before. I cannot remember his name. He only stayed a short while and was then exchanged for another one. When the prisoners arrived, some were healthy and some were not, but none showed any signs of ill-treatment or malnutrition. I think that during the time I was there there were no cells for solitary confinement, but, as I say, the camp was only in its initial stages. The same rules as to German political and German prisoners were applied to the Poles and, later, to the Russians. There was no difference. One of the stone buildings was reserved for a hospital. This stone building did not differ in any way from the other buildings. Besides the one doctor I have mentioned, there was another doctor supplied from the interned people, among whom there were many doctors and medical students. It was not within my power to give any orders to the medical staff as the doctors came immediately under the Kommandant. The rate of deaths was roughly one per cent, in the summer or possibly one and a half per cent — this was a weekly average. These were natural deaths and it depended upon what was wrong with them when they came in. Reports were made by the camp doctor and I, as adjutant, saw them. I received an average of 30 of these reports per week. The prisoners who had died were burnt. There were prisoners working in the crematorium under orders of guards. The ashes were sent to the relatives if they required them.

There were very few releases from this camp whilst I was there. These releases were authorized only by the Gestapo in Berlin, for political prisoners; or by the police authorities for ordinary criminals. The Gestapo organization who dealt with the camp was the Gestapo Departmental Headquarters at Katowice. Whether there was another Headquarters between Katowice and the Central H.Q. in Berlin, I do not know. The Gestapo men were either civilians in plain clothes, or uniforms, with no distinguishing marks. Some of them wore an S.D. badge. The S.D. and the Gestapo were two different things. I depended upon the S.S. for my orders. So did the Kommandant of the camp. The Gestapo, however, dealt with the political prisoners within the camp. All corporal punishment had to be authorized from Berlin. The camp authorities could not authorize any corporal punishments. In the beginning, corporal punishment was administered by the guards, but, later on, this was forbidden by Berlin, and the prisoners had to administer the punishment themselves. I do not know why this order came from Berlin. It was signed by Gruppenführer Glucks and came from Oranienburg, Berlin.

Dachau. Between 15th and 20th November, 1940, I went back to Dachau. So far I had always been employed in the office, first as clerk, then as adjutant, and now I should get to know the work immediately connected with the prisoners. I was to be trained to become a Lagerführer. My transfer was authorized by the Central S.S. organization in Berlin. When I arrived in Dachau the camp was in perfect running order and consisted of 30 or 32 wooden buildings, all told, for housing the prisoners, including the hospital, etc. The number of prisoners in one barrack varied between 300 and 450. The total number of prisoners was between 13,000 and 14,000. There were three companies of S.S. (120 to 150 men in each company) to guard them, and the administrative personnel consisted of about 100 or 120. The officers of the Guards Companies were not professional S.S. They were people who had been called up from trades or professions, put in the Army, and then detailed to S.S. They were then from the S.S. detailed to their particular duties, *e.g.* concentration camps; they did not volunteer for these particular duties. They received their orders from the Kommandant who, in turn, received his orders from Berlin, Oranienburg. The Kommandant's name was S.S. Obersturmführer Piorkowski. The next in rank after the Kommandant was the Lagerführer, Hauptsturmfuhrer Eill. I do not remember his Christian name. There was one officer in charge of administration, Hauptsturmführer Wagner. Then there were three company commanders whose names I cannot remember.

The prisoners were all men and consisted of criminals and political prisoners as before, and a new type, namely Poles and Russians, who had been prisoners of war and who were detailed for certain work, *e.g.* farming jobs, and who had committed minor crimes such as trying to escape or refusing to work, and they were therefore sent to the concentration camp. These prisoners of war were interned because they had committed these crimes. At this time there were only prisoners from the Eastern front, namely Poles and Russians. It has been pointed out to me that the war in Russia only broke out in June, 1941, whereas I left again in

April, 1941. If this is so I must have mixed it up with Auschwitz. I was only there as a sort of trainee and had very little to do with the organization of the place. I cannot remember any prison-breaks. The death rate I cannot remember because it had nothing to do with me, but I know it was a very good camp.

There was a furniture factory and prisoners worked as carpenters and joiners, also as tailors and cobblers. Prisoners were only allowed out outside the camp in exceptional cases, such as for gardening. There were about forty to fifty new intakes per week whilst I was there. There were few transfers and very few releases. The prisoners came from the Gestapo in Munich. If they were criminals they came from the Police, also in Munich. Parties, organized by the camp administration, who visited the camp and going round the camp, were a regular feature about two or three times a week. These parties were formed mostly of prominent guests from abroad, statesmen and politicians from countries allied to Germany. No high-ranking German officials ever visited the camp.

Natzweiler, April, 1941, to 10th or 15th May, 1944. My appointment at Natzweiler was Lagerfuhrer and in October, 1942, I was appointed camp Kommandant. I had been promoted to the rank of Hauptsturmfuhrer before I was appointed Kommandant. When I arrived at the camp the Kommandant was Sturmbahnfuhrer Huettig. The officer in charge of administration was Obersturmfuhrer Faschingbauer. The doctor was Obersturmfuhrer Eiserle. The O.C. Guards Company was Obersturmfuhrer Peter. The administrative personnel consisted of 20 to begin with, and 70 to 75 in the end. The camp is a very small one. There were no prisoners when I arrived as the camp had just been built. When I left in May, 1944, there were 2500 to 3000 prisoners, comprising the three usual categories: political, anti-socials, criminals and, later, Polish and Russian prisoners of war who had committed minor crimes or tried to escape or refused to work. There were also a few hundred prisoners from Luxembourg. I cannot quite say for certain whether there were any French prisoners there or not. The prisoners arrived with papers and their nationality was on these papers, but I cannot remember any details because I did not go through the papers myself. None of these people came into the camp direct; they all came from other concentration camps. I can, therefore, not say what they were in for, but as far as I know they were of the same three types as I have described before.

I cannot remember that, at any rate, prisoners have been lent for experiments to a doctor in Strasbourg. I cannot remember Professor Pickard of Strasbourg. It is quite impossible that experiments of any kind on prisoners have been carried out without my knowledge, as in both my appointments as Lagerfuhrer and later as Lager Kommandant, I would have known. Obergruppenfuhrer Glucks from the Ministry in Berlin came to inspect the camp twice in the beginning, once in the summer of 1941 and once in the spring of 1942. The visit of Gruppenfuhrer Pohl took place at the end of April or the beginning of May, 1944. The only things that Glucks enquired into were how many political prisoners, how many anti-socials there were. Foreigners figured as political prisoners. He did not ask for their nationalities. I do not know of any British prisoners having been there. I have never seen a document which shows British as the nationality of any prisoners in the camp.

There were 15 wooden barracks in the camp and up to 250 prisoners to each of these barracks. The camp was on top of the hill and my office was in the camp boundary. I lived in the village at the bottom of the hill with my family. The officers were all married and lived with their families in the village. One change in the personnel which I can remember was that Obersturmfuhrer Peter, who commanded the company of guards, was transferred and replaced by an Obersturmfuhrer called Meier. I do not know any of the Rottenfuhrer who were there. There was a crematorium at the camp. The death rate depended upon the season. There were about 7 to 8 per week in the good season and about 15 to 18 in the bad season. They all died natural deaths. The same procedure of informing the relatives and the authority that had sent them to the camp was followed in this camp as in the others described before.

There was only one medical officer on the staff (Obersturmfuhrer Eiserle), and four or five medical orderlies (German). There were doctors and medical students among the prisoners who assisted the M.O. Many persons of over 50 years died of natural causes, such as heart diseases. Compared with other camps, the death rate in this camp was very low. I used to go into the doctor's surgery and he explained the various things, like medical supplies, he had there, but as it was in Latin I did not really know what it was all about. He never complained about any lack of medical supplies. There were two barracks set aside for the hospital, one for the people who were only weak and the other one as a real hospital. There were 60 to 75 beds in the real hospital. The surgeon had facilities for carrying out minor operations but not major operations. For these people were sent to Strasbourg. A document was signed when a person went there and it was signed again when he returned, and the death rate was shown in the books of the camp.

There were 20 to 25 prison-breaks whilst I was there, and ten of the prisoners who tried to escape were shot. Eight or nine were recaptured and brought back and the others got away. The eight or nine who were recaptured got between 14 and 21 days' detention, according to their age and physical condition. In four or five cases out of twenty, they were either whipped or beaten. The culprit got 10 or 15 lashes in each case. This was supervised by the Lagerführer and the camp doctor. When I was Lagerführer I supervised this myself. Generally speaking, when corporal punishment was administered, the number of lashes given varied between 5 and 25. The number was laid down in the order coming from Berlin. Twenty-five was the maximum. The doctor had to be present when corporal punishment was administered. I cannot recollect where a prisoner was unable to stand his punishment and fainted. If such a case had arisen, it would have been the doctor's duty to interfere as that was why he was there. The punishment was administered with ordinary wooden sticks, 3 or 4 feet long and about as thick as my thumb. The sticks were made of solid wood, as you find them in the woods around the camp. The punishment was administered by another prisoner, who was chosen at random, and in the following manner: the prisoner was made to bend down over a table, and the lashes were given on his backside, without his clothes having been removed previously. I never had any difficulties with prisoners who had to administer this punishment. They were given the order and they complied with it. If they had refused to comply with the order I could not have punished them for this refusal. The orders from Berlin were that so many lashes had to be administered by another prisoner, but the order did not say what should be done if one of the prisoners refused to beat one of his comrades.

There were no set rules for what crimes corporal punishment could be administered. It was up to the Kommandant to apply to Berlin for authority for corporal punishment to be administered. The application to Berlin had to say what kind of offence the prisoner had committed and what punishment he had been given already for offences committed previously. This letter had to be signed by the Kommandant. The sort of offences for which I would have applied to Berlin for authority for corporal punishment to be given was: "This prisoner has already three or four times stolen food from his fellow prisoners" or for untidiness or for disobedience or for attacking a guard. The first thing that happened when somebody broke out of the camp and was brought back, was that the Criminal Investigation Department made investigation to find out whether he had committed any crimes whilst at large, and then he was brought before the Kommandant without any trial and the Kommandant ordered punishment. Every man who tried to escape had to be reported to Berlin and likewise had to be reported when he was brought back. The Kommandant could give him 21 days' detention without referring to higher authority, but could give corporal punishment only with authority from Berlin. Every member of the guard was armed with a rifle and there were machine-guns on the turrets. Whips and sticks were forbidden. The guards just carried rifles.

When the prisoners came in in a bunch they were all put in the same block. Eventually, they were sorted out into three groups, politicals, anti-socials and criminals, but never according to their nationalities. There were no strict rules as to that point, but it developed like this as we went along. The three above-mentioned categories were kept apart only in their living quarters. They worked together, fed together and could talk to each other. In the beginning the prisoners worked only in the camp itself. Later we opened a quarry nearby. Other work that was done was that aeroplane engines were taken to pieces and those parts were salvaged which could be used again. Fifteen to twenty prisoners were released while I was there. The order for releases came from Berlin. I do not know why the order came. They were all political prisoners and of German nationality.

The camp was surrounded by barbed wire — 3 metres high. There were towers at the corners of the camp with machine-guns. There was one row of barbed wire where the guards patrolled and then another row of barbed wire. The wire was not electrified in the beginning because there was no current, but later, when current was available, this was done, in the spring of 1943. I was Kommandant then. Two months before I left the camp eight or nine dogs arrived, who were used to assist the guard. They were mainly employed in the quarry to prevent prisoners from escaping. They were controlled by the guards. I remember two incidents where prisoners tried to escape from the quarry, but I cannot remember that they were shot. During the whole of my three years I had only two shootings in the quarry. The other eight prisoners who tried to escape, whom I have already mentioned, tried to escape from the camp itself and not from the quarry.

The only hanging that took place was in the summer of 1943 and it was done on orders from Berlin. Two Gestapo agents brought a prisoner to the camp and showed me an order, signed by somebody in Berlin, saying that this man had to be delivered to my camp and had to be hanged. I cannot remember by whom this order was signed. I therefore detailed two prisoners to carry out the execution. A scaffold was built in the camp and the execution was carried out in my presence. The people present were: the camp doctor (Obersturmführer Eiserle), who certified that the cause of death was hanging, the two Gestapo agents who had brought the prisoner, the two prisoners who carried out the execution, and myself. I cannot remember the name of the prisoner; I think his nationality was Russian. I cannot remember his name because he never appeared in my books. He was only delivered to be hanged. It is quite impossible that any other executions took place whilst I was camp Kommandant. The other prisoners of the camp were not paraded for this execution. No authorized shootings or any other executions took place at the camp on orders from Berlin. I have never heard of any special, narrow cells where men were hanged by their arms. There were no special buildings for prisoners who were under arrest, and no solitary confinement cells. It is quite impossible that any execution by hanging prisoners by their arms was carried out without my knowledge. The only prison we had was a block which was separated by barbed wire from the rest and this one was used for people who had contravened camp discipline.

All the prisoners in this camp were men. I have never heard of a prisoner called Fritz Knoll at this camp. He was not a foreman, but he may have been one of the prisoners. I cannot remember his name. If someone had died on a working party it would have been reported to the office and the office would have reported to me, but I cannot remember such an incident having occurred. Every instance of a prisoner dying at work or through any other cause would be reported to the office, by the office to the Criminal Investigation official and by him to the Kommandant. My command and control over all happenings in the camp at Natzweiler was so complete, and my staff had such definite orders, that the execution of any prisoners without my knowledge during the time when I was Kommandant is an utter impossibility.

Only S.S. personnel were allowed to inspect the camps. Nobody else was allowed anywhere near it. This included army officers who were forbidden to enter any concentration camp. One could only go into a concentration camp with authority from the S.S. General Commanding in Berlin. S.D. personnel were not allowed in the camp either, without authority from Berlin. With the exception of Gruppenfuhrer Glücks, who came from the Ministry in Berlin, and Obergruppenfuhrer Pohl, nobody visited the camp for the two years I commanded it. Apart from these visits, I was answerable to no one, except on paper, to Berlin. I cannot remember any particulars of the visit of Obergruppenfuhrer Pohl at the beginning of May, 1944. He came to inspect the camp and just had a good look round.

During the time I was Lagerfuhrer I received the Kriegsverdienstkreuz (2nd Class) in the spring of 1943. There was no particular reason for this decoration. It was mainly for being Lagerführer for two years in that camp. I was put forward for the decoration by the Kommandant. I have also got the Kriegsverdienstkreuz (1st Class), which I received in January, 1945. During the whole of the time I was at Natzweiler I was responsible for the camp. When I left I handed over to my successor. He was Sturmbannführer Hartjenstein. The handing-over proceedings took place in my office, and I handed over the whole camp to him. The books were not handed over formally to my successor, they were not mentioned.

Auschwitz, 10th to 15th May, 1944, *till 29th November,* 1944. Auschwitz was an enormous camp to which many smaller camps in the vicinity belonged. As the responsibility for the whole camp could not be taken by one man, it was split, and I was put in charge of one part of the camp. I was Kommandant of that part, but as I came under the supreme commander of the whole camp, who was my superior officer, my duties were those of a Lagerführer, though my appointment was called Kommandant. I had under me in my part of the camp the hospital and the agricultural camp, which was an enormous camp and contained many thousand acres. The number of prisoners under my immediate control varied between 15,000 and 16,000 and 35,000 and 40,000, comprising male and female.

There were between 350 and 500 deaths a week. The death rate was higher among the men, the reason being that the influx from the working camp consiste mainly of sick people. When I speak of the death rate in Auschwitz, I mean the all these people died of natural causes, that is to say either from illness or old age The death rate was slightly above normal, due to the fact that I had a camp wit sick people who came from other parts of the camp. The only reason I can see for the higher death rate, not only at Auschwitz but at all concentration camps i comparison with civil prisons, was that prisoners had to work, whereas in civ prisons they had not to work.

In Auschwitz the prisoners went out to work at 5 a.m. in the summer an returned at 8 p.m., sometimes even later. They worked seven days a week, but o Sundays they returned at 1, 2 or 3 o'clock in the afternoon. The work was of a agricultural nature and all the work there was done by prisoners. The whole cam contained about 90,000 to 100,000 prisoners, but this is only a rough estimate My superior officer, and the Kommandant of the whole camp, was Obersturm bannführer Hoess. There were men, women and children in the camp. The majorit of prisoners under my immediate control were Easterners, *i.e.* Poles and Russian I have no reason to believe that there were any prisoners of war among them although there might have been without my knowing it. As far as I can remembe there were no British internees. I think the British prisoners were in the concen tration camp at Sachsenhausen and in another camp near Hamburg called Neuen gamme. It is possible that there were some French people in my camp, but cannot say for certain. There were more women than men prisoners.

I had three companies of S.S. under me to guard the camp. Some of th guards were men of the Waffen S.S., and there were women employed by the S.S as wardresses. There were roughly 420 male S.S. guards and about 40 to 50 wome guards. The men and women prisoners who were outside the camp in the agricu tural part were invariably guarded by men. The women guards only guarded th prisoners within the compound. There were about 10 to 14 doctors for the whol camp, out of which two were detailed to my particular part of the camp. Ther was a hospital in each part of the camp, but the biggest was in my part. I canno say exactly how many beds there were in the hospital; this depended on how clos you could put the beds together.

Prisoners were housed in wooden buildings with three-tier beds. The me were separated from the women and the children were with their mothers. Marrie people were separated. There were 150 buildings all told, men and women camp together; about 80 or 90 were for men and about 60 for women; 25 or 30 build ings were set aside for the hospitals. The camp was only being started, and it wa planned to enlarge it considerably.

All prisoners who died were cremated. There was no sort of service hel when they died. They were just burnt. The cremations were carried out by pr soners. All I had to do when a prisoner died was to inform Obersturmbannführe Hoess and he would deal with it. I had no administration in Auschwitz. All th prisoners were known by numbers only. I had nothing to do with meting ou punishment in Auschwitz; that was all done through Hoess. When I came t Auschwitz there was no corporal punishment for women, but I have heard mentioned, and it was talked about in the camp, that there had been corpora punishment for women before, and that it had been abolished. The only way i which I was informed corporal punishment for women was not allowed was tha conversation in the camp to which I have referred. I cannot remember with who this conversation took place. If a case would have arisen in which a women woul have committed one of the crimes for which a man would have been beaten, would have pointed out to the women guards that corporal punishment could no be administered to women. The only authority on which I could have placed th was that conversation shortly after my arrival. Even if corporal punishment fo women would have been allowed, I would never have put it into practice, as suc a thing is inconceivable to me. The punishment administered to women, if the had committed any of the crimes for which men were beaten, was that they wer transferred to another working party where they had a dirtier type of work longer hours.

When a request for labour came from Berlin, the prisoners had to parad before the doctor. I was very often present at these parades, but not always. Th examination took place by the prisoners filing by the doctor without undressin Then the decision whether a man or a woman was fit enough to be sent to wor was made. If, however, somebody had to be examined to ascertain whether h was fit to receive corporal punishment, a proper medical examination was carrie out. The reason why no proper medical examination could be carried out in th case of detailing people for labour was that the requests ran into thousands an the doctor would have been busy for days. This method of choosing people for work was the normal method applied in all concentration camps. There was nothing unusual about it.

There were four or five cases of people trying to escape whilst I was there. These attempts were made separately. Some of these prisoners got away. No prisoners were shot trying to escape in my part of the camp. No prisoners were flogged; there were no executions, shootings or hangings in my part. I went through the camp frequently on inspections. The doctor alone was responsible for certifying the cause of death if a prisoner died. The doctors changed continuously. One of these doctors was Hauptsturmführer Mengele. I carried out inspections of the bodies of people who had died through natural causes in my capacity as Kommandant when I was wandering round the camp. Whoever died during the day was put into a special building called the mortuary, and they were carried to the crematorium every evening by lorry. They were loaded on the lorry and off the lorry by prisoners. They were stripped by the prisoners of their clothes in the crematorium before being cremated. The clothes were cleaned and were re-issued where the people had not died of infectious diseases. During my inspections I never saw prisoners who had died through physical violence. When a prisoner died, a doctor had to certify the time of death, the cause and the details of the disease. A doctor signed a certificate and sent it to the Central Camp Office. These certificates did not go through my hands. The two doctors worked daily from 8 o'clock in the morning until 8 or 9 at night. All efforts were made by these doctors to keep the prisoners alive. Medical supplies and invigorating drugs were applied. Two different doctors took charge of my part of the camp every day. I remember one very well, because he had been the longest period in my particular part of the camp and he had also served under my predecessor, Hartjenstein. I do not know how long he had been there. His name was Hauptsturmführer Mengele, as mentioned before.

The camp wire was electrified and the dogs were only used outside the camp compound to guard prisoners who were working on agricultural jobs. It was never reported to me that prisoners had to be treated for dog bites. No interrogations were carried out in the camps, and I have never done any interrogating at all whilst I was Kommandant. I sometimes sent people away for interrogation to the Criminal Investigation Officer, in which case they went to the Central Camp Office and were brought back after the interrogation had been completed. I do not know who did the interrogating.

I have heard of the allegations of former prisoners in Auschwitz referring to a gas chamber there, the mass executions and whippings, the cruelty of the guards employed, and that all this took place either in my presence or with my knowledge. All I can say to all this is that it is untrue from beginning to end.

Belsen, 1st December, 1944, *till 15th April,* 1945. On 29th November 1944, I went to Oranienburg, Berlin, to report to Gruppenfuhrer Glücks. His appointment was Chef der Amtsgruppe D, which means that he was the officer in charge of the organization of all concentration camps within the Reich. He was responsible to Obergruppenfuhrer Pohl, whose appointment was Chef der Wirtschaftsverwaltungshauptamtes der S.S. (head of the Administration Department of the S.S. at the Ministry): equivalent to a General in the Army. He said to me: "Kramer, you are going to Belsen as Kommandant. At Belsen there are, at the moment, a lot of Jewish prisoners who will eventually be exchanged". It was later, when I was in Belsen, that I learned that these Jewish prisoners were being exchanged against German nationals abroad. The first exchange took place between 5th and 15th December, 1944, and was carried out under the personal supervision of an official who came from Berlin for that purpose. I cannot remember his name. His rank was "Regierungs-Rat". The first transport contained about 1300 to 1400 prisoners. Glücks said to me at the interview in Berlin: "It is intended to turn Belsen into a camp for sick prisoners. This camp will take all sick prisoners and internees from all concentration camps in Northern and North-Western Germany, and also all sick persons among these prisoners who are working either in firms or with industrial firms". He was referring to Arbeitseinsatzstellen, which means prisoners who have been allotted to peasants or industrial firms, coal mines, and the quarries for labour and for whom special camps have been erected on the premises. Responsibility for feeding and for accommodation is entirely the responsibility of the firm. Responsibility for administration remained with the parent concentration camp. He said: "There are considerable numbers of prisoners working with industrial firms who are sick or physically unfit to do the work they are detailed for. All these prisoners will be drafted into Belsen Camp. It puts an unnecessary burden upon the industrial firms concerned and therefore these prisoners must be transferred. Which prisoners and how many Belsen is eventually going to hold I cannot tell you at the moment, because that will have to be worked out as we go along. The general rule is to be that every prisoner who through illness is absent from his work for more than 10 or 14 days will be transferred to Belsen. If and when these prisoners recover in Belsen, they will either be formed into new detachments and sent out to new jobs or returned to their old work, whichever may be more expedient. You see that this is going to be a very big task for you. I suggest that you go to Belsen now to look at the camp and see how you get along. If you want any help you can either come back to Berlin or write".

This is where the duty conversation came to an end. Glücks then asked me how my wife and children were, and I enquired into the well-being of his family. I also asked whether it would be possible when I took over Belsen Camp to move my family there. He told me that I would have to go to Belsen and have a look. If I could find a suitable house I should write to him and he would authorize the move of my household. This conversation took place between Gruppenführer Glücks and myself, there was nobody else present. These were the only instructions I received and I did not ask for any more. I did not think I would require any more instructions and was quite satisfied with my orders.

After the interview with Glücks I spoke to three officers whom I knew personally. They were: Standartenführer Maurer (he was in charge of the allocation of prisoners to camps and for labour); Hauptsturmführer Sommer (he worked in Maurer's department); and Sturmbannführer Burger (he was the man who supervised the administration in the various concentration camps). I did not have any conversation on duty matters with either of the three above-named people. They were friends of mine, and as I happened to be in the house, I went to their various offices to say "Hallo". The leading doctor was a Standartenfuhrer Dr. Lolling. He was the M.O. in charge of all concentration camps. I cannot remember any names of other people, but I can remember these four names because they either came to visit the camps or I saw their names on various letters coming from the Ministry.

I then travelled to Belsen, where I was received by Obersturmfuhrer Schaaf. He was the officer in charge of administration. The next morning I went to the office and met Sturmbannführer Haas, the Kommandant, who knew that I was arriving from Berlin to take over complete charge of Belsen. I asked him how many prisoners the camp contained, and he said, "Roughly 15,000". He said that it was not much use to discuss matters in the office and suggested a tour through the camp. On that tour he pointed out changes and improvements which he still wanted to make. The camp was about 1½ kilometres long and between 300 and 350 metres wide. There were roughly 60 barracks, including accommodation for guards and stores; 40 to 45 were for the accommodation of the prisoners. The prisoners were made up of men, women and children; families were allowed to live together; otherwise men were separated from women. Six buildings in the men's camp, three in the family camp, and two in the women's camp served as hospitals. There was a crematorium in the camp.

I do not know of what nationality the prisoners were when I arrived, because there were no files or papers of any kind in the camp. It was impossible for me to know what kind of prisoners there were as they had been sent to Belsen because they were ill, from all concentration camps over the country. Many of them had lost their identification marks, and as there were no records it was absolutely impossible to tell who was who. I started to keep my own records of the prisoners, but these records were all destroyed on orders which I received from Berlin about the end of March. I do not remember who signed these orders.

The personnel consisted of one Guard Company S.S. The O.C. of the Company was Hauptscharführer Meyer. He came from somewhere near Hanover. He was of average height, about 1 m. 70; he wore spectacles, had hardly any hair and was about 50. Then there was Hauptsturmführer Vogler. He was the officer in charge of administration who took over from Schaaf, whom I mentioned before as officer in charge of administration on my arrival. The officer in charge of the Criminal Department was Untersturmführer Frericks. The Lagerführer (Obersturmführer Stresse) was transferred a few days after my arrival, and I was without a Lagerfuhrer for over two months and had to do the job myself with only one N.C.O. as assistant, whose appointment was Rapportführer; he was Oberscharführer Reddhaser. The M.O. was Sturmbannführer Schnabel. A Hauptscharführer acted as dentist. He was later on promoted Untersturmführer. His name was Linsmeier. There were no other officers and I had no Adjutant. There were 60 to 70 N.C.Os., 20 to 25 of whom were in the Guards S.S. Company and the others employed on administrative duties. One of the N.C.Os. employed was the N.C.O. who was Office Clerk to the Officer in charge of Administration. He was Unterscharführer Kuckertz. There was another senior N.C.O. in my office. His name was Unterscharführer Rang. He acted as Untersturmführer and Adjutant. Other N.C.Os. whom I remember are Oberscharfuhrer Hilmer (N.C.O. Administration); Unterscharführer Lademacher (also N.C.O. Administration); Unterscharführer Wille (also N.C.O. Administration); and Unterscharführer Müller, who was in charge of the food stores. When I took over Belsen there were six officers, including myself. I had no senior N.C.Os. When I took over there were three women on the staff. I cannot remember their names at the moment.

The death rate when I arrived was between 40 and 60 a week. When I entered the camp the Lagerführer had to report to me and had to say: "There are so many in the camp; so many died yesterday; which leaves so many". On my arrival a book was kept in which these figures were entered, but was later dispensed with. This book I had taken over from my predecessor. It was kept by the acting Lagerführer in his office. There was also another book in which the strength was recorded. The acting Lagerführer held a parade every morning to count the prisoners. On this parade every Blockfuhrer reported the strength of his unit and the number of deaths that had occurred the previous day, and the Rapportführer added up the strength of the various blocks on a sheet of paper, making a grand total. This report included the number of deaths that had occurred the previous day. There were approximately 40 Blockführer on parade every day.

In January I took over a new camp, adjoining the old camp, in which there were 40 to 50 new blocks. I did not get any more staff when I took this camp over. Only later, when camps in Silesia were evacuated, guards arrived with prisoners, thus putting up the strength of personnel. I was not always informed when transports of prisoners arrived; especially transports of prisoners evacuated from Silesia arrived without warning. There were transports with only 100 or 200 people, and others with 1500, 2000, 2500, etc. I had food reserves in the camp, and when a new batch of prisoners arrived I had to fall back on these reserves until I had reported the new strength and thus got additional food for the higher number of prisoners. There was no regular food transport; the railway should have brought the food whenever there was a train available. I am unable to say how many prisoners I had after this month because it was my orders that I had to send out prisoners for work as fast as possible. The incoming prisoners were therefore balanced by those being sent out for work and the figures fluctuated every day. Every prisoner who was fit to work was sent out with working parties ("Arbeitseinsatz") to industrial firms. The other prisoners worked only inside the camp and for the maintenance of the camp.

On 1st December when I took over there were roughly 15,000 people in the camp; roughly 200 died in December; on 1st January there were roughly 17,000 people in the camp; 600 died in January; on 1st February there were 22,000 prisoners in the camp. From the 15th February onwards I am unable to say how many prisoners I had as no more books were kept, as this proved utterly impossible in view of the transports streaming in from camps in Silesia which were being evacuated and, as I have already said, the records which I had maintained I destroyed in March.

I do not know the number of deaths which occurred in this period at all, but the conditions in Belsen got worse from the middle of February till the middle of April, 1945, when the Allies came. I inspected the camp daily during this period and was fully aware of the conditions and the great number of people who were dying. The death rate during the months of February, March and April gradually mounted until it reached 400 or 500 a day. This figure was due to the fact that if people were healthy I had to send them out on working parties and only retain the sick and dying. I was notified by the Stationmaster that a transport had arrived and I would have to collect the prisoners. The transports arriving were checked in by the guards only by numbers and not by names. About twice a week food was indented for from local depots and a return sent to the Ministry in Berlin, which was based on the figures given by the guards, who checked the people on entering the camp.

All prisoners received three meals a day. I cannot tell what the daily ration was as this was laid down by the food depot and was standardized. I never checked up on the rations from the depots, but I made sure that each prisoner had one litre of vegetable stew for the main meal, and in the morning the prisoner had coffee and bread, if available, and for the evening meal coffee and bread, again if available, and cheese or sausage. If the prisoners had worked on this diet it would have been insufficient for them to survive, but as they did not work I think it was enough to keep them alive. I thought they could stand this diet for about six

273

weeks, and after six weeks I was hoping to get some more food. The rations described above were the normal rations in any concentration camp at that time. The main point on which the food deteriorated was bread, as this was lacking entirely for two or three days running several times. It was absolutely impossible for me to procure enough bread to feed the number of prisoners I had. In the early days the bread had been supplied by local bakeries at Belsen. Later there were so many prisoners in the camp that the local bakeries could not supply the required quantity any longer, and I sent out lorries to Hanover and other places to fetch bread, but even then I was not able to get half the bread I required to feed prisoners on normal rations. Apart from bread, the rations were never cut down. Flour was supplied in lieu of bread and was employed in making meals. It turned out, however, that had we made bread of this flour the death rate would not have been so high. I went to the depot in Celle and then to the next higher authority in Hanover and put them in the picture as to what was going on in Belsen. I also pointed out to them that if a catastrophe was going to happen, I would not only disclose the facts but also make them responsible. I cannot remember whom I saw at either of these places. I have never applied to Berlin in these matters because they could not have helped me in any way. This was entirely a matter for the ration people in Celle and in Hanover. My visits to these depots resulted in extra rations of potatoes and turnips arriving some time later.

I remember one case of cannibalism quite well. It was reported to me that a prisoner had entered the mortuary and that parts of one body were missing. I put a guard on the dead bodies at night and that guard arrested a man the same night who had approached a dead body. This man was arrested, but before he could be interrogated next morning he hanged himself. Whether there were more cases of cannibalism I cannot tell, but I put a guard on the mortuary from that night onwards. That guard consisted of prisoners. I thought that the prisoners would guard the bodies against other prisoners. Whether they did or did not do so I cannot tell. The mortuary was not always in the same building, as the prisoners fluctuated to such a great extent. I had to shift the accommodation continuously and therefore the building detailed as a mortuary was not always the same. If changes took place, this building was cleaned by the prisoners and used for their accommodation the next day.

The camp doctor reported sick and was replaced by Dr. Klein at the middle of February. Roughly, on 1st March another M.O. arrived. His name was Hauptsturmführer Horstmann. Two days before the Allies arrived Horstmann left with the troops and only Dr. Klein remained. Apart from those two (Klein and Horstmann), there were no S.S. doctors in the camp. At the end of January Dr. Lolling, from the Ministry in Berlin, arrived on an inspection tour. I pointed out to him that if, as I was told in Berlin, Belsen was going to be a camp for sick people. I needed more doctors. He said that there were none available at the moment, but that as soon as he had some he would send them. Dr. Lolling inspected the camp and was fully aware of the conditions prevailing there at the time when he inspected it. He spent a whole day walking through the camp with Dr. Schnabel and inspected it thoroughly. The measures taken were that Dr. Lolling took a list of requirements with him and said he would see to it that we got the necessary medical supplies. Even though I was Kommandant I did not know anything about the supply of medical equipment and medical stores. This I left entirely to the M.O. All medical supplies were asked for direct from Berlin (Dr. Lolling's department). This is all I know about this matter.

During my stay at Belsen there were 15 to 20 prison-breaks. Some of the prisoners trying to escape were shot whilst trying to escape. I do not know how many. Towards the end of December an order arrived from Berlin forbidding corporal punishment altogether. From that moment onwards no corporal punishment was meted out.

Between 20th and 28th February the M.O. notified me that spotted fever had broken out in the camp. This fact was verified by a Bacteriological Institute in Hanover. I therefore closed the camp and sent a report to Berlin. The answer from Berlin was that I had to keep the camp open to receive transports coming from the East, fever or no fever. The second time I wrote to Berlin was between 1st and 10th March, when I sent a complete report on the conditions prevailing in the camp. These two occasions were the only occasions on which I ever made any representations to higher authority. These two letters were addressed to the Verwaltungsgruppe B in Berlin. I did not go to Berlin myself as I was instructed at my interview in November, because that would have taken three or four days and there was nobody to carry on in my absence.

As far as I can remember, Gruppenführer Pohl inspected Belsen Camp about 20th March. He came with one other officer. I conducted Pohl right through the camp and pointed out conditions as they were. He did not come because of the letter I had written. He came on a routine inspection tour — "Just to have a look at the camp". Whether the letter I had written to the Central Office in Berlin was mentioned during our conversations I cannot tell. I pointed out conditions to him, and he said that something must be done. The first measure he suggested was to close the camp and put no more people into it. I suggested two measures to Pohl to cope with the situation: *(a)* no further transports to come in; and *(b)* the exchange of the Jews in the camp to take place immediately. The result of this was that he dictated a letter from my office, addressed to Berlin, saying that the exchange of Jewish prisoners had to take place immediately. This exchange did eventually take place during the last days of March, I do not know against whom these prisoners were to be exchanged, but they left Belsen going to Theresienstadt. Between 6000 and 7000 people were sent away to be exchanged (three train-loads). These 6000 or 7000 constituted the entire number of Jewish prisoners who were to be exchanged. They were transported in three train-loads, each train consisting of 45 to 50 trucks. I had orders to send off three consignments on three different days. Each time I detailed a few guards — I cannot remember how many — and there was an N.C.O. in charge of each train, probably a Scharführer, but I cannot remember. I do not know to whom these N.C.O.s had to report at the other end. All I knew was I had to send off three train-loads. I never saw these N.C.Os. whom I sent away, again.

I pointed out to Pohl that I wanted more beds and more blankets, and he agreed that in this matter, like as in the other matters, immediate help was required. The doctor and the officer in charge of administration also spoke to Pohl. The officer in charge Administration pointed out his difficulties in obtaining food, whereas the doctor was satisfied with the position as he had just received a new consignment of medical stores. Pohl held his appointment in Berlin for roughly two years. Glücks was there much longer as he had been there already under Eike. Eike was later sent to the Western Front and afterwards to the Eastern Front, where he was killed.

I do not know what nationality any of the prisoners were of at Belsen as there were no papers sent with them and the only check was done by numbers. I therefore cannot tell whether there were any British subjects among the prisoners, but it is possible that there were. I have never heard of a prisoner called Keith Meyer, who was a British subject.

The female staff increased in number the same as the male staff, as women guards arrived with women transports from the East. All women in the camp were under my command, the same as the men. Twenty to 22 wardresses were still at Belsen when the Allies arrived, and approximately 26,000 women prisoners. Unless I received complaints from the prisoners themselves I had no means of ascertaining what treatment was meted out by the female guards, but I had complete confidence in those guards. The only criticism I had to make was that they were a bit too familiar with the female prisoners. I had the same confidence in the male guards. They were 100 per cent correct, and I have never received any complaints from the prisoners. In February or March — I cannot remember the exact date — Oberaufseherin Volkenrath arrived and was put in charge of the women guards. I had complete confidence in her.

There was a crematorium in the camp and as long as coke was available all dead bodies were cremated. When there was no more coke available they were buried in mass graves. I have never seen a Red Cross official in any of the camps I have been to. I cannot tell why not. If a Red Cross official had called I would have rung up Berlin immediately to ask whether he was permitted to enter the camp, as nobody could enter the camp without permission from Berlin. What the answer would have been I cannot tell.

There were no standing orders from Berlin for any of the concentration camps I have been to as to: *(a)* the space allotted to individual prisoners; *(b)* sanitation, or *(c)* working conditions. This was completely left to the discretion of the Kommandant. I can remember no standing orders or instructions from Berlin except with regard to visitors to the camp and to punishments. In all other matters the Kommandant had complete discretion. When Belsen Camp was eventually taken over by the Allies I was quite satisfied that I had done all I possibly could under the circumstances to remedy the conditions in the camp.

FURTHER STATEMENT OF JOSEF KRAMER

1. I relinquished command of Struthof-Natzweiler in May, 1944, and handed over to Sturmbannführer Hartjenstein. At this time and for at least a year previously Buck was commanding Schirmeck, but there was no official connec-

tion between Schirmeck and Struthof. There was a Gestapo officer attached to me during my period at Struthof; his name was Wochner and he was sent by the Gestapo at Stuttgart. According to the district allocation Struthof should have been, in my opinion, in Strasbourg Gestapo area, but I believe that in any case Strasbourg Gestapo depended on Stuttgart.

2. With reference to the orders received to gas certain women and despatch them to Strasbourg University, as sworn by me before Commandant Jadin of the French Army, I give the following details: The orders I received were in writing signed by order of Reichsführer Himmler by Gruppenführer Glücks. As nearly as I can remember they stated that a special transport would arrive from Auschwitz and that the people on this transport were to be killed and their bodies sent to Strasbourg to Professor Hirt. It further said that I should communicate with Professor Hirt as to how the killing was to take place. This I did and was given by Hirt a container of gas crystals with instructions how to use them. There was no regular gas chamber in Struthof, but he described to me how an ordinary room might be used. I do not know any more of the Professors concerned with Hirt, but I do know that there was in one of the departments a Professor Bickerbach.

3. The first time I saw a gas chamber proper was at Auschwitz. It was attached to the crematorium. The complete building containing the crematorium and gas chamber was situated in Camp No. 2 (Birkenau), of which I was in command. I visited the building on my first inspection of the camp after being there for three days, but for the first eight days I was there it was not working. After eight days the first transport, from which gas chamber victims were selected, arrived, and at the same time I received a written order from Hoess, who commanded the whole of Auschwitz Camp, that although the gas chamber and crematorium were situated in my part of the camp, I had no jurisdiction over it whatever. Orders in regard to the gas chamber were, in fact, always given by Hoess, and I am firmly convinced that he received such orders from Berlin. I believe that had I been in Hoess's position and received such orders, I would have carried them out, because even if I had protested it would only have resulted in my being taken prisoner myself. My feelings about orders in regard to the gas chamber were to be slightly surprised, and wonder to myself whether such action was really right.

4. In regard to conditions at Belsen, I say once more that I did everything I could to remedy them. In regard to the food, the prisoners throughout March and April, 1945, got their full entitlement, and in my opinion this entitlement was perfectly sufficient for the healthy prisoner, but from the middle of February onwards sick people began to come in and I felt they should have more food. I sent my Messing N.C.O., Unterscharführer Müller, to the food depots in Celle and Hanover, but he was told that no further food could be issued because we were already getting our entitlement. I did, in fact, get some food from the food store in the Wehrmacht Camp at Belsen, but it would have been no use my asking for more from them because they were not my correct authorized depot.

5. In regard to accommodation, when I was ordered to take 30,000 more people in early April, when the camp was already more than full, I appealed to Lieutenant-General Beineburg in the Kommandantur in the Wehrmacht Camp at Belsen and it was he who arranged for 15,000 prisoners to be lodged in the barracks in that camp. He had to get special permission over the telephone to do this. I never appealed to the General for help on the food situation or any other difficulties because I knew that he would not have been able to help me, in that he had no jurisdiction. I do not consider that I should have appealed to him because I knew that he could not have helped. Furthermore, I do not believe that anybody in Germany could have altered the food entitlement for the prisoners in the camp because I do not believe that the food was available. It surprises me very much to hear that there were large and adequate stocks of food in the Wehrmacht Camp. Nevertheless, I still feel that an appeal to the General would have been useless.

6. I have been told that some of my S.S. staff were guilty of ill-treatment and brutality towards the prisoners. I find this very difficult to believe and I would trust them absolutely. To the best of my belief they never committed any offences against the prisoners. I regard myself as responsible for their conduct and do not believe that any of them would have infringed my orders against ill-treatment or brutality.

7. The Hungarian troops took over guard duties around the perimeter of my camp during the few days before the British arrived. I agree that during this period more shooting took place than was customary when the Wehrmacht were doing guard. I remember the incident on 15th April, 1945, in the late afternoon, when I went with British officers to the potato patch and was ordered to remove

the dead body of a prisoner from that patch. I think it is wrong that this man should have been shot and have no doubt at all that it was either the Wehrmacht or the Hungarians who were responsible.

8. The rifle range which is visible at the north-west corner of my camp was used fairly regularly by the Wehrmacht two or three days a week.

APPENDIX E
THE ROLE OF THE VATICAN

The implications of a lie on the scale of the Jewish extermination hoax cannot be constrained to bear on isolated subjects such as Israel or World War II revisionism. Before not many years it was realized that, during and after the war, Pope Pius XII had never spoken out in condemnation of the supposed exterminations of Jews. This fact naturally raised some problems for the propaganda history of World War II. The specific event that ignited general controversy was Rolf Hochhuth's play *Der Stellvertreter (The Deputy)*. Supposedly based on the "Gerstein statement", the play performs a completely unscrupulous job of character assassination on Pius XII by relating events inconsistent with the "statement", thereby piling invention on invention. However the Hochhuth play was unquestionably the catalyst for the discussion of a fairly important fact, although the ensuing discussion, carried on among people who had been completely taken in by the hoax, never clarified anything and only amplified the confusion.

It is no more necessary, here, to explain why Pius XII did not speak up about exterminations of Jews, than it is necessary to explain why he did not protest the extermination of Eskimoes. However the role of the Vatican is of some interest to our subject, so a few words are appropriate.

First a few background remarks. During the period 1920–1945 the Vatican considered Communism to be the principal menace loose in the world. This being the case, it was open to friendly relations with the Fascists after their assumption of power in Italy in 1922 and the Concordat of 1929, reversing the earlier pre-Fascist anti-clerical policies of Italian Governments, was the basis for relations which remained generally good until Mussolini fell from power in 1943.

When Hitler came to power in 1933 the Vatican had similar hopes for an anti-Communist regime that would make domestic peace with the Church. At first, it appeared that events would unfold as in Italy, and the Concordat of 1933 with Hitler (still in force), guaranteeing the Church a portion of tax revenues and further defining the proper spheres of Church and State, reinforced this expectation.

Things did not turn out so well, however. Although the Concordat had defined the Church's rights in the sphere of education, and youth culture in general, to the satisfaction of the Vatican, the Nazis found it difficult to live with such terms, and found various ways of undercutting the Catholic position without formally repudiating the terms of the Concordat. For example, the Catholic Youth associations were forbidden to engage in sport, on the shrewd calculation that such restrictions of such associations to the realm of the truly spiritual would guarantee that they would wither. There were also various means of intimidation employed against parents who insisted on sending their children to Catholic schools. Moreover Nazi publications such as *Das Schwarze Korps* (the SS magazine) and *Der Stuermer* were openly anti-Christian, and constantly heaped abuse on the Pope and the Catholic clergy in general, favorite charges being that the holy men were homosexuals or were having amorous liaisons with Jewesses. Although the Nazis never welched on the most important provision of the Concordat, the commitment on tax revenues, the mutual hostility became so great that many felt that there was always a good possibility for a second *Kulturkampf* (Bismarck's unsuccessful attempt of the 1870's to break the power of the Roman Church in Germany).

The Nazi-Vatican hostility led, in 1937, to the most unusual Papal encyclical *Mit brennender Sorge*. Issued in German rather than the usual Latin, it was among the strongest attacks that the Vatican had ever made on a specific State. The Pope at the time was Pius XI and Eugenio Cardinal Pacelli, who was to become Pope Pius XII in 1939, was the Vatican Secretary of State. Pacelli, a diplomat of world-wide experience, for ten years Papal Nuncio in Germany and fluent in German, was already regarded as the obvious heir to Pius XI and his pre-eminence in the area of international diplomacy was unquestioned. *Mit brennender Sorge* was written under his supervision.[1]

Despite the unquestioned hostility between the Church and the Nazis, it should be kept in mind that Communism, in the eyes of the Vatican, was still the prime enemy. With an antagonist such as the German Nazis, there was room for maneuver for the Church but the Communists, up to that date, had shown themselves to be total and deadly enemies. Moreover, Germany was not the only European State that the Vatican was displeased with. France and Czechoslovakia had strongly anti-clerical Governments. Thus, when war came, the Vatican (although, of course, officially neutral) could not be enthusiastic for either side. Since Communism was considered the prime enemy, it is probably correct that the Vatican rather preferred the Axis side, but in their eyes this was definitely a choice of lesser evils. Moreover, there was a considerable diversity of preferences within the Church. For example the wartime Papal Nuncio in Berlin, Msgr. Cesare Orsenigo, was evidently satisfied with the German victory over France in 1940, and expressed to the German Foreign Office his hope that the Germans would march into Paris through Versailles. On the other hand the Jesuit-controlled Vatican radio was so anti-German that the British considered it a virtual extension of their own propaganda service.[2]

So much for the political background of the Vatican's situation during the war; we return to consideration of the fact of Pope Pius' silence on exterminations of Jews. It would not be feasible to review here the views of all who have contributed to the controversy, so we shall restrict ourselves in this respect. First, there is the Vatican itself, which is represented mainly by the nine volumes of wartime documents that it published in the years 1967–1975, *Actes et documents du Saint Siège relatifs à la seconde guerre mondiale.* The principal editor of this series has been Robert A. Graham, an American Jesuit and former editor of the Jesuit magazine *America.* Graham, who accepts the extermination legend, has emerged as the principal spokesman for the Vatican in these matters. It is unfortunate that the only volumes of the nine that are devoted entirely to war victims are the last two, published in 1974–1975, which carry the subject no further than December 1943.

Among the numerous authors in the controversy, the various positions are well represented by two recent books, *The Vatican in the Age of the Dictators* by Anthony Rhodes (London, 1973), a defender of the Vatican, and *The Pope's Jews* by Sam Waagenaar (London, 1974), a critic of the Pope.

The official Vatican position, as set forth in the Introduction to the eighth volume of *Actes et documents,* is as follows:

During his brief visit to the Vatican on 26 September (1942), the personal representative of President Roosevelt, Myron Taylor, renewed an official request for information. They had received, from the Geneva office of the Jewish Agency for Palestine, information on the desperate situation of the Polish Jews and the Jews deported to Poland. The report, dated 30 August, described the liquidation of the Warsaw ghetto, executions in a camp called Belick, in Lwow and in Warsaw. The destination of the deportations was death: "The Jews deported from Germany, Belgium, Holland, France and Slovakia", said the report, "were sent to the slaughterhouse, while the aryans deported to the East from Holland and France were actually used for labor". The memorandum from Taylor to Cardinal Maglione (Vatican Secretary of State) said: "I would be very grateful to Your Eminence if it were possible to tell me if the Vatican has any information which tends to confirm the report contained in this memorandum. If so, I would like to know if the Holy Father has some suggestions touching on some practical means of using the forces of public opinion of the civilized world in order to prevent the continuation of this barbarism".

Cardinal Maglione had to reply, on 10 October, that he had on his part no particular information confirming the Geneva report. In effect, the most detailed information, received those days by the Vatican, was the same as that received by the United States. The sources were the Polish Ambassador to the Vatican and the Jewish organizations themselves. "The reports on severe measures adopted against non-aryans have also come to the Holy See from other sources, but at present it has not been possible to verify their accuracy". Under these conditions, the second question on practical means to put into operation did not call for a reply.

Very significant are the notes set down by Maglione after having received the Taylor document: "I do not believe that we have any information which confirms these grave tidings. Right?" For his part the "minutante" (recorder or archivist) wrote: "There is Mr. Malvezzi's." The information of Malvezzi, official of an Italian firm, recently returned from Poland, was grave but general, and did not harmonize with the Geneva report.

That which the Cardinal Secretary of State heard as "severe measures" can be interpreted in the light of the documents of these two years. The information received in the Vatican consisted of second or third hand reports, taken seriously however, concerning the brutal treatment imposed on the Jews of Hungary, Croatia, Slovakia, France and other countries. What was the ultimate destination of the deportees, what was the plan of the Nazis, then remained an enigma. When, for example, in the month of March, Msgr. Burzio, the Charge d'affaires in Slovakia, spoke of the deportees as going to "a certain death", it is clear that he based this assertion on the inhuman conditions of the departures and the brutality of the guards. After such a beginning, it was easy to imagine that the old, the sick and the children were not able to live long, even if typhus did not cut them down in the overpopulated and unsanitary camps. In the same sense was taken the remark of the Croatian police chief Eugene Kvaternik, according to whom the Germans had already caused two million Jews to die and that the same fate awaited the Croatian Jews. Afterwards, these words have been confirmed as only too exact. It is obvious, however, that the representative of the Holy See, Father Abbe Marcone, in reporting them to the Vatican, did not believe or was unable to believe that they should be taken literally. One took them at least as a grave intimation of the tragedy which appeared only in general outline.

The end of the year 1942 saw several public declarations on the deportations. On 17 December, the United Nations published in London a declaration on the rights of man, in which it denounced, in strong but general terms, the treatment inflicted on the Jews. On 24 December Pope Pius XII made, in his Christmas Eve message, a very clear allusion to the deportations, concerning which the world, at that time, was able only with difficulty to form an idea.

This Vatican explanation is not acceptable. It is of course true that only occasional scraps bearing on exterminations of Jews appear in their documents. Moreover no reasonable person would deny that most of these scraps must be classified as inventive propaganda, for the claims of exterminations are either coupled in some sense with other claims that nobody would defend today, or are associated with other oddities demolishing their credibility. For example, a note of 2 January 1943 to the Vatican from Wladislas Raczkiewicz, the President of the Polish exile government in London, claimed that the Germans had embarked on a general extermination of the Polish population in addition to its Jewish minority (in agreement with our analysis of Chapter III, the note mentions the Auschwitz concentration camp with an implication that it is not one of the sites of exterminations).[3] We have already noted, in Chapter III, that Msgr. Burzio, the Papal Chargé d'affaires in Slovakia, sent some invented tales back to Rome. Additional scraps of this sort are reviewed below.

One must of course accept the Vatican claim that such information as they had during the war could not have been taken as decent evidence of exterminations; that has already been proved in this book. However, that is not the point. The Vatican spokesmen today assert not merely that their information did not reveal an extermination program, but that the exterminations happened, on a continental scale, without reliable information about them coming to the Vatican. It is this claim that is completely ridiculous and simply cannot be entertained for more than a few seconds.

It is not possible for an extermination program of the type claimed to have transpired without the Vatican learning of it. The slaughters are supposed to have taken place mainly in Catholic Poland, where the Church had its agents, Catholic priests, in every village, situated in such a way (hearing gossip, confessionals, etc.) that no such thing as the exterminations could possibly have happened without the entire Polish Catholic clergy knowing about them. It is true that the Germans imposed a censorship on communications to or from Poland, so that the Polish clergy and the Vatican could not communicate with customary freedom, as explained in the Introduction to volume three of *Actes et documents,* but as also there explained, there were many ways of circumventing the censorship, notably through Italians who had business of various sorts in Poland and points east, and through messages carried by private persons from Poland to the office of the Papal Nuncio in Berlin, who communicated with the Vatican through privileged diplomatic channels.

Rhodes realizes that the claim of ignorance of the exterminations is not tenable and concedes (since he assumes the exterminations happened) that Pius XII must have known about them. The explanation for the failure to speak up unambiguously seems to Rhodes to be a fear that any public and explicit condemnation would have made the situation of Catholics in Germany and the occupied territories worse. Rhodes then asserts that "in his *private* messages to Heads of States in connection with the persecution of the Jews, Pius XII certainly 'spoke up'" (Rhodes' italics), and then gives two examples of such private messages, bearing on Slovakia and on Hungary, which however contain nothing about exterminations, but speak only of deportations and persecutions of Jews in general terms.[4]

Rhodes' picture of a timid Pius, afraid to speak up against the Nazis and their programs, does not hold up for many reasons. As shown by the documents Rhodes quotes, he must claim that the Pope was also too timid to speak up in confidential diplomatic communications. Moreover the historical record does not support Rhodes' picture of a Catholic Church terrorized into silence by the Nazis. The German Bishops were by no means terrorized into silence. While, in parallel with their counterparts in Allied countries, they never opposed the German war effort, they were quite vocal during the war in their opposition to the religion-related policies and values of the National Socialist regime, and expressed their opposition in the Catholic press in Germany and in pulpits throughout Germany. In December 1942 the German Bishops, meeting in their annual conference in Fulda, sent a declaration to the German Government denouncing the persecution of Catholic Churches in occupied countries. In January 1943 Konrad Count von Preysing, Bishop of Berlin, made a public condemnation of Nazi racial theories and policies. In August 1943 the German Bishops publicly denounced the Nazi policies hostile to Catholic education, and this denunciation was read in public all over Germany.[5] The inescapable fact is that the Catholic Church was not terrorized into silence.

Timidity does not explain why Pope Pius failed to condemn the alleged exterminations after the Nazis had been defeated. The Pope's speech to the College of Cardinals on 2 June 1945 was a long and blistering attack on the defeated Nazis, and yet the only thing in the speech that could possibly be interpreted as a reference to exterminations was a reference to "applications of national socialist teachings, which even went so far as to use the most exquisite scientific methods to torture or eliminate people who were often innocent". However reading further in the speech it becomes clear that the Pope, like so many other people at the time, was thinking of the catastrophic scenes found in the German camps at the end of the war. The only specific victims mentioned are the Catholic priests interned at Dachau, a high percentage of whom perished there for reasons abundantly covered in this book. Although Pope Pius did mention that one Polish auxiliary bishop died of typhus, his remarks leave the impression that he believed that the deaths in the camps were intentional on the part of the Nazis, and the priests interned at Dachau are described by Pius as having "endured indescribable sufferings for their faith and for their vocation". There is nothing in the address about exterminations of any racial, religious or national group.[6]

While it is the case that the record does not indicate that the Roman Church was terrorized into silence during the war, the Vatican was nevertheless vulnerable to pressures to some degree, as is made evident by an examination of the circumstances behind the declaration of Pope Pius' which came closest to sounding like a condemnation of exterminations, his Christmas Eve message of 1942.

In Chapter III and above we saw that, in the autumn of 1942, the Allies inquired of the Vatican whether it had any information supporting the extermination claims that Rabbi Wise and some others had been making for several months, and that the Vatican had no such information. While Pope Pius and the Secretary of State, Luigi Cardinal Maglione, no doubt smelled *Greuelpropaganda* immediately upon hearing such stories, the Vatican material reproduced above shows that they at least made some effort to inquire into the matter. Also, the Papal Nuncio in Italy, Msgr. Francesco Borgongini-Duca, met on 10 November 1942 with Guido Buffarini, Undersecretary in the Italian Ministry of the Interior, for the purpose of discussing the general military and political situation. The situation of the Jews was discussed and Borgongini-Duca reported to Maglione that[7]

He then spoke to me concerning the speech of Hitler (in Munich on 8 November) and, I having asked him if in allusions to retaliations, they might mean asphyxiating gas, he twice replied to me decidedly no.

Thus the Vatican had essentially no information, in the autumn of 1942, tending to confirm the extermination claims, and it took this position in its exchanges with Allied representatives, when the matter came up. In Chapter III we noted that there was one anonymous note, supposedly from a Vatican source, produced in late November, which supported the extermination claims. However, since that was not the Vatican position, the note was no doubt a forgery in some sense. If it did come from a source inside the Vatican, it may have been authored by Virgilio Scattolini, an employee of the Vatican newspaper *l'Osservatore Romano,* who posed as a Vatican insider during the war in order to sell his fabricated "information"; suitably tailored for the buyer, to all comers, and who for a while was considered "our man in the Vatican" by the OSS.[8] A lesser possibility is that the note came from the priest Pirro Scavizzi, who is discussed below.

The information that the Vatican had in December 1942, relative to Nazi persecutions of Jews, is well represented by a message composed by Msgr. Giuseppe Di Meglio of the staff of Orsenigo, Papal Nuncio in Berlin, and delivered to the Vatican by Di Meglio on 9 December 1942. The message deals at length with the German policies toward the Jews and it is a good assumption that such material was written in response to a request, to Orsenigo from the Vatican, for such information. The Berlin Nunciature was doubtless considered about the best source of such information within the Church since, as we noted above, a good deal of the communication between Poland and the Vatican was through Orsenigo's Berlin office. The heart of the part of the message that dealt with the Jews was:[9]

Since many fled, before the arrival of the German troops, from the Polish territories occupied by the Russians and from territories properly Russian, one estimates that presently, in the Reich and the occupied territories, including the Protectorate of Bohemia-Moravia, there are more than four million Jews, i.e., one fourth of the entire world Jewish population.

Measures.

1. Institution of ghettos.

Internal quarters of some cities have been designated for the Jews as their official homes, with the right of administration, police forces, and appropriate means of communication.

Of the ghettos established up to now, the most important are those of Litzmannstadt (Lodz) and Warsaw. Some ghettos are also found in the Baltic countries and in the occupied Russian territories.

2. Concentration camps.

Since, as is evident, places cannot be found for all Jews in the city ghettos, immense concentration camps have been created where they lead a harsh life; little food is given them; they are assigned to extremely hard work – conditions which quickly lead many to death.

It is said that such concentration camps are found up to now in Poland, that the eastern territories, particularly Poland, have been established in the plans of the German Government as the definitive place of residence for the Jewish population of Europe.

Generally, in order to not attract the attention of the population too much, they are forced to leave in the middle of the night; they are permitted to take little clothing with them and only a small sum of money.

3. The Star.

Since the month of September 1941, a mark of identification has been compulsory for all Jews: a yellow star, six pointed, to be worn on the breast, with the inscription in the center, *Jude*!

The sight of these wretches who, pale and emaciated (their food rations are much less than those of the Germans; some foodstuffs are denied to them entirely), walk the streets at predesignated hours of the day or, when travelling, cluster together in corners, awakens a profound sense of horror and pity.

Inhuman treatment in the occupied territories and in the countries politically subject to Germany:

An Italian journalist, returned from Rumania, gave me, some time ago, a long account concerning the brutal methods adopted in that country, mainly by German instigation, against the Jews.

He related to me that a train was completely filled with Jews; every opening was then closed, so that no air could enter. When the train arrived at its destination, there were only a few survivors, those, that is, who, finding themselves near some incompletely sealed opening, had been able to breathe a bit of air . . .

Di Meglio closed this part of his message by noting the anti-Christian character of Alfred Rosenberg's *Institut fuer Erforschung des juedischen Einflusses auf das deutsche kirchliche Leben* (Institute for Investigation of Jewish influence in German Religious Life), and also by noting the unconcern of the German clergy with the tribulations of the Jews.

In several respects Di Meglio's information was obviously erroneous. For example we can gain a fair idea of the actual conditions of the deportations of Rumanian Jews from the Report of the Red Cross, both from the excerpt reproduced in Chapter V here and from other sections,[10] and also from the writings of Ginsburg. It is certain that the events in the story related

283

by the anonymous Italian journalist were invention. Di Meglio seems willing to accept the worst.

Di Meglio's treatment of the role of the concentration camps admits some misinterpretations of the actual conditions. For one thing, he suggested that many Jews were sent to concentration camps because there was insufficient space for them in the ghettos; this is not correct. Jews, among others, were sent to the camps in Poland as labor needs required. Di Meglio also gave the impression that the camps were primarily for quartering Jews, which is also incorrect. He also probably exaggerated the poverty of the diet in the camps but, as we saw in Chapter IV, he was at least correct on the matter of the high death rate in the camps, at the time he wrote his account, although overwork was not the cause of the deaths.

In other words, Di Meglio's description of the situation was the general or approximate truth, with some inaccuracies, and colored by his willingness to believe the worst. It is clear that he had no information on the existence of an extermination program even remotely resembling the one that was then taking shape in the Allied propaganda and was being related to the Vatican by various Allied diplomats and Jewish organizations.

The Pope's Christmas address made a passing remark, without specific reference to the Jews, on "the hundreds of thousands who, through no fault of their own, and solely because of their nation or race, have been condemned to death or progressive extinction". Berlin had mixed reactions to the address; the RSHA considered it a direct assault on the Nazi regime, while the Foreign Office appears to have considered it so much holy hot air. The Allies, we recall from our Chapter III, had officially embraced the extermination claims on 17 December, in a statement in which "the number of victims" was "reckoned in many hundreds of thousands" of Jews, and they were not satisfied with the Pope's statement, and thought it was not explicit enough.[11] From our point of view, however, the Christmas remark seems at first puzzlingly strong, in view of the picture of the situation that the Vatican had received from the Berlin Nunciature, and also in consideration of the oddity that the Pope's strongest remark of such a category should have been made so early in the war and then not repeated.

An explanation for the appearance of the "death or progressive extinction" remark in the Pope's Christmas address is found in the Vatican's wartime documents. In late 1942 and early 1943 one of the Vatican's principal diplomatic objectives was to secure a pledge from the Allies not to bomb Rome. The British were particularly insistent on their right to bomb Rome, as compared to the Americans, who had a large Catholic minority that constituted a very important component of the political base of Roosevelt's New Deal. The British took the position that Rome could not be given special consideration and would be bombed if and when military factors indicated such action. In pursuit of its objective, the Vatican dealt not only with the Allies, attempting to divert them from their apparent course, but also with the Germans and Italians, attempting to persuade them to remove any operations of a military nature from Rome (there was little or no war industry in the city, but there were military command headquarters and military barracks). In December 1942 the Italian Government agreed to relocate its military headquarters away from Rome. Feeling that some progress toward their objective had been made, Cardinal Maglione met on 14 December with the British Minister to the Vatican, Sir F. D'Arcy Osborne, in order to communicate this development to the British and to further discuss the bombing issue. Osborne, however, was unimpressed and pointed out that there remained Italian troops quartered in the city. Maglione's notes on the meeting summarized the exchange thus:[12]

The Minister pointed out that one has the impression that the Holy See is particularly preoccupied with the Italian cities, when it speaks of bombings, because they are Italian.

I made him observe: (1) that for Rome there are special considerations. I recounted them to him (and I did not fail to repeat to him that if Rome is bombed, the Holy See will protest); (2) that the Holy See now intervenes against the bombing of the civilian population of the Italian cities because such bombings are in progress. The Minister must not forget that the Holy Father spoke against bombing of defenseless populations on other occasions: when the English cities were being bombed everybody knew that the bombings of the English cities did not escape really harsh words from the Holy Father.

The Minister recognized the justice of my observation and, then, exclaimed: But why doesn't the Holy See intervene against the terrible slaughter of the Jews?

I recalled for him that the Holy Father had already asserted, in his messages, the right to life, to a peaceful existence, and to a sufficient share in the goods of this world, for all men, whatever their race or religion.

One must not ignore, I added, how much the Holy Father has done and is doing to alleviate the plight of the poor Jews. These people know it and frequently thank the Holy See for how much it is doing for them.

The Minister insisted on this point: it would be necessary that the Holy See intervene to stop the massacres of the Jews. (end of note)

Later the same day Osborne ran into Msgr. Domenico Tardini, Secretary of the Congregation of Extraordinary Ecclesiastic Affairs (the Vatican Foreign Office) and, regarding the departure of the Italian military command headquarters from Rome, Osborne assured Tardini that "It changes nothing!" Tardini summarized his conversation with Osborne in his notes and concluded that[13]

The removal of the military commands may help put better in evidence that whoever bombs Rome is barbaric (and thus it is well that the Holy See be an interested party), but it will not spare Rome from the bombs.

We thus see the background of the Pope's Christmas Eve remark. To the Vatican, it appeared from the exchange between Osborne and Maglione that the English were in effect proposing a deal: the Pope condemns extermination of Jews and the Allies do not bomb Rome, a persuasive position that can convince even a Holy Father. Aside from any possible ethical considerations, it was obvious to the Vatican that it could not wreck its official neutrality by publicly accusing the Germans of completely fabricated offenses and, in any case, the Germans were still the dominant military power on the Continent at that time, so the remark appeared in the Christmas address without specific reference to Jews or Germany (along with other remarks that sounded more or less anti-German without being specific). However the Allied bombing threat to Rome did not diminish after Christmas 1942. Thus except for a brief similar remark, ignored by the world press, which occurred in a long papal address of 2 June 1943, no more talk of this nature came from the Vatican. Pope Pius made a favorable reference to the Christmas remark in his letter of 30 April 1943 to his friend von Preysing, but even in that confidential communication his specific words were milder than those of the Christmas remark.[14]

Although the Vatican was entirely justified in interpreting Osborne's remarks as a specific proposition, it is most likely that this was a misinterpretation nevertheless, and that Osborne did not imagine himself as offering a deal. It is possible, for example, that Osborne felt that Maglione had a relatively strong position and thus he grasped at something somewhat out of context in order to supplement his side of the verbal exchange. The official Allied declaration on exterminations of Jews came three days later and thus the matter was no doubt somewhat in the air in the diplomatic corps and came to Osborne rather naturally.

Rome was first bombed on 19 July 1943 (by the Americans), the targets being the rail centers that German and Italian troops had started passing through after the Allied landings in Sicily on 9 July. In subsequent raids bombs occasionally fell on the Vatican, but the damage to historical and religious monuments, in the Vatican and elsewhere in Rome, was slight.

The only other point of some interest in regard to the role of the Vatican is that its efforts in extending aid to Jews were fairly extensive, as discussed by Rhodes. However Waagenaar should also be read in this connection, on account of Rhodes' failure to make some points. However, from the point of view of analyzing the extermination legend, the only significant inference to draw from such activities of the Vatican is that they offer further data showing that, the Vatican being somewhat involved in Jewish affairs in Europe at the time, the exterminations could not possibly have happened without the Vatican knowing of them.

While the significant points regarding the role of the Vatican are not many and have been covered, there are a few odd matters that we may as well set forth while we are on this subject.

A strange character appearing in the Vatican's wartime documents is Pirro Scavizzi, a very ordinary priest who rode Italian military hospital trains that shuttled back and forth between Italy and the eastern front. He was called an "almoner" and he administered to the wounded Italian soldiers whatever incantations are delivered in such circumstances. Since he did so much travelling, however, he was frequently used as a courier, and his frequent near contact with, and regular delivery of messages to high ranking prelates seems to have fired his imagination.

The first oddity we run into was in February-March 1942. Scavizzi produced a letter, allegedly from Adam Sapieha, Archbishop of Cracow, on the subject of the sufferings of Catholic priests under the brutal Germans. As related in *Actes et documents,* however, the circumstances were most peculiar:[15]

> . . . the Archbishop renounced all precaution and described . . . the rigor of the Nazi oppression and the tragedy of the concentration camps. But after having deposited this testimony with . . . Scavizzi, he grew fearful and sent Scavizzi a message asking him to burn the document "for fear that it fall into the hands of the Germans, who would have shot all the Bishops and perhaps others". The Abbé Scavizzi destroyed the note in question, but not without first having made a copy in his own hand and having added at the same time his own testimony on the tragedy and the despair which constituted the daily course of existence of the Catholics of Poland.

Scavizzi's producing of a letter which he had burned, in honoring the request of the author of the letter, necessarily makes one a bit uneasy about him, but let us bear with him a bit. He next appears in connection with a letter he wrote to Pope Pius from Bologna on 12 May 1942:[16]

> In regard to the present Nuncio, the Cardinal (Orsenigo, Nuncio in Berlin) deplored the silence about it and expressed the judgment that He (the Pope) is too timorous and not interested in such grave tidings.
> The anti-Jewish campaign is implacable and constantly grows worse, with deportations and even mass executions.
> The massacre of the Jews in the Ukraine is already complete. In Poland and Germany they also intend to carry it to completion, with a system of mass killings.

We have seen above that this did not represent the information of the Berlin Nunciature, so Scavizzi was just projecting opinions of his own onto Orsenigo. However even if Orsenigo had held such views, it is ludicrous in the extreme to imagine that he would have confided them to Scavizzi, even for Scavizzi's personal information, not to mention for transmission to the Pope via Scavizzi. One is now entitled to raise suspicions regarding Scavizzi's reliability.

Scavizzi next appears on 7 October 1942, when he wrote a "report on the situation in Poland" that managed to get into the Vatican files:[17]

> The Jews: The elimination of the Jews, with mass killings, without regard for children or even for babies, is almost total. As for the remainder of them, who are all marked by white armbands, civilized life is impossible. They are not permitted to shop, enter business establishments, take streetcars or taxis, attend spectacles or frequent non-Jewish homes. Before being deported or killed, they are condemned to forced hard labor, even if they are of the cultivated class. The few remaining Jews appear serene, almost ostentatiously proud. It is said that more than two million Jews have been killed.

At this point, one develops a second suspicion, namely, that the Vatican took as knowledge what we have set forth as our first suspicion about Scavizzi: that little weight should be attached to Scavizzi's statements. They had such material from Scavizzi in their files but did not consider it as confirming the claims of the Zionist organizations, as is made clear above.

Possibly because the Vatican wartime documents are still in the process of editing for publication at the time this is being written, Scavizzi makes no more appearances in them. However in 1964 (he died around 1967) he claimed, in an Italian magazine, that, during the war, the Pope had *confided* to him, Pirro Scavizzi, on the apparently negative implications of a proposed excommunication of Hitler (a nominal Catholic) for his exterminations of Jews![18] That does it. Scavizzi was obviously a weaver of self-inflating tall tales designed to make him appear rather more important than his humble station in riding the hospital trains would have suggested. It therefore becomes clear that our second suspicion must be correct; Scavizzi was considered by the Vatican to be a harmless nut who could be trusted to administer last rites, and even to deliver messages, but not to keep facts straight. It is mildly humorous that, judging from their editorial comments, the editors of *Actes et documents* seem to take Scavizzi seriously. However, since the interpretation of Scavizzi as a teller of tall tales fairly leaps out at the reader from the documents, it is possible that the editors have other thoughts on the subject of Scavizzi that they have not expressed.

There is, however, one point of not negligible importance in connection with Scavizzi's reports, particularly the report of 12 May 1942 concerning what Orsenigo allegedly confided to him. It is not likely that Scavizzi independently invented the extermination legend, although it is remotely possible. If he did not invent the extermination claims appearing in his letter of 12 May 1942, he must have heard them somewhere, a fact of some interest, since his report is dated over a month before Zionist organizations in the West started talking this way (the first known such statement from the World Jewish Congress was on 29 June 1942, as we noted in Chapter III). This suggests that such propaganda was in circulation in Eastern Europe earlier than June 1942. This, indeed, is in agreement with the account of Dawidowicz, according to whom extermination claims for the Wartheland (the annexed part of Poland south of the Corridor), claiming killings via gasmobiles at Chelmno, first appeared in the four page Jewish underground publication, the *Veker*, which printed these first extermination claims on pages three and four in issues published in February 1942. Claims of exterminations in the General Government of Poland (via gassing at Belzec) appeared in the underground publication *Mitteylungen* in early April 1942.[19] The evidence, thus, suggests that the extermination legend owes its birth to obscure Polish Jewish propagandists, but the nurturing of the legend to the status of an international and historical hoax was the achievement of Zionist circles centered primarily in the West, particularly in and around New York.

Since it appears that extermination propaganda was in existence in Poland in the spring of 1942, and since much of the information that reached the Vatican from Poland came through the office of the Papal Nuncio in Berlin, such stories might have reached Orsenigo at the time. Indeed, a letter of Orsenigo's to Msgr. Giovanni Montini (the present Pope Paul VI, who often substituted for Maglione during the war), dated 28 July 1942, was devoted mainly to deploring the difficulty of ascertaining exactly what was happening in regard to the Jews. After commenting on the occasional practice of the Nazis of suddenly and without warning ordering selected Jews to pack up for deportation, he wrote:[20]

As is easy to understand, this lack of advance notice opens the door to the most maccabre suppositions on the fate of the non-aryans. There are also in circulation rumors, difficult to verify, of disastrous journeys and even of massacres of Jews. Also every intervention in favor only of the non-aryan Catholics has thus far been rejected with the customary reply that baptismal water does not change Jewish blood and that the German Reich is defending itself from the non-aryan race, not from the religion of the baptized Jews.

Among such sinister rumors there is no lack of some less bleak: thus for example there is talk that in Holland, where deportations of the non-aryans have now commenced, an outspoken protest by the clergy, with which the Catholic Bishops associated themselves, succeeded in getting the baptized non-aryans excepted from the deportations. Likewise it was reported that in the notorious ghetto of Litzmannstadt, in the Wartheland, a Polish priest, who with a spirit of apostolical heroism had requested it, was granted permission to enter and remain there for the care of the souls of the non-aryan Catholics.

An editorial footnote remarks that the story from Holland was false. We remark in passing that a considerable portion of the Vatican concern for aiding Jews, in this period, was specifically for the families of Jewish background that had converted to Catholicism, and whose situation was particularly tragic, since it seemed that nobody wanted them; the Germans considered them Jews, and the Jews considered them renegades.

The preceding remarks of Orsenigo make it clear that Scavizzi had at least misrepresented him, but also make it clear that he had heard certain horrid rumors, although it is not clear what he meant by "massacres" (*eccidi in massa*). There were, of course, as we noted in Chapter VII, occasional massacres of Jews during the war, and the reports he had received may have pertained to them, or they might have had their origin in the extermination propaganda that had recently started coming from Jewish underground organizations in Poland. It is even possible that he was thinking of some report that Scavizzi had made at the Berlin Nunciature in connection with the "information" he transmitted in his letter of 12 May 1942. In any case, the Di Meglio letter of 9 December 1942 shows that the Nunciature, at that time, had accepted no extermination claims (except possibly for the story from Rumania), if such claims reached it.

There are just a couple more points worth discussion, in relation to the Vatican documents. During the war the Vatican representative in Greece and Turkey was Msgr. Angelo Roncalli, the later Pope John XXIII. On 8 July 1943 he reported to the Vatican from Istanbul as follows:[21]

1. In accord with my rule of circumspection in my contacts with various people, even those entitled to special respect, I avoid meetings not strictly necessary or singularly useful. For example I saw von Papen (German Ambassador to Turkey) only once in six months, and only hastily and in passing on the occasion of my Easter visit to Ankara. At the time there was much talk of the Katyn affair which, according to von Papen, should have made the Poles reflect on the advantage of their turning to the Germans. I replied with a sad smile that it was necessary first of all to make them overlook the millions of Jews sent to Poland and *soppressi* there, and that in any case this was a good occasion for the Reich to improve its treatment of the Poles.

Now that von Papen has returned, as has the entire diplomatic corps, from Ankara to Istanbul and the Bosphorus, occasions for meetings will not be lacking.

2. Now and then the fine Baron von Lersner comes to see me . . .

Roncalli then proceeded to discuss matters not relevant to our subject.

When this document was published by the Vatican, the press reported that Roncalli had remarked on "the millions of Jews sent to Poland and annihilated there",[22] a fair enough translation, but a few words on the point of the translation are worthwhile. The Italian verb *sopprimere* (whose past participle appears in Roncalli's note) is cognate to the English "to suppress" and the French *supprimer* (which is relevant since Roncalli and von Papen probably spoke to each other in French). The Italian and French words are equivalent in meaning, but they are not equivalent to the English word since, when applied to people, *sopprimere* and *supprimer* carry some implication of killing in large numbers. However when applied to people they are not entirely equivalent to "extermination" or "annihilation"; both French and Italian have words cognate to and equivalent to these two English words. To apply *sopprimere* to a large group of people carries an implication only of large numbers of killings, and may or may not mean "extermination", depending on the context. Thus one must allow the possibility that Roncalli was thinking of something other than the sorts of extermination claims that the Allies had made, and which Roncalli had certainly heard by then. For example, he may have been thinking in terms of such things as the then recent and highly publicized German suppression of the Warsaw ghetto rebellion, in the course of which the Germans killed many Jews. However I am inclined to reject such an interpretation; it seems more likely to me that Roncalli was indeed thinking in terms of exterminations such as the Allies had claimed.

If, however, one reads the Roncalli account carefully, against its proper diplomatic background, it becomes clear that it is not really very important what, very specifically, Roncalli was thinking about when he made this remark. He describes a chance meeting between two diplomats, one of whom, he, did not wish a meeting. In accord with his "rule of circumspection" his words would therefore have been chosen to "avoid meetings". What Roncalli in effect said to von Papen was that, if the latter wished to prolong the meeting, Roncalli was going to be difficult. Roncalli communicated to von Papen, in diplomatic language, the attitude he sets forth in plain and direct language in the first sentence of his report. Roncalli's remark was a diplomatic parry of a certain well known type, wherein it is not really important to determine, in better than vague terms, what the speaker was referring to, or to determine whether or not the speaker himself accepted the truth of the allegation in question. All that is relevant in the exchange is that Roncalli did not want to talk to von Papen, and that was all he communicated to von Papen. If, on the other hand, Roncalli had wished to speak to von Papen, he certainly would not have *opened* his side of the exchange with such necessarily antagonistic remarks, either in reference to exterminations or in reference to bloody suppression of ghetto revolts, and quite independently of any of his own opinions on the subject of alleged German atrocities and brutalities.

Since the Vatican was an observer of and participant in the events of World War II it was inevitable that the extermination stories, which the whole world heard, were heard also by the Vatican. The stories are thus naturally reflected in passages found in the Vatican/documents and, when we encounter such passages there, they should be viewed in the context of the possible specific motivations of the person making the remark and also of the evolution of the propaganda as analyzed in this book, especially in Chapter III. Roncalli, as his report clearly implies in its first sentence, was merely trying to get rid of von Papen, at their 8 July 1943 encounter in Ankara, when he repeated the extermination claim which, as he well knew, had not been specifically endorsed by the Vatican despite Allied pressures.

Another letter we encounter in the Vatican documents was written to Pope Pius in August 1942 by the Ukranian Roman Catholic Archbishop André

Szeptyczkyi. The letter dwells at great length on supposed German atrocities and the reader will be very puzzled, especially in regard to motivation, until the last lines are read and Szeptyczkyi finally comes to the whole point of his letter. He remarks on his failures over a three year period to obtain from the Pope an Apostolic Benediction (i.e. a papal endorsement, most important in religious politics) and then points out that his sufferings and strivings under the "evil" Germans should certainly be adequate grounds for granting one at last.[23]

That the few passages appearing in the Vatican documents and bearing on exterminations of Jews merely reflect the evolution of the propaganda, as analyzed in this book, is very clear. In Chapter III (p. 99) we noted that Burzio passed on to the Vatican, from Slovakia, tales about soap factories when such tales were a feature of the propaganda. Another example is a set of notes made by Maglione on 5 May 1943 recording extermination stories. The occasion for composing the notes is not clear, i.e. the reader cannot tell from what has been published whether Maglione was recording his own impressions or merely allegations made by somebody else (other documents written by Maglione around that time do not suggest that he believed the extermination stories). In any case, gas chamber exterminations at Treblinka and near Brest-Litovsk are noted. The editors of *Actes et documents,* obviously puzzled, remark[24]

The information, probably delivered by an Italian official, would seem quite old, since it mentions neither Birkenau nor Auschwitz, where the greater part of the exterminations were concentrated at the time.

Further on this theme, the editors remark that in 1943[25]

the Allied propaganda, which dwelled abundantly on the German atrocities, was completely silent, for reasons which have never been satisfactorily analyzed, on Auschwitz.

Just as it was inevitable that some of the propaganda would manifest itself in the Vatican's documents, it was also inevitable that some of the truth, in regard to the matters we are concerned with here, would find its way into that part of the Vatican archives selected for publication. Thus the documents suggest that the Vatican did after all have some access to Jews in Poland, not only Polish Jews but also Italian Jews who were deported after the German occupation of Rome on 8 September 1943.[26] Also the editors of volume 9 of *Actes et documents* (on the subject of war victims in 1943) note that friends and relatives of deported Jews were known to have later received mail from them, that the members of the Dutch resistance who were "in constant contact with the Jews of their country (reported) simply that the deportees were enlisted for work in the camps, while the aged were sent to ghettos", and that the Jewish leaders in Rome were unaware of any extermination program and feared deportations only in connection with such things as "the rigors of winter and the fragile health of many deportees", as is confirmed by "many letters received then at the Vatican, and which today form a thick dossier in the archives . . . no mention is made of their brutal extermination". We also read that Father Marie-Benoît (a priest who was deeply involved in wartime aid to Jews) made a report in July 1943 on deportations of Jews from France and remarked that the Auschwitz and nearby camps were work camps where "the morale among the deportees is generally good and they are confident of the future".[27]

Since Auschwitz extermination propaganda only started in 1944 we will probably encounter Auschwitz extermination claims in the Vatican's wartime documents when the Vatican publishes documents for 1944-1945, because that is all there is, bearing on exterminations, in the documents of this critically situated source: propaganda.

NOTES

In this work we have avoided extravagant notes and have attempted to say everything worth saying in the text. The notes provided here are thus very succinct.

Since many notes direct the reader to Nuernberg trial documents, we have attempted to indicate those cases where the text of the document in question may appear in some relatively easily accessible source. With the exception of documents in the NI, NG and NO series and other exceptions that are noted, the texts of documents referenced here are printed in the 42 volume IMT set. The documents in the NI, NG and NO are the majority of documents referenced, and the notes indicate where the texts may be found in those cases where it is known that they have been reproduced in some book; in most such cases the documents are printed in the 15 volume NMT set. If no such reprinting is indicated, then we are not aware of a reproduction of the document, so the investigator must in such a case go through the annoying procedure of obtaining copies through the inter-library loan department of a large research library.

I. TRIALS, JEWS AND NAZIS
1. Kennedy, 216-219; 236-239 in Memorial Edition.
2. Grayzel, 792.
3. Rassinier (1961), 9,175; Rassinier (1962), 112.
4. *Nation Europa*, vol.23 (Oct 73), 50; vol.25 (Aug 75), 39. The Ginsburg beating incident is well known and is mentioned by App, 20.
5. Ruppin, 30-33.
6. *N.Y. Times* (22 Feb 48), 4.
7. *World Almanac* (1931), 192; (1942), 588; (1952), 394; (1962), 251.
8. *World Almanac* (1931), 197; (1942), 593; (1952), 437; (1962), 258.
9. *World Almanac* (1952), 438.
10. US-WRB (1945), 64-69; *N.Y. Times* (10 June 44), 1; (13 June 44), 1; (10 Aug 44), 5; (24 Oct 44), 14; (25 Oct 44), 13; Myer, 108-123.
11. Reitlinger, 534, 542-544.
12. Reitlinger, 327.
13. NG-2586-G in NMT, vol.13, 212.
14. Rassinier (1964), 220.
15. Kelley, 76-77; *N.Y. Times* (2 Jan 58), 18; Robertson, 266.
16. Rassinier (1962), 83. See also Dawidowicz, 121.
17. Taylor (15 Aug 49), 1-3; *N.Y. Times* (1 Feb 45), 4.
18. Davidson, 6,18,21n.
19. *N.Y. Times* (21 June 45), 6; (16 Dec 45), sec.4, 8; *New Yorker* (17 Nov 45), 24; *Survey Graphic* (Jan 46), 4-9; *Reader's Digest* (Feb 46), 56-64.
20. Taylor (Apr 49), 248-255; Select Committee, 1536.
21. *N.Y. Times* (17 Oct 43), 16; (20 May 45), 15.
22. Kolander; Taylor (15 Aug 49), 4,10,13,14.
23. Utley, 185-200; *Chicago Tribune* (30 Apr 48), 12; (13 Feb 49), 3; (14 Feb 49), 3; (17 Feb 49), 8; *N.Y. Times* (31 Oct 48), sec.4, 8.
24. *N.Y. Times* (30 Jul 48), 5; (7 Oct 48), 15; (7 Jan 49), 1,9; (2 Mar 49), 1,14; (5 Mar 49), 1,4; (5 May 49), 8.
25. *N.Y. Times* (5 Mar 49), 4; (30 Apr 49), 2; (6 Sep 49), 9; (7 Sep 49), 9; (8 Sep 49), 9.
26. Arendt, 201,251 (221,274 in 1964 edition); Aretz, 28-29.
27. Taylor (Apr 49), 272-276.
28. DuBois, 182. *Chicago Tribune* (23 Feb 48), 1,2; (24 Feb 48), 3; (25 Feb 48), 4; (26 Feb 48), 1,8; (28 Feb 48), 4,8; (29 Feb 48), 2; *N.Y. Times* (23 Feb 48), 5; (25 Feb 48), 10; (29 Feb 48), 10; (6 Mar 48), 6.
29. Taylor (Apr 49), 272-276.
30. Marcus; *Encyclopedia Judaica*, vol.11, 945; Berkman, 44-45; *Saturday Evening Post* (4 Dec 48), 179.
31. Taylor (15 Aug 49), 13,14,34,35.
32. DuBois, 19-22, 31,53,63,69-70,74-75; Berkman, 195-199,157-159.

33. Marcus; Berkman, 191-193,199; John & Hadawi, vol.2, 209n,367; Zink, 209,210; *N.Y. Times* (8 Apr 43), 12; (16 Apr 43), 10; (17 Mar 46), 15; (16 Sep 47), 10; (29 Apr 48), 16; Blum, 383.
34. Colvin, vii,1-6; *N.Y. Times* (23 Dec 56), 1; (6 Jul 69), 11. See Sturdza, 161-162, for an episodic illustration of Canaris at work.
35. Reitlinger, 28; Red Cross (1947), 99; Eichmann, session 75, V1,W1.
36. Arendt, 136 (152 in 1964 edition).

II. CAMPS

1. Veale, 133-136; Martin, 121.
2. Reitlinger, 122,402; Hilberg, 570-571; DuBois, 127.
3. Burney, 9; Buber, 188; Lenz, 31; Cohen, 120-122.
4. Sington, 117-118.
5. Fyfe, 152.
6. Sington, 48.
7. Fyfe, 17.
8. Hilberg, 561-564; Reitlinger, 94,147-150,154.
9. Cohen, 26-28;
10. Red Cross (1948), vol.1, 546-547.
11. 1469-PS and NO-1990 in NMT, vol.5, 382,389.
12. Cohen, xiii.
13. Aronéanu, 212.
14. 1469-PS in NMT, vol.5, 382.
15. Reitlinger, 364-365,406; Hilberg, 377-379,632-633.
16. A. Frank, 285.
17. Aronéanu, 207,213,214,217,220.
18. Burney, 10-14.
19. Hoehne, 383-387 (434-436 in paperback).
20. Burney, 10.
21. 3420-PS; 3422-PS. For pictures see, e.g., Andrus, photographs. A "macabre collection" of specimens from Buchenwald is also pictured in Pelissier, 64opp.
22. 3421-PS; IMT, vol.3, 515; quoted Shirer, 984.
23. *N.Y. Times* (24 Sep 48), 3; (1 Oct 48), 11; (8 Oct 48), 10; (22 Oct 48), 5; (27 Dec 48), 1,12; (20 Dec 50), 15; (16 Jan 51), 1; (3 Sep 67), 1.
24. Burney, 106-109.
25. Lenz, 32,42,78; 1063-PS.
26. Red Cross (1948), vol.1, 620; vol.3, 83,184; Red Cross (1947), 82-84.
27. Red Cross (1947), 134-137.
28. Red Cross (1947), 144-146,149-152.
29. Lenz, 270; Gun, 63-64.
30. M.J. Smith, 94-95.
31. IMT, vol.5, 167-173; Rassinier (1962), 78.
32. Burney, 107; Red Cross (1947), 151.
33. Gordon, 23-25.
34. Red Cross (1947), 150.
35. Letter by Pinter in Catholic weekly *Our Sunday Visitor* (14 Jun 59), 15.
36. *Die Zeit* (26 Aug 60), 14 (letter by M. Broszat); Rassinier (1962), 79. Rassinier's reference to *Die Zeit* (19 Aug 60) is incorrect, as indicated here.
37. Howard, 3,11-22,44,60-62; NMT, vol.7, 79-80.
38. Craven, 172.
39. Howard, 35-37.
40. Dunbrook, 50; Naunton, 107.
41. DuBois, 154-155.
42. Reitlinger, 110,128; NO-034 in NMT, vol.5, 356-358.
43. Reitlinger, 114-115; DuBois, 156.
44. Central Commission, Figs. 2,4; Langbein, 929.
45. Central Commission, 30; Reitlinger, 492; NO-021 in NMT, vol.5, 385.
46. DuBois, 217-218,223-227; Reitlinger, 115.
47. NMT, vol.8, 1183-1184.
48. Red Cross (1947), 92; Red Cross (1948), vol.1, 546-551.
49. Central Commission, 31; Reitlinger, 123,492; 1469-PS and NO-021 in NMT, vol.5, 382,385.
50. NI-11412-A in NMT, vol.8, 311-312.
51. NO-1290 in NMT, vol.5, 371.
52. Cohen, 180; Christophersen, 34. See also the discussion of the Dachau brothel in Gun, 38-40.
53. NMT, vol.9, 121; Central Commission, 37.

54. DuBois, 164,220-224.
55. DuBois, 141; NMT, vol.6, 207,223; NMT, vol.9, 120; US-WRB (1944), pt.I, 1-2; Christophersen, 23-25.
56. Reitlinger, 115,157; Hilberg, 565,574.
57. Central Commission, 31.
58. Central Commission, 27-29; DuBois, 130; Friedman, 33.
59. DuBois, 341; Naunton, 107; Bebb & Wakefield, 945.

III. WASHINGTON AND NEW YORK

1. Howard, 4-7,216; U.S. Special Committee, 24.
2. Howard, chapters 2-9.
3. Howard, 82-83.
4. Howard, 104-108.
5. Naunton, 104.
6. DuBois, 284.
7. As stated, the rubber crisis "filled the press", but the following stories seem to summarize the crisis adequately: *Business Week* (31 Jan 42), 22+; (14 Mar 42), 15+; (30 May 42), 15+; (20 Jun 42), 15+; (15 Aug 42), 15+; (19 Sep 42), 15+; (19 Dec 42), 28+; *Newsweek* (6 Apr 42), 46+; (13 Apr 42), 56+; (1 June 42), 46+; (21 Sep 42), 58+; *N.Y. Times* (11 Jan 42), sec.7, 6+; (26 Jul 42), sec.7, 3+; *Fortune* (June 42), 92+; *Nature Magazine* (May 42), 233+; *Harper's* (Dec 42), 66+.
8. Naunton, 108; Howard, 210-213.
9. Howard, 221-222; Coit, 120-121,162-222,513-520.
10. Howard, 227-228; U.S. Special Committee, 13,18,50-51; Dunbrook, 40-46.
11. The photograph appears in Schoenberner, 162 (206 in paperback), and in Central Commission, Fig.39.
12. C.B. Smith, 166-171 and photographs.
13. Hilberg, 631; Reitlinger, 493-495.
14. Unless otherwise noted, out treatment of the early extermination propaganda, related developments in Washington and New York and the conflicts between the State Department, on the other hand, and Zionists and the Treasury Department on the other, and the events leading up to the establishment of the War Refugee Board, is based on Morse, 3-99; Feingold, 167-247; DuBois, 183-189; Blum, 207-227; Israel; 173-174, 216-217, 306-337; Morgenthau.
15. Guggenheim's affidavit is in despatch no. 49 of 29 October 1942, of the retired files of the U.S. Consulate, Geneva, which are in the archives of the Foreign Affairs Document and Reference Center, Department of State, Washington. Squire's memorandum of his interview with Burckhardt is attached to Squire's personal letter of 9 November 1942 to Harrison, which is in the same file.
16. The questions put to Burckhardt, and his answers, are IMT document Kaltenbrunner 3.
17. The statement of the "Vatican source" is in the U.S. National Archives as Department of State file 740.00116 EW/726.
18. Hull, 471-473.
19. *Morgenthau Diary*, 6.
20. *N.Y. Times* (23 Jan 44), 11.
21. *Morgenthau Diary*, 6-9.
22. DuBois, 198-199; Red Cross (1947), 20,23,59-60; US-WRB (1945), 9-10, 56-61.
23. US-WRB (1945), 46-56.
24. *Morgenthau Diary*, 805-810; Aretz, 366-368.
25. Barnes. Quoted in Anonymous, 3.
26. Blum, 343,383.
27. *Das Reich* (14 Jun 42), 2; Jaeckel, 62-63.
28. Calic, 34-35. Hitler also made relevant remarks in *Mein Kampf.*
29. Hitler, 848.
30. *N.Y. Times* (29 Oct 42), 20; *New Yorker* (18 Apr 42), 62; (12 Sep 42), 53; (24 Oct 42), 64f; (28 Nov 42), 82; (5 Dec 42), 82.
31. Reitlinger, 176-186.
32. Reitlinger, 439.
33. DuBois, 197.
34. *N.Y. Times* (1 Nov 43), 5; (11 Dec 43), 1; (13 Dec 43), 11; (3 Jan 44), 9.
35. Reitlinger, 533,545,546.
36. *Time* (12 Jul 54), 98.100; *New Republic* (20 Dec 54), 22; *N.Y. Times* (7 Apr 53), 20; (12 Apr 53), 33; Eichmann, session 85, A1-L1; IMT, vol.11, 228.
37. R.H. Smith, 214-215.
38. Reitlinger, 367,370-371,378.
39. Reitlinger, 352.
40. DuBois, 137-138,186-188.
41. NMT, vol.5, 820; Reitlinger, 466; Borwicz, 66-76.

42. US-WRB (1945), 24-33. For contacts of Slovakian Jews with Poland, especially Cracow, and with Budapest, see Neumann's book and also the testimony of Freudiger: Eichmann, session 51, Wwl-Eee; session 52, A1-Bb1. Wallenberg discussed in Poliakov and Wulf (1955), 416-420.
43. R.H. Smith, 2,12,23,62,125,239; Kimche & Kimche. 108.
44. IMT, vol.3, 568.
45. DuBois, 173-175.
46. Neumann, 178-183.
47. *N.Y. Times* (30 Nov 57), 21; *Encyclopedia Judaica,* vol.16, 418-419.
48. Reitlinger, 115n,182,590-591.
49. Eichmann, session 52, M1,N1,W1-Aal; session 71, Ffl; session 72, Il-M1; session 109, J1-L1,R1,S1. The affidavit is reproduced by Vrba & Bestic, 273-276.
50. Naumann, 290-291; Langbein, vol.1, 122-125; vol.2, 968,971.
51. *N.Y. Times* (27 Apr 74), 7. *Actes et documents,* vol.8, 476,486-489; vol.9, 40,178n.

IV. AUSCHWITZ

1. 3868-PS.
2. IMT, vol.11, 396-422.
3. Hilberg, 575; Reitlinger, 113.
4. Reitlinger, 113,502,516-517; Red Cross (1947), 95,98,103-104.
5. Langbein, vol.2, 930-931; Naumann, 19opp; US-WRB (1944), pt.1, 22.
6. IMT, vol.6, 211.
7. Reitlinger, 119.
8. 008—USSR; Friedman, 14.
9. Reitlinger, 472-478; US-WRB (1945), 39-40.
10. US-WRB (1945), 49-50.
11. IMT, vol.11, 398.
12. Hilberg, 556-560; Reitlinger, 107ff; documents R-129, NO-719 and 1063(F)-PS in NMT, vol.5, 298-303.
13. Reitlinger, 109,115.
14. Reitlinger, 147ff.
15. DuBois, 213. Some of the chemistry of Zyklon ("Cyclon") is discussed in the article on CYANIDE in the *Encyclopedia Britannica* for 1943.
16. Hilberg, 567-571.
17. IMT, vol.6, 225-332.
18. Hilberg, 570; Reitlinger, 154-156.
19. Hardenbergh, 252-254,257-259; Knipling.
20. IMT, vol.6, 211,225,360-364; Rassinier (1962) 80,224; Rassinier (1964), 105n; Rassinier (1965), 38-48; Reitlinger, 161n.
21. NMT, vol.1, 865-870; IMT, vol.27, 340-342.
22. Hilberg, 570.
23. Reitlinger, 161; 1553-PS.
24. Friedlaender, vii-xii.
25. Friedlaender, xi.
26. Friedlaender, x.
27. Reitlinger, 162f. See also *Vierteljahreshefte f. Zeitgeschichte* (Apr 53), 189n, which is cited in article in *Nation Europa* (May 63), 50+ (q.v.).
28. Hilberg, 567; Reitlinger, 155-156; documents NO-4344 and NO-4345 in NMT, vol.5, 362-364.
29. Hilberg, 565; Reitlinger, 158n.
30. Langbein, vol.2, 930-931; Naumann, 19opp.
31. Reitlinger, 155-158.
32. US-WRB (1944), pt.1, 19-21,37-38; Reitlinger, 182-183; Blumental, 105.
33. IMT, vol.6, 218.
34. Reitlinger, 183.
35. *Yad Vashem Studies,* vol.7, 109,110n,113.
36. Reitlinger, 181-182; Boehm, 292-293.
37. Reitlinger, 118-121. Reitlinger remarks on the "mystery" presented by the data in the Netherlands Red Cross reports, which is presented and discussed here in Appendix C. The letters from Auschwitz are considered by de Jong.
38. Cohen, 38-39.
39. Red Cross (1947), 91-92.
40. NMT, vol.8, 320.
41. DuBois, 53,173,231; US-WRB (1945), 48-55.
42. Lerner, 152-153.
43. Friedman, 13-14.
44. Cohen, 119.

45. Cohen, 60.
46. Friedman, 14-15; Reitlinger, 172; Hilberg, 587; Blumental, 109-110. One of the documents are reproduced in Poliakov & Wulf (1955), 198.
47. NO-4634 in NMT, vol.4, 1166; Eichmann, session 79, W1-Y1.
48. IMT, vol.11, 336-339.
49. Poliakov & Wulf (1956), 299-302; Eichmann, session 79, Y1-Bb1; session 101, Hh1-Mm1; session 107, U1-V1; session 109, F1-H1,N1,01; NG-5077.
50. Most of the Korherr report is reproduced in Poliakov & Wulf (1955), 240-248. Eichmann, session 77, Y1,Z1.
51. Reitlinger, 557. Documents reproduced in Poliakov & Wulf (1955), 197-199.
52. IMT, vol.11, 400-401.
53. IMT, vol.11, 420; Central Commission, 87-88.
54. Central Commission, 83-84; Rassinier (1962), 85-86. Rassinier does not cite a source, so he presumably got it from Central Commission.
55. Reitlinger, 157-158; Hilberg, 565; NO-4472.
56. Central Commission, 83; Rassinier (1962), 86; NO-4461.
57. Reitlinger, 159; NO-4353, NO-4400 & NO-4401 in NMT, vol.5, 353-356; NO-4445; NO-4448. Photograph also in Schoenberner and in Nyiszli.
58. Friedman, 54.
59. NMT, vol.5, 619-620.
60. 008-USSR.
61. NO-4466 in NMT, vol.5, 624.
62. Friedman, 20,74,78; Hilberg, 632.
63. 008-USSR; Central Commission, 88; US-WRB (1944), pt.1, 14-16; Fyfe, 158; Blumental, 100.
64. Rassinier (1962), 245-249.
65. DuBois, 221. NO-1245.
66. Cohen, 81,125. See also Fyfe, 159. And Appendix D here.
67. NMT, vol.5, 624-625. See also Blumental, 100.
68. Polson, 138,143-145.
69. Polson, 138-139.
70. DuBois, 340-341.
71. IMT, vol.11, 421.
72. DuBois, 218,230,232.
73. Polson, 137-146.
74. Reitlinger, 158-159.
75. Polson, 142.
76. 008-USSR; Central Commission, 89.
77. Johnson & Auth, 259-261.
78. Polson, 141.
79. *N.Y. Times* (30 Aug 44), 1.
80. NMT, vol.5, 622-623.
81. Hilberg, 566.
82. Grosch's testimony is supposed to be in the Case 4 transcript, 3565-3592, but these pages were missing in the transcript copy I consulted. Presumably he testified in agreement with his affidavit NO-2154.
83. NO-2154 quoted in Rassinier (1962), 84ff, and also in Poliakov & Wulf (1955), 136. Grosch's pre-court wavering is reported in the Ortmann memorandum attached to NO-4406.
84. Central Commission, 41,43; Naumann, 194,254; German edition of Naumann, 540.
85. IMT, vol.6, 211.
86. Reitlinger, 125; NO-021 in NMT, vol.5, 385. See also Fyfe, 729, or Appendix D herein.
87. DuBois, 192,220.
88. US-WRB (1944), pt.1, 30,32; Reitlinger, 122.
89. DuBois, 209.
90. Reitlinger, 122-123. The death book is at the *Rijksinstituut voor Oorlogsdocumentatie,* and is discussed by the Netherlands Red Cross, vol.1, 8-12.
91. US-WRB (1944), pt.1, 32.
92. e.g. Burney, 108-109.
93. Reitlinger, 127; 2172-PS.
94. NO-1523 and NO-1285 in NMT, vol.5, 372-376.
95. 1469-PS in NMT, vol.5, 379-382.
96. NO-1935 in NMT, vol.5, 366-367.
97. Fyfe, 729, or Appendix D herein. Case 6 transcript, 14326.
98. Hesseltine, 152,156,192,203; *Encyclopedia Britannica,* 11th ed., vol.1, 960.
99. Amery, vol.5, 252,253,601; vol.6, 24,25.
100. *Encyclopedia Britannica,* 12th ed., vol.32 (third volume supplementing 11th ed.), 157.

101. Komitee der Antifaschistischen, 86; M.J. Smith, 95; NO-3863 and NO-3860 in NMT, vol.5, 613-616; Internationales Buchenwald-Komitee, 206-207 and Fig. 55; Musiol, Figs. 88-91.
102. Documents NO-1242 and NO-4463, cited by Hilberg, 566; Fyfe, 731 or Appendix D herein.

V. THE HUNGARIAN JEWS

1. Red Cross (1948), vol.3, 523.
2. Reitlinger, 512-513; Red Cross (1947), 99-100.
3. Reitlinger, 176-177; Shirer (1960), 991.
4. Reitlinger, 148.
5. US-WRB (1945), 49.
6. Reitlinger, 447-487,542; Hilberg, 509-554,599-600.
7. NG-2586-G in NMT, vol.13, 212; NO-5194, part of the Korherr report, which is reproduced in Poliakov & Wulf (1955), 240-248; NG-5620, cited by Hilberg, 513.
8. Ruppin, 30-31,68.
9. Craven, 280-302,641f; Carter (see Index under "Auschwitz").
10. C.B. Smith, 167.
11. Craven, 172-179.
12. Reitlinger, 421-422; Hilberg, 528; Rassinier (1962), 229-230; Sachar, 463-464; John & Hadawi, vol.2, 36n.
13. IMT, vol.4, 355-373; U.S. Chief of Counsel, vol.8, 606-621.
14. NMT, vol.14, 1023,1027.
15. N.Y. Times (26 Feb 47), 4; Hilberg, 350f; NMT, vol.14, 1057f; Steengracht 86.
16. NMT, vol.14, 1031.
17. Hilberg, 714,715; Reitlinger, 443,566,567; Eichmann, session 85, A1,B1,O1-R1; London *Times* (20 Nov 64), 16; *N.Y. Times* (20 Nov 64), 8. London *Daily Telegraph* (7 Nov 75), magazine section, 17.
18. *N.Y. Times* (22 Feb 40), 22; (26 Aug 40), 17; (30 Mar 44), 6; (14 Nov 45), 8; (17 Jan 46), 14; Select Committee, 1534-1535; *Current Biography* (1943), 370; *Who's Who in World Jewry* (1965), 498.
19. Kempner, 1-12; *N.Y. Times* (28 Sep 41), sec.2, 6; (20 Jan 45), 10.
20. R.H. Smith, 217,222; *Yad Vashem Studies*, vol.5, 44; *N.Y. Times* (6 Oct 46), sec.6, 8; (7 Oct 46), 2; (18 Mar 47), 4; Select Committee, 1536, 1539.
21. *Current Biography* (1948), 533-534; *N.Y. Times* (7 Feb 43), 34.
22. *Current Biography* (1948), 534; *N.Y. Times* (14 Oct 46), 44; (23 Oct 46); 8; (26 Oct 46), 1; (27 Oct 46), 16; (3 Nov 46), 13; *Newsweek* (4 Nov 46), 26.
23. *N.Y. Times* (12 Mar 47), 6; (13 Mar 47), 17; (14 Mar 47), 12; (15 Mar 47), 11; (18 Mar 47), 4; (19 Mar 47), 5; (26 Mar 47), 4; *Chicago Tribune* (19 Mar 47), 20.
24. Utley, 172,177; Gaus (Case 11 transcript, 5123-5167) denied the coercion but, as Magee commented in court, "we have the questions and answers that the witness gave" in the relevant interrogation. The von Thadden and Haefliger declarations were made in the sessions of 3 March and 11 May 1948, respectively, and the corresponding parts of the trial transcript are quoted by Bardèche, 120ff, who gives other examples of coercion and intimidation of witnesses at Nuernberg.
25. *N.Y. Times* (8 Nov 47), 10; (4 Apr 48), 46; *Nation* (27 May 50), 528; (2 Dec 50), 499.
26. *N.Y. Times* (17 Dec 49), 1; (22 Jul 50), 32.
27. *N.Y. Times* (30 Sep 49), 21; (12 Jan 51), 7; (2 Feb 51), 8.
28. Belgion, 64-78.
29. IMT, vol.10, 648.
30. Select Committee, 1536-1548.
31. *N.Y. Times* (25 Apr 52), 5; *Chicago Tribune* (24 Apr 52), pt.4, 1.
32. *N.Y. Times* (15 Nov 52), 2; (23 Dec 52), 1.
33. *Encyclopedia Judaica*, vol.10, 904; *N.Y. Times* (31 Mar 71), 1; (5 Dec 72), 16.
34. *N.Y. Times* (6 Oct 46), sec.6, 8; (7 Oct 46), 2.
35. Taylor (15 Aug 49), 38+.
36. NMT, vol.13, 487-508; Reitlinger, 566.
37. Lublin (Maidanek) propaganda appeared in *Life* (28 Aug 44), 34; (18 Sep 44), 17; *Newsweek* (11 Sep 44), 64; *Reader's Digest* (Nov 44), 32; *Time* (21 Aug 44), 36; (11 Sep 44), 36; *Sat. Rev. Lit.* (16 Sep 44), 44.

VI. ET CETERA

1. Hilberg, 562; Reitlinger, 137,567; Rassinier (1962), 80n.
2. NMT, vol.1, 876.
3. NO-824 (Hitler order), NO-846 (Faulhaber letter), NO-844 (report on rumors).
4. *N.Y. Times* (7 Dec 41), 45.
5. IMT, vol.20, 487-515.

6. Fyfe, 157.
7. Gilbert's book should be read in its entirety, but pp. 15,39,46,47,64,78,152,175, 242,273-275,291 are of particular interest.
8. Hilberg, 599; Reitlinger, 460-463; IMT vol.16, 445, 520.
9. Speer, 375-376,512.
10. Speer, xvii; de Jong.
11. *N.Y. Times Book Review* (23 Aug 70), 2,16.
12. In Goering's testimony, see especially IMT, vol.9, 515-521,609-619.
13. Kelley, 54-58.
14. IMT, vol.11, 273-276, 335.
15. IMT, vol.22, 494-496.
16. Case 6 transcript, 197.
17. NMT, vol.5, 664-676.
18. DuBois, 230-231; NMT, vol.8, 312-321; Case 6 transcript, 14321-14345.
19. Eichmann, session 78, N1-O1; session 98, T1-W1.
20. Eichmann, session 103, Jjl; session 106, V1.
21. Eichmann, session 72, Aal-Kkl1; session 73, A1-R1; session 74, Hhl-Iil; session 88, L1-P2 and appendices; session 104, T1-V1; session 105, W1-Z1; *Life* (28 Nov 60), 19+; (5 Dec 60), 146+.
22. Eichmann, session 85, J1-K1,T1-U1; session 87, M1-O1,Y1; session 88, G1-H1.
23. Aretz, 58; Naumann, 8.
24. Naumann, 8-26,416-417.
25. Laternser, 85-94.
26. Naumann, 412-413,418-419,422-423. Reitlinger, 551,561.
27. Michelet, 151-157,313-314.
28. Belgion, 80-81.
29. Bardèche, 12,73; Davidson, 44-47,51.
30. Eichmann, session 75, U1. For the fanatical measures taken to isolate Eichmann from the outside world during his imprisonment in Israel see, e.g., the London *Jewish Chronicle* (2 Sept 60), 15.
31. Solzhenitsyn has given the definitive account of the historical development of the Communist political "trial". See also Conquest, 82-147.
32. Reitlinger, 450-452; Hilberg, 524; Schmidt, 248.
33. Last page of testament reproduced by Trevor-Roper, 180. Discovery and text of testament reported in *N.Y. Times* (30 Dec 45), 1; (31 Dec 45), 1,6. Text also given by Shirer (1947), 180-181.
34. 1919-PS in IMT, vol.29, 110-173 (in German). Excerpts in English translation in NMT, vol.13, 318-327.
35. IMT, vol.11, 561.
36. NMT, vol.13, 318.
37. NMT, vol.13, 457-487.
38. Reitlinger, 317.
39. NMT, vol.5, 666,675.
40. Lochner, 126,138,147f,241,viii. Oven's remarks are in *Nation Europa* (Apr 75), 53-56.
41. Veale, 220-224; Reitlinger, 83, 198; Dawidowicz, 125.
42. Reitlinger, 82-84,199-201; Hilberg, 187-188,194-195.
43. Reitlinger, 213.
44. IMT, vol.3, 560; vol.26, 102-105. Poliakov & Wulf (1955), 140ff.
45. Solzhenitsyn, 112n.
46. IMT, vol.3, 559.
47. Reitlinger, 201, note 70 on page 611.
48. NMT, vol.13, 269-272 (excerpts only).
49. IMT, vol.37, 670-717; NMT, vol.4, 154.
50. Hilberg, 252n; Reitlinger, 232-233. Documents 135-R and 3633-PS reproduced in Poliakov & Wulf (1955), 190ff.
51. Hilberg, 709; Reitlinger, 560; 3428-PS in NMT, vol.4, 191-193.
52. Reitlinger, 213-214.
53. NMT, vol.4, 168-169,187,190.
54. *N.Y. Times* (16 July 43), 7.
55. IMT, vol.4, 311-355.
56. IMT, vol.22, 478-480,491-494,509-510,538.
57. NMT, vol.4, 223-312.
58. NMT, vol.4, 313-323,547-555.

VII. THE FINAL SOLUTION

1. NMT, vol.13, 243-249.

2. Hilberg, 619 or 621.
3. Sachar, 365-368,412-417; John & Hadawi, vol.1, 295-326.
4. NMT, vol.13, 169-170.
5. e.g. Shirer (1960), 964.
6. NMT, vol.13, 212-213. Poliakov & Wulf (1955), 119-126.
7. See particularly the *N.Y. Times* (28 Feb 41), 4; (18 Oct 41), 4; (28 Oct 41), 10; (9 Feb 42), 5; (15 Mar 42), 27; (6 Aug 42), 1.
8. Rothe, 173-196.
9. NO-1611 and NO-1882 in NMT, vol.5, 616-619.
10. Reitlinger, 149,279; Hilberg, 318,619 or 621.
11. Reitlinger, 84-97; Hilberg, 262-263.
12. Reitlinger, 102-109; Hilberg, 264-265; NMT, vol.13, 213.
13. Grayzel, 785-786.
14. Koehl, 131-132.
15. Koehl, 146.
16. Koehl, 130,184.
17. Reitlinger, 533-546; Hilberg, 670.
18. Reitlinger, 367,377.
19. *Yad Vashem Studies,* vol.3, 119-140.
20. Kimche & Kimche, 63.
21. Steengracht 64 in NMT, vol.13, 300. NO-1247 cited by Reitlinger, 308, and quoted by Hilberg, 254. Steengracht 65 (or NO-1624) does not appear to be reproduced anywhere.
22. In the "survivor" literature, see in particular Glatstein *et. al.,* 25-32,43-112; Gringauz (1949 & 1950); Friedman & Pinson.
23. *N.Y. Times* (18 Oct 41), 4.
24. The best source to consult to see the nature of and motivation for the anti-Jewish pogroms, and the German measures to suppress them, seems to be Raschhofer, 26-66. See also Burg (1962), 50.
25. *N.Y. Times* (31 Apr 46), 8.
26. *N.Y. Times* (20 Jul 45), 9; (7 Sep 45), 5; (25 Nov 45), 32; (10 Mar 46), 2; (17 Apr 46), 27; (13 May 46), 18; (17 May 46), 5; (2 Dec 46), 5.
27. Reitlinger, 534,542-543; *N.Y. Times* (8 Jul 45), 1; (24 Mar 46), 3.
28. Koehl, 198-199; NMT, vol.5, 692-741; vol.4, 954-973.
29. *N.Y. Times* (28 Jun 45), 8.
30. Davie, 33.
31. US-WRB (1945), 3-4,12-13.
32. Rosenman, 399.
33. *N.Y. Times* (21 Sep 45), 7.
34. *N.Y. Times* (23 Dec 45), 1.
35. US-WRB (1945), 9,16-45,61-69,72-74.
36. John & Hadawi, vol.2, 34.
37. Koehl, 219-220.
38. Zink, 121-122.
39. *N.Y. Times* (26 Oct 46), 5.
40. Kimche & Kimche, 88-89; John & Hadawi, vol.2, 23-26,34-36; *Morgenthau Diary,* 79.
41. *N.Y. Times* (14 Aug 46), 10; (21 Aug 46), 1,5; (23 Aug 46), 18.
42. *N.Y. Times* (1 Oct 45), 2; (2 Oct 45), 1; (3 Oct 45), 1.
43. Kimche & Kimche, 101-103.
44. Kimche & Kimche, 97-98.
45. Kimche & Kimche, 85-88.
46. Kimche & Kimche, 81-83.
47. *N.Y. Times* (24 Jun 46), 12.
48. *N.Y. Times* (10 Aug 46), 4; (27 Aug 46), 6; (2 Nov 46), 7.
49. *N.Y. Times* (2 Dec 46), 3; (3 Dec 46), 13.
50. *N.Y. Times* (2 Nov 46), 7; Kimche & Kimche, 95.
51. John & Hadawi, vol.2, 45,179.
52. *World Almanac* (1950), 193; (1958), 364-365; Prittie, 149-150; McDonald, 142-143.
53. Kimche & Kimche, 15-19.
54. *N.Y. Times* (23 Dec 45), 1.
55. U.S. Displaced Persons Commission, v,248.
56. This data comes ultimately from the *Annual Report* of the U.S. Immigration and Naturalization Service. In this case I employed the summaries given in the *Information Please Almanac* (1969) and the *Statistical Abstract of the U.S.* (Sep 72).
57. Aretz, 337-346.
58. Reitlinger, 521.

VIII. REMARKS

1. Hilberg, 632.
2. Colorado Springs *Sun* (30 Jan 73), 6.
3. *N.Y. Times* (12 Aug 72), 23.
4. *N.Y. Times* (6 Oct 61), 10; (14 Oct 61), 10; (17 Oct 61), 35; (4 Nov 61), 11; R.H. Smith, 237n.
5. *N.Y. Times* (8 May 74), 16.
6. Fuks.
7. *Cambridge Ancient History,* vol.10, 296; Packer; Carcopino, 16-21; T. Frank, vol.2, 245; vol.4, 158f; vol.5, 218n.
8. *Encyclopedia Judaica,* vol.4, 735.
9. McCown.
10. Babylonian *Talmud, Sanhedrin* 93b or p. 627 in the translation edited by I. Epstein.
11. *N.Y. Times* (18 Jan 75), 6.
12. Vogel, 56,88-100.

APPENDIX A. THE "GERSTEIN STATEMENT"

1. Rassinier (1964), 93-106.
2. Hilberg, 622; Reitlinger, 163. Poliakov and Wulf (1955), 114.
3. *Vierteljahreshefte f. Zeitgeschichte* (Apr 53), 178-182. Mosse, 245. *N.Y. Times* (1 Feb 67), 39.
4. Rassinier (1964), 35-39.

APPENDIX E. THE ROLE OF THE VATICAN

1. Rhodes, 171-210.
2. Rhodes, 246.
3. *Actes et documents,* v.7, 179.
4. Rhodes, 347.
5. *N.Y. Times* (22 Jan 43), 6; (13 May 43), 8; (5 Sep 43), 7; (6 Sep 43), 7.
6. *N.Y. Times* (3 Jun 45), 22.
7. *Actes et documents,* vol.7, 82.
8. *Catholic Historical Rev.,* vol.59 (Jan 74), 719f.
9. *Actes et documents,* vol.8, 738-742.
10. Red Cross (1948), v.3, 520ff.
11. Rhodes, 272ff; Waagenaar, 409, 435f.
12. *Actes et documents,* vol.7, 136ff. Waagenaar, 413, quotes from the Osborne-Maglione exchange, but he does not quote it in its proper context of the bombing threat to Rome.
13. *Actes et documents,* vol.7, 138f.
14. *Actes et documents,* vol.2, 326; vol. 9, 40; Rhodes, 348f.
15. *Actes et documents,* vol.3, 15f. Rhodes, 288.
16. *Actes et documents,* vol.8, 534.
17. *Actes et documents,* vol.8, 669n.
18. Rhodes, 345; Waagenaar, 431.
19. Dawidowicz, 295ff.
20. *Actes et documents,* vol.8, 607f.
21. *Actes et documents,* vol.7, 473f.
22. *N.Y. Times* (5 Apr 73), 1,5.
23. *Actes et documents.* vol.3, 625-629.
24. *Actes et documents,* vol.9, 39,274.
25. *Actes et documents,* vol.9, 42.
26. *Actes et documents,* vol.9, 493,499,632-636.
27. *Actes et documents,* vol.9, 38,42f.

REFERENCES

Actes et documents du Saint Siège relatifs à la seconde guerre mondiale, 8 vols., Libreria Editrice Vaticana, Vatican City, 1967–1974.

L. S. Amery, general editor, *The Times History of the War in South Africa,* 7 vols., Sampson Low, Marston & Co., London, 1907 (vol.5), 1909 (vol.6).

Burton C. Andrus, *I Was the Nuremberg Jailer,* Coward-McCann, N.Y., 1969.

Anonymous, *The Myth of the Six Million,* Noontide Press, Los Angeles, 1969.

Jacob Apenszlak, ed., *The Black Book of Polish Jewry,* American Federation for Polish Jews, 1943.

Austin J. App, *The Six Million Swindle,* Boniface Press, 8207 Flower Ave., Takoma Park, Md. 20012. 1973.

Hannah Arendt, *Eichmann in Jerusalem,* Viking, N.Y., 1963 (revised and enlarged edition in 1964).

Emil Aretz, *Hexen-Einmal-Eins einer Luege,* 3rd ed., Verlag Hohe Warte – Franz von Bebenburg, Muenchen, 1973.

Eugène Aronéanu, ed., *Camps de Concentration,* Service d'Information des Crimes de Guerre, Paris, 1946.

Maurice Bardèche, *Nuremberg II, ou Les Faux Monnayeurs,* Les Sept Couleurs, Paris, 1950.

Harry Elmer Barnes, "The Public Stake in Revisionism," *Rampart J. of Individualist Thought,* vol.3, no.2 (Summer 1967), 19–41.

R. L. Bebb & L. B. Wakefield, "German Synthetic Rubber Developments" in G. S. Whitby, C. C. Davis & R. F. Dunbrook, eds., *Synthetic Rubber,* 937–986, John Wiley, N.Y. and Chapman & Hall, London, 1954.

Montgomery Belgion, *Victor's Justice,* Henry Regnery, Hinsdale, Illinois, 1949.

Ted Berkman, *Cast a Giant Shadow,* Doubleday, Garden City, N.Y., 1962.

Bibliography of the Holocaust and After, Israel Book and Printing Center, Tel Aviv.

John Morton Blum, *From the Morgenthau Diaries. Years of War 1941–1945* (3rd vol. in a series), Houghton Mifflin, Boston, 1967.

Nachmann Blumental, ed., *Dokumenty i Materialy,* vol.1, Obozy (Camps), Wydawnictwa Centralnej Zydowskiej Komisji Historycznej, Lodz, 1946.

Eric H. Boehm, ed., *We Survived,* Yale University Press, New Haven, 1949.

Michel Borwicz, *Ecrits des Condamnés à Mort Sous l'Occupation Allemande,* Presses Universitaires de France, Paris, 1954.

Randolph A. Braham, ed., *The Destruction of Hungarian Jewry,* 2 vols., Pro Arte, N.Y., 1963.

Brown Book: War and Nazi Criminals in West Germany, Verlag Zeit im Bild, Berlin (DDR), 1965. Listed title may not include words *"Brown Book".*

Margaret Buber, *Under Two Dictators,* Dodd, Mead & Co., N.Y.

J. G. Burg, *Schuld und Schicksal,* Damm Verlag, Muenchen, 1962.

J. G. Burg, *Suendenboecke,* G. Fischer, Muenchen, 1967.

J. G. Burg, *NS-Verbrechen,* G. Fischer, Muenchen, 1968.

Christopher Burney, *The Dungeon Democracy,* Duell, Sloan & Pearce, N.Y., 1946.

Edouard Calic, *Secret Conversations with Hitler,* John Day, N.Y., 1971.

Cambridge Ancient History, various editors, 12 vols., 1st ed., Cambridge, 1923–1939.

Jérôme Carcopino, *Daily Life in Ancient Rome,* Yale, New Haven, 1940.

Kit C. Carter and Robert Mueller, *The Army Air Forces in World War II – Combat Chronology – 1941-1945,* Albert F. Simpson Historical Research Center, Air University, and Office of Air Force History, 1973. Superintendent of Documents stock number 0870-00334.

Central Commission for Investigation of German Crimes in Poland, *German Crimes in Poland,* vol.1, Warsaw, 1946.

William Henry Chamberlin, *America's Second Crusade,* Henry Regnery, Chicago, 1950.

Thies Christophersen, *Die Auschwitz Luege,* 2nd ed., Kritik-Verlag, Mohrkirch, 1973. English translation from Western Unity Movement, P.O. Box 156, Verdun 19, Quebec, Canada, 1974.

Elie A. Cohen, *Human Behavior in the Concentration Camp,* W. W. Norton, N.Y., 1953.

Margaret L. Coit, *Mr. Baruch,* Riverside Press, Cambridge, Mass., 1957.

Benjamin Colby, *'Twas a Famous Victory,* Arlington House, New Rochelle, N.Y., 1974.

Ian Colvin, *Master Spy,* McGraw-Hill, N.Y., 1951.

Robert Conquest, *The Great Terror,* Macmillan, N.Y., 1968.

Vesley Frank Craven, James Lea Cate & U.S.A.F. Historical Div., eds., *The Army Air Forces in World War II*, vol.3, University of Chicago, 1951.

Eugene Davidson, *The Trial of the Germans*, Macmillan, N.Y., 1966.

Maurice R. Davie, *Refugees in America*, Harper, N.Y., 1947.

Lucy S. Dawidowicz, *The War Against the Jews, 1933–1945*, Holt, Rinehart and Winston, N.Y., 1975.

Andrea Devoto, *Bibliografia dell'Oppressione Nazista Fino al 1962*, Leo S. Olschki, Firenze, 1964.

Quincy L. Dowd, *Funeral Management and Costs*, University of Chicago, 1921.

Josiah E. DuBois, Jr., *The Devil's Chemists*, Beacon Press, Boston, 1952.

R. F. Dunbrook, "Historical Review" in G. S. Whitby *et. al.* (see Bebb and Wakefield above), 32–55.

Eichmann. *The Attorney-General of the Government of Israel vs. Adolf, the son of Adolf Karl Eichmann*, Minutes of Sessions, Jerusalem, 1962.

Encyclopedia Judaica, 16 vols., Keter Pub. House, Jerusalem, and Macmillan, N.Y., 1971.

Isidore Epstein, ed., *The Talmud* (Babylonian), many vols., Soncino Press, London, 1936.

Henry L. Feingold, *The Politics of Rescue*, Rutgers U. Press, New Brunswick, 1970.

Anne Frank, *Diary of a Young Girl*, Doubleday, Garden City, N.Y., 1952.

Tenney Frank, ed., *An Economic Survey of Ancient Rome*, 6 vols., Johns Hopkins, Baltimore, 1933–1940.

Saul Friedlaender, *Kurt Gerstein: The Ambiguity of Good*, Alfred A. Knopf, N.Y., 1969.

Filip (or Philip) Friedman, *This was Oswiecim*, United Jewish Relief Appeal, London, 1946.

Philip Friedman and Koppel S. Pinson, "Some Books on the Jewish Catastrophe", *Jewish Social Studies*, (Jan 50), 83–94.

Gregory (Grzegorz) Frumkin, *Population Changes in Europe Since 1939*, George Allen & Unwin, London, and Augustus M. Kelley, N.Y., 1951.

Alexander Fuks, "Aspects of the Jewish Revolt in A.D. 115–117", *J. Roman Studies*, vol. 51, 1961, 98–104.

David Maxwell Fyfe, ed., *The Belsen Trial* (vol. 2 of *War Crimes Trials*), William Hodge, London, 1949. Sometimes listed under "Josef Kramer" or under Raymond Phillips (the editor of vol.2 of the set).

G. M. Gilbert, *Nuremberg Diary*, Farrar, Strauss & Co., N.Y., 1947.

Jacob Glatstein, Israel Knox and Samuel Margoshes, eds., *Anthology of Holocaust Literature*, Jewish Pub. Society of America, Philadelphia, 1969.

John E. Gordon, "Louse-Borne Typhus Fever in the European Theater of Operations, U.S. Army, 1945", in Forest Ray Moulton, ed., *Rickettsial Diseases of Man*, Am. Acad. for the Advancement of Science, Washington, D.C., 1948, 16–27.

Michael Grant, *The Jews in the Roman World*, Weidenfeld and Nicolson, London, 1973.

Solomon Grayzel, *A History of the Jews*, Jewish Pub. Society of America, Philadelphia, 1947.

Samuel Gringauz, "The Ghetto as an Experiment of Jewish Social Organization," *Jewish Social Studies*, (Jan 49), 3–20.

Samuel Gringauz, "Some Methodological Problems in the Study of the Ghetto", *Jewish Social Studies*, (Jan 50), 65–72.

Nerin E. Gun, *The Day of the Americans*, Fleet Pub. Corp., 1966.

William A. Hardenbergh, "Research Background of Insect and Rodent Control," in *Preventive Medicine in World War II, vol. II, Environmental Hygiene*, John Boyd Coates, Jr. & Ebbe Curtis Hoff, eds., Office of the Surgeon General, Washington, D.C., 1955, 251.

Richard Harwood, *Did Six Million Really Die?*, Historical Review Press, Richmond, Surrey, 1974.

William Best Hesseltine, *Civil War Prisons*, Ohio State University Press, Columbus, 1930.

Raul Hilberg, *The Destruction of the European Jews*, Quadrangle Books, Chicago, 1961 & 1967.

Adolf Hitler, *My New Order*, Raoul de Roussy de Sales, ed., Reynal & Hitchcock, N.Y., 1941.

Heinz Hoehne, *The Order of the Death's Head*, tr. by Richard Barry, Ballantine Books, N.Y., 1971.

Frank A. Howard, *Buna Rubber: The Birth of an Industry*, D. Van Nostrand, N.Y., 1947.

Cordell Hull, *Memoirs*, vol.1, Macmillan, N.Y., 1948.

IMT (International Military Tribunal), *Trial of the Major War Criminals*, IMT, Nuremberg, 42 vols., 1947–1949. May be listed under "U.S. Army. Civil affairs division.

Trial of the major war criminals . . .."

Internationales Buchenwald-Komitee, *Buchenwald*, Roederberg-Verlag, Frankfurt, 1960.

Fred L. Israel, ed., *The War Diary of Breckenridge Long*, University of Nebraska Press, Lincoln, 1966.

Eberhard Jaeckel, *Hitler's Weltanschauung*, Wesleyan University Press, Middletown, Conn., 1972.

Robert John & Sami Hadawi, *The Palestine Diary*, 2 vols., New World Press, N.Y., 1970.

Allen J. Johnson & George H. Auth, *Fuels and Combustion Handbook*, First ed., McGraw-Hill, N.Y., 1951.

Louis de Jong, "Die Niederlande und Auschwitz", *Vierteljahreshefte fuer Zeitgeschichte*, vol.17, no.1 (Jan 69), 1—16. In English translation in *Yad Vashem Studies*, vol.7, 39—55.

Douglas M. Kelley, *22 Cells in Nuremberg*, Greenberg, N.Y., 1947.

Robert M. W. Kempner, *Nazi Subversive Organization, Past and Future*, stencil, privately published, 30 October 1943.

John F. Kennedy, *Profiles in Courage*, Harper, N.Y., 1955. Memorial edition 1964.

Jon Kimche & David Kimche, *The Secret Roads*, Farrar, Straus & Cudahy, N.Y., 1955. Introduction by David Ben-Gurion.

E. F. Knipling, "DDT and Other Insecticides for the Control of Lice and Fleas Attacking Man," in Moulton (see Gordon), 215—223.

Robert L. Koehl, *RKFDV: German Resettlement and Population Policy 1939—1945*, Harvard University Press, Cambridge, Mass., 1957.

Morris W. Kolander, "War Crimes Trials in Germany," *Pennsylvania Bar Assn. Quarterly*, vol.18, (April 47), 274—280.

Komitee der Antifaschistischen Widerstandskaempfer in der DDR, *Sachsenhausen*, Kongress-Verlag, Berlin, 1962.

Leszek A. Kosinski, "Changes in the Ethnic Structure of East Central Europe, 1930—1960", *Geographical Review*, vol. 59, 1969, 388—402. Also "Migration of Population in East-Central Europe, 1939—1955", *Canadian Slavonic Papers*, vol. 11, 1969, 357—373.

Helmut Krausnick, Hans Buchheim, Martin Broszat & Hans-Adolf Jacobsen, *The Anatomy of the SS State*, Walker, N.Y., 1968.

Hermann Langbein, *Der Auschwitz Prozess. Eine Dokumentation*, 2 vols., Europa Verlag, Wien, 1965.

Hans Laternser, *Die andere Seite im Auschwitz Prozess 1963/65*, Seewald Verlag, Stuttgart, 1966.

Johann M. Lenz, *Christ in Dachau* (tr. Countess Barbara Waldstein), Missionsdruckerei St. Gabriel, Moedling bei Wien, 1960.

Daniel Lerner, *Psychological Warfare Against Nazi Germany*, M.I.T. Press, Cambridge, Mass., 1971.

Louis P. Lochner, ed., *The Goebbels Diaries*, Doubleday, Garden City, N.Y., 1948. Republished by Greenwood Press, Westport, Conn., 1970.

David Marcus, "War Crimes" article in *Britannica Book of the Year — 1947*, 819—821, Encyclopedia Britannica, Chicago.

James J. Martin, *Revisionist Viewpoints*, Ralph Myles, Colorado Springs, 1971.

C. C. McCown, "The Density of Population in Ancient Palestine", *J. Biblical Lit.*, vol. 66, 1947, 425—436.

James G. McDonald, *My Mission in Israel*, Simon & Schuster, N.Y., 1951.

Jules Michelet, *Satanism and Witchcraft*, Citadel Press, N.Y., 1939.

Henry Morgenthau, Jr., "The Morgenthau Diaries — Part VI", *Collier's*, (1 Nov 47), 22+

Morgenthau Diary (Germany), 2 vols. published by U.S. Senate Committee on the Judiciary, U.S. Government Printing Office, Washington, D.C., 20 November 1967. Superintendent of Documents nos. Y4.J 89/2:M 82/2/v.1 and v.2. The book *Das Morgenthau Tagebuch*, ed. Hermann Schild, Druffel-Verlag, Leoni am Starnberger See, 1970, consists mainly of excerpts from the two volumes, translated into German.

Arthur D. Morse, *While Six Million Died*, Random House, N.Y., 1968.

George L. Mosse, *The Crisis of German Ideology*, Grosset and Dunlap, N.Y., 1964. Printing of 1971.

Teodor Musiol, *Dachau, 1933—1945*, Instytut Slaski w Opulo, Katowice.

Dillon S. Meyer, *Uprooted Americans*, University of Arizona Press, Tucson, 1971.

Bernd Naumann, *Auschwitz* (tr. Jean Steinberg), Frederick A. Praeger, N.Y., 1966. Original German edition from Athenaeum Verlag, Frankfurt, 1965.

W. J. S. Naunton, "Synthetic Rubber" in *History of the Rubber Industry*, P. Schidrowitz & T. R. Dawson, eds., pub. for The Institute of the Rubber Industry by W. Heffer & Sons Ltd., Cambridge, U.K., 1952, 100–109.

Netherlands Red Cross, *Auschwitz,* Hoofdbestuur van de Vereniging het Nederlandsche Roode Kruis, 6 vols., The Hague, 1947–1953.

Oskar Neumann (or J. Oskar Neumann), *Im Schatten des Todes,* Tel-Aviv, 1956.

NMT (Nuernberg Military Tribunal), *Trials of War Criminals,* U.S. Government Printing Office, Washington, D.C., 1950, 15 vols.. May be listed under "U.S. Defense Dept., Adjutant General. Trials of war criminals . . .."

Miklos Nyiszli, *Auschwitz,* Frederick Fell, N.Y., 1960.

James E. Packer, "Housing and Population in Imperial Ostia and Rome", *J. Roman Studies,* vol. 57, 1967, 80–95.

Jean Pelissier, *Camps de la Mort,* Editions Mellottée, Paris, 1946.

Léon Poliakov & Josef Wulf, *Das Dritte Reich und die Juden,* Arani-Verlags, Berlin-Grunewald, 1955.

Léon Poliakov & Josef Wulf, *Das Dritte Reich und Seine Diener,* Arani-Verlags, Berlin-Grunewald, 1956.

C. J. Polson, R. P. Brittain & T. K. Marshall, *Disposal of the Dead,* 2nd ed., Charles C. Thomas, Springfield, Illinois, 1962.

Terence Prittie, *Eshkol: The Man and the Nation,* Pitman, N.Y., 1969.

Hermann Raschhofer, *Political Assassination,* Fritz Schlichtenmayer, Tuebingen, 1964.

Paul Rassinier, *Le Mensonge d'Ulysse,* 5th ed., La Librairie Française, Paris, 1961.

Paul Rassinier, *Ulysse Trahi par les Siens,* La Librairie Française, Paris, 1961 (not referenced on any specific point here).

Paul Rassinier, *Le Véritable Procès Eichmann,* Les Sept Couleurs, Paris, 1962. German translation *Zum Fall Eichmann: Was ist Wahrheit?,* Druffel-Verlag, Leoni am Starnberger See, 1963.

Paul Rassinier, *Le Drame des Juifs Européens,* Les Sept Couleurs, Paris, 1964. German translation *Das Drama der Juden Europas,* Hans Pfeiffer Verlag, Hanover, 1965. English translation *Drama of the European Jews,* Steppingstones Publications, Box 612, Silver Spring, Md., 20901, 1975.

Paul Rassinier, *l'Opération Vicaire,* La Table Ronde, Paris, 1965.

Red Cross. International. *Documents sur l'activité du CICR en faveur des civils detenus dans les camps de concentration en Allemagne (1939–1945),* Geneva, 1947.

Red Cross. International. *Report of the International Committee of the Red Cross on its Activities During the Second World War (Sept. 1 1939–June 30, 1947),* 3 vols., Geneva, 1948.

Gerald Reitlinger, *The Final Solution,* 2nd ed., Vallentine, Mitchell, London, 1968.

Anthony Rhodes, *The Vatican in the Age of the Dictators 1922–45,* Hodder and Stoughton, London, 1973.

Wilmot Robertson, *The Dispossessed Majority,* Howard Allen, Cape Canaveral, Florida, 1972. Revised 1973.

Samuel I. Rosenman, *Working With Roosevelt,* Harper, N.Y., 1952.

Wolf Dieter Rothe, *Die Endloesung der Judenfrage, Band 1, Zeugen,* E. Bierbaum Verlag, Frankfurt, 1974.

Arthur Ruppin, *The Jewish Fate and Future,* Macmillan, London, 1940.

Abram Leon Sachar, *The History of the Jews,* 5th ed., Alfred A. Knopf, N.Y., 1964.

Paul Schmidt, *Hitler's Interpreter,* William Heinemann, London, 1951.

Gerhard Schoenberner, *The Yellow Star,* Transworld, London, 1969. Also in paperback from Bantam, N.Y., 1969. Originally published in German as *Der Gelbe Stern,* 1960 & 1969.

Select Committee to Conduct an Investigation of the Facts, Evidence, and Circumstances of the Katyn Forest Massacre, *The Katyn Forest Massacre,* part 5, U.S. Government Printing Office, Washington, D.C., 1952. Maybe be listed under "U.S. House of Representatives; Katyn Forest Massacre".

William L. Shirer, *End of a Berlin Diary,* Alfred A. Knopf, N.Y., 1947.

William L. Shirer, *The Rise and Fall of the Third Reich,* Simon & Schuster, N.Y., 1960.

Derrick Sington, *Belsen Uncovered,* Duckworth, London, 1946.

Constance Babington Smith, *Evidence in Camera,* Chatto & Windus, London, 1958.

Marcus J. Smith, *Dachau, The Harrowing of Hell,* University of New Mexico Press, Albuquerque, 1972.

R. Harris Smith, *O.S.S.,* University of California Press, Berkeley, 1972.

Aleksandr I. Solzhenitsyn, *The Gulag Archipelago,* Harper & Row, N.Y., 1973.

Albert Speer, *Inside the Third Reich,* Macmillan, N.Y., 1970.

Michel Sturdza, *The Suicide of Europe,* Western Islands, Belmont, Mass., 1968. A censored and edited translation of the Rumanian language original, *Romania si sfarsitul Europei,* Madrid, 1966.

303

Yuri Suhl, ed., *They Fought Back*. Crown, NY, 1967.

Telford Taylor, "The Nuremberg War Crimes Trials", in *International Conciliation* (Apr 49), 241-375. Reproduced in following reference.

Telford Taylor, *Final Report to the Secretary of the Army on the Nuernberg War Crimes Trials Under Control Council Law No. 10*, U.S. Government Printing Office, Washington, D.C. (15 August 1949). Preceding reference reproduced pp. 121-237.

H.R. Trevor-Roper, *The Last Days of Hitler*, Macmillan, N.Y., 1947.

U.S. Chief of Counsel for the Prosecution of Axis Criminality, *Nazi Conspiracy and Aggression*, 11 vols., U.S. Government Printing Office, Washington, D.C. 1946-1948.

U.S. Displaced Persons Commission, *The DP Story*, U.S. Government Printing Office, Washington, D.C., 1952.

U.S. Special Committee to Study the Rubber Situation, *Report of the Rubber Survey Committee*, U.S. Government Printing Office, 10 September 1942. The bulk of the report is reproduced in Charles Morrow Wilson, *Trees and Test Tubes, the Story of Rubber*, Henry Holt, N.Y., 1943, 261-330.

US-WRB (U.S. War Refugee Board), *German Extermination Camps – Auschwitz and Birkenau*, Executive Office of the President, Washington, D.C., November 1944. This is the "WRB report", which is also supposed to be document 022-L.

US-WRB (U.S. War Refugee Board), *Final Summary Report of the Executive Director*, Executive Office of the President, Washington, D.C., 15 September 1945.

Freda Utley, *The High Cost of Vengeance*, Regnery, Chicago, 1949.

Frederick J.P. Veale, *Advance to Barbarism*, C.C. Nelson, Appleton, Wisconsin, 1953. New edition from Devin-Adair, N.Y., 1968.

Rolf Vogel, ed., *The German Path to Israel*, Oswald Wolff, London, 1969. Foreword by Konrad Adenauer.

Rudolf Vrba & Alan Bestic, *I Cannot Forgive*, Grove, N.Y., 1964.

Sam Waagenaar, *The Pope's Jews*, Alcove Press, London, 1974.

Yad Vashem (or *Washem*) *Studies*, 8 vols., Jerusalem, 1957-1970.

Yigael Yadin, *Bar-Kokhba*, Random House, N.Y. and Weidenfeld and Nicolson, London, 1971.

Harold Zink, *American Military Government in Germany*, Macmillan, N.Y., 1947.

INDEX

Gas chambers: 6, 35, 44-47, 58, 62, 65, 68, 77-79, 82, 87-90, 92, 98, 101-112, 116, 118, 120-122, 129, 132, 147-150, 172f, 176, 180, 183, 186, 191, 202, 214, 215, 220, 223, 240, 242, 248, 252-256, 260, 271, 276, 282, 290.
Gasmobiles or gassing vans: 35, 68, 88, 198, 202, 287.
General Government of Poland: 30, 113, 210, 213, 215, 222, 287. See also Poland.
Geneva, Switzerland: 61-62, 279, 280.
Geneva Conventions: 36, 49, 68, 134, 138. See also Hague Conventions.
Gerstein, *Obersturmfuehrer* Kurt: 105-107, 173, 174, 251-258, 264.
Gestapo (*Geheime Staatspolizei*, Secret State Police): 30, 32, 33, 79, 95, 101-102, 112, 140, 181, 182, 195, 200, 233, 251, 266, 269, 276.
Gilbert, Dr. G.M.: 177, 179.
Ginsburg, Josef (J.G. Burg, author): 11, 239, 283.
Gipsies: 124, 130, 220.
Globocnik, *Gruppenfuehrer* Odilo: 252.
Gluecks, *Gruppenfuehrer* Richard (Inspector of Concentration Camps): 32, 104, 108, 126, 153, 266-273.
Goebbels, Dr. Joseph (German Minister for Propaganda): 17, 30, 68-71, 73, 89, 195, 197, 255.
Goering, *Reichsmarschall* Hermann (Commander of the Luftwaffe, Chief of the Four Year Plan, Deputy to Hitler and designated successor): 9, 17-18, 30, 161, 167, 177, 179, 180, 189, 195, 204-206, 210, 211, 214, 215.
Goldstein, Rabbi Israel: 76, 80.
Graham, Msgr. Robert A.: 279.
Grayzel, Dr. Solomon (historian): 215.
Greece: 37, 82, 84, 101, 137, 146, 207, 216, 230, 231, 236, 237, 288.
Greifelt, *Obergruppenfuehrer* Ulrich: 19, 33.
Greiser, Artur (*Gauleiter* of the Wartheland): 113.
Grodno, Poland: 82, 220, 222.
Grosch, *Sturmbannfuehrer* Wolfgang: 122.
Gross Rosen camp (Germany): 91, 108, 127.
Guenther, *Sturmbannfuehrer* Rolf: 252, 254-255, 257.
Guggenheim, Prof. Paul: 60-61.
Gun, Nerin E.: 45.
Gurs camp (France): 135.
Gusen camp. See Mauthausen-Gusen camp.

Hadamar, Germany: 179, 251.
Hadrian (Roman Emperor, 117-138 A.D.): 246-247.
Haganah (pre-Israel Jewish army in Palestine): 28.
Hague, The: 53-54.
Hague Conventions: 68, 134, 141. See also Geneva Conventions.
Halberstadt camp (Germany): 37.
Hamburg: 12, 70, 90, 151, 163, 186, 203, 251, 256.
Hargreaves, Reginald (author): 72.
Harmense (Auschwitz subsidiary): 49, 51.
Harrison, Leland: 60, 61-62, 64-66, 88.
Hartheim Castle, Austria: 47.
Harwood, Richard (author): 12.
Hemingway, Ernest (author): 71.
Herzogenbusch camp (Germany): 127.
Hess, Rudolf (Deputy leader of Nazi Party): 18, 249.
Heydrich, *Obergruppenfuehrer* Reinhard: 17, 19, 30-32, 101, 104, 113, 145, 181, 198, 200, 205, 206, 211-214.
Hilberg, Prof. Raul (political scientist): 7, 9, 10, 11, 17, 19, 61, 101, 105, 107, 120, 122, 126, 152, 160, 173, 174, 214, 216-217, 240, 241, 247.
Hildebrandt, *Obergruppenfuehrer* Richard: 33, 219, 220.
Hilldring, Gen. John H.: 29.
Himmler, *Reichsfuehrer-SS* Heinrich:17, 19, 30-32, 50, 91, 98-99, 104, 108, 112-115, 126, 131, 145, 152, 160, 170, 176, 177, 180, 181, 193, 194, 195, 198, 199, 200, 202, 205, 208, 210, 211, 214, 240, 253, 254-255, 276.
Hiroshima, Japan: 203.
Hirschfeld, Hans: 244, 245.
Hirt, Prof. August (Director of Strasbourg Anatomical Institute): 276.
Hiss, Donald: 64, 66.
Hitler, Adolf: 14, 17, 19, 30, 31, 48, 60, 62, 64, 69-73, 76-78, 86, 107, 108, 138, 146, 166, 174, 176, 177, 180, 181, 189, 192, 193, 198, 200, 203, 205, 206, 209, 211, 214, 244, 245, 253, 256, 265, 278, 282, 287.

311

Pohl, *Obergruppenfuehrer* Oswald: 19, 32, 101-102, 104, 108, 117, 126, 128, 130, 176, 182, 193, 195, 268-271, 275.
Poland: 14-16, 20, 30, 32-33, 35, 37, 44, 47, 49, 58, 61, 62, 64, 68, 75-79, 81-84, 86, 101, 103, 112-113, 116, 124, 134, 137, 140, 146f, 149, 151, 158, 166, 173, 174, 175, 192, 207, 210, 212-214, 215, 217-219, 220-221, 223-226, 228, 230-231, 236, 239-240, 252, 254, 261-263, 265, 280, 281, 282-284; 286-290. Polish exile govt. (London): 60, 75, 166, 280.
Poliakov, Léon: 10, 33, 112, 248.
Ponger, Kurt: 81.
Pope. See Vatican, Pius XII.
Portugal: 30f, 57, 139.
Posen, "Himmler's" speech in: 193, 194, 195 (193-195).
Prague: 75, 196, 212, 252.
Preysing, Konrad Count von: 254, 281, 285.
Prisoners of War: 57, 68, 102, 113, 127-128, 134, 141, 146, 154.
    American: 6, 89, 166, 168.
    British: 6, 36, 49, 89, 111, 165, 268, 269, 275.
    French: 36.
    German: 240.
    Polish: 49, 267.
    Russian: 36, 49, 101, 128-130, 258, 266.
Purvis, Melvin: 20.

Race and Settlement Main Office. See RuSHA.
Raisko (Auschwitz subsidiary): 49-51, 120.
Rasch, *Brigadefuehrer* Dr. Otto: 197.
Rassinier, Prof. Paul (geographer): 10-12, 17, 25, 107, 117, 216, 239, 256, 258.
Ravensbrueck camp (Germany): 67, 127, 255, 260.
Rawa Ruska, Poland: 78.
Reconstruction Finance Corporation: 54.
Red Cross (German): 134, 222.
Red Cross (International): 44-45, 49, 61, 67, 76, 103, 109-111, 133-145, 149f, 153, 158, 166f, 170f, 181, 197, 210, 217, 239, 275, 283.
Red Cross (Netherlands): 89, 109, 125, 127, 216, 260, 263.
Red Cross (Polish): 166.
Red Cross (Rumanian): 140-141.
Red Cross (Slovak): 137.
Red Cross (Swedish): 138.
Das Reich: 69, 89.
Reich Security Main Office. See RSHA.
Reichskommissar fuer die Festigung des deutschen Volkstums: see RKFDV.
Reichssicherheitshauptamt (Reich Security Main Office). See RSHA.
Reitlinger, Gerald R. (author): 9, 11, 15, 16, 19, 33, 61, 79, 81, 82, 92, 95, 98-99, 101, 103-107, 109-110, 117, 120, 125-126, 149, 152, 160, 173, 174, 183, 194, 199, 200, 212, 214, 216-217, 225, 228, 237, 240, 241, 242, 247, 260.
Rhodes, Anthony E. (author): 279, 281, 286.
Ribbentrop, Joachim von: 9, 18, 26, 153, 154-156, 159, 162, 205-208, 209.
Richter, *Obersturmbannfuehrer* Gustav: 209-210.
Riegner, Gerhard: 60-62, 66, 96.
Rifkind, Judge Simon H.: 230.
Riga, Latvia: 109, 127, 196, 219, 220, 222.
RKFDV (*Reichskommissar fuer die Festigung des deutschen Volkstums*): 33.
Roehm, Capt. Ernst (SA leader, executed in 1934): 103.
Rogge, O. John: 161-164, 166.
Roman Catholic Church. See Vatican.
Roman Empire: 245-247.
Rome: 208, 246, 284-286, 290.
Rommel, *Feldmarschall* Erwin: 31.
Roncalli, Msgr. Angelo: 288, 289.
Roosevelt, Franklin D.: 17, 20, 29, 59, 61, 62, 66, 75, 82, 86, 146, 150, 162, 226, 280, 284.
Rosenberg, Alfred (German Minister for the Occupied East): 73, 173, 194, 199, 215, 283.
Rosenfeld, Col. A.H.: 24-25.
Rosenman, Samuel: 20.
Rothe, Wolf Dieter (author): 12, 212.
Rotterdam: 70.

313